GOING DEEP

20 Classic Sports Stories

by GARY SMITH

Sports Illustrated

{ GOING DEEP }

20 Classic Sports Stories

{ *by* GARY SMITH }

SPORTS ILLUSTRATED BOOKS

*This book is dedicated with love and with gratitude
to Sally, my wife/editor/shrink/pal*

Contents

Contents

—

Introduction

BY RICK REILLY

I KNOW YOU'RE NOT GOING TO BELIEVE THIS BUT Gary Smith doesn't look, act or sound anything like a genius. Yes, he is a genius. Yes, he is America's greatest magazine writer. And yes, he is the only living writer today who never fails to blow me away with the depth, detail and sheer lock-yourself-in-the-bathroom-until-you're-done-reading drama of the stories he weaves. It's just that he doesn't come across as that guy.

I remember the day I was going to meet him for the first time, in 1985. I worshipped the man. To this day when I see a Gary Smith piece in my SPORTS ILLUSTRATED, I holler "Yes!!!", flop down on the landing in front of the door, and devour it until it's finished. I love trying to figure out how he does it, how he can start in the middle—with the guy hanging from a cliff—then backtrack to how he got there, then get him off the cliff, only to suddenly be facing a lion, and, then, finally, throw the guy a rope, with which he has just enough strength left to pull himself out.

And spun through it all—in just the right doses—are these psychiatric trips he takes you on into the recesses of some poor guy's soul, where we can talk to his demons and poke around in his secrets. And all of it real and honest and so penetrating that you can't help think, God, please don't let this guy ever profile me.

I'm not the only one who thinks Smith has perfected the art. Four of his stories—"Shadow of a Nation," "Crime and Punishment," "Moment of Truth" and "Lying in Wait"—have won National Magazine Awards, the most won by any individual in the history of the award. One story ("Someone to Lean On") was the basis for a movie, one for a documentary film ("Damned Yankee"), and two others have been optioned for movies ("The Rapture of the Deep" and "Higher Education").

So, that day we first met, I figured that anybody who could do all that would be wearing a black trench coat, smoking a hand-rolled cigarette, carrying a Freud tome in his left hand and an absinthe in his right. I expected to extend my quivering hand, have him stare straight through me—as though he'd discovered how intellectually transparent I really was—knit his brow, say, "I don't believe in cultural artifice," and return to his Sigmund.

But, no, that isn't within four area codes of what Gary Smith was like that day, nor any day since. He was wearing an old Who T-shirt that was so threadbare you could almost see through it, jean shorts and flip-flops. He treated my fawning compliments like anthrax cupcakes, wanted nothing to do with them, couldn't wait for me to be done with them. All he wanted to do was laugh, play hoops and figure out where we were drinking that night. And that is pretty much what we've done in the 20-something years since.

Gary Smith broods upon the sorrows and obsessions and depths of lives, yes, but that doesn't keep him from doing a giant cannonball into the deep end of his own. There's nothing he's not up for. It was Gary Smith at the Barcelona Olympics who cajoled a dozen of us at a throbbing dance hall to start taking off our credentials, our hats, our shirts, our shoes, our socks, our belts, and our watches to make a giant pile to dance around, as though it were some kind of spiritual fire. It was Gary Smith in Sydney who once forced not one but three espressos down my throat at midnight in order that I stay up with him until 8 a.m., the only finishing hour he felt was respectable. It was Gary Smith in North Carolina who was supposed to introduce me for an award and instead showed up with his mother and seven of his eight siblings, grabbed me off the stage, hog-tied and blindfolded me and held me hostage until I confessed to various sins and inadequacies.

Lord, there are so many more Gary Smith stories—running with bulls, kidnapping a bus and forcing it to take us to a karaoke bar, unspeakable adventures involving rental cars. But my lasting memory of him is one day in Orlando, when he came up with this game in which we'd heave personal items out our eighth-story Marriott window and the other guy, standing on the ground below, had to a) name the item as it fell; and b) catch it, in order to accrue maximum points. You haven't lived until you've seen Gary Smith diving full-out into a lilac bush screaming, "My lactose intolerant pills!"

I only bring this up because as you read these amazing, psychoanalytical and ultimately life-affirming profiles, you will shake your head and say to yourself, "What kind of mind *thinks* like this?" and try to form a picture of the mad scientist in your head.

And I'm here to tell you: Don't think Jung, think young.

{ Part One }

Higher Education

Who was this coach and what was his game?
Deep in Ohio's Amish country, the unlikeliest of men
changed a town's ideas about race and how to live.

THIS IS A STORY ABOUT A MAN, AND A PLACE WHERE magic happened. It was magic so powerful that the people there can't stop going back over it, trying to figure out who the man was and what happened right in front of their eyes, and how it'll change the time left to them on earth.

See them coming into town to work, or for their cup of coffee at Boyd & Wurthmann, or to make a deposit at Killbuck Savings? One mention of his name is all it takes for everything else to stop, for it all to begin tumbling out. . . .

"I'm afraid we can't explain what he meant to us. I'm afraid it's so deep we can't bring it into words."

"It was almost like he was an angel."

"He was looked on as God."

There's Willie Mast. He's the one to start with. It's funny, he'll tell you, his eyes misting. He was so sure they'd all been hoodwinked that he almost did what's unthinkable now—run that man out of town before the magic had a chance.

All Willie had meant to do was bring some buzz to Berlin, Ohio, something to look forward to on a Friday night, for goodness' sake, in a town without high school football or a fast-food restaurant, without a traffic light or even a place to drink a beer, a town dozing in the heart of the largest Amish settlement in the world. Willie had been raised Amish, but he'd walked out on the religion at 24—no, he'd peeled out, in an eight-cylinder roar, when he just couldn't bear it anymore, trying to get somewhere in life without a set of wheels or even a telephone to call for a ride.

He'd jumped the fence, as folks here called it, become a Mennonite and started a trucking company, of all things, his tractor-trailers roaring past all those horses and buggies, moving cattle and cold meat over half the country. But his greatest glory was that day back in 1982 when he hopped into one of his semis and moved a legend, Charlie Huggins, into town. Charlie, the coach who'd won two Ohio state basketball championships with Indian Valley South and one with Strasburg-Franklin, was coming to tiny Hiland High. Willie, one of the school's biggest hoops boosters, had banged the drum for Charlie for months.

And yes, Charlie turned everything around in those winters of '82 and '83, exactly as Willie had promised, and yes, the hoops talk was warmer and stronger than the coffee for the first time in 20 years at Willie's table of regulars in the Berlin House restaurant. They didn't much like it that second year when Charlie brought in an assistant, a man who'd helped him in his summer camps, who was black. But Charlie was the best dang high school coach in three states; he must've known something that they didn't. Nor were they thrilled by the fact that the black man was a Catholic, in a community whose children grew up reading tales of how their ancestors were burned at the stake by Catholics during the Reformation in Europe more than 400 years ago. But Charlie was a genius. Nor did they cherish the fact that the Catholic black man was a loser, 66 times in 83 games with those hapless kids at Guernsey Catholic High, near Cambridge, before that school went belly-up. But Charlie...

Charlie quit. Quit in disgust at an administration that wouldn't let players out of their last class 10 minutes early to dress for practice. But he kept the news to himself until right before the '84 school year began, too late to conduct a proper search for a proper coach. Willie Mast swallowed hard. It was almost as if his man, Charlie, had pulled a fast one. Berlin's new basketball coach, the man with the most important position in a community that had dug in its heels against change, was an unmarried African-American Catholic loser. The *only* black man in eastern Holmes County.

It wasn't that Willie hated black people. He'd hardly known any. "All I'd heard about them," he'll tell you, "was riots and lazy." Few had ever strayed into these parts, and fewer still after that black stuffed dummy got strung up on the town square in Millersburg, just up the road, after the Civil War. Maybe twice a year, back in the 1940s and '50s, a Jewish rag man had come rattling down Route 39 in a rickety truck, scavenging for scrap metal and rags to sell to filling stations 30 miles northeast in Canton or 60 miles north in Cleveland, and brought along a black man for the heavy lifting. People stared at him as if he were green. Kids played Catch the Nigger in their schoolyards without a pang, and when a handful of adults saw the color of a couple of Newcomerstown High's players a few years before, you know what word was ringing in those players' ears as they left the court.

Now, suddenly, this black man in his early 30s was standing in the middle of a gym jammed with a thousand whites, pulling their sons by the jerseys until their nostrils and his were an inch apart, screaming at *them*. Screaming, "Don't wanna hear your shoulda-coulda-wouldas! Get your head outta your butt!" How dare he?

Worse yet, the black man hadn't finished his college education, couldn't even teach at Hiland High. Why, he was working at Berlin Wood Products, the job Charlie had arranged for him, making little red wagons till 2 p.m. each day. "This nigger doesn't know how to coach," a regular at the Berlin House growled.

Willie agreed. "If he wins, it's because of what Charlie built here," he said. "What does he know about basketball?"

But what could be done? Plenty of folks in town seemed to treat the man with dignity. Sure, they were insular, but they were some of the most decent and generous people on earth. The man's Amish coworkers at the wood factory loved him, after they finally got done staring holes in the back of his head. They slammed Ping-Pong balls with him on lunch hour, volleyed theology during breaks and dubbed him the Original Black Amishman. The Hiland High players seemed to feel the same way.

He was a strange cat, this black man. He had never said a word when his first apartment in Berlin fell through—the landlord who had agreed to a lease on the telephone saw the man's skin and suddenly remembered that he rented only to families. The man had kept silent about the cars that pulled up to the little white house on South Market Street that he moved into instead, about the screams in the darkness, the voices threatening him on his telephone and the false rumors that he was dating their women. "They might not like us French Canadians here," was all he'd say, with a little smile, when he walked into a place and felt it turn to ice.

Finally, the ice broke. Willie and a few pals invited the man to dinner at a fish joint up in Canton. They had some food and beers and laughs with him, sent him on his merry way and then . . . what a coincidence: The blue lights flashed in the black man's rearview mirror. DUI.

Willie's phone rang the next morning, but instead of it being a caller with news of the school board's action against the new coach, it was *him*. Perry Reese Jr. Just letting Willie know that he knew exactly what had happened the night before. And that he wouldn't go away. The school board, which had caught wind of the plot, never made a peep. Who *was* this man?

Some people honestly believed that the coach was a spy—sent by the feds to keep an eye on the Amish—or the vanguard of a plot to bring blacks into Holmes County. Yet he walked around town looking people in the eyes, smiling and teasing with easy assurance. He never showed a trace of the loneliness he must have felt. When he had a problem with someone, he went straight to its source. Straight to Willie Mast in the school parking lot one night. "So you're not too sure about me because I'm black," he said, and he laid everything out in front of Willie, about racism and how the two of them needed to get things straight.

Willie blinked. He couldn't help but ask himself the question folks all over town would soon begin to ask: Could I do, or even dream of doing, what this man is doing? Willie couldn't help but nod when the black man invited him along to scout an opponent and stop for a bite to eat, and couldn't help but feel good when the man said he appreciated Willie because he didn't double-talk when confronted—because Willie, he said, was real. Couldn't help but howl as the Hiland Hawks kept winning, 49 times in 53 games those first two years, storming to the 1986 Division IV state semifinal.

Winning, that's what bought the black man time, what gave the magic a chance to wisp and curl through town and the rolling fields around it. That's what gave him the lard to live through that frigid winter of '87. That was the school year when he finally had his degree and began teaching history and current events in a way they'd never been taught in eastern Holmes County, the year the Hawks went 3–18 and the vermin came crawling back out of the baseboards. Damn if Willie wasn't the first at the ramparts to defend him, and damn if that black Catholic loser didn't turn things right back around the next season and never knew a losing one again.

How? By pouring Charlie Huggins's molasses offense down the drain. By runnin' and gunnin', chucking up threes, full-court pressing from buzzer to buzzer—with an annual litter of runts, of spindly, short, close-cropped Mennonites! That's what most of his players were: the children, grandchildren and great-grandchildren of Amish who, like Willie, had jumped the fence and endured the ostracism that went with it. Mennonites believed in many of the same shall-nots as the Amish: A man shall not be baptized until he's old enough to choose it, nor resort to violence even if his government demands it, nor turn his back on community, family, humility, discipline and orderliness. But the Mennonites had decided that unlike the Amish, they could continue schooling past the eighth grade, turn on a light switch or a car ignition, pick up a phone and even, except the most conservative of them, pull on a pair of shorts and beat the pants off an opponent on the hardwood without drifting into the devil's embrace.

The Hawks' Nest, Hiland's tiny old gym, became what Willie had always dreamed it would be: a loony bin, the one place a Mennonite could go to sweat and shriek and squeal; sold out year after year, with fans jamming the hallway and snaking out the door as they waited for the gym to open, then stampeding for the best seats an hour before the six o'clock jayvee game; reporters and visiting coaches and scouts sardined above them in wooden lofts they had to scale ladders to reach; spillover pouring into the auditorium beside the gym to watch on a video feed as noise thundered through the wall. A few dozen teenage Amish boys, taking advantage of the one time in their lives when some elders allowed them to behold the modern world and 16-year-old cheerleaders' legs, would be packed shoulder to shoulder in two corners of the gym at the school they weren't permitted to attend. Even a few Amish men, Lord save their souls, would tie up their horses and buggies across the street at Yoder's Lumber and slink into the Nest. And plenty more at home would tell the missus that they'd just remembered a task in the barn, then click on a radio stashed in the hay and catch the game on WKLM.

Something had dawned on Willie, sitting in his front-row seat, and on everyone else in town. The black man's values were virtually the same as theirs. Humility? No coach ever moved so fast to duck praise or bolt outside the frame of a team picture. Unselfishness? The principal might as well have taken the coach's salary to pep rallies and flung it in the air—most of it ended up in the kids' hands anyway. Reverence? No congregation ever huddled and sang out the Lord's Prayer with the crispness and cadence that the Hawks did before and after every game. Family? When Chester Mullet, Hiland's star guard in '96, only hugged his mom on parents' night, Perry gave him a choice: Kiss her or take a seat on the bench. Work ethic? The day and season never seemed to end, from 6 a.m. practices to 10 p.m. curfews, from puke buckets and running drills in autumn to two-a-days in early winter to camps and leagues and an open gym every summer day. He out-Amished the Amish, out-Mennonited the Mennonites, and everyone, even those who'd never sniffed a locker room in their lives, took to calling the black man Coach.

Ask Willie. "Most of the petty divisions around here disappeared because of Coach," he'll tell you. "He pulled us all together. Some folks didn't like me, but I was respected more because he respected me. When my dad died, Coach was right there, kneeling beside the coffin, crossing himself. He put his arm right around my mom—she's Amish—and she couldn't get over that. When she died, he was the first one there. He did that for all sorts of folks. I came to realize that color's not a big deal. I took him for my best friend."

And that man in Willie's coffee clan who'd held out longest, the one given to calling Coach a nigger? By Coach's fifth year, the man's son was a Hawk, the Hawks were on another roll, and the man had seen firsthand the effect Coach had on kids. He cleared his throat one morning at the Berlin House; he had something to say.

"He's not a nigger anymore."

THE MAGIC didn't stop with a nigger turning into a man and a man into a best friend. It kept widening and deepening. Kevin Troyer won't cry when he tells you about it, as the others do. They were all brought up to hold that back, but maybe his training was better. He just lays out the story, beginning that autumn day 10 years ago when he was 16, and Coach sat him in the front seat of his Jeep, looked in his eyes and said, "Tell me the truth."

Someone had broken into both Candles Hardware and R&R Sports and stolen merchandise. Whispers around town shocked even the whisperers: that the culprits were their heroes, kids who could walk into any restaurant in Berlin and never have to pay. They'd denied it over and over, and Coach had come to their defense . . . but now even he had begun to wonder.

A priest. That's what he'd told a few friends he would be if he weren't a coach. That's whose eyes Kevin felt boring into him. How could you keep lying to the man who stood in the lobby each morning, greeting the entire student body, searching everyone's eyes to see who needed a headlock, who needed lunch money, who needed love? "Don't know what you did today, princess," he'd sing out to a plump or unpopular girl, "but whatever it is, keep it up. You look great."

He'd show up wearing a cat's grin and the shirt you'd gotten for Christmas—how'd he get into your bedroom closet?—or carrying the pillow he'd snagged right from under your head on one of his Saturday morning sorties, when he slipped like smoke into players' rooms, woke them with a pop on the chest, then ran, cackling, out the door. Sometimes those visits came on the heels of the 1 a.m. raids he called Ninja Runs, when he rang doorbells and cawed "Gotcha!", tumbling one family after another downstairs in pajamas and robes to laugh and talk and relish the privilege of being targeted by Coach. He annihilated what people here had been brought up to keep: the space between each other.

His door was never locked. Everyone, boy or girl, was welcome to wade through those half dozen stray cats on the porch that Coach gruffly denied feeding till his stash of cat food was found, and open the fridge, grab a soda, have a seat, eat some pizza, watch a game, play cards or Ping-Pong or Nintendo . . . and talk. About race and religion and relationships and teenage trouble, about stuff that wouldn't surface at Kevin Troyer's dinner table in a million years. Coach listened the way other folks couldn't, listened clean without jumping ahead in his mind to what he'd say next, or to what the Bible said. When he finally spoke, he might play devil's advocate, or might offer a second or third alternative to a kid who'd seen only one, or might say the very thing Kevin didn't want to hear. But Kevin could bet his mother's savings that the conversations wouldn't leave that house.

Coach's home became the students' hangout, a place where they could sleep over without their parents' thinking twice . . . as long as they didn't mind bolting awake to a blast of AC/DC and a 9 a.m. noogie. There was no more guard to drop. Parents trusted Coach completely, relied on him to sow their values.

He sowed those, and a few more. He took Kevin and the other Hawks to two-room Amish schools to read and shoot hoops with wide-eyed children who might never get to see them play, took the players to one another's churches and then to his own, St. Peter, in Millersburg. He introduced them to Malcolm X, five-alarm chili, Martin Luther King Jr., B.B. King, crawfish, Cajun wings, John Lee Hooker, Tabasco sauce, trash-talk fishing, Muhammad Ali.

And *possibility*. That's what Coach stood for, just by virtue of his presence in Berlin: possibility, no matter how high the odds were stacked against you, no matter how whittled your options seemed in a community whose beliefs had barely budged in 200 years, whose mailboxes still carried the names of the same Amish families that had come in wagons out of Pennsylvania in the early 1800s—Yoders and Troyers and Stutzmans and Schlabachs and Hostetlers and Millers and Mullets and Masts. A place where kids, for decades, had graduated, married their prom dates and stepped into their daddies' farming or carpentry or lumber businesses without regard for the fact that Hiland High's graduating classes of 60 ranked in the top 10 in Ohio proficiency tests nearly every year. Kevin Troyer's parents didn't seem to care if he went to college. Coach's voice was the one that kept saying, "It's your life. There's so much more out there for you to see. Go places. Do things. Get a degree. Reach out. You have to take a chance."

The kids did, more and more, but not before Coach loaded them with laundry baskets full of items they'd need away from home, and they were never out of reach of those 6 a.m. phone calls. "I'm up," he'd say. "Now you are too. Remember, I'm always here for you."

He managed all that without raising red flags. He smuggled it under the warm coat of all that winning, up the sleeve of all that humility and humor. Everyone was too busy bubbling over the 11 conference titles and five state semifinals. Having too much fun volunteering to be henchmen for his latest prank, shoving Mr. Pratt's desk to the middle of his English classroom, removing the ladder to maroon the radio play-by-play man up in the Hawks' Nest loft, toilet-papering the school superintendent's yard and then watching Coach, the most honest guy in town, lie right through all 32 teeth. He was a bootlegger, that's what he was. A bootlegger priest.

"Kevin . . . tell the truth."

Kevin's insides trembled. How could he cash in his five teammates, bring down the wrath of a community in which the Ten Commandments were still stone, own up to the man whose explosions made the Hawks' Nest shudder? How could he explain something that was full of feeling and empty of logic—that somehow, as decent as his parents were, as warm as it felt to grow up in a place where you could count on a neighbor at any hour, it all felt suffocating? All the restrictions of a Conservative Mennonite church that forbade members to watch TV, to go to movies, to dance. All the emotions he'd choked back in a home ruled by a father and mother who'd been raised to react to problems by saying, "What will people think?" All the expectations of playing for the same team that his All-State brother, Keith, had carried to its first state semi in 24 years, back in 1986. Somehow, busting into those stores in the summer of '91 felt like the fist Kevin could never quite ball up and smash into all that.

"I . . . I did it, Coach. We . . ."

The sweetest thing eastern Holmes County had ever known was ruined. Teammate Randy Troyer, no relation to Kevin, disappeared when word got out. The community gasped—those six boys could never wear a Hawks uniform again. Coach? He resigned. He'd betrayed the town's trust and failed his responsibility, he told his superiors. His "sons" had turned to crime.

The administration begged him to stay. Who else was respected enough by family court judges, storekeepers, ministers and parents to find resolution and justice? Coach stared across the pond he fished behind his house. He came up with a solution both harder and softer than the town's. He would take Randy Troyer under his own roof, now that the boy had slunk back after two weeks of holing up in Florida motels. He'd be accountable for Randy's behavior. He'd have the six boys locked up in detention centers for two weeks, to know what jail tasted and smelled like. But he would let them back on the team. Let them feel lucky to be playing basketball when they'd really be taking a crash course in accountability.

Kevin found himself staring at the cinder-block wall of his cell, as lonely as a Mennonite boy could be. But there was Coach, making his rounds to all six lost souls. There was that lung-bursting bear hug, and another earful about not following others, about believing in yourself and being a man.

The Berlin Six returned. Randy Troyer lived in Coach's home for four months. Kevin walked to the microphone at the first pep rally, sick with nerves, and apologized to the school and the town.

Redemption isn't easy with a 5' 11" center, but how tight that 1991–92 team became, players piling into Coach's car every Thursday after practice, gathering around a long table at a sports bar a half hour away in Dover and setting upon giant cookie sheets heaped with 500 hot wings. And how those boys could run and shoot. Every time a 20-footer left the hands of Kevin Troyer or one of the Mishler twins, Nevin and Kevin, or the Hawks' star, Jr. Raber, Hiland's students rose, twirling when the ball hit twine and flashing the big red 3's on their T-shirts' backs.

Someday, perhaps in a generation or two, some Berliner might not remember every detail of that postseason march. Against Lakeland in the district championship, the Hawks came out comatose and fell behind 20–5, Coach too stubborn to call a timeout—the man could never bear to show a wisp of doubt. At halftime he slammed the locker-room door so hard that it came off its hinges, then he kicked a crater in a trash can, sent water bottles flying, grabbed jerseys and screamed so loud that the echoes peeled paint. Kevin and his mates did what all Hawks did: gazed straight into Coach's eyes and nodded. They knew in their bones how small his wrath was, held up against his love. They burst from that locker room like jackals, tore Lakeland to bits and handily won the next two games to reach the state semis. The world came to a halt in Berlin.

How far can a bellyful of hunger and a chestful of mission take a team before reality steps in and stops it? In the state semifinal in Columbus, against a Lima Central Catholic bunch loaded with kids quicker and thicker and taller and darker, led by the rattlesnake-sudden Hutchins brothers, Aaron and all-stater Anthony, the Hawks were cooked. They trailed 62–55 with 38 seconds left as Hiland fans trickled out in despair and Lima's surged to the box-office windows to snatch up tickets for the final. Lima called timeout to dot its *i*'s and cross its *t*'s, and there stood Coach in the Hiland huddle, gazing down at a dozen forlorn boys. He spoke more calmly than they'd ever heard him, and the fear and hopelessness leaked out of them as they stared into his eyes and drank in his plan. What happened next made you know that everything the bootlegger priest stood for—bucking the tide, believing in yourself and possibility—had worked its way from inside him to inside them.

Nevin Mishler, who would sit around the campfire in Coach's backyard talking about life till 2 a.m. on Friday nights, dropped in a rainbow three with 27 seconds left to cut the deficit to four. Timeout, calm words, quick foul. Lima's Anthony Hutchins blew the front end of a one-and-one.

Eleven seconds left. Jr. Raber, whose wish as a boy was to be black, just like Coach, banked in a driving, leaning bucket and was fouled. He drained the free throw. Lima's lead was down to one. Timeout, calm words, quick foul. Aaron Hutchins missed another one-and-one.

Nine ticks left. Kevin Troyer, who would end up going to college and becoming a teacher and coach because of Coach, tore down the rebound and threw the outlet to Nevin Mishler.

Seven seconds left. Nevin turned to dribble, only to be ambushed before half-court by Aaron Hutchins, the wounded rattler, who struck and smacked away the ball.

Five seconds left, the ball and the season and salvation skittering away as Nevin, who cared more about letting down Coach than letting down his parents, hurled his body across the wood and swatted the ball back toward Kevin Troyer. Kevin, who almost never hit the floor, who had been pushed by Coach for years to give more, lunged and collided with Anthony Hutchins, then spun and heaved the ball behind his back to Jr. Raber as Kevin fell to the floor.

Three seconds left. Jr. took three dribbles and heaved up the impossible, an off-balance 35-footer with two defenders in his face, a shot that fell far short at the buzzer . . . *but he was fouled*. He swished all three free throws, and the Hawks won, they won—no matter how many times Lima fans waiting outside for tickets insisted to Hiland fans that it couldn't be true—and two days later won the only state title in school history, by three points over Gilmour Academy, on fumes, pure fumes.

In the aisles, people danced who were forbidden to dance. The plaque commemorating the crowning achievement of Coach's life went straight from his hands into those of Joe Workman, a water and towel boy. Kevin Troyer and his teammates jumped Coach before he could sneak off, hugging him and kissing him and rubbing his head, but he had the last laugh. The 9 a.m. noogies would hurt even more those next nine years, dang that championship ring.

SOMEONE WOULD come and steal the magic. Some big-cheese high school or college would take Coach away—they knew it, they just knew it. It all seems so silly now, Steve Mullet says. It might take Steve the last half of his life to finish that slow, dazed shake of his head.

Berlin, you see, was a secret no more by the mid-1990s. Too much winning by Coach, too many tourists pouring in to peer at the men in black hats and black buggies. Two traffic lights had gone up, along with a Burger King and a couple dozen gift shops, and God knows how many restaurants and inns with the word *Dutch* on their shingles to reel in the rubberneckers. Even the Berlin House, where Willie Mast and the boys gathered, was now the Dutch Country Kitchen.

Here they came, the city slickers. Offering Coach big raises and the chance to hush that whisper in his head: Why keep working with disciplined, two-parent white kids when children of his own race were be-

ing devoured by drugs and despair for want of someone like him? Akron
Hoban wanted him. So did Canton McKinley, the biggest school in the
city where Coach had grown up, and Canton Timken, the high school he
attended. They wanted to take the man who'd transformed Steve Mullet's
family, turned it into something a simple and sincere country fellow had
never dreamed it might be. His first two sons were in college, thanks to
Coach, and his third one, another guard at Hiland, would likely soon be
too. Didn't Steve owe it to that third boy, Carlos, to keep Coach here?
Didn't he owe it to all the fathers of all the little boys around Berlin?

Coach had a way of stirring Steve's anxiety and the stew of rumors.
He would walk slow and wounded through each April after he'd driven
another team of runts to a conference crown, won two or three postseason
games, and then yielded to the facts of the matter, to some school with
nearly twice as many students and a couple of 6' 5" studs. "It's time for a
change," he'd sigh. "You guys don't need me anymore."

Maybe all missionaries are restless souls, one eye on the horizon, looking for who needs them most. Perhaps Coach was trying to smoke out
even the slightest trace of misgivings about him, so he could be sure to
leave before he was ever asked to. But Steve Mullet and eastern Holmes
County couldn't take that chance. They had to act. Steve, a dairy farmer
most of his life, knew about fencing. But how do you fence in a man when
no one really understands why he's there, or what he came from?

Who was Coach's family? What about his past? Why did praise and
attention make him so uneasy? The whole community wondered, but in
Berlin it was disrespectful to pry. Canton was only a 45-minute hop away,
yet Steve had never seen a parent or a sibling of Coach's, a girlfriend or
even a childhood pal. The bootlegger priest was a man of mystery and
moods as well as a wide-open door. He'd ask you how your grandma,
sister and uncle were every time you met, but you weren't supposed to
inquire about his—you just sensed it. His birthday? He wouldn't say. His
age? Who knew? It changed every time he was asked. But his loneliness,
that at last began to show.

There were whispers, of course. Some claimed he'd nearly married a
flight attendant, then beat a cold-footed retreat. A black woman appeared
in the stands once, set the grapevine sizzling, then was never glimpsed
again. Steve and his pals loved to tease Coach whenever they all made the

20-mile drive to Dinofo's, a pizza and pasta joint in Dover, and came face to face with that wild black waitress, Rosie. "When you gonna give it up?" she'd yelp at Coach. "When you gonna let me have it?"

He'd grin and shake his head, tell her it would be so good it would spoil her for life. Perhaps it was too scary, for a man who gave so much to so many, to carve it down to one. Maybe Jeff Pratt, the Hiland English teacher, had it right. Loving with detachment, he called it. So many people could be close to him, because no one was allowed too close.

A circle of women in Berlin looked on him almost as a brother—women such as Nancy Mishler, mother of the twins from the '92 title team, and Peg Brand, the school secretary, and Shelly Miller, wife of the booster club's president, Alan. They came to count on Coach's teasing and advice, on his cards and flowers and prayers when their loved ones were sick or their children had them at wit's end, and they did what they could to keep him in town. "I wish we could find a way to make you feel this is your family, that this is where you belong," Peg wrote him. "If you leave," she'd say, "who's going to make our kids think?" The women left groceries and gifts on his porch, homemade chocolate-chip cookies on his kitchen table, invited him to their homes on Sundays and holidays no matter how often he begged off, never wanting to impose.

But they all had to do more, Steve decided, picking up his phone to mobilize the men. For God's sake, Coach made only $28,000 a year. In the grand tradition of Mennonites and Amish, they rushed to answer the community call. They paid his rent, one month per donor; it was so easy to find volunteers that they had a waiting list. They replaced his garage when a leaf fire sent it up in flames; it sent him up a wall when he couldn't learn the charity's source. They passed the hat for that sparkling new gym at Hiland, and they didn't stop till the hat was stuffed with 1.6 million bucks. Steve Mullet eventually had Coach move into a big old farmhouse he owned. But first Steve and Willie Mast had another brainstorm: road trip. Why not give Coach a couple of days' escape from their cornfields and his sainthood, and show him how much they cared?

That's how Steve, a Conservative Mennonite in his mid-40s, married to a woman who didn't stick her head out in public unless it was beneath a prayer veil, found himself on Bourbon Street in New Orleans. Standing beside Willie and behind Coach, his heartbeat rising and stomach fluttering as he watched Coach suck down a Hurricane and cock his head outside a string of bars, listening for the chord that would pull him inside.

Coach nodded. This was the one. This blues bar. He pushed open the door. Music and smoke and beer musk belched out. Steve looked at Willie. You could go to hell for this, from everything they'd both been taught. Willie just nodded.

They wedged into a whorl of colors and humanity. When Steve was a boy, he'd seen blacks only after his parents jumped the fence, became Mennonites and took the family in their car each summer to a city zoo. Nothing cruel about blacks was ever said. Steve's parents simply pulled him closer when they were near, filled him with a feeling: Our kind and theirs don't mix. Now there were blacks pressed against his shoulders, blacks on microphones screaming lust and heartache into Steve's ears, blacks pounding rhythm through the floorboards and up into his knees. People touching, people gyrating their hips. You could go to hell for this. Steve looked at Willie as Coach headed to the bathroom. "I can't take this," Steve said.

"It's Coach's time, bub," Willie said.

Coach came back, smelled Steve's uneasiness and knew what to do. "Liven up," he barked and grinned. They got some beers, and it was just like the Hawks' radio play-by-play man, Mark Lonsinger, always said: Coach stood out in a room the instant he walked in, even though he did everything to deflect it. Soon Coach had the folks nearby convinced that he was Black Amish, a highly obscure sect, and Steve, swallowing his laughter, sealing the deal with a few timely bursts of Pennsylvania Dutch, had them believing the three of them had made it to New Orleans from Ohio in a buggy. Before you knew it, it was nearly midnight, and Steve's head was bobbing, his feet tapping, his funk found deep beneath all those layers of mashed potatoes. You know what, he was telling Willie, this Bourbon Street and this blues music really aren't so bad, and isn't it nice, too, how those folks found out that Mennonites aren't Martians?

When they pulled back into Coach's driveway after days filled with laughter and camaraderie, Steve glanced at Willie and sighed, "Well, now we return to our wives."

"You're the lucky ones," said Coach. "Don't you ever forget that."

Steve realized something when they returned from the road: It wasn't the road to ruin. He felt more space inside himself, plenty enough room for the black friends his sons began bringing home from college for the weekend. He realized it again the next year, when they returned to Bourbon Street, and the next, when they went once more, and the one after that as well. "Some things that I was taught were strictly no-nos . . . they're not sins," Steve will tell you. "All I know is that it all seemed right to do with him."

Funny how far that feeling had fanned, how many old, deep lines had blurred in Berlin, and what occurred in a dry community when Coach overdid it one night four years ago and tried one last time to leave. "I screwed up," he told school superintendent Gary Sterrett after he got that second DUI, 14 miles up the road in Sugar Creek. "You need to take my job."

What happened was sort of like what happened the time the ball rolled toward the Hawks' bench in a game they were fumbling away that year at Garaway High, and Coach pulled back his leg and kicked the ball so hard that it hissed past a referee's ear and slammed off the wall, the gym hushing in anticipation of the technical foul and the ejection. But nothing happened. The two refs had such enormous respect for Coach, they pretended it away.

He apologized to every player and to every player's parents for the DUI. Steve never mentioned it. The community never said a word. It was pretended away.

THEY'VE COMBED through the events a thousand times, lain in bed at night tearing themselves and God to shreds. There were clues, after all, and it was their job to notice things Coach was too stubborn to admit. They thought, when he holed up in his motel room for three days in Columbus last March, that it was merely one of his postseason moods, darker than ever after falling one game shy, for the third straight year, of playing for the state title. They thought he was still brooding two months later when, preoccupied and suffering from a cold he couldn't shake, he started scrambling names and dates and getting lost on country roads.

It all came to a head one Saturday last June, when he climbed into another rented tux because Phil Mishler, just like 50 or 60 kids before him, had to have Coach in his wedding party. At the reception, Coach offered his hand to Tom Mullet and said, "I'm Perry Reese Jr., Hiland High basketball coach." Tom Mullet had been Hiland's assistant athletic director for 10 years.

Phone lines buzzed that Sunday. People began comparing notes, discovering new oddities. On Monday night two of Coach's best friends, Dave Schlabach and Brian Hummel, headed to Mount Hope and the old farmhouse Coach had moved into just outside Berlin, the only house with lights in a community of Amish. They found him shivering in a blanket, glassy-eyed and mumbling nonsense.

Their worst possible fears . . . well, it went beyond all of them. Brain tumor. Malignant. Inoperable. Four to eight months to live, the doctors at Canton's Aultman Hospital said. You can't bring down a sledgehammer faster than that.

Jason Mishler, Coach's starting point guard the past two years, was the first kid to find out. He stationed himself in the chair beside Coach's bed, wouldn't budge all night and most of the next day. His cousin Kevin Mishler, from the state championship team, dropped his vacation on Hilton Head Island, S.C., and flew back. Dave Jaberg, who had played for Hiland a few years before that, dropped the bonds he was trading in Chicago and drove for six hours. Jr. Raber was on the first plane from Atlanta. Think a moment. How many teachers or coaches would you do that for?

The nurses and doctors were stupefied—didn't folks know you couldn't fit a town inside a hospital room? Coach's friends filled the lobby, the elevator, the halls and the waiting room. It was like a Hiland basketball game, only everyone was crying. Coach kept fading in and out, blinking up at another set of teary eyes and croaking, "What's new?"

What do people pray for when doctors don't give them a prayer? They swung for the fences. The Big M, a miracle. Some begged for it. Some demanded it. A thousand people attended a prayer vigil in the gym and took turns on the microphone. Never had so much anger and anguish risen from Berlin and gone straight at God.

Steroids shrank the tumor enough for Coach to return home, where another throng of folks waited, each telling the other tales of what Coach had done to change his life, each shocked to find how many considered him their best friend. When he walked through his front door and saw the wheelchair, the portable commode, the hospital bed and the chart Peg Brand had made, dividing the community's 24-hour care for Coach into six-hour shifts, he sobbed. The giving was finished. Now all he could do was take.

Go home, he ordered them. Go back to your families and lives. He called them names. They knew him well enough to know how loathsome it was for him to be the center of attention, the needy one. But they also knew what he would do if one of them were dying. They decided to keep coming anyway. They were family. Even more in his dying than in his living, they were fused.

They cooked for him, planned a trip to New York City he'd always dreamed of making, prayed and cried themselves to sleep. They fired off e-mails to churches across the country, recruited entire congregations who'd never heard of Coach to pray for the Big M. Louise Conway, grandmother of a player named Jared Coblentz, woke up three or four times a night, her heart thumping so hard that she had to drop to her knees and chew God's ear about Coach before she could drop back to sleep. People combed the Internet for little-known treatments. They were going to hoist a three at the buzzer and get fouled.

Coach? He did the strangest thing. He took two radiation treatments and stopped. He refused the alternative treatments, no matter how much people cried and begged and flung his own lessons in his face. Two other doctors had confirmed his fate, and damned if he was going to be helpless for long if he could help it. "Don't you understand?" he told a buddy, Doug Klar. "It's O.K. This is how it's supposed to be."

He finally had a plan, one that would make his death like his life, one that would mean the giving wasn't finished. He initiated a foundation, a college scholarship fund for those in need, started it rolling with his $30,000 life savings and, after swallowing hard, allowed it to be named after him on one condition: that it be kept secret until he was dead.

He had no way to keep all the puzzle pieces of his life in boxes now; dying shook them out. Folks found out, for instance, that he turned 48 last August. They were shocked to meet two half sisters they'd never heard of. They were glad finally to see Coach's younger sister, Audrey Johnson, whose picture was on his refrigerator door and who was studying to be a social worker, and his younger brother, Chris, who helps run group homes for people who can't fend for themselves and who took a leave of absence to care for Coach.

It turned out that Audrey had made a couple of quiet visits a year to Coach and that the family had gathered for a few hours on holidays; there were no dark or splintering secrets. He came from two strict parents who'd died in the '80s—his dad had worked in a Canton steel mill—and had a mixed-race aunt on one side of the family and a white grandfather on the other. But there were never quite enough pieces of the puzzle for anyone to put them together on a table and get a clean picture.

Coach's family was shocked to learn a few things too. Like how many conservative rural white folks had taken a black man into their hearts. "Amazing," said Jennifer Betha, his half sister, a supervisor for Head Start. "And so many loving, respectful, well-mannered children around him. They were like miniature Perrys! Our family was the independent sort, all kind of went our own ways. I never realized how easy it is to get to Berlin from Canton, how close it is. What a waste. Why didn't we come before?"

Coach had two good months, thanks to the steroids. Berlin people spent them believing that God had heard them, and that the miracle had come. Coach spent the months telling hundreds of visitors how much he cared about them, making one last 1 a.m. Ninja Run and packing his life into 10 neat cardboard boxes.

The first week of August, he defied doctors' orders not to drive and slipped into the empty school. Gerald Miller, his buddy and old boss at the wagon factory, found him later that day at home, tears streaming down his cheeks. "Worst day of my life," Coach said. "Worse than finding out about this thing in my head. I cleaned out my desk. I can't believe it. I'm not gonna teach anymore. I'm done."

In early September the tumor finally had its way. He began slurring words, falling down, losing the use of his right hand and leg, then his eyesight. "How are you doing?" he kept asking his visitors, on blind instinct. "Is there anything I can do for you?" Till the end he heard the door open and close, open and close, and felt the hands, wrapped around his, doing that too.

On the day he died, November 22, just over a week before the Hawks' first basketball game and 17 years after he first walked through their doors, Hiland looked like one of those schools in the news in which a kid has walked through the halls with an automatic weapon. Six ministers and three counselors walked around hugging and whispering to children who were huddled in the hallway crying or staring into space, to teachers sobbing in the bathrooms, to secretaries who couldn't bear it and had to run out the door.

AN OLD nettle digs at most every human heart: the urge to give oneself to the world rather than to only a few close people. In the end, unable to bear the personal cost, most of us find a way to ignore the prickle, comforting ourselves that so little can be changed by one woman or one man anyway.

How much, in the end, was changed by this one man? In Berlin, they're still tallying that one up. Jared Coblentz, who might have been the Hawks' sixth man this year, quit because he couldn't play for anyone other than Coach. Jason Mishler was so furious that he quit going to church for months, then figured out that it might be greedy to demand a miracle when you've been looking at one all your life. Tattoo parlors added Mennonites to their clientele. Jr. Raber stares at the R.I.P. with a P beneath it on his chest every morning when he looks into the mirror of his apartment in Atlanta. Jason Mishler rubs the image of Coach's face on the top of his left arm during the national anthem before every game he plays at West Liberty State in West Virginia.

The scholarship fund has begun to swell. Half the schools Hiland has played this season have chipped in checks of $500 or $600, while refs for the girls' basketball games frequently hand back their $55 checks for the pot.

Then there's the bigger stuff. Kevin Troyer has decided that someday, rather than teach and coach around Berlin, he'll reverse Coach's path and do it with black kids up in Canton. Funny, the question he asked himself that led to his decision was the same one that so many in Berlin ask themselves when they confront a dilemma: What would Coach do? Hard to believe, an outsider becoming the moral compass of a people with all those rules on how to live right.

And the even bigger stuff. Like Shelly and Alan Miller adopting a biracial boy 10 years ago over in Walnut Creek, a boy that Coach had taken under his wing. And the Keims over in Charm adopting two black boys, and the Schrocks in Berlin adopting four black girls, and the Masts just west of town adopting two black girls, and Chris Miller in Walnut Creek adopting a black girl. Who knows? Maybe some of them would have done it had there never been a Perry Reese Jr., but none of them would have been too sure that it was *possible*.

"When refugees came to America," the town psychologist, Elvin Coblentz, says, "the first thing they saw was the Statue of Liberty. It did something to them—became a memory and a goal to strive for your best, to give your all, because everything's possible. That's what Coach is to us."

At the funeral, just before Communion, Father Ron Aubry gazed across St. Peter, Coach's Catholic church in Millersburg. The priest knew that what he wanted to do wasn't allowed, and that he could get in trouble. But he knew Coach too. So he did it: invited everyone up to receive the holy wafer.

Steve Mullet glanced at his wife, in her simple clothing and veil. "Why not?" she whispered. After all, the service wasn't the bizarre ritual they had been led to believe it was, wasn't all that different from their own. Still, Steve hesitated. He glanced at Willie Mast. "Would Coach want us to?" Steve whispered.

"You got 'er, bub," said Willie.

So they rose and joined all the black Baptists and white Catholics pouring toward the altar, all the basketball players, all the Mennonites young and old. Busting laws left and right, busting straight into the kingdom of heaven.

POSTSCRIPT: *Berlin, Ohio still pays honor to the beloved Coach. Hiland High School built a new gym in his honor, the Perry Reese Jr. Community Center, and every Martin Luther King Jr. Day weekend the town holds a 20-team basketball tournament designed to bridge the gap between inner city and rural schools. The memorial fund he started with $30,000 has grown sevenfold. Every spring the fund awards two scholarships—one based on need, the other on basketball skill—to two college-bound Hiland grads. And Perry Reese's name lives on in another way. Says Shelly Miller, "At least five kids have been named after him. But I've stopped counting."*

The Chosen One

*Tiger Woods was raised to believe that his destiny was
to change the world. Could he fulfill his father's mighty vision
or would the relentless forces of celebrity grind him down?*

I T WAS ORDINARY. ALL SO ORDINARY. IT WAS A SALAD, A
dinner roll, a steak, a half potato, a slice of cake, a clinking
fork, a podium joke, a ballroom full of white-linen-tablecloth
conversation. Then a thick man with tufts of white hair rose
from the head table. His voice trembled and his eyes teared and his
throat gulped down sobs between words, and everything ordinary was
cast out of the room.

He said, "Please forgive me . . . but sometimes I get very emotional when I
talk about my son. . . . My heart . . . fills with *so . . . much . . . joy* . . . when I
realize . . . that this young man . . . is going to be able . . . to help so many

38

people. . . . He will *transcend* this game . . . and bring to the world . . . a humanitarianism . . . which has never been known before. The world will be a better place to live in . . . by virtue of his existence . . . and his presence. . . . I acknowledge only a small part in that . . . in that I know that I was personally selected by God himself . . . to nurture this young man . . . and bring him to the point where he can make his contribution to humanity. . . . This is my treasure. . . . Please accept it . . . and use it wisely. . . . Thank you."

Blinking tears, the man found himself inside the arms of his son and the applause of the people, all up on their feet.

IN THE history of American celebrity, no father has ever spoken this way. Too many dads have deserted or died before their offspring reached this realm, but mostly they have fallen mute, the father's vision exceeded by the child's, leaving the child to wander, lost, through the sad and silly wilderness of modern fame.

So let us stand amidst this audience at last month's Fred Haskins Award dinner to honor America's outstanding college golfer of 1996, and take note as Tiger and Earl Woods embrace, for a new manner of celebrity is taking form before our eyes. Regard the 64-year-old African-American father, arm upon the superstar's shoulder, right where the chip is so often found, declaring that this boy will do more good for the world than any man who ever walked it. Gaze at the 20-year-old son, with the blood of four races in his veins, not flinching an inch from the yoke of his father's prophecy but already beginning to scent the complications. The son who stormed from behind to win a record third straight U.S. Amateur last August, turned pro and rang up scores in the 60s in 21 of his first 27 rounds, winning two PGA Tour events as he doubled and tripled the usual crowds and dramatically changed their look and age.

Now turn. Turn and look at us, the audience, standing in anticipation of something different, something pure. *Quiet.* Just below the applause, or within it, can you hear the grinding? That's the relentless chewing mechanism of fame, girding to grind the purity and the promise to dust. Not the promise of talent, but the bigger promise, the father's promise, the one that stakes everything on the boy's not becoming separated from his own humanity and from all the humanity crowding around him.

It's a fitting moment, while he's up there at the head table with the audience on its feet, to anoint Eldrick (Tiger) Woods—the rare athlete to establish himself *immediately* as the dominant figure in his sport— as SPORTS ILLUSTRATED's 1996 Sportsman of the Year. And to pose a question: Who will win? The machine . . . or the youth who has just entered its maw?

TIGER WOODS will win. He'll fulfill his father's vision because of his mind, one that grows more still, more willful, more efficient, the greater the pressure upon him grows.

The machine will win because it has no mind. It flattens even as it lifts, trivializes even as it exalts, spreads a man so wide and thin that he becomes margarine soon enough.

Tiger will win because of God's mind. *Can't you see the pattern?* Earl Woods asks. *Can't you see the signs?* "Tiger will do more than any other man in history to change the course of humanity," Earl says.

Sports history, Mr. Woods? Do you mean more than Joe Louis and Jackie Robinson, more than Muhammad Ali and Arthur Ashe? "More than any of them because he's more charismatic, more educated, more prepared for this than anyone."

Anyone, Mr. Woods? Your son will have more impact than Nelson Mandela, more than Gandhi, more than Buddha?

"Yes, because he has a larger forum than any of them. Because he's playing a sport that's international. Because he's qualified through his ethnicity to accomplish miracles. He's the bridge between the East and the West. There is no limit because he has the guidance. I don't know yet exactly what form this will take. But he is the Chosen One. He'll have the power to impact nations. Not people. *Nations*. The world is just getting a taste of his power."

Surely this is lunacy. Or are we just too myopic to see? One thing's clear: We're witnessing the first volley of an epic encounter, the machine at its mightiest confronting the individual groomed all his life to conquer it and turn it to his use. The youth who has been exposed to its power since he toddled onto *The Mike Douglas Show* at three, the set of *That's Incredible!* at five, the boy who has been steeled against the silky seduction to which so many before him have succumbed. The one who, by all appearances, brings more psychological balance, more sense of self, more conscious-ness of possibility to the battlefield than any of his predecessors.

This is war, so let's start with war. Jungle, foliage up to a man's armpits, sweat trickling down his thighs, leeches crawling up them. Lieutenant Colonel Earl Woods, moving through the night with his rifle ready, won-dering why a U.S. Army public information officer stationed in Brooklyn decided in his mid-30s that he belonged in the Green Berets and ended up doing two tours of duty in Vietnam. Wondering why his first marriage has died and why the three children from it have ended up without a dad around when it's dark like this and it's time for bed—just as Earl ended up as a boy after his own father died. Wondering why he keeps plotting ways to return to the line of fire—"creative soldiering," he calls it—to eyeball death once more. To learn once again about his dark and cold side, the side that enables Earl, as Tiger will remark years later, "to slit your throat and then sit down and eat his dinner."

Oh, yes, Earl's one hell of a cocktail. A little Chinese, a little Cherokee, a few shots of African-American; don't get finicky about measurements, we're making a vat here. Pour in some gruff and a little intimidation, then some tenderness and warmth and a few jiggers of old anger. Don't hold back on intelligence. And stoicism. Add lots of stoicism, and even more of responsibility—"the most responsible son of a bitch you've ever seen in your life" is how Earl puts it. Top it all with "a bucket of whiskey," which is what he has been known to order when he saunters into a bar and he's in the mood. Add a dash of hyperbole, maybe two, and to hell with the ice, just *whir*. This is one of those concoctions you're going to remember when morning comes.

Somewhere in there, until a good 15 years ago, there was one other ingredient, the existential Tabasco, the smoldering *why*? The Thai sec-retary in the U.S. Army office in Bangkok smelled it soon after she met Earl, in 1967. "He couldn't relax," says Kultida (Tida) Woods. "Search-ing for something, always searching, never satisfied. I think because both his parents died when he was young, and he didn't have Mom and Dad to make him warm. Sometimes he stayed awake till three or four in the morning, just thinking."

In a man so accustomed to exuding command and control, in a Green Beret lieutenant colonel, *why*? has a way of building up power like a river dammed. Why did the Vietcong sniper bracket him that day—first bullet a few inches left of one ear, second bullet a few inches right of the other—but never fire the third bullet? Why did Earl's South Vietnamese combat buddy, Nguyen Phong—the one Earl nicknamed Tiger, and in whose memory he would nickname his son—stir one night just in time to awaken Earl and warn him not to budge because a viper was poised inches from his right eye? What about that road Earl's jeep rolled down one night, the same road on which two friends had just been mutilated, the road that took him through a village so silent and dark that his scalp tingled, and then, just beyond it . . . hell turned inside-out over his shoulder, the sky lighting up and all the huts he had just passed spewing Vietcong machine-gun and artillery fire? He never understands what is the purpose of Lieutenant Colonel Woods's surviving again and again. He never quite comprehends what is the point of his life, until. . . .

Until the boy is born. The boy who will get all the time that Earl was unable to devote to the three children from his first marriage. He will be the only child from Earl's second marriage, to the Thai woman he brought back to America, and right away there are signs. What other six-month-old, Earl asks, has the balance to stand in the palm of his father's hand and remain there even as Daddy strolls around the house? Was there another 11-month-old, ever, who could pick up a sawed-off club, imitate his father's golf swing so fluidly and drive the ball so wickedly into the nylon net across the garage? Another four-year-old who could be dropped off at the golf course at 9 a.m. on a Saturday and picked up at 5 p.m., pockets bulging with money he had won from disbelievers 10 and 20 years older, until Pop said, "Tiger, you can't *do* that"? Earl starts to get a glimmer. He is to be the father of the world's most gifted golfer.

But *why*? What for? Not long after Tiger's birth, when Earl has left the military to become a purchaser for McDonnell Douglas, he finds himself in a long discussion with a woman he knows. She senses the power pooling inside him, the friction. "You have so much to give," she tells him, "but you're not giving it. You haven't even scratched the surface of your potential." She suggests he try est, Erhard Seminars Training, an intensive self-discovery and self-actualizing technique, and it hits Earl hard, direct mortar fire to the heart. What he learns is that his overmuscular sense of responsibility for others has choked his potential.

"To the point," says Earl, "that I wouldn't even buy a handkerchief for myself. It went all the way back to the day my father died, when I was 11, and my mother put her arm around me after the funeral and said, 'You're the man of the house now.' I became the father that young, looking out for everyone else, and then she died two years later.

"What I learned through est was that by doing more for myself, I could do much more for others. Yes, be responsible, but *love* life, and give people the space to be in your life, and allow yourself room to give to others. That caring and sharing is what's most important, not being responsible for everyone else. Which is where Tiger comes in. What I learned led me to give so much time to Tiger, and to give him the space to be himself, and not to smother him with dos and don'ts. I took out the authority aspect and turned it into companionship. I made myself vulnerable as a parent. When you have to earn respect from your child, rather than demanding it because it's owed to you as the father, miracles happen. I realized that, through him, the giving could take a quantum leap. What I could do on a limited scale, he could do on a global scale."

At last, the river is undammed, and Earl's whole life makes sense. At last, he sees what he was searching for, a *pattern*. No more volunteering for missions—he has his. Not simply to be a great golfer's father. To be destiny's father. His son will change the world.

"What the hell had I been doing in public information in the Army, posted in Brooklyn?" he asks. "Why, of course, what greater training can there be than three years of dealing with the New York media to prepare me to teach Tiger the importance of public relations and how to handle the media?"

Father: Where were you born, Tiger?

Son, age three: I was born on December 30, 1975, in Long Beach, California.

Father: No, Tiger, only answer the question you were asked. It's important to prepare yourself for this. Try again.

Son: I was born in Long Beach, California.

Father: Good, Tiger, good.

The late leap into the Green Berets? "What the hell was that for?" Earl says. "Of course, to prepare me to teach Tiger mental toughness."

The three children by the first marriage? "Not just one boy the first time," says Earl, "but two, along with a girl, as if God was saying, 'I want this son of a bitch to *really* have previous training.'"

The Buddhist wife, the one who grew up in a boarding school after her parents separated when she was five, the girl who then vowed that her child would know nothing but love and attention? The one who will preach inner calm to Tiger simply by turning to him with that face—still awaiting its first wrinkle at 52? Whose eyes close when she speaks, so he can almost see her gathering and sifting the thoughts? The mother who will walk every hole and keep score for Tiger at children's tournaments, adding a stroke or two if his calm cracks? "Look at this stuff!" cries Earl. "Over and over you can see the plan being orchestrated by someone other than me because I'm not this damn good! I tried to get out of that combat assignment to Thailand. But Tida was meant to bring in the influence of the Orient, to introduce Tiger to Buddhism and inner peace, so he would have the best of two different worlds. And so he would have the knowledge that there were two people whose lives were totally committed to him."

What of the heart attack Earl suffered when Tiger was 10 and the retired lieutenant colonel felt himself floating down the gray tunnel toward the light before he was wrenched back? "To prepare me to teach Tiger that life is short," Earl says, "and to live each day to the maximum, and not worry about the future. There's only *now*. You must understand that time is just a linear measurement of successive increments of *now*. Anyplace you go on that line is *now*, and that's how you have to live it."

No need to wonder about the appearance of the perfect childhood coach, John Anselmo; the perfect sports psychologist, Jay Brunza; the perfect agent, Hughes Norton; the perfect attorney, John Merchant; and the perfect pro swing instructor, Butch Harmon. Or about the great tangle of fate that leads them all to Tiger at just the right junctures in his development. "Everything," says Earl, "right there when he needs it. *Everything*. There can't be this much coincidence in the world. This is a directed scenario, and none of us involved in the scenario has failed to accept the responsibility. This is all destined to be."

His wife ratifies this, in her own way. She takes the boy's astrological chart to a Buddhist temple in Los Angeles and to another in Bangkok and is told by monks at both places that the child has wondrous powers. "If he becomes a politician, he will be either a president or a prime minister," she is told. "If he enters the military, he will be a general."

Tida comes to a conclusion. "Tiger has Thai, African, Chinese, American Indian and European blood," she says. "He can hold everyone together. He is the Universal Child."

This is in the air the boy breathes for 20 years, and it becomes bone fact for him, marrow knowledge. When asked about it, he merely nods in acknowledgment of it, *assents* to it; *of course* he believes it's true. So failure, in the rare visits it pays him, is not failure. It's just life pausing to teach him a lesson he needs in order to go where he's inevitably going. And success, no matter how much sooner than expected it comes to the door, always finds him dressed and ready to welcome it. "Did you ever see yourself doing this so soon?" a commentator breathlessly asks him seconds after his first pro victory, on October 6 in Las Vegas, trying to elicit wonder and awe on live TV. "Yeah," Tiger responds. "I kind of did." And sleep comes to him so easily: In the midst of conversation, in a car, in a plane, off he goes, into the slumber of the destined. "I don't see any of this as scary or a burden," Tiger says. "I see it as fortunate. I've always known where I wanted to go in life. I've never let anything deter me. This is my purpose. *It will unfold.*"

No sports star in the history of American celebrity has spoken this way. Maybe, somehow, Tiger *can* win.

THE MACHINE will win. It must win because it too is destiny, five billion destinies leaning against one. There are ways to keep the hordes back, a media expert at Nike tells Tiger. Make broad gestures when you speak. Keep a club in your hands and take practice swings, or stand with one foot well out in front of the other, in almost a karate stance. That will give you room to breathe. Two weeks later, surrounded by a pen-wielding mob in La Quinta, Calif., just before the Skins Game, the instruction fails. Tiger survives, but his shirt and slacks are ruined, felt-tip-dotted to death.

The machine will win because it will wear the young man down, cloud his judgment, steal his sweetness, the way it does just before the Buick Challenge in Pine Mountain, Ga., in September. It will make his eyes drop when the fans' gaze reaches for his, his voice growl at their clawing hands, his body sag onto a sofa after a practice round and then rise and walk across the room and suddenly stop in bewilderment. "I couldn't even remember what I'd just gotten off the couch for, two seconds before," he says. "I was like mashed potatoes. Total mush."

So he walks away. Pulls out on the eve of the Buick Challenge, pulls out of the Fred Haskins Award dinner to honor him, and goes home. See, maybe Tiger *can* win. He can just turn his back on the machine and walk away. Awards? Awards to Tiger are like echoes, voices bouncing off the walls, repeating what a truly confident man has already heard inside his own head. The Jack Nicklaus Award, the one Jack himself was supposed to present to Tiger live on ABC during the Memorial tournament last spring? Tiger would have blown it off if Wally Goodwin, his coach at Stanford during the two years he played there before turning pro, hadn't insisted that he show up.

The instant Tiger walks away from the Buick Challenge and the Haskins dinner, the hounds start yapping. See, that's why the machine will win. It's got all those damn heel-nippers. Little mutts on the PGA Tour resenting how swiftly the 20-year-old was ordained, how hastily he was invited to play practice rounds with Nicklaus and Arnold Palmer. And big dogs snapping too. Tom Kite quoted as saying, "I can't ever remember being tired when I was 20," and Peter Jacobsen quoted, "You can't compare Tiger to Nicklaus and Palmer anymore because they never [walked out]."

He rests for a week, stunned by the criticism—"I thought those people were my friends," he says. He never second-guesses his decision to turn pro, but he sees what he surrendered. "I miss college," he says. "I miss hanging out with my friends, getting in a little trouble. I have to be so guarded now. I miss sitting around drinking beer and talking half the night. There's no one my own age to hang out with anymore because almost everyone my age is in college. I'm a target for everybody now, and there's nothing I can do about it. My mother was right when she said that turning pro would take away my youth. But golfwise, there was nothing left for me in college."

He reemerges after the week's rest and rushes from four shots off the lead on the final day to win the Las Vegas Invitational in sudden death. The world's waiting for him again, this time with reinforcements. Letterman and Leno want him as a guest; *GQ* calls about a cover; *Cosby*, along with almost every other sitcom you can think of, offers to write an episode revolving around Tiger, if only he'll appear. Kids dress up as Tiger for Halloween—did anyone ever dress up as Arnie or Jack?—and Michael Jordan declares that his only hero on earth is Tiger Woods. Pepsi is dying to have him cut a commercial for one of its soft drinks; Nike and Titleist call in chits for the $40 million and $20 million contracts he signed; money managers are eager to know how he wants his millions invested; women walk onto the course during a practice round and ask for his hand in marriage; kids stampede over and under ropes and chase him from the 18th hole to the clubhouse; piles of phone messages await him when he returns to his hotel room. "Why," Tiger asks, "do so many people want a piece of me?"

Because something deeper than conventional stardom is at work here, something so spontaneous and subconscious that words have trouble going there. It's a communal craving, a public aching for a superstar free of anger and arrogance and obsession with self. It's a hollow place that chimes each time Tiger and his parents strike the theme of father and mother and child love, each time Tiger stands at a press conference and declares, "They have raised me well, and I truly believe they have taught me to accept full responsibility for all aspects of my life." During the making of a Titleist commercial in November, a makeup woman is so moved listening to Earl describe his bond with Tiger that she decides to contact her long-estranged father. "See what I mean?" cries Earl. "Did *you* affect someone that way today? Did anyone else there? It's destiny, man. It's something bigger than me."

What makes it so vivid is context. The white canvas that the colors are being painted on—the moneyed, mature and almost minority-less world of golf—makes Tiger an emblem of youth overcoming age, have-not overcoming have, outsider overcoming insider, to the delight not only of the 18-year-olds in the gallery wearing nose rings and cornrows, but also—of all people—of the aging insider haves.

So Tiger finds himself, just a few weeks after turning pro at the end of August, trying to clutch a bolt of lightning with one hand and steer an all-at-once corporation—*himself*—with the other, and before this he has never worked a day in his life. Never mowed a neighbor's lawn, never flung a folded newspaper, never stocked a grocery shelf; Mozarts just don't, you know. And he has to act as if none of this is new or vexing because he has this characteristic—perhaps from all those years of hanging out with his dad at tournaments, all those years of mixing with and mauling golfers five, 10, 20, 30 years older than he is—of never permitting himself to appear confused, surprised or just generally a little squirt. "His favorite expression," Earl says, "is, 'I knew that.' " Of course Pop, who is just as irreverent with Tiger as he is reverent, can say, "No, you didn't know that, you little s---." But Earl, who has always been the filter for Tiger, decides to take a few steps back during his son's first few months as a pro because he wishes to encourage Tiger's independence and because he is uncertain of his own role now that the International Management Group (IMG) is managing Tiger's career.

Nobody notices it, but the inner calm is beginning to dissolve. Earl enters Tiger's hotel room during the Texas Open in mid-October to ask him about his schedule, and Tiger does something he has never done in his 20 years. He bites the old man's head off.

Earl blinks. "I understand how you must feel," he says.

"No, you don't," snaps Tiger.

"And I realized," Earl says later, "that I'd spent 20 years planning for this, but the one thing I didn't do was educate Tiger to be the boss of a corporation. There was just no vehicle for that, and I thought it would develop more slowly. I wasn't presumptuous enough to anticipate *this*. For the first time in his life, the training was behind the reality. I could see on his face that he was going through hell."

The kid is fluid, though. Just watch him walk. He's quick to flow into the new form, to fit the contour of necessity. A few hours after the outburst he's apologizing to his father and hugging him. A few days later he's giving Pop the O.K. to call a meeting of the key members of Tiger's new corporation and establish a system, Lieutenant Colonel Woods in command, chairing a 2½-hour teleconference with the team each week to sift through all the demands, weed out all the chaff and present Tiger five decisions to make instead of 500. A few days after that, the weight forklifted off his shoulders, at least temporarily, Tiger wins the Walt Disney World/Oldsmobile Classic. And a few weeks later, at the Fred Haskins Award dinner, which has been rescheduled at his request, Tiger stands at the podium and says, "I should've attended the dinner [the first time]. I admit I was wrong, and I'm sorry for any inconvenience I may have caused. But I have learned from that, and I will never make that mistake again. I'm very honored to be part of this select group, and I'll always remember, for both good and bad, this Haskins Award; for what I did and what I learned, for the company I'm now in and I'll always be in. Thank you very much." The crowd surges to its feet, cheering once more.

SEE, MAYBE Tiger *can* win. He's got the touch. He's got the feel. He never writes down a word before he gives a speech. When he needs to remember a phone number, he doesn't search his memory or a little black book; he picks up a phone and watches what number his fingers go to. When he needs a 120-yard shot to go under an oak branch and over a pond, he doesn't visualize the shot, as most golfers would. He looks at the flag and pulls everything from the hole back, back, back . . . not back into his mind's eye, but into his hands and forearms and hips, so they'll do it by feel. Explain how he made that preposterous shot? He can't. Better you interview his knuckles and metacarpals.

"His *handicap*," says Earl, "is that he has such a powerful creative mind. His imagination is *too* vivid. If he uses visualization, the ball goes nuts. So we piped into his creative side even deeper, into his incredible sense of feel."

"I've learned to trust the subconscious," says Tiger. "My instincts have never lied to me."

The mother radiates this: the Eastern proclivity to *let* life happen, rather than the Western one to *make* it happen. The father comes to it in his own way, through fire. To kill a man, to conduct oneself calmly and efficiently when one's own death is imminent—a skill Earl learns in Green Berets psychological training and then again and again in jungles and rice paddies—one removes the conscious mind from the task and yields to the subconscious. "It's the more powerful of the two minds," Earl says. "It works faster than the conscious mind, yet it's patterned enough to handle routine tasks over and over, like driving a car or making a putt. It knows what to do.

"Allow yourself the freedom of emotion and feeling. Don't try to control them and trap them. Acknowledge them and become the beneficiary of them. Let it all outflow."

Let it all because it's all there: The stability, almost freakish for a close-of-the-millennium California child—same two parents, same house all his 20 years, same best friends, one since second grade, one since eighth. The kid, for god's sake, never once had a babysitter. The conditioning is there as well, the two years of psychological boot camp during which Earl dropped golf bags and pumped cart brakes during Tiger's backswings, jingled change and rolled balls across his line of vision to test his nerves, promising him at the outset that he only had to say "Enough" and Earl would cut off the blowtorch, but promising too that if Tiger graduated, no man he ever faced would be mentally stronger than he. "I *am* the toughest golfer mentally," Tiger says.

The bedrock is so wide that opposites can dance upon it: The cautious man can be instinctive, the careful man can be carefree. The bedrock is so wide that it has enticed Tiger into the habit of falling behind—as he did in the final matches of all three U.S. Junior Amateur and all three U.S. Amateur victories—knowing in his tissue and bones that danger will unleash his greatest power. "Allow success and fame to happen," the old man says. "Let the legend grow."

TO HELL with the Tao. The machine will win, it has to win, because it makes everything happen before a man knows it. Before he knows it, a veil descends over his eyes when another stranger approaches. Before he knows it, he's living in a walled community with an electronic gate and a security guard, where the children trick-or-treat in golf carts, a place like the one Tiger just moved into in Orlando to preserve some scrap of sanity. Each day there, even with all the best intentions, how can he help but be a little more removed from the world he's supposed to change, and from his truest self?

Which is . . . *who*? The poised, polite, opaque sage we see on TV? No, no, no; his friends hoot and haze him when they see that Tiger on the screen, and he can barely help grinning himself. The Tiger they know is perfectly 20, a fast-food freak who never remembers to ask if anyone else is hungry before he bolts to Taco Bell or McDonald's for the 10th time of the week. The one who loves riding roller coasters, spinning out golf carts and winning at cards no matter how often his father accuses him of "reckless eyeballing." The one who loves delivering the dirty joke, who owns a salty barracks tongue just a rank or two beneath his father's. The one who's flip, downright cocky. When a man in a suit walks up to him before the Haskins Award dinner and says, "I think you're going to be the next great one, but those are mighty big shoes to fill," Tiger replies, "Got big feet."

A typical exchange between Tiger and his agent, Norton:

"Tiger, they want to know when you can do that interview."

"Tell them to kiss my ass!"

"All right, and after that, what should I tell them?"

"Tell them to kiss my ass again!"

"O.K., and after that. . . ."

But it's a cockiness cut with humility, the paradox pounded into his skull by a father who in one breath speaks of his son with religious awe and in the next grunts, "You weren't s--- then, Tiger. You ain't s--- now. You ain't never gonna be s---."

"That's why I know I can handle all this," Tiger says, "no matter how big it gets. I grew up in the media's eye, but I was taught never to lose sight of where I came from. Athletes aren't as gentlemanly as they used to be. I don't like that change. I like the idea of being a role model. It's an honor. People took the time to help me as a kid, and they impacted my life. I want to do the same for kids."

So, if it's a clinic for children instead of an interview or an endorsement for adults, the cynic in Tiger gives way to the child who grew up immersed in his father's vision of an earth-altering compassion, the seven-year-old boy who watched scenes from the Ethiopian famine on the evening news, went right to his bedroom and returned with a $20 bill to contribute from his piggy bank. Last spring busloads of inner-city kids would arrive at golf courses where Tiger was playing for Stanford, spilling out to watch the Earl and Tiger show in wonder. Earl would talk about the dangers of drugs, then proclaim, "Here's Tiger Woods on drugs," and Tiger would stagger to the tee, topping the ball so it bounced crazily to the side. And then, presto, with a wave of his arms Earl would remove the drugs from Tiger's body, and his son would stride to the ball and launch a 330-yard rocket across the sky. Then Earl would talk about respect and trust and hard work and demonstrate what they can all lead to by standing 10 feet in front of his son, raising his arms and telling Tiger to smash the ball between them—and, *whoosh*, Tiger would part not only the old man's arms but his haircut too.

They've got plans, the two of them, big plans, for a Tiger Woods Foundation that will fund scholarships across the country, set up clinics and coaches and access to golf courses for inner-city children. "I throw those visions out there in front of him," Earl says, "and it's like reeling in a fish. He goes for the bait, takes it and away he goes. This is nothing new. It's been working this way for a long time."

"That's the difference," says John Merchant, Tiger's lawyer and a family friend. "Other athletes who have risen to this level just didn't have this kind of guidance. With a father and mother like Tiger's, he *has* to be real. It's such a rare quality in celebrities nowadays. There hasn't been a politician since John Kennedy whom people have wanted to touch. But watch Tiger. He *has* it. He actually listens to people when they stop him in an airport. He looks them in the eye. I can't ever envision Tiger Woods selling his autograph."

Maybe. Just maybe Tiger can win.

LET'S BE honest. The machine will win because you can't work both sides of this street. The machine will win because you can't transcend wearing 16 Nike swooshes, can't move human hearts while you're busy pushing sneakers. Gandhi didn't hawk golf balls, did he? Jackie Robinson was spared that fate because he came and went while Madison Avenue was still teething. Ali became a symbol instead of a logo because of boxing's disrepute and because of the attrition of cells in the basal ganglia of his brain. Who or what will save Tiger Woods?

Did someone say *Buddha*?

Every year near his birthday, Tiger goes with his mother to a Buddhist temple and makes a gift of rice, sugar and salt to the monks there who have renounced all material goods. A mother-of-pearl Buddha given to Tiger by his Thai grandfather watches over him while he sleeps, and a gold Buddha hangs from the chain on his neck. "I like Buddhism because it's a whole way of being and living," Tiger says. "It's based on discipline and respect and personal responsibility. I like Asian culture better than ours because of that. Asians are much more disciplined than we are. Look how well behaved their children are. It's how my mother raised me. You can question, but talk back? *Never.* In Thailand, once you've earned people's respect, you have it for life. Here it's, What have you done for me lately? So here you can never rest easy. In this country I have to be very careful. I'm easygoing, but I won't let you in completely. There, I'm Thai, and it feels very different. In many ways I consider that home.

"I believe in Buddhism. Not every aspect, but most of it. So I take bits and pieces. I don't believe that human beings can achieve ultimate enlightenment, because humans have flaws. I don't want to get rid of all my wants and desires. I can enjoy material things, but that doesn't mean I need them. It doesn't matter to me whether I live in a place like this"—the golf club in his hand makes a sweep of the Orlando villa—"or in a shack. I'd be fine in a shack, as long as I could play some golf. I'll do the commercials for Nike and for Titleist, but there won't be much more than that. I have no desire to be the king of endorsement money."

On the morning after he decides to turn pro, there's a knock on his hotel room door. It's Norton, bleary-eyed but exhilarated after a late-night round of negotiations with Nike. He explains to Tiger and Earl that the benchmark for contract endorsements in golf is Greg Norman's reported $2½ million-a-year deal with Reebok. Then, gulping down hard on the *yabba-dabba-doo* rising up his throat, Norton announces Nike's offer: $40 million for five years, *eight mil a year.* "Over three times what Norman gets!" Norton exults.

Silence.

"Guys, do you realize this is more than Nike pays any athlete in salary, even *Jordan*?"

Silence.

"Finally," Norton says now, recalling that morning, "Tiger says, '*Mmmm-hmmm*,' and I say, 'That's *it*? Mmmm-hmmm?' No 'Omigod.' No slapping five or 'Ya-hooo!' So I say, 'Let me go through this again, guys.' Finally Tiger says, 'Guess that's pretty amazing.' That's *it*. When I made the deal with Titleist a day later, I went back to them saying, 'I'm almost embarrassed to tell you this one. Titleist is offering a little more than $20 million over five years.'"

On the Monday morning after his first pro tournament, a week after the two megadeals, Tiger scans the tiny print on the sports page under Milwaukee Open money earnings and finds his name. *Tiger Woods: $2,544.* "That's *my* money," he exclaims. "I *earned* this!"

See? Maybe Tiger *can* win.

HOW? HOW can he win when there are so many insects under so many rocks? Several more death threats arrive just before the Skins Game, prompting an increase in his plainclothes security force, which is already larger than anyone knows. His agent's first instinct is to trash every piece of hate mail delivered to IMG, but Tiger won't permit it. Every piece of racist filth must be saved and given to him. At Stanford he kept one letter taped to his wall. Fuel comes in the oddest forms.

The audience, in its hunger for goodness, swallows hard over the Nike ad that heralds Tiger's entrance into the professional ranks. The words that flash on the screen over images of Tiger—*There are still courses in the United States I am not allowed to play because of the color of my skin. I've heard I'm not ready for you. Are you ready for me?*—ooze the very attitude from which many in the audience are seeking relief. The media backlash is swift: The Tiger Woods who used to tell the press, "The only time I think about race is when the media ask me"—whoa, what happened to *him?*

What happened to him was a steady accretion of experiences, also known as a life. What happened, just weeks before he was born, was a fusillade of limes and BBs rattling the Woods house in Cypress, Calif., one of the limes shattering the kitchen window, splashing glass all around the pregnant Tida, to welcome the middle-class subdivision's first non-Caucasian family.

What happened was a gang of older kids seizing Tiger on his first day of kindergarten, tying him to a tree, hurling rocks at him, calling him monkey and nigger. And Tiger, at age five, telling no one what happened for several days, trying to absorb what this meant about himself and his world.

What happened was the Look, as Tiger and Earl came to call it, the uneasy, silent stare they received in countless country-club locker rooms and restaurants. "Something a white person could never understand," says Tiger, "unless he went to Africa and suddenly found himself in the middle of a tribe." What happened was Tiger's feeling pressured to leave a driving range just two years ago, not far from his family's California home, because a resident watching Tiger's drives rocket into the nearby protective netting reported that a black teenager was trying to bombard his house.

What happened was the cold shoulder Earl got when he took his tyke to play at the Navy Golf Course in Cypress—"a club," Earl says, "composed mostly of retired naval personnel who knew blacks only as cooks and servers, and along comes me, a retired lieutenant colonel outranking 99 percent of them, and I have the nerve to take up golf at 42 and immediately become a low handicap and beat them, and then I have the *audacity* to have this kid. Well, they had to do something. They took away Tiger's playing privileges twice, said he was too young, even though there were other kids too young who they let play. The second time it happened, I went up to the pro who had done it and made a bet. I said, 'If you'll spot my three-year-old just one stroke a hole, nine holes, playing off the same tees, and he beats you, will you certify him?' The pro started laughing and said, 'Sure.' Tiger beat him by two strokes, got certified, then the members went over the pro's head and kicked him out again. That's when we switched him to another course."

Beat them. That was his parents' solution for each banishment, each Look. Hold your tongue, hew to every rule and *beat them.* Tiger Woods is the son of the first black baseball player in the Big Seven, a catcher back in the early '50s, before the conference became the Big Eight. A man who had to leave his Kansas State teammates on road trips and travel miles to stay in motels for blacks; who had to go to the back door of restaurant kitchens to be fed while his teammates dined inside; who says, "This is the most racist society in the world—I *know* that." A man who learned neither to extinguish his anger nor spray it but to quietly convert it into animus, the determination to enter the system and overcome it by turning its own tools against it. A Green Berets explosives expert whose mind naturally ran that way, whose response, upon hearing Tiger rave about the security in his new walled community, was, "*I* could get in. I could blow up the clubhouse and be gone before they ever knew what hit them." A father who saw his son, from the beginning, as the one who would enter one of America's last Caucasian bastions, the PGA Tour, and overthrow it from within in a manner that would make it smile and ask for more.

"Been planning that one for 20 years," says Earl. "See, you don't turn it into hatred. You turn it into something positive. So many athletes who reach the top now had things happen to them as children that created hostility, and they bring that hostility with them. But that hostility uses up energy. If you can do it without the chip on the shoulder, it frees up all that energy to create."

It's not until Stanford, where Tiger takes an African-American history course and stays up half the night in dormitories talking with people of every shade of skin, that his experiences begin to crystallize. "What I realized is that even though I'm mathematically Asian—if anything—if you have one drop of black blood in the United States, you're black," says Tiger. "And how important it is for this country to talk about this subject. It's not *me* to blow my horn, the way I come across in that Nike ad, or to say things quite that way. But I felt it was worth it because the message needed to be said. You can't say something like that in a polite way. Golf has shied away from this for too long. Some clubs have brought in tokens, but nothing has really changed. I hope what I'm doing can change that."

But don't overestimate race's proportion in the fuel that propels Tiger Woods. Don't look for traces of race in the astonishing rubble at his feet on the Sunday after he lost the Texas Open by two strokes and returned to his hotel room and snapped a putter in two with one violent lift of his knee. Then another putter. And another. And another and another—eight in all before his rage was spent and he was ready to begin considering the loss's philosophical lesson. "That volcano of competitive fire, that comes from me," says Earl. A volcano that's mostly an elite athlete's need to win, a need far more immediate inside Tiger Woods than that of changing the world.

No, don't overestimate race, but don't overlook it, either. When Tiger is asked about racism, about the effect it has on him when he senses it in the air, he has a golf club in his hands. He takes the club by the neck, his eyes flashing hot and cold at once, and gives it a short upward thrust. He says, "It makes me want to stick it right up their asses." Pause. "On the golf course."

THE MACHINE will win because there is so much of the old man's breath in the boy . . . and how long can the old man keep breathing? At 2 a.m., hours before the second round of the Tour Championship in

Tulsa on October 25, the phone rings in Tiger's hotel room. It's Mom. Pop's in an ambulance, on his way to a Tulsa hospital. He's just had his second heart attack.

The Tour Championship? The future of humanity? The hell with 'em. Tiger's at the old man's bedside in no time, awake most of the night. Tiger's out of contention in the Tour Championship by dinnertime, with a second-round 78, his worst till then as a pro. "There are things more important than golf," he says.

The old man survives—and sees the pattern at work, of course. He's got to throw away the cigarettes. He's got to quit ordering the cholesterol special for breakfast. "I've got to shape up now, God's telling me," Earl says, "or I won't be around for the last push, the last lesson." The one about how to ride the tsunami of runaway fame.

The machine will win because no matter how complicated it all seems now, it is simpler than it will ever be. The boy will marry one day, and the happiness of two people will lie in his hands. Children will follow, and it will become his job to protect three or four or five people from the molars of the machine. Imagine the din of the grinding in five, 10, 15 years, when the boy reaches his golfing prime.

The machine will win because the whole notion is so ludicrous to begin with, a kid clutching an eight-iron changing the course of humanity. No, of course not, there won't be thousands of people sitting in front of tanks because of Tiger Woods. He won't bring about the overthrow of a tyranny or spawn a religion that one day will number 300 million devotees.

But maybe Pop is onto something without quite seeing what it is. Maybe it has to do with timing: the appearance of his son when America is turning the corner to a century in which the country's faces of color will nearly equal those that are white. Maybe, every now and then, a man gets swallowed by the machine, but the machine is changed more than he is.

For when we swallow Tiger Woods, the yellow-black-red-white man, we swallow something much more significant than Michael Jordan or Charles Barkley. We swallow hope in the American experiment, in the pell-mell jumbling of genes. We swallow the belief that the face of the future is not necessarily a bitter or bewildered face; that it might even, one day, be something like Tiger Woods's face: handsome and smiling and ready to kick all comers' asses.

We see a woman, 50-ish and Caucasian, well-coiffed and tailored—
the woman we see at every country club—walk up to Tiger Woods before
he receives the Haskins Award and say, "When I watch you taking on all
those other players, Tiger, I feel like I'm watching my own son" . . . and
we feel the quivering of the cosmic compass that occurs when human
beings look into the eyes of someone of another color and see their own
flesh and blood.

———◆———

POSTSCRIPT: *With 65 career wins, 14 majors and counting, Tiger Woods has
finished at No. 1 in the world in all but three years of his professional career.
He remained exceptionally close to his father until May 2006, when Earl died
at age 74 after an eight-year battle with prostate cancer. The Tiger Woods
Learning Center opened in Anaheim in February 2006 and has since helped
over 23,000 students—85% of them Hispanic—to develop life skills in subjects
as varied as forensic science, robotics and rocket design.*

Lying in Wait

*A dirty secret followed George O'Leary as he climbed the coaching
ladder to his dream job at Notre Dame—then took just five days to bring
him crashing down. Did he pay a fair price for a few lies?*

HERE, THEN, TO START THE STORY OF THE
Notre Dame football coach's flaming fall from
grace? Upon George O'Leary's hotel bed that
night, as his hand keeps rubbing his face and his
lips whisper, "Oh, Jesus . . . oh, Jesus . . . what will my mother say?" Or
at the Minnesota Vikings office of George's old high school quarterback,
who quietly shuts the door so no one will hear him sob?

No. They're both too close.

Perhaps on the laptop screen of the columnist in Chicago as the words
"low-rent fraud" flash to life in his third sentence? Or on the sketch

59

pad of *The Orange County Register* cartoonist as he draws George with a Pinocchio nose at a job interview, saying, "I can fly if I concentrate really hard."

No. They're both too far away.

How about in the kitchen of a white Cape Cod in Liverpool, N.Y.? Yes, that's it, the kitchen where an old Italian has just come to a halt, electrocuted by the radio news of the lies on George O'Leary's résumé and of his resignation on December 14, five days after taking his dream job at Notre Dame. Luke LaPorta sags into a chair. His eyes close, and 23 years collapse: He's sitting in his office as athletic director at Liverpool High in the summer of 1978, asking his young Irish Catholic football coach a question so loaded, so personal, that he can barely squeeze it from his throat: "George . . . are there any inconsistencies in how you've represented yourself?"

Luke knows the answer. The school superintendent, Virgil Tompkins, has called him aside and informed him of inaccuracies in George's claims about his playing career and postgraduate credits, and now the heat's on Luke, who hired George over 84 other applicants the year before. But Luke still hopes against hope that it's all a misunderstanding, because if this man's a liar, then the world's flat and the moon's square and eagles are no better than cockroaches.

George flushes red. "A lot of people do that," he replies.

Luke comes from a Long Island neighborhood teeming with ethnic groups. So does George. Both know the dictionary of meanings contained in the small gestures and the eye flickers of first-generation immigrants. George's shoulders shrug, his lips purse, and his eyes cut to one side. Luke knows what George's look means:

That's all I'm going to say. That's the way of the world. You and I, we understand each other. There's no need to do anything. We'll just let it lie . . . right?

Maybe some other language has a word for what runs through Luke. It's something close to nausea and not far from deep sorrow. He knows it's true: Everyone lies. He knows that if he chooses compassion, he chooses complicity. His last name, in Italian, means "the door." Now he stands at the portal of George O'Leary's career, holding his fate. LaPorta can open. LaPorta can shut.

Luke sits, guts turning, in his office in June 1978. He sits, guts turning, in his kitchen in December 2001. Again he weighs a life against a lie.

A LETTER rests in Luke's wrinkled hands. It arrived just a few days after George O'Leary stared out his hotel room's second-story window and decided that 20 feet wasn't enough to do the job.

Dear Coach LaPorta,

I want to thank Coach O'Leary for all he did for my son Rich. . . . Because of Coach O'Leary, my son behaved himself in high school and became one of his class's leaders. He developed respect for his parents (that alone was wonderful), valued his physical body, became one of a team, and stretched himself to produce "110%." . . . As an adult, my son carried his leadership and teaching skills to other boys and girls and has coached in methods O'Leary instilled in him as a teen. He is both a better parent and a better coach because of Coach O'Leary.

I am saddened to hear of Coach O'Leary's difficulties. My prayer is that they don't stop Coach from doing what he does best—coach! Because somewhere there are other teens and young men who would benefit from it. . . .

I also thank you for your wisdom in hiring O'Leary. . . .

Sincerely,

Barbara Wiggins,

Rich Wiggins's Mom

LUKE IS 77. He's determined the fates of liars and birth-certificate forgers—coaches and parents who try to pass off their 14-year-olds for 12-year-olds—during his quarter century on the board of Little League Baseball International. As a boy during the Depression, working at his family's gas station, he was astonished when adults volunteered to pump their own gas so they could squeeze out an extra nickel's worth and then plead that their hands had slipped. But then, Luke himself filched dimes from the till, from his own blood, and clamped his lips when his grandfather confronted him.

What should he have done that day, that moment after George gave him that look? Could he have averted the personal catastrophe that lay in silent wait for George for the next 23 years, gathering, girding? What would *you* have done?

Say nothing. That's all the old man wants of you for now. First you must know George and the soil that grew his lies, maybe your lies, my lies. First you must know the net effect of his 55 years on earth and lay that against the net effect of the sin.

Here. Take one. Read it. It's George's curriculum vitae. Not the bogus one claiming that he lettered in football for three years at the University of New Hampshire and holds a master's degree in education from New York University. Not a bare-bones list of jobs and dates. A man is so much more than that—doesn't *vitae* mean "of life"? Then you can decide. Then you'll have the right to make Luke's choice.

GEORGE J. O'LEARY
BIRTH DATE: AUGUST 17, 1946
STATUS: MARRIED WITH FOUR CHILDREN
EXPERIENCE: 1953–60 ALTAR BOY

GEORGE WAS seven when he first played with fire. "*Who* had the matches?" demanded his mother. George and his four siblings shrugged and shook their heads. A liar? In Peggy O'Leary's house? A liar would kneel in salt or get an earful of God and His mother. There *had* to be accountability in Peggy O'Leary's house.

She wasn't a cartoon ogre. She was a splendidly spunky sort—still is—a dandy fox-trotter with sparkling blue eyes and no hesitation about laughing at herself. A woman born to raise boys, all four of them: a classic Irish mom. She pointed to the bathtub and the singe marks made by the matches. "The Blessed Mother's watching!" she cried. Our Lady. *Notre Dame.* The statuette in the living room. "She'll tell me who did it!" Mrs. O'Leary cried.

George swallowed. He was about to become an altar boy. A few days passed, George tiptoeing around his mother and God's mother until the supper dishes were done. That's when the family always knelt under Our Lady's gaze and said the rosary, the boys machine-gunning their 10 Hail Marys apiece so they could get back to playing ball and dying a thousand deaths as their sister, Margaret, stretched each *theeeee* and *thyyyyy* from here to kingdom come.

Then it happened. George reached again for the matchbox above the sink. Every kid played with matches, but George had been warned, and now he was going to play with fire a second time. Mrs. O'Leary burst into the kitchen, grabbed him and banished him to his bedroom. "When your father comes home," she shouted, "you'll be taken away to live in the Home for Wayward Children!"

Dusk fell. Dad entered the high-rise projects where the O'Learys lived on the Lower East Side of Manhattan. A wee scrap of a man, just over 5½ feet tall and 140 pounds, but full to the brim with pep and piss and pun was George the Father. He'd drop to the floor in his 50s to bang out push-ups, clapping his hands after each one, and when he blinked the telltale twinkle from his eye and told his kids that the jagged scar across his gut—the result of an ulcer operation that removed three quarters of his stomach—actually stemmed from his belly dive onto a grenade to save a buddy during World War II, they believed him. After all, he'd been a paratrooper, and who on earth was a more loyal soul than he?

Dad headed to George's bedroom, hotfooted by his wife's glower. He shut the door and confronted his son. Dad was renowned for his brutal honesty, but Dad, God rest his soul, was a pushover. The sight of a forlorn child seemed to mine misery from the ninth year of his own life, when his father had vanished. "You can't play with matches, George," he rebuked his son. Job done, he melted. It wasn't really that serious, Son, and give Mom a day or two, she'd lighten up, and maybe he could sneak young George a bite to eat or slip him a nickel for candy.

George's older brother, Peter, the one with a striking IQ and magnificent wrists, was a .500-hitting high schooler whom opponents would defend with four outfielders. Terry, a year younger than George, was a straight-A student with a blue-ribbon jump shot, a future Suffolk County high school tournament MVP. Margaret, three years younger, was sweetness itself, no worries there. George? Well, let's be honest: George was no slickie. *Thick* and *blunt* were the adjectives his family hung on him, a mostly B and C student who couldn't dance or carry a tune in a houseful of hams and who was teased for the half inch of elevation he got on his jump shot. But, Jesus, Mary and Joseph, there was no more loyal brother or buddy in a tight spot and no more hard-nosed bundle of will and self-assurance on a ball field. He'd play two-on-two tackle football on pavement, and then when he wrenched his neck in a helmet-to-helmet collision during his sophomore year in high school, the bedside contraption rigged by the family doctor to hold George's neck in traction lasted two days. "This is bull," snapped George, who dismantled the device, practiced the next day and played the following weekend.

By then there were eight children, and the O'Learys had outgrown the Manhattan apartment and moved to a modest Cape Cod in blue-collar Central Islip, Long Island. But a kid still couldn't hide anything in that home, not with four boys jammed into one bedroom, four girls into another, a grandma and great uncle in the third bedroom, George's mother and father in the last one and the church waiting outside the door with hellfire. George didn't even try to carve out his own place. He bunched elbow-to-elbow with all the other males on Saturdays in front of the black-and-white television, hollering the Irish home against the best that the WASPs could throw at them, no one ever saying it, only feeling it: Notre Dame football was everything honest and right, and if *that* Fighting Irish Catholic 11 could *own* the American pie, then the dozen crammed in this house could at least have a slice of it.

When the game on TV ended, the boys tumbled outside and lived it all over again, deep into dark. Then came Sunday and even more Irish in the house, grandparents born and bred in the old land, along with aunts and uncles and cousins, gathering in the basement to sing the old songs on birthdays, anniversaries and holidays.

So how could an entire roast beef just *disappear* one day? It couldn't! Out with it, demanded Mrs. O'Leary. Her children blinked at her, all denying knowledge. Well, then, we'll see. For three days she served sad leftovers for supper, waiting for the children to crack, but by then they'd been hardened, known suppers during lean times that were just a plateful of mashed potatoes tinted ominously red by baby-food beets.

The Blessed Mother works in mysterious ways, her wonders to perform. Sarge, the family mutt, sauntered in from the backyard with the string from the roast beef dangling from his arse, and the O'Learys at last sat down to some decent grub.

Have you located it yet? Where could a lie, an exaggeration that would make a national disgrace of a man, take root in that house? A home where no one dared preen or puff himself, where Dad dismissed airs or boasts with just three letters—"SPS," for Self-Praise Stinks—and any boy who made himself out to be one inch more than he was risked humiliation. "All right, who is it?" Mrs. O'Leary asked, chortling one day as she finished the laundry. "Who's the big head who thinks he needs an extra-large jock?"

No one owned up. Not George, not Terry, not Peter, and for damn sure not Sarge.

1964–68 SANDBAGGER, BARTENDER, ROAD PAVER, LANDSCAPER, MOVER, STUDENT

WHEN YOU'RE 18, there's no explaining it. Sometimes everything you love is everything you hate. Maybe it was the smell of four boys in a bedroom just after a ball game, maybe it was singing the same song from the Auld Sod for the 32nd time, maybe it was that eternal flame underneath that infernal pot of Mrs. O'Leary's boiling potatoes. Maybe it was the fact that Dubuque was the only college that showed a glimmer of interest in George. Maybe that's why he was suddenly on the road, the first O'Leary to leave the fold, barreling through a cornfield on a 24-hour Greyhound bus ride to Iowa, a boy who'd never been farther from home than the Jersey shore.

A *glimmer*, mind you. Not a scholarship. A thousand bucks in financial aid, a bit of an insult, really, after George had quarterbacked his high school team—more on grit than on grace—to an undefeated season. At Dubuque he found himself one of five quarterbacks, promptly converted to bottom-of-the-depth-chart fullback, an out-of-place Noo Yawker on a bad Division III team cheered by a few hundred fans, the glory of his senior season and the warmth of his big family fading, fading . . . gone.

He knew more than the damn coach did. He was sure of it. He barely stepped on the football field all fall. No, that's a lie. He cut across it at night to get to the Disabled American Veterans Bar to quaff a half-dozen Hamm's. The future coach of Notre Dame? They'd have howled in the locker room if you'd pointed at *him* and said *that*. He scraped by academically, quit football and wouldn't have returned for his sophomore year if he hadn't felt so listless that he couldn't stir himself to apply to another school. There was one highlight that second year: the road trip. To South Bend. He walked the hallowed grounds of Notre Dame and sensed the magic that his grades and football skills wouldn't let him touch.

A third helping of Iowa was out of the question. His dad, who'd worked his way up from school custodian to school board president and postmaster of Central Islip, had come to be known as the Godfather, the townsman with the most connections and the deepest devotion to arranging jobs for any man he deemed a good man. He saw the lost look in his boy's eyes and grew uneasy. He turned to Walt Mirey, an administrator in the Central Islip school district who'd played football at New Hampshire. Somehow Dad had to wedge the kid through college. Mirey got him into his alma mater. Dad exhaled. So long, George!

George? What was he doing back at the front door? A week and a half into August preseason camp, George quit the team and took a bus home. Cripes, what was the point? He'd be ineligible for a year because of the transfer, owed a bundle for student loans and couldn't bear another four-eyed professor slowly squeezing his privates in a midterm vise.

He walked through the door. He couldn't meet his father's stare. He hated letting down the kind of man who, the first time he ever flew in an airplane, jumped out of it, on a paratrooper training mission in Georgia. The kind who always forgave you.

"So. . .what're you going to do, George?" his father asked.

"I don't know. Go in the service, maybe."

"You need to get back to college, George. You're not a quitter. You're better than that."

Three days of unbearable silence later George returned to New Hampshire. His playing life was over, his pilot light barely aflame, but in the next two years he worked enough as a part-time bartender, landscaper, mover and paver to know what he *didn't* want, so he hit the books, or at least tapped them, enough to get a B.S. in phys ed.

And he met a girl. Bumped into her at a party and was so taken by her that just before the next bash at his frat house, he concocted a doozy. He talked Sharon Littlefield into coming as a blind date for a nonexistent friend of his, then offered his regrets when she showed up and the buddy didn't—but, hey, now that she was there, why not be *his* date? She didn't mind, because there was nothing slick about his deception; truth is, he was a little rough around the edges. She liked his blue eyes, his blond hair and his swagger, and she so prized her own privacy and independence that it was O.K. that he was a loner. They married before he graduated. She would look back on that first date, four children later, as such a wonderful little lie.

1969-74 PHYS-ED TEACHER, DRIVER'S ED TEACHER,
ASSISTANT FOOTBALL COACH

SURPRISE! THE son of Central Islip's school board president secured his first real job in 1969—as a teacher and assistant football coach at Central Islip High. "It was almost," says George's youngest brother, Tom, "as if he'd become Dad's project."

Take a young man. Place him in front of a group of kids just a few years younger than he is. He must give them direction when he's barely begun to find his own. He must seal off all his own doubts so they'll believe and follow. Make sure they never do what he did: quit. What's a young coach but an elaborate bluff, a careful construction of small lies? What's a successful coach but one so convincing that even he comes to believe the bluff, and turns it into truth?

But this was a *good* lie, right? A boy becoming a man in a world where everyone lies had to figure that out. This sort of lie his country rewarded, for its coaches played the role that tribal elders—the ones entrusted to take boys and turn them, through rites of passage, into men—played in other lands. George started driving up and down the East Coast, attending football clinics at which these elders held court, in quest of knowledge and a model.

In Washington, D.C., he found one. Here was fire, here was aura, here was Woody Hayes. You *have* to do it right, the Ohio State coach thundered, and your players *have* to do it right, *every* time! Accountability! Integrity! Trust! In four more towns George heard Woody roar. Woody's slogans became George's slogans. Woody's hero, Patton, became George's. Woody's realization—that raw honesty could be an astonishingly effective motivating tool—became George's eureka. George caught fire. Then breathed it.

He descended the cellar steps of Ralph G. Reed Junior High School, a few blocks from C.I. High. Beneath the low ceiling pipes he painted a wide purple circle on the floor. That's what George began doing, drawing circles. If you weren't in the circle, weren't with him on his mission, as his old high school teammate and coaching partner, Tommy Black, put it, "you might think that he had a stick up his ass." But if you were in the circle, you'd thrash anything that threatened it. George filled the purple circle with weights and bars and benches, raised them on platforms, lit them with track lights to make the circle more sacred, christened it the Pride Area and demanded that his players return to it three days a week, year round. No conversation was permitted there. Only screaming. George and dozens of boys raised an ear-shattering din as they encircled a puff-cheeked offensive lineman straining to surpass his personal-best bench press—*You can do it, Tommy. It's fourth-and-one! How much do you want it? How much?!*

"Wow," thought Billy Neuse, a Long Island guy who used to slam Hamm's with George in Dubuque and caught up with him one day in Central Islip, "is that the same guy?"

1975–79 HIGH SCHOOL HEAD COACH

WATCH CLOSELY now. George just left the web of family and favors, of connections and loyalty. George just left Dad.

His heels clacked through the cavernous halls of Liverpool High in upstate New York. A man could get lost there: Nearly 4,000 students surged through the corridors, and most of them couldn't tell George how to find the main office. A man could be found there: Ten miles away stood Syracuse University and something impossible to see from Central Islip—a major-college football program.

It was 1977. He was 31. He looked at the sea of strange faces. They hadn't a clue that he'd labored six years as an assistant, waiting for the C.I. head coach to step aside, then gone 16-1-1 in two seasons as head coach and been named Suffolk County coach of the year. No one knew him in Liverpool, the way no one had known his grandparents 70 years earlier when they had left behind a land where everything was set in stone to come to one where everything was fluid and people kept moving, kept selling themselves to strangers, jockeying for position, an upgrade. Where a man was free to tell anyone anything to prove his worth, or his product's worth, and the line between marketing and lying was so fine that he could find himself right on top of it before he knew he was there, then lurch across it by sheer momentum. As George's brother Tom would ask, "Is anyone trying to tell me that résumés are truthful? In the America we live in, the willingness to lie on a résumé is an indication of how much you want the job."

Something was missing in the persona George had built, some mortar that would better hold the bricks in place, some grout that would make the wall more impenetrable. A man who made quitting seem so repulsive, so weak, who convinced so many boys that anything was possible if they refused to quit. . . . Why, *he* couldn't have quit, could he? So, sure, he said now, here where no one knew him, sure, he'd played college ball at New Hampshire. Somehow the lie contained a deeper truth about George, an updated one. The man he'd become would've gutted it out at New Hampshire, not to mention Dubuque—which he didn't mention at all.

Funny, the lie didn't really stick in the altar boy's throat. It didn't torture Mrs. O'Leary's son. Hell, how had Dad, virtually blind in his left eye, passed the physical to become a paratrooper? By memorizing the eye chart! By pulling a fast one to get his foot in the door. And if Dad hadn't hit a tree on his last training jump and the doctor who examined him hadn't discovered his visual disability, he probably would've been killed in Italy like so many of his training partners and that deception would've been hailed in his eulogy as proof of his courage and patriotism.

In truth, the subject of George's past rarely arose. "He was such an awe-inspiring coach, it seemed like he was born that way," says Tim Green, an All-America defensive lineman who played under George in high school and college, then became a lawyer, writer and TV commentator. "People were terrified of him. One time at practice someone said ouch. George said, '*Ouch*? Who the hell just said *ouch*? My goddam wife doesn't say ouch! My goddam little girl doesn't say ouch! Everybody hit the ground! One hundred up-downs!' Sure, some walked away from him bruised, but we all walked away from him better. To have great rewards you must have great effort. George showed me how. He gave me the blueprint."

He inherited a 1–9 squad at Liverpool. He began to change what the players saw when they looked in the mirror. He would yank their face masks and head-slap them with his clipboard when they lost focus. He would station a kid in the center of a ring of players, a circle of fire, and call out names so they'd charge and drill the boy from all angles, one by one. He sent them out of the team bus with the Notre Dame fight song ringing in their ears, full of belief in themselves. They went 3–6 his first year, then went 8–1 and won their conference title.

At a summer camp based in a suffocating converted barn 100 miles from Liverpool, George instituted dawn wake-ups and bunk inspections and three-a-day practices and late-night team meetings. It worked because George demanded even more of himself than of the boys, and because he'd crack them up, in the midst of their misery, with stiletto one-liners. It worked because George cared so much, because he asked how your mom and dad were doing and if there was anything else he could do to help you get that scholarship, and because come Saturday in autumn, you kicked the crap out of anyone who had the audacity to think he belonged on the same grass as you, after all you'd been through. In George's third year his team went 10–0, surrendered just *33 points* all season and was ranked No. 2 in the state as George, for the second straight year, was named Onondaga County coach of the year.

His wife received a phone call. It was their daughter's kindergarten teacher, worried because the family portrait that little Trish had been asked to draw included her mother and three siblings—but no father. Was there trouble at home? No. Sharon tried to explain: The marriage was fine, and Trish did see her dad now and then, but usually when he was on the sideline, and usually all she saw was the back of his head.

George received a letter. "You are the kind of person with whom it is a pleasure to be associated—both professionally and personally," wrote Liverpool High executive principal David Kidd. "Your dedication, ethics and loyalty are recognized by everyone."

1979–94 ASSISTANT COACH, SYRACUSE
DEFENSIVE COORDINATOR, GEORGIA TECH
ASSISTANT COACH, SAN DIEGO CHARGERS

IT WASN'T enough.

George's ballpoint hovered over four blank lines. The heading above them, on the Syracuse University personal information form, read *Athletic background (sports played in high school, college, professional; letters won, honors, championships etc. Please be specific).*

He'd made it. The big leap. The rare jump from high school coach to major-college assistant, bypassing the usual rungs—graduate assistant, Division III coach—that took a man there. Just in time, too, after the coach at Baldwinsville High had sneaked into the woods and snapped pictures of George holding practices out of season and gotten Liverpool's sports teams put on probation for a year. It was April 1980. George had been in his new job for three months, wowing Syracuse coach Frank Maloney as a defensive line coach and a recruiter. It wasn't enough.

George's ballpoint came down. *Basketball 3 yrs.—All-League—County Champion.* His team, in fact, had lost in the Suffolk County championship game on George's missed shot at the buzzer. It wasn't enough.

College, he wrote. This information would go into his bio in game programs and the media brochure. Other coaches on the staff would read it. They'd all played college ball. *Univ. of New Hampshire,* he wrote. His players would read it too. He wasn't a quitter. He was better than that: *3 yr lettered,* he wrote. More mortar. More grout. How could he dream that a child not yet born would grow up to become a student assistant in the Syracuse sports information department, would fax this very sheet of paper to a reporter 21 years later and demolish George's life?

George spat a stream of brown juice into a Styrofoam cup. A new habit. One more thing, besides the college football letters, he now had in common with the Syracuse defensive coaches. He began filling out a second document, entitled *Personal Data Sheet,* in which he was asked to spell out his academic credentials. He began to list the graduate schools he'd attended and the credits he'd earned. He had 31. It wasn't enough. *Presently have B.S. +48,* George wrote, adding 17 credits.

Hell, it was no big deal, just another coach's ploy, wasn't it? Like thrusting his badly scarred left hand with its permanently bent pinkie—the result of a tumble at age five, when he landed on a broken bottle at the bottom of a sump—into the face of a player who seemed always to complain of injuries and screaming, "See that? *That's* college football!" Just a way of creating more authority, more aura, more *men.* Just another tool. Right?

George hatched a first-round NFL draft pick on the Syracuse defensive line, Tim Green, and two second-rounders: Mike Charles and Blaise Winter—an abused kid, born with a cleft palate, for whom George became a father figure. George became assistant head coach. George became hot property. Funny: That past he'd puffed up? No one who hired him after that would ask to see his résumé. Bobby Ross didn't ask when he snatched George from Syracuse and made him his defensive coordinator at Georgia Tech in 1987, nor when George's defense refused to allow a touchdown in the *first 19 quarters* of '90 as Tech began its march to a share of the national championship. Ross sure didn't peruse the résumé before he took George to the Chargers as his defensive line coach in '92 and San Diego's front four promptly led the AFC in sacks on its way to the Chargers' first playoff appearance in a decade. Homer Rice, then athletic director at Georgia Tech, never gave the résumé a glance when he coaxed George back to cure Tech's defense in '94. The man *produced*, at every level. The man was real.

But, still, something must've been missing. George still didn't have what he lusted for; he remained an assistant. In 1987 a member of Tech's sports information department, preparing coaches' bios for the fall football program, popped into George's office to ask a few questions. When the interview was done, the boy who couldn't stop playing with matches had a master's degree.

1995–2001 HEAD COACH, GEORGIA TECH

IT WAS ticking now. So softly that even he couldn't hear it. So softly that no one could, and nearly every article and anecdote about George hinged on his extraordinary honesty, his *painful* honesty, and all the perpendicular adjectives—upstanding, upright, up-front, straightforward—echoed again and again. How could anyone hear the time bomb ticking as George paced before his team in 1995, his authority threatened for the first time as a college head coach, his face contorted in a snarl, his cheeks red as fire, his tobacco juice spraying his shirt, and he screamed out his paramount rule, his *only* rule: "DON'T LIE TO ME!"

Someone had sung to George: The training rules he'd put into effect that weekend had been violated. "I want anyone who was drinking," he cried, "to stand up!" Now he'd see if his bedrock values—trust, accountability, integrity—had sunk in. "*Now!*"

Ryan Stewart, one of George's leaders, a senior strong safety on his way to the NFL, agonized in his seat. He'd had a beer and a half. If he stood, he'd be up at 5:30 running or monkey-rolling or somersaulting, maybe till he vomited. If he stood, he'd force the three teammates who'd split the six-pack with him to stand up too. The silence gathered. George's face was no longer red. It was purple. "*Who didn't understand what I said?*"

The fear thickened. If George already knew that Ryan had been drinking, and Ryan didn't stand, everything between them would be broken, and his pro career might be jeopardized. Ryan loved playing for George. George made Ryan believe in himself. Ryan was about to cry.

He stood. The three other beer-and-a-halfers stood. Then six were standing. Then 10. Then a dozen. Lies couldn't last under George. His blue eyes bulged. "*The whole team will be punished!*" he roared.

It was George's world now. It was *his* field you played on, he'd remind you, *his* food you ate, *his* dorm you roomed in, *his* time when you woke, worked, ate and fell asleep. The first day of August camp he gave each of his players a packet: Every day for the next five months, their lives were scheduled. Every opponent had already been game-planned, every practice mapped out. Practices lasted two hours and seven minutes: 24 five-minute periods, sprinting between stations. He might let you miss one. *If* you ratted out a teammate.

You didn't dare show up for a meeting or a meal or a team bus exactly when his itinerary told you to. You'd miss it by 15 minutes and get left behind—it happened even to the athletic director. George's meetings ended, literally, before they were scheduled to start. You didn't dare come his way with facial hair, earrings, headphones or a hat on backward. You didn't let a cellphone ring in a team meeting unless you wished to see it bounce off the wall and go to pieces on the floor. You didn't utter a word in a coaches' meeting without assuming he'd chicken-scratch it onto one of the four legal notepads he brought to each session and sail it back at you at a meeting two months later. You didn't move a plant or lift a blind in his office. He'd know. You didn't work or play under him unless you'd learned to walk on all sorts of surfaces—on pins, on needles, on eggshells and through fire.

Ten cups of coffee and 10 fingernails—that's what he went through each day. Four hours' sleep, and he started all over again: 16-hour days, seven days a week, his Irish music blasting on the car ride home to keep him awake, his two dogs waiting frantically by the door for the man whose pockets bulged with pig's ears, cookies, beef jerky and biscuits for them. Once a year he'd take off a half day to drink beer, sing the old songs and zing one-liners at pals. Once a year: St. Patrick's Day. Irish souvenirs and proverbs covered his office desk and walls, but he never had the time to go to Ireland. For years his friends and relatives had kidded him, asking the Fighting Irishman when he'd take over the

Fighting Irish, because if ever a man was made for a place, it was George for Notre Dame.

Sure, that was a dream, but who had time for dreaming? The lights went out during a Georgia Tech evening practice in '95, then flashed back on. An electrician, trying to pinpoint the problem, inserted his screwdriver into the fuse box by the field. An explosion sent him tumbling down an embankment, smoke curling from beneath his hat, and brought the football trainers on the run. Players stopped in mid-drill and stared in fear as the electrician rose slowly to his feet. "He's O.K.!" screamed George. "Run the damn play!"

Obsession is contagious. Tech won an ACC title and, beginning in 1997, five straight bowl berths. The legions grew, players who'd dive on grenades for George. Off to the side stood casualties such as Dustin Vaitekunas, a 6' 7" offensive lineman whose grit left George so unimpressed two years ago that he flipped a ball to the kid and sent four defensive linemen at him so he'd know how it felt to be an unprotected quarterback. Vaitekunas didn't get up for 10 minutes; he quit the team, and his mother threatened to have George arrested for assault. Media and academic types were outraged, scarcely believing George's claim that he hadn't intended for his front four to flatten the boy. But his players—who depended on brotherhood and commitment as they stood on a field where any one of 11 men might attack from any side—rallied around George. As long as he stayed on a football field, George could be justified. "If he was on fire, I wouldn't walk across the street to piss on him," says Michael Dee, a Tech safety in the mid-'90s, "but I'd want him as my coach."

Maybe now George could chance it. Maybe now that he earned more than a million a year on a multiyear contract, now that he'd won two ACC coach of the year awards and national coach of the year in 2000, he could quietly ask that his two lies be stricken from Tech's publicity material.

His wife had noticed the falsehood about his playing career. "Ah, the guy in the sports information department at Syracuse told me to make it look good," George fibbed. His mom and dad had noticed it too. "Ah, it's not important. I don't know how it got in there," George said. "I gotta get it out." He thought about it. But he couldn't risk it. Fame had removed his control of the lies; they had flown everywhere now, on paper and in cyberspace.

His children believed the lies. His brothers and old pals from Central

Islip figured they were just part of the hype machine. When George's more recent friends asked about his college career, he'd say, "I could hit you, but I couldn't catch you," then nod toward the scar on his knee and allude to a football injury—but not mention that the blow had actually occurred years after college, when he was coaching. The wave of his hand and his silence discouraged more questions, and who had questions about New Hampshire football anyway?

It was the perfect lie, and George the perfect agent for it: Who would suspect subterfuge from a sledgehammer? Who'd suspect it from a religious man with no tolerance for preening, the same modest man at a million a year as he had been at $14,322? If his secretary hadn't pulled his coach of the year awards out of a box and displayed them in his office, nobody would have laid eyes on them.

The one man George wished to shine for—the one he called minutes after every game—was dying a slow, gasping death from emphysema when Tech named George head coach. Dad never saw the glory. George leaned over his coffin and pinned a Georgia Tech button to his lapel. He was shocked, days later, to find himself sobbing with the team priest, unable to sleep. Shocked at how many mourners had materialized with previously untold tales of Mr. O'Leary's acts of kindness.

More and more George found himself slipping his barber $100 for a haircut to help him through hard times, or tucking a C-note beneath a plate after finding out that his harried waitress had five kids at home, or inviting a custodian home for Thanksgiving dinner and to sleep over. "Don't tell anyone," he'd tell people who witnessed such acts. He wanted no one to glimpse inside the wall he'd built, a wall so thick that he couldn't hear those last . . . few . . . ticks. . . .

Notre Dame called. Its athletic director, Kevin White, who'd grown up just a few miles from Central Islip, had interviewed 50 people who were sure of three things: George's honesty, his character and his ability. Notre Dame offered to buy out George's $1.5 million contract with Georgia Tech. Notre Dame wanted George.

A strange thing happened. George hesitated. It was the quiet uneasiness of a man who owned his reality and wondered if he should let go of it for anything, even his dream. "Imagine if Dad were here to see this," said his brothers and brother-in-law. "It's Notre Dame, George. It's Notre Dame."

DEC. 9–13, 2001 HEAD COACH, NOTRE DAME

THE MOMENT he set foot on campus, all his doubts vanished—he knew this was right. He entered the grotto where the blue-sashed Virgin Mary stood amid stones blackened by the candle soot of a century of adoration. The day before, he had signed on to begin the crowning chapter of his life, at Our Lady's university. On *her* day, December 8, the Feast of the Blessed Mother. He looked skyward. The Golden Dome gleamed. It was true, what they said about this place. Everything was magic.

He entered the basilica. The choir, rehearsing, hurled its song at the gilded angels and saints upon the soaring ceiling. He could hear and smell a hundred Sundays at the altar of his childhood, a thousand dusks of saying the rosary surrounded by his kneeling family. The emotion rose in his throat and tightened the knot on his blue-and-gold necktie. He knelt alone to offer thanks. At 55, he'd clawed his way forward to his past. He was home.

He entered the basketball arena. The pep band burst into the fight song he used to play to send his high school troops to battle. The cheerleaders tumbled. The crowd, clad in BY GEORGE, IT'S O'LEARY! T-shirts, rose, and so did the hair on his neck.

He flew back home to Atlanta, packed up his life and his Irish regalia and returned to South Bend two days later. At dusk on his first day on the job, he was interrupted quietly, apologetically, by the Notre Dame sports information director, John Heisler. A call had just come from Jim Fennell, a reporter for the Manchester *Union Leader* in New Hampshire. He was tracking down men who'd had the honor of playing college football 33 years ago with Notre Dame's newest coach, but, funny, his old teammates said George had never played.

George blinked. *Blindsided.* Now he had to lie again. Well, he said, it was true, he hadn't really played, uh . . . there was that knee injury one year, and then the other year he was sick, mononucleosis. Somebody must've made a mistake in the bio. Heisler left. George looked down at his thick, chafed hands. He worked until 2 a.m.

The next day, figuring the worst was over, he left for Alexandria, Va., to recruit running back Tommy Clayton. George still didn't understand. Notre Dame, George. *Notre Dame.* A phone call came late that afternoon. It was Lou Nanni, the university's vice president of public affairs and communications. Fennell had called back, holding a 21-year-old document that Syracuse had faxed to him. The lie had been written by George. Could he explain?

No, George couldn't, he must've written it, but, but. . . . Lou, this is just a speed bump, right? No, said Nanni. Calls from media outlets everywhere were pouring into the university. Nanni was surprised at what happened next. George offered to resign.

Hold on, said Nanni. They would prepare a statement admitting George's weakness as a young coach. They'd take some terrible blows, but they'd weather them together. George left to meet the recruit's parents, his gut in a knot. Nanni called back, read the statement, then asked, "George, is there anything else in your bio that's not accurate?"

A pause. A lifetime hanging. The master's degree—should he lie? "George, there's going to be incredible scrutiny on this by the media," said Nanni. "If we don't get this all clear now, it *will* come out anyway."

George's voice cracked, and words began to tumble from his lips— something about credits and a degree—that didn't quite make sense. "George," said Nanni, in a nightmare of his own. "If someone were to look hard at the records concerning the master's degree at NYU, would it be fair to say they're not going to find your name there?"

Another pause. For the first time it occurred to George: He'd wandered off his field. He could survive a lie inside a white-lined rectangle, but now he was playing in someone else's ivory tower. Yes, George finally said, his voice deathly quiet and far away. They wouldn't find it.

Nanni blanched and got off the phone. White, the athletic director, called George moments later to verify.

"I'm sorry," George kept saying, "I'm sorry, I'm sorry."

White was reeling. He had to speak to the university president, Father Edward Malloy. He'd call back in a few minutes, he said.

George waited. Forty minutes of forever passed. The phone rang. A trust had been broken, said White. False academic credentials at Notre Dame were a death knell. He accepted George's resignation.

George hung up. That was it. He was done. Just a couple of little matches. . .and everything was up in flames. Sure, he might've had to resign from any other university, but the fact that it had happened at Notre Dame, that was the wind turning this into a conflagration, sending it burning from page 4C in the newspapers to page 1A.

His hand began to work across his face. It was just after midnight. All the consequences, one horror and humiliation after the next, began to spread through him. The joke, the sick joke, was on him. Notre Dame hadn't cared whether he had a master's degree or whether he'd lettered in college football. The lies had been wasted. George O'Leary: the chipmunk trying to pass for a squirrel, when everyone saw him as a lion.

His mind reeled to the assistants he'd brought from Tech to Notre Dame, suddenly jobless. To the lives of his entire staff at Tech, thrown asunder for nothing. To himself, unemployed, unemployable, holding the bag for the $1.5 million buyout that Notre Dame wouldn't pay now. To his family name—ruined. Oh, Jesus, his mother, his mother. . . .

He stared out the second-floor window. He considered the distance. Eighth floor, maybe, he thought. But not from here. He stood. He had to get out of there, leave, go somewhere, *now*. No. Not allowed. Aviation regulations. Mandatory rest time. Notre Dame's private pilots couldn't fly till 4 a.m. For four hours he sat there, holding on through the dark, trying to survive.

He flew to South Bend, grabbed a few belongings, hurried back to the plane to return to Georgia in the sickly light of dawn. He got into his car at a private airport near Atlanta and began the hour-and-a-half drive to his lake house. Tears began streaming down his cheeks.

The phone was ringing as he entered the empty house. Oh, God. Mom. Eighty years old. "George. . .what happened?" she cried. She heard him struggling not to break down.

"Mom . . . I made a mistake. But it was never a factor in getting any job."

"But. . . . "

"I really don't want to talk about it, Mom."

He went to the finished basement. His 29-year-old son, Tim—who, like his younger brother, Marty, had played for their father at Tech—came through the front door, fearful for George. He found him on a sofa in the basement, staring into nothingness, notepad in lap, pen in hand, reaching to write a list when there was nothing left to list.

His wife and daughters arrived. They dared not hug him. They couldn't even go near him. He was almost catatonic. The phone rang endlessly. Tim turned away the callers. Sharon was too tearful to speak. George's friends arrived, but he refused to see them.

Friday blurred into Saturday. George hadn't moved from the sofa. He wouldn't eat. Wouldn't change his clothes. Couldn't look in a mirror to shave or wash up or comb his hair. It was frightening to watch a man try to hold in that much grief, that much shame, that much anger. His brothers Peter and Tom arrived from New York, pushed past Tim and went downstairs. His friends showed up again. Everyone was crying. George sat and stared at his own wake.

Days passed. His friends feared that his basement would be his tomb. In bits and pieces he began to hear what the world was saying. It was even worse than he'd dreaded. America seemed more shocked by lying from a football coach than from a politician or a businessman. The country still attached honor to sports. There was glee as well, cackling at the sight of two American institutions going down at once: the crusty old-fashioned football coach and, my God, *Notre Dame.* Jay Leno called him "George O'Really?" The radio talk shows went wild. The O'Learys in New York shuddered and hurried past front pages blaring LIAR, LIAR and NOTRE SHAME. In 12 months George had gone from national coach of the year to national joke of the year.

Perhaps all the laughter was the nervous release of a deep uneasiness. People with big plans everywhere opened their laptops, called up their résumés and began hitting the delete button. Rick Smith, a newly named Georgia Tech assistant, didn't edit his bio fast enough and went from a 150-grand-a-year defensive coordinator to a 60-buck-a-day substitute teacher.

Two weeks after the horror began, George started to comb his hair and clean up. He went to a different store to get doughnuts in the morning, hoping people wouldn't recognize him, and he slipped out of Sunday Mass early to avoid meeting the eyes of the priest. As he drove, he prayed the rosary on a set of old brown beads worn smooth by his father's hands on his deathbed.

His old players felt as if they'd been kicked in the stomach, but when they caught their breath, most stood up, eyes blazing, for George. His brother Peter, the president of the Suffolk County Detectives Association, on Long Island, said, "It was like me being named FBI director and three days later being fired because I farted in church." Peggy O'Leary lit candles and cried herself to sleep over a son who wouldn't come to the phone when she called on Christmas Day. What she'd told him 50 years ago—funny how it had turned out to be right. Even when no one else has seen you, even when you're sure you've gotten away with a lie, you won't get it past the Blessed Mother. Our Lady. Notre Dame.

And George? He kept waking up at night, raging at the world and at himself: "Two sentences in my bio. Two sentences insignificant to what I was doing. Academic fraud, they're calling it. How could that be, when I never used it to get a job? Nobody ever asked for a résumé before they hired me to coach in college or the pros. I never profited from it. Look, I was stupid, I screwed up. I'm responsible for everything. But where's forgiveness? I keep kicking myself: You did it to yourself. You were set—financially, emotionally. For 30 years you put in 16 hours a day, to end up like this? Now you're nothing. Why? I was just trying to get ahead. To prove something to people who didn't know me. I just didn't believe in myself enough."

2002 ASSISTANT COACH, MINNESOTA VIKINGS

A WHITE-HAIRED man moved swiftly through the airport in Atlanta with a cellphone pressed to his ear, pretending to hold a conversation so none of the people staring at him would approach. He stepped onto an airplane to Minneapolis that morning in mid-January and arranged his purgatory. George O'Leary had sown too much loyalty to be abandoned in hell.

Mike Tice, George's old high school quarterback who'd wept when he heard the shocking news, wanted this man at his side as he took over the Vikings, the purple and gold—the same colors to which the two had brought glory at Central Islip High. "I get the benefit of it all," said Tice. "I get to have a better coach than me."

A few weeks later George reported for his first day on the job. The sky was black. The temperature was 15 degrees. The time was 6:30 a.m. He hadn't felt the tingle yet but was pretty sure it would come. He pulled into the Vikings' parking lot, first one there, 30 seconds before Tice.

So what do we have here? A man who was tarred and feathered—and is already largely rehabilitated. A man off the hook for the $1.5 million payout, which Georgia Tech let slide, and earning roughly $300,000 a year. A man who's walking into a circle where men will take a step forward to slap him on the back and say, "What a bunch of bull," and "What a raw deal you got over something so small"—while people outside the circle will take a step back and see, from a wider angle, that it's not small, because what becomes of a society if no one's word means a thing?

What no one can know is what will happen on the field, George's old safe place, the first time he snarls and demands complete honesty from a player who knows his sin.

AND LUKE? Over in Liverpool, N.Y., the old Italian continued to toss and turn at night, thinking of George and all the kids he'd steered to manhood, weighing the decision that he and his superintendent had made a quarter century ago—that the net worth of a man like George was more, much more, than the cost of his weakness. And shaking his head in sad wonder at the fear that whispers the oldest and biggest lie to us all: You're not good enough, you're not good enough, you're not good enough. And deciding that, still, he and his boss had been right to let George get away with playing with matches, even in the face of all that had come to pass, because . . . well, because his grandmother was right.

"'*Piglia i buoni*,' she always said to me," says Luke. "It means, 'Take the good'—in people. You have to give them the benefit of the doubt. You have to give the rose a chance to bloom, or it's a dark world."

So. That was Luke's choice. Now it's your turn.

———◆———

POSTSCRIPT: *George O'Leary kept his position with the Minnesota Vikings for two years before returning to the college game in 2004, taking over as head coach at the University of Central Florida. His first year in Orlando, the team finished 0–11. The next season UCF earned a bowl berth and O'Leary was named coach of the year in Conference USA. In the '07 season, he took the 10–3 Knights to their second bowl game.*

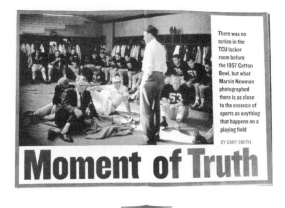

There was no
action in the
TCU locker
room before
the 1957 Cotton
Bowl, but what
Marvin Newman
photographed
there is as close
to the essence of
sports as anything
that happens on a
playing field

BY GARY SMITH

Moment of Truth

Moment of Truth

---

*No one stirred in the TCU locker room minutes before the 1957
Cotton Bowl, but what Marvin Newman photographed there came closer
to capturing the essence of sports than any slam-bang action shot.*

{ THE PHOTO ABOVE CAN BE SEEN IN FULL INSIDE THE BOOK JACKET }

OU HEARD ME RIGHT: COME IN. NO, YOU WON'T
disturb a soul in this locker room. They're all lost in that
place most folks go maybe once or twice in a lifetime,
when their mamas or daddies die or their children are
born, a place they don't go nearly as often as they should. Trust me, these
boys will never know you're here. All right, maybe that fellow in white
will notice, the one looking your way, but Willard McClung would be the
last to make a peep.

82

See, that's one reason we picked this, out of all the crackerjack pictures we might've chosen, as our favorite sports photograph of the century. Not claiming it's better than that famous one of Muhammad Ali standing and snarling over Sonny Liston laid out like a cockroach the morning after the bug man comes. Or that picture of Willie Mays catching the ball over his shoulder in the '54 World Series, or any number of others. But you can walk around inside this picture in a way you can't in those others, peer right inside the tunnel these boys have entered. Their boxer shorts are hanging right there, on the hooks behind their heads, but their faces are showing something even more personal than that. Almost reminds you of a painting by Norman Rockwell.

Can you smell it? No, not the jockstrap sweat, or the cigar reek wafting off the coach, Orthol Martin—better known as Abe, or Honest Abe—in the brown hat. It's the smell of men about to go to war. What I'm inviting you into is 12:50 p.m. at the Cotton Bowl on January 1, 1957, just a few minutes after the boys have returned from pregame warmups, just a quarter of an hour before a legend is born. A roomful of young men from Texas Christian University are about to try and stop the best football player in history, a fellow from Syracuse by the name of Jim Brown, in his last college game—but only his second in front of the entire nation, thanks to the NBC cameras waiting outside.

No denying it, a lot of folks might whip right past this in a collection of sports pictures, rushing to get to those slam-bang plays at home plate or those high-flying Michael Jordan circus shots. But it's funny. The older you get, the more you realize that *this* is what sports are most about: the moments *before*, the times when a person takes a flashlight to his soul and inspects himself for will and courage and spirit, the stuff that separates men such as Jordan and Ali from the rest more than anything in their forearms or their fingers or their feet. *Who am I?* And, *Is that going to be enough?* That's what you're peeking at through the door, and believe me, those are two big and scary questions, the two best reasons for all of god's children to play sports, so they can start chewing on them early. Because once the whistle blows and a game begins, everything's just a blur, a crazy ricochet of ball and bodies that springs—inevitably, you might say—from whatever it is that these boys are discovering right here, right now.

But you're still hesitating, a little intimidated by all those cleats and helmets and knees. Come on, there are things I want to show you. See? Told you nobody would bat an eye. You're *in*.

MAYBE IT was like this for you, too, back when you played. All the posturing and bluffing and the silly airs that human beings put on get demolished in a moment like this. A team is never more a *team* than it is now, yet look at the looks on the Horned Frogs! Ever see so many guys look so alone?

Look at Buddy Dike, number 38, just behind old Abe. He's the Frogs' starting fullback and inside linebacker, and he's just gotten a good look at Jim Brown's 46-inch chest and 32-inch waist in warmups. Doctors advised Buddy never to play football again after he ruptured a kidney tackling another phenom of the era, Penn State's Lenny Moore, two years earlier. The kidney healed and hemorrhaged four more times, doubling Buddy over with pain, making blood gush out his urethra, bringing him within a whisker of bleeding to death, yet here he is, with a look on his face that might not be seen again until the day he loses his 18-year-old son in a car wreck.

There are 32 more young men suited up in this room, besides the 17 you're looking at. Almost every one's a kid from a small town or ranch or farm in west or south Texas, where all his life he's watched everyone drop everything, climb into automobiles and form caravans for only two occasions: funerals and football games. Nine of the 11 TCU starters—remember, they have to play both ways—are seniors, most of them staring into the biggest and last football game of their lives. Eleven wars are about to burst out on every play, because that's what football is, and what those wars hinge on, more than most folks realize, is the question lurking in the shadows of this room: Who has the most tolerance for pain?

That's a loaded question about manhood, and a matter of geography too. Jim Brown be damned, the Southwest Conference team that loses to an Eastern school in the Cotton Bowl in the 1950s might as well run right past the locker room door at the end of the game, exit the stadium and just keep going, till it's lost in the prairie.

Let's take a good look at old Abe. Country boy from Jacksboro, Texas, who played end at TCU in the late 1920s and kept to the grass on campus, claiming the sidewalk was too hard for his feet. Some folks take him for a hick, but be careful, every shut eye isn't asleep. Notice, Abe's not working the boys into one of those tent-preacher lathers. Not his style. The season after this one, just before the Horned Frogs take the field at Ohio State with 80,000-plus fans licking their fangs, all Abe will tell his boys is "Laddies, you're playin' the best team in *the* United States of America"—then walk away. Another game, what he'll say is, "These are big guys. Hope you don't get hurt." He's a master of the subtle psychological ploy, a man who lacks both the strategic genius and the double-knotted sphincter of your other big football honchos, but who maneuvers a college of 4,700 students, most of them female, into three Cotton Bowls in four seasons between '55 and '58 and humbles elephants such as Southern Cal and Penn State and Texas along the way. "You just believe in human beings, that they're all pretty good folks, and you just try to keep 'em that way"—that's how Abe sums up his coaching philosophy in the Cotton Bowl program they're hawking outside that locker room right now.

In practice he'll drop to his hands and knees and crawl into the huddle, gaze up at his gang like a gopher and declare, "Boys, run a 34." Late in a game, when the Froggies are driving for a score they need desperately, old Abe will come down off the chair he always sits on—fanny on the seat back, feet on the seat—take another chomp of the unlit cigar he alternately sucks and rolls between his palms until it disintegrates, and walk down the sideline murmuring to his troops, "Hold your left nut, laddies—we need this one."

Oh, sure, Abe can get riled. But the vilest oath he ever musters—with his fist clenched and his thumb in an odd place, on top of his index finger instead of around his knuckles—is "Shistol pot!" which is a spoonerism for *pistol shot*, in case you need a translation. Usually Abe just walks a player away from the group with an arm around the boy's shoulders and quietly says, "Now, you know better 'n that." You know what troubles the fellows most at a moment like this, 15 minutes before kickoff? The thought that they might let down Abe.

All right, let's be honest, not everyone's dying to please the boss, not in any locker room in the world. See number 67, Norman Ashley, sitting third from the left against the back wall? He's in Abe's doghouse for late hits in practice and for tackling quarterback Chuck Curtis so hard one day that Curtis peed blood. Ashley will never play a lick, and he knows it. He'll end up spending four decades in Alaska flying a Piper Super Cub just big enough for him, his rifle, his rod and his hunting dog, searching for places where there are no whistles and no prey that a man can't bring down. And over on the other side, second from your right, that's center Jim Ozee, who started all season till today. Damn near half a century later, when he's a grandpa tossing raisins to the mockingbird that visits him in his backyard in Fort Worth each day, he'll still remember, "That's despair on my face. I'm offended by Abe at this moment. I couldn't figure why I wasn't starting. I didn't hear anything he said. . . ."

" . . . *wanna thank you fellas. Seniors in this room . . . no need to tell you how I feel 'bout you. You were my first recruitin' class, came in green just like me, and accomplished some great things. Now you're 'bout to split up, go your separate ways, and this'll be the game you remember the rest of your days. Life's about to change, laddies. You're never gonna capture this moment again. . . .* "

Two in this room will end up in early coffins when their hearts quit: Dick Finney, on your far right, and John Mitchell, second from your left, the lad inspecting the fingernails he's just chewed. Two other players will lose sons in car accidents, which is worse than a heart attack. Another, Jack Webb, seated in the deep corner just to the left of the youngster holding his chin in his hand, will relish the tension of moments like this so much that he'll become a fighter pilot, only to lose his life when his jet crashes in the Philippines. Two will get rich, then go bankrupt. Allen Garrard, number 84, the guy seated on the floor near the corner, will get multiple sclerosis and draw on moments like this 40 years from now, when his car blows a tire in a rainstorm in the dead of night and he has to hobble painfully on his cane far beyond the 200 feet he's usually able to walk. Of course, Abe himself, when he's in his 70s, will be found draped across his bed by his wife one morning when his ticker quits.

See that fellow on the floor behind Abe, number 53, Joe Williams? Can you tell? A year ago he lost his mom, who attended every game he ever played, in a car accident, and he's worried sick about his dad, sleepwalking awake ever since she died, who's somewhere in the stands high above this room. Here's what Joe will say 42 years from now, when his hair's as white as snow and arthritis has racked his joints with pain and stolen his right hand: "I should've expressed my gratitude to Abe. I'm still living by the principles he taught us. I'm not gonna give in. I'm still coming out of bed swinging even though I might not hit a thing. He guided us through those years. He looked out for us the way our parents presumed he would.

"You know something? Nothing ever again will match the intensity, the passion of moments like this. What it takes to overcome yourself—because if you listen to your body, you'll always be a coward. Don't get me wrong, I love my wife and kids, but I'd give anything to go back. More than who you're looking at now, that guy in the picture, *that's* me. *That's* who I really am."

" *. . . HASN'T BEEN an easy road for us this season, laddies. Stubbed our toe real bad, and a lot of folks started calling us a second-rate team. But we didn't roll up in a ball, and by going through what we did and coming together, we're more a team now 'n we've ever been. . . .* "

This is how the boys will recollect Abe's speech four decades later. His sermon doesn't dwell on details, but here are the facts: You're listening to a coach who was hung in effigy and made it to the Cotton Bowl in the same season. Right now, as Possum Elenburg, the fellow gnawing his knuckles on your far left, puts it, "Abe's done a rare thing—got all his coons up the same tree." He's got them all ruminating on a season that began with the Horned Frogs as heavy favorites in the Southwest Conference, returning a slew of starters from the nation's sixth-ranked team the year before, busting out to a 3–0 start with a 32–0 blitzing of Kansas, a 41–6 crushing of Arkansas and a 23–6 spanking of Alabama. Next came TCU's blood enemy, Texas A&M, with Bear Bryant at the wheel, the team that had handed the Frogs their only regular-season defeat the year before.

So now it was payback time, a gorgeous Saturday in College Station, the Aggies' stadium jammed and the 3–0 Frogs cross-eyed crazy in their locker room. And what happened? Sometime during the first quarter, all the friction between the two squads was more than the sky could hold, and the ugliest wall of black clouds you ever saw came rolling in from the north. The wind began to howl so hard that flagpoles bent into upside-down L's, and the ref had to put a foot on the ball between plays to keep it from sailing to Mexico. The rain came in sheets so thick that the subs on the sideline couldn't see the starters on the field, and then the rain turned to hail so helmet-drumming heavy that the linemen couldn't hear the signals from the quarterback screeching at their butts. Postpone the game? This is Texas, y'all! This is football!

The Frogs knifed through winds that gusted up to 90 mph, penetrated the A&M two-yard line on three drives behind their All-America running back, Jim Swink—and couldn't get it in! On one series Swink crossed the goal line twice—the Frogs had the film to prove it—but either the refs couldn't see or it was too slippery to get a good grip on your left nut in a monsoon. TCU finally scored in the third quarter but missed the extra point, and the Aggies stole the game with a fourth-quarter touchdown, 7–6.

Ever drive a car into the exit of a drive-in theater when you were 16, not knowing about those metal teeth? That's the sound that leaked out of the Froggies after that. Miami rocked them 14–0 the next week, Baylor scared the daylights out of them before succumbing 7–6, and then Texas Tech, a team that didn't belong in the same county with the Frogs, pasted them 21–7. Another ferocious storm fell on the team bus on the way home from Lubbock, and the Frogs crawled through it, wondering if their senior-laden squad had lost focus, become more concerned with the honeys they were fixing to marry and the careers they were fixing to start than with the mission at hand.

Back on campus, there dangled poor Abe from a rope lashed to a tree not far from the athletic dorm, brown hat and sport coat over a pillow head and sheet body. It was a startling sight at a university that many players had chosen because it had the homey feel of a big high school, a cow-town college where guys wore cowboy hats and boots, or jeans rolled up at the cuffs and penny loafers. Just like that, the dispirited Frogs had a cause. Their starting quarterback, Chuck Curtis—that's him, number 46, sitting two to the left of Abe—along with end O'Day Williams and backup end Neil Hoskins, the youngster two to the left of Curtis, with his chin in his hand, went out to do a little rectifyin'. Curtis slashed down the effigy with a pocket knife, then led his mates, rumor by rumor, to the perpetrator, who turned tail after a little shouting and shoving. Two days later the Frogs called a players-only meeting at the dining hall, where the subs vented their frustration over lack of playing time, and Cotton Eye Joe Williams, the captain, promised to take their beef to Abe. The players all agreed that an attack on Abe was like an attack on their daddies, and they closed ranks.

To Cotton Eye's suggestion that the second fiddlers fiddle more, Abe said, Great idea. To the notion that the boys were steamed about the hanging effigy, Abe said, Couldn't've been me, I'm a lot better lookin' than that. To the proposition that the Froggies might still make it to the Cotton Bowl—A&M had been hit with NCAA sanctions for recruiting violations and wouldn't be eligible—Abe said, Let's go make hay. That's what the Frogs did, slapping Texas in the face 46–0, elbowing a ripsnorting Rice squad by three and thumping SMU 21–6 to finish 7–3, second to A&M, and scoop up the Aggies' fumbled Cotton Bowl bid. Then came a month to heal and prepare, a half-hour Greyhound bus ride to Dallas a few days before the big one, the formal dance and then the downtown parade on the fire engine, eyeing that big load on the other fire truck, the one that scored a record-breaking 43 points against Colgate: Jim Brown.

FINALLY ALL the buildup is over. The Southwest Conference princesses in convertibles and the high-stepping high school bands are drumming up one last buzz among the 68,000 waiting outside the locker room. But here inside there's only quiet, broken by a soft sob just outside the frame, from the Frogs' All-America lineman Norman Hamilton—who'll swear decades later that no matter what his teammates recollect, he didn't cry before games.

Quiet, broken by the calm drawl of Honest Abe. Whose calm is a lie, so keep your eye on him, because any minute he might just sneak off to the john and throw up. That's what Virgil Miller—he's number 18, the little guy in the dark corner with his head down—will find Abe doing before a game a few years later, when Virgil returns to visit the coach. "Ever get nervous like that?" Abe will ask Virgil. It's safe, since Virgil has graduated and gone.

It's almost like going to church, being here, isn't it? Nope, it's more religious than church, because half of the people here aren't faking it. Maybe folks who never played can't understand how you can be 15 minutes from tearing somebody's head off, 15 seconds from vomiting and a half inch from God, all at the same time. But Chuck Curtis knows. Forty-two years from now, when this picture is placed under his eyes, he'll say, "Look at us. Compared to players today? We weren't great athletes. But we were a team from top to bottom, all giving entire respect to our leader and wanting the same thing wholeheartedly. A sincere group of young men. It'd take a miracle to get the feeling we had in that moment again. With that attitude, there's not a sin that's not erased." When he looks up, there will be tears in his eyes.

Henry B. (Doc) Hardt, he'd understand. He's the old-timer wearing his brown Sunday best and that purple-and-white ribbon on his left arm, so lost in his meditation that he doesn't know that his pants leg is climbing up his calf and that three decades have vanished since he last suited up for a football game—he'd snatch a helmet and storm through that door if Abe would just say the word. That's reverence, the look of a man with four Methodist minister brothers and a missionary sister. Doc's the head of the TCU chemistry department and the Frogs' NCAA faculty representative, the man who makes sure the flunkers aren't playing and the boosters aren't paying, and he's so good at it that he'll become president of the NCAA a few years after this game. Huge hands, grip like a vise and a kind word for everyone, even when he hobbles on a cane to Frogs games a quarter century later. Nice to know he'll make it to 90.

But you need to meet the rest of the boys. Just behind Doc's left shoulder is Mr. Clean: Willard McClung, the quiet assistant to renowned trainer Elmer Brown. Brown's busy right now shooting up guard Vernon Uecker's ankle with novocaine, but Willard would be glad to go fetch a glass of Elmer's concoction for those whose steak and eggs are about to come up, a cocktail the boys call "the green s---." Trouble is, Elmer's green s--- usually comes up along with everything else.

Willard's the only man here who never played, the only one not crawled inside himself—no coincidence there. His ankles were too weak for him to play ball, but he was determined to jimmy his way into moments like this, so he climbed aboard a train his senior year of high school, a fuzzy-cheeked kid from Minden, La., and rode all day to reach the National Trainers' Convention in Kansas City. Trainers were so thrilled to see a kid show up that Elmer Brown finagled him a scholarship at TCU.

That's Frankie Hyde just behind Doc Hardt's right shoulder, the blond studying the hairs on his left calf. He's the Frogs' scout-team quarterback and an all-around good guy. Doesn't know that he'll hurt his shoulder a few months from now in spring training, that he'll never suit up for a football game again. Doesn't know that Abe's steering his rudder, that he'll end up coaching football just like six of the 17 players in the picture. That he'll end up guiding wave after wave of teenage boys through this moment, some who'll start chattering like monkeys, some who'll go quieter than the dead, some who'll slam their shoulder pads into lockers and poles, some who'll pray like a priest on his third cup of coffee, some who'll get too sick to play. Take it from Frankie: "People who don't experience this don't know themselves like they should."

Or take it from Hunter Enis, the handsome raven-haired boy leaning forward in the dark corner, the one who'll make a bundle in oil: "Sure, there's times in business when you'll work together with a group of men to meet a goal. But that's not about anything as important as this. It's just about money."

Or Possum Elenburg, the sub on the far left, sitting there thinking, Heck, yes, it'd be nice to get in and quarterback a few plays on national TV, but heck, no, I don't want to have to play defense and risk getting burned deep like I did against Texas Tech. Forty-two years later, here's Possum: "This is reality stripped to its nakedness. There's no place to hide. Time is standing still. It's funny, but all your life people tell you that football's just a game, that so many things more important will happen to you in life that'll make sports seem insignificant." Listen to Possum. He's a man who came within a quarter inch of losing his life in '60 when an oil rig crashed into his skull and paralyzed his right side for a year, a man who lost a fortune overnight when oil prices crashed on his head two decades later. "But it's not true, what people tell ya," he says. "I'm fixing to be tested in this moment, and I'm gonna be tested again and again in my life, and I'm gonna get nervous and wonder about myself every single time. Your priorities as a kid are just as important to you as your priorities as a 60-year-old man, because all your aspirations and goals are on the line. At any age, each thing that's important to you . . . is important to you, and each fight needs to be fought with every effort."

WE'RE LOOKING at a roomful of bladders fixing to bust, but it's just a hoax—any doctor could explain the phenomenon. It's just anxiety sending a surge of adrenaline to the nerve endings in the bladder, causing it to tighten and creating the feeling that you gotta go. These boys are like a pack of hunting dogs spraying all over the place just before the hunt, only dogs are lucky enough not to have all those laces and hip pads and jockstraps to fumble with.

" . . . *don't need to remind you, laddies, what happened to us in the Cotton Bowl last year, and what that felt like. Not many folks in life get a second chance, but we've got it right here, today . . . the chance to redeem ourselves. . . .*"

Redemption. That's all that thumps through the hearts and heads of two players who happen to be sitting elbow to elbow: Chuck Curtis and, on his right, Harold (Toad) Pollard, number 16, with the dirty-blond crew cut and the eye black. See, Toad's missed extra point was the margin of defeat in TCU's 14–13 Cotton Bowl loss to Mississippi last year. And Toad's missed extra point in the monsoon at A&M cost the Frogs that 7–6 heartache. Before you get the idea that Toad's a lost cause, you need to know that he led the nation's kickers in scoring last season and that his nickname is Abe's bungled version of Toad's true moniker, the Golden Toe. But ever since that wide-right boot in the Cotton Bowl, Toad has walked around imagining that the entire campus is thinking or saying, "There goes the guy who missed the extra point." Every morning last summer, before his 3-to-11 shift as a roughneck in the oil fields, he toted a tee to a high school field and kicked 40 through the pipes, alone, to prepare for his redemption. "It's a lot more hurt," he'll admit years later, "than a person would realize." Especially since Toad always seems to be clowning, doing that dead-on Donald Duck imitation. But right now he's more nervous than he's ever been, trying to swallow back the notion that he could bungle another critical extra point and be stuck with seeing himself in the mirror every time his hair needs combing the rest of his life.

It's a double-wide hot seat over there, cooking Chuck Curtis's fanny too. Because it was in this very room, at this very moment at the Cotton Bowl last year, that Abe concluded his pregame talk by reminding Chuck-a-luck, as he was fond of calling his quarterback, that he was absolutely *not* to run back the kickoff, that he was to pitch it back to Swink. But Chuck-a-luck, who believed fiercely in his ability to perform or charm his way out of any fix, walked out of this room and fielded that kickoff on the run, down near his shins, and decided that all that forward momentum shouldn't be wasted on a backward lateral, and actually traveled a few yards before—*crunch!*— he took a lick that cracked three ribs and partially dislocated his shoulder, and the Frogs' star quarterback was gone on the game's first play.

Of course, Dick Finney, the backup quarterback—that's him on your farthest right, the one who used to call audibles with fruits instead of numbers ("Apples! Oranges! *Bananas!*")—came trotting into the huddle with that bird-eating grin of his and declared, "Have no fear, Finney's here." But fear truly was in order, because although Diamond Dick ran like a jackrabbit, he also passed like one, and Ole Miss stacked everybody but the trombone players on the line to create a terrible constipation that day.

Imagine what that did to Chuck Curtis, a strapping 6' 4", 200-pound All-Conference signal-caller, a Pentecostal preacher's son who could sell a bikini to an Eskimo. In a few years he'll be buying cattle like crazy, owning a bank, winning three state championships as a high school coach and selling automobiles to boot, joking with a former Frogs teammate who protests that he can't afford to pay for a car, "Hey, ol' buddy, I didn't ask you to *pay* for a car—I just wanna *sell* you a car." In the '70s, when he comes up on charges of making false statements on bank-loan applications, there will be preachers preaching in his favor on the courthouse steps, alongside his Jacksboro High football team, cheerleaders and band, all crooning the school's alma mater, and he'll get off with a $500 fine. But no amount of preaching or singing or selling can hide the fact that Chuck-a-luck's ego, more than Toad's blown extra point, cost his teammates the '56 Cotton Bowl, and that he'll have to wear that around like a stained pair of chaps for the rest of his life . . . unless, in about 10 minutes, he can maneuver the Frogs past Jim Brown.

NOW TURN around. It's long past time you met Marvin Newman, the well-groomed fellow with the side of his snout pressed against that camera. Nearly forgot about him, he's been so quiet, but none of this would've been possible without him. Funny guy, Marvin: your classic pushy New Yorker when there's something he really wants, but when what he really wants is to disappear into the woodwork—presto, Marvin's a mouse. You can barely hear the click of that Leica he's pointing toward Abe.

He can't use a flash—that would be like taking a hammer to a moment like this. So he has to spread his legs, brace his knees, lock his elbows against his sides and hold his breath to keep that camera stone still. He has to become the tripod, because the quarter second that the shutter needs to be open to drink in enough light is enough to turn Chuck-a-luck and Toad and Buddy and Joe into a purple smear if Marvin's paws move even a hair. Doesn't hurt that he's only 29, because the hands won't let you do that at 59. Doesn't hurt that he rarely drinks, either, because more than a few magazine shooters would still have the shakes at 10 minutes to one in the afternoon on New Year's Day.

He's a Bronx kid, a baker's only son who knew at 19 that he wasn't going to keep burying his arms to the elbows in a wooden vat of rye dough, wasn't going to do what his father and grandfather and great-grandfather had done, even if his old man nearly blew a fuse when that first $90 camera was delivered to the door.

Who knows, maybe that's part of why he lies in hotel beds for hours, boiling with plans A, B, C and Z on the night before an assignment, brain-storming about how to come home with an image nobody else would have thought of. Maybe that's why he has to come up with something at this Cotton Bowl as heart-touching as the picture he nailed at last year's, that classic shot of Ole Miss's Billy Kinnard coming off the field after beating TCU by one point and planting a kiss on Ole Miss cheerleader Kay Kinnard, who just happened to be his new bride. So, recollecting from last New Year's Day how mouthwatering the light was in that locker room, Marvin made it his first item of business when he saw Abe in Dallas to start schmoozing, start persuading Abe how discreet he'd be, how lickety-split he'd get in and get out, and how much his boss was counting on him . . . so could he *please* slip into the Frogs' locker room just before kickoff? Heck, Abe didn't need schmoozing. *Sure, Marvin! Why not drop by at halftime, too?*

Sure, he'll take snaps more famous than this. He'll bag that black-and-white shot of the World Series-winning homer soaring off Bill Mazeroski's bat as the scoreboard shows all the pertinent facts—3:36 p.m, ninth inning, score tied—of Game 7 between the Pittsburgh Pirates and the New York Yankees in 1960. He'll catch eyes all over the country with his picture of the newly widowed Jackie Kennedy clutching John-John's hand as they watch JFK's coffin go by. But 40-plus years after this New Year's Day in Dallas, he'll remember this picture almost as if he took it yesterday.

"They completely forgot about me," he'll say, sitting over the photo in his Manhattan apartment at age 71. "When photography works well, you can go inside the psyche of the people in the picture. You can see beyond the moment. I always loved this picture. I knew it was special. There hadn't been many photographs taken inside locker rooms, so I knew I was privileged. I couldn't have been standing more than 10 feet from Abe Martin. . . ."

" . . . *but we're not gonna shut down Jim Brown, boys. Not with one tackler. We're gonna have to swarm him. We'll slow him down. We'll go right at him when we've got the ball. He's not a great defensive player. We'll tire him out. We won't stop him. We'll outscore him. This game can put us right back where we belong, with the best teams in the country. Look inside yourselves and ask, Do I really want it? If you do, laddies, the goose hangs high. Now let's have the prayer.*"

SOME OF you might not quite grasp what's sitting and waiting for the Frogs in the room down the hall. Jim Brown stands 6' 2" and weighs 225 pounds, which is at least 35 pounds more than the average halfback of his day, not to mention 22 pounds heavier than the average player on the biggest line in the country, Notre Dame's. He runs 100 yards in 10 seconds flat, high-jumps 6' 3", hurls the discus 155 feet and once won six events for Syracuse in a track meet, which gave him the notion that it might be fun to enter the national decathlon championship, which he did on 10 days' practice and placed fifth. He scored 33 in a Syracuse basketball game and will be drafted by the NBA's Syracuse Nationals, not bad for a fellow who at the time was considered to have been the greatest lacrosse player in U.S. history. He's just finishing up a senior season in which he averaged 6.2 yards per carry, and he will average a record 5.2 yards per carry for the Cleveland Browns over the next nine years, leading the NFL in rushing in eight of those, before he'll hang it up, as MVP, at age 30. Forgive me if you knew all that, but some legends get so large, the particulars get lost.

Now, some of the Frogs are deeply worried about Brown. Others have been fooled by the three game films they've seen, because Brown looks slower on celluloid than he does when you're reaching for his heels. Still others think he's very good, but he can't possibly be better than John David Crow of Texas A&M.

Brown's sitting very still and silent right now. He's the sort of man who contains a lot more than he lets out, till he steps on the field, and maybe some of what he's holding in has to do with a question that's struck you already, looking around the TCU locker room: Where are all the black folks? There's not one playing football in the Southwest Conference, and there won't be one on scholarship till nine years down the road, after Chuck Curtis becomes an SMU assistant coach and recruits Jerry Levias. In fact, it was only two years before this that the first blacks played in TCU's stadium, when Penn State brought Lenny Moore and Rosey Grier to town and they had to sleep at a motel way out on Jacksboro Highway, because the team couldn't find a downtown Fort Worth hotel that would have them.

That wasn't going to happen to Brown. He decided before the Orangemen arrived in Dallas that he'd refuse to be separated from his teammates, but it hadn't come to that. Syracuse was staying in a hotel on the edge of Dallas that accepted the whole squad.

Sure, Brown's thoughts are fixed on football right now, 15 minutes before kickoff, but it would be a lie to say that another question isn't nibbling on his mind: What's going to happen when he's circled by nearly 70,000 white Texans, some of them wearing cleats? Abe hasn't said a thing to his boys about color. Before the game against Moore and Grier in '54, all he said was, "They're darn good football players, so it wouldn't make much sense to say something to get 'em mad."

Brown will never be the sort to live on the fumes of his past, or reminisce much at all. But even at 63, when he's running across America directing Amer-I-Can—an organization he founded to tackle gang problems and help prisoners get ready for life outside the walls—some of what coursed through him in that Cotton Bowl locker room will still be with him.

"I was concerned how their players would carry themselves, if there'd be any epithets," he'll say. "But I wasn't going to make that any kind of extra motive, or try to prove something. Racism is sickness, and I'm not gonna prove something to sickness. I was a performer with my own standards, and living up to them was all I worried about. For me, the time just before a game was always tense, like going to war without death. I always felt humbled. It's a very spiritual moment. I'd try to go into a pure state. No negative thoughts, even toward the other team. No rah-rah, because rah-rah's for show. Your butt's on the line, and you either stand up and deal with it, or . . . or you can't. You become a very difficult opponent for anyone or anything when you know that you can."

LET ME tell you what happened that day, right after Marvin's last click. Chuck Curtis went wild. He called a run-pitch sprint-out series that no one expected from a drop-back quarterback without much foot speed, and he threw two touchdown passes to stake the Frogs to a 14–0 lead.

Then it was Brown's turn. The tip that TCU coaches had passed on to the Frogs after studying film—that just before the snap Brown leaned in the direction he was about to go—was accurate, but it wasn't worth a Chinese nickel. As Brown carried a couple of more Frogs for rides, Abe spun toward his boys on the sideline and nearly swallowed his cigar, then howled, "Shistol pot! Can't anybody tackle him?"

Against Brown, everything the Frogs had learned about hitting a man in the thighs and wrapping him up went down the sewer—there was just too much power there. First tackler to reach him had to hit him high, delay him for a second, take some of the forward momentum out of those thighs, then wait for reinforcements to hit him low.

Brown bashed in from the two for Syracuse's first touchdown, kicked the extra point, then hurled a 20-yard pass that set up his own four-yard touchdown run and booted another point after to tie the ball game 14–14 just before intermission. Lonnie Leatherman, a backup end for the Frogs, would shake his head from here to the year 2000, yelping, "He ran through the whole stinkin' team! That man was bad to the bone! He was unbelievable! These are great football players, and they couldn't tackle him. Norman Hamilton was an All-America and couldn't tackle him."

A savage moment came early in the second half. Syracuse was on the TCU 40 and rolling—Brown had just made another first down on a fourth-down plunge—when Buddy Dike, with his battered kidney, threw caution to the wind. He hit Brown head-on, producing a sound Hamilton would never forget. "Like thunder," he'd recall. "Never heard a sound that loud from two men colliding. I thought, How can they ever get up?"

Dike's face mask snapped in two, the pigskin burst from Brown's grasp and TCU recovered it. Brown would not miss a play. The inspired Froggies again targeted Brown when he was on defense, flooding his side of the field with three receivers. Years later Leatherman would make no bones about it. "Brown was horrible on defense," he'd say. Joe Williams would be a trifle kinder: "Maybe their coaches didn't want to offend him by teaching him defense."

Curtis closed a drive by sweeping around the left end for a score, and Jim Swink found paydirt for the Frogs a few minutes later. Toad Pollard stepped on the field for the extra point. He was 3 for 3, and his side was up 27–14, but with nearly 12 minutes left and Brown yet to be corralled, the kicker's gut quivered with evil memories. To Jim Ozee, finally getting a few minutes at center, it seemed like eternity between his snap and the thud of Toad's toe against the ball. "What took you so long?" Ozee demanded seconds after the kick sailed true.

"I wanted to be sure," Toad said, breathing heavily—as if he knew that Brown would rip off a 46-yard return on the kickoff, then slam in from the one and bust open Toad's lip a few moments later. As if he knew that Syracuse would roar right down the field on its next possession, finally figuring a way to reach the end zone without Brown, on a touchdown pass with 1:16 left. As if he knew that Chico Mendoza, the lone Mexican-American on the Frogs' roster, would storm in from right end just after Syracuse's third touchdown and block Brown's point-after try, making the team that lost by one extra point in the Cotton Bowl in 1956 the winner by one extra point in 1957, by a score of 28–27. "All those white boys out there," Leatherman would point out, "and the Mexican and the black were the key players."

Brown would finish with 132 yards on 26 carries, three kick-off returns for 96 more yards, three extra points, the whole country's admiration . . . and no slurs. "They were nice human beings," he'd say of the Frogs. But Chuck-a-luck, who finished 12 of 15 through the air, would see Brown speak at the University of Texas-Arlington years later and leave sniffing that "he sounded like one of those Black Panthers."

Toad would remember "floating" at the postgame banquet, thinking he was saved from a lifetime of negative thoughts, but in his 60s that extra point he missed in the '56 Cotton Bowl would still occupy his mind more than the four he made in '57, and every kick he watched on TV would make his foot twitch up, as if the kick were his.

TCU? The Frogs wouldn't win another bowl game for 41 years. The rules changed on Abe: Free substitution and the end of the two-way player meant that a college needed at least 22 studs, and that a small school with a scrawny budget and even less national TV exposure had almost no prayer, no matter how sincere its players were 15 minutes before kickoff. When Abe quit nine years later, people said the game had passed him by.

Come 1999, that bare locker room would no longer be a locker room, that Southwest Conference would no longer exist, and that New Year's Day game would be known as the Southwestern Bell Cotton Bowl Classic, with a website.

ONE LAST thing. There's a saying Texans used to share about men in locker rooms awaiting battle, and pardon my French, but it goes like this: Brave men piss, cowards s---.

Which were you? Which was I? Guess I just can't walk out of this picture without asking questions like that. But I'll shut up now, in case you want to go back and catch Chuck-a-luck going watery-eyed as he leads the team prayer. Hurry, though. It's going hard on nine minutes to one.

———————

POSTSCRIPT: *Marvin Newman, still a working photographer at 80, recently published a book and held a one-man show in New York City. In 1999, he returned to that very locker room and re-created the picture with its living members for SI. "It was a little scary," Newman says. "But once the players knew I had been the photographer, they treated me with great respect. The photograph brought back all their memories of a time that so many of them felt was the best of their youth."*

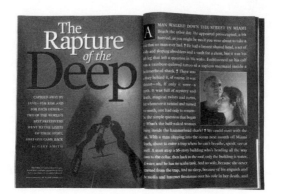

The Rapture of the Deep

Carried away by love—for risk and for each other—two of the world's best freedivers pushed to the furthest limits of their strange and frightening sport. Only one came back.

MAN WALKED DOWN THE STREET IN MIAMI BEACH the other day. He appeared preoccupied, a bit hurried, as you might be too if you were about to take a risk that no man ever had.

He had a bronze shaved head, a set of wide and sloping shoulders and a vault for a chest, but it was his left leg that left a question in his wake. Emblazoned on his calf was a rainbow-colored tattoo of a topless mermaid inside a hammerhead shark.

There was a story behind it, of course. It was almost—oh, if only it were—a myth. It was full of mystery and death, magical twists and turns, but whenever it twisted and turned too much, one had only to remember the simple question that began it: What's the half-naked woman doing inside the hammerhead shark?

We could start with the risk. With a man slipping into the ocean next month off Miami Beach, about to enter a trap where he can't breathe, speak, see or smell. A man atop a 56-story building who's heading all the way down to the cellar, then back to the roof, only the building is water, all water, and he has no scuba tank. And no wife, because she never returned from the trap. And no sleep, because of his anguish and the media and Internet firestorms over his role in her death, and the resulting lawsuit. Yes, we could start by asking how it happens that the *last* thing a man in the midst of such grief should be doing becomes his only way out of it and why—here, today, a few billion years into the evolution of life on earth—we've come to this, the ritualized risking of death: *extreme sports*.

But I've always felt it's better to start with the half-naked woman.

Fully clothed, at this point, of course. Twenty-one years old. Staring in disbelief at a poster at a university in La Paz, Mexico, seven years ago. *Him*. On the poster. The centerpiece of her marine-biology thesis on how the human body adapts to survive at extreme depths. The risk taker. Pi-PEEN, as Spanish speakers pronounced his nickname. Pipín Ferreras.

Who could Audrey Mestre turn to and tell what was stirring inside her? Look, that's him, this legendary Cuban she'd been up all night reading about for months, this guy who could fill his lungs with 8.2 liters of air—nearly twice as much as a normal human being—and dive deeper than anyone else on earth; this guy who'd been in movies and TV shows and scientists' studies, this total stranger she'd started *dreaming* about and somehow . . . fallen in love with. Coming to Cabo San Lucas, the poster said, to attempt another world-record dive, just a few hours' drive away. What coincidence! No. That couldn't be. What *fate*.

She found herself on a bus packed with peasants and dogs and chickens, chugging toward Cabo. O.K., she wouldn't make a fool of herself. Wouldn't stay long, wouldn't act on this fantasy flitting through her head: the mermaid and the fish man.

She got off the bus, checked into a cheap hotel and headed toward the wharf. Amazing. Pipín was offering to give novices a couple of hours of instruction and then let them observe one of his training dives. It was like Michael Jordan's saying, "Anyone want to let me teach you to play ball, then stand under the basket and watch me scrimmage?" Audrey watched, close up, as he slid into the water and ventilated to prepare for his dive, his lungs and windpipe producing the sound of a bicycle tire being pumped with air: in with the oxygen he'd need to last for nearly three minutes and the 858 feet of water, round-trip, he hoped to cover. Out with the carbon dioxide and the thoughts that could kill him. Because where he was going, panic could burn up those 8.2 liters of air in seconds, emotion could devour them in a minute, and even a stray thought could stir his heartbeat and consume the oxygen he'd need to make those last few feet.

She watched him wrap his knees around the crossbar of an aluminum sled, close his eyes and raise one hand to the metal frame overhead: a religious posture. She knew by heart the religion's history, how man for centuries had been diving for sponge and fish and pearls until Raimondo Bucher, a Hungarian air force officer naturalized as an Italian citizen, dived 30 meters on a dare in 1949. With that act, man realized he could dive for something far more important than sponge or fish or pearls—he could dive for *ego*—and competitive freediving, or submerging without the aid of an air tank, was born.

Pipín took one last gulp of air, then vanished. But Audrey had absorbed her subject so completely that she could shut her eyes and see it all: The sled gathering speed, gliding down a cable anchored with a 100-pound weight, a contraption Pipín had helped devise so that he—and fewer than a dozen others in the world who dedicated themselves to No Limits, the most extreme of the freediving disciplines—could bore deeper and faster than legs and fins could propel him. Pipín flying past a few scuba divers stationed at intervals along the cable, safety assistants who could do only so much if trouble occurred, because you can't make an unconscious man breathe. Pipín letting water flood his nasal passages and ear tubes to stave off the searing pain and equalize the relentlessly increasing pressure that could rupture his eardrums. Pipín's heart rate slowing to 50 ... 40 ... 30 ... 20 beats a minute, his lungs shriveling to the size of potatoes. His hand, when he reached the bottom, opening an air-tank valve that inflated a lift bag that would rocket him back up.

He burst through the surface in his neoprene wet suit, a missile from the abyss. He barely seemed to notice her.

MAYBE SHE could go just a little deeper. Ask him a question or two, make her thesis shine. She watched from across the table as he sat beside his girlfriend, the blonde knockout, the jazz singer.

What good fortune that Pepe Fernández, the chief of Pipín's safety divers, had gotten an eyeful of Audrey in her bathing suit and invited her to tag along with the crew for dinner and drinks. No. What fate.

The jazz singer rose to sing with her band. Audrey took a deep breath. She'd grown up just outside Paris, the only child of scuba-diving parents and the granddaughter of a champion spearfisherman, crazy for dancing and for water and for her dream of merging the two: becoming an Olympic synchronized swimmer. But she'd contracted typhoid fever at 14 after her family moved to Mexico City, just as she entered her growth spurt, and it had left her with scoliosis and a spine that swerved like an *S*.

For four years she was trapped, pinched inside a hard plastic corset. Her right eyelid drooped and her vision went double as her bewildered body produced antibodies that could locate no infection and settled in her eye. She couldn't bear it, finally—all the wrecking of her body and her dream. She was found in the school bathroom, blood puddling from her slit wrists.

There was, she came to realize, one place where she could escape the trap. For hours each day in the summers she spent on the Mediterranean coast with her grandfather, she flung off the corset, strapped on the scuba tank and slipped into the sea, and everything again seemed possible. She swam through the fire of shame and came out the other side, a sweet and shy 18-year-old. In the pictures she sketched, she was a mermaid.

She stared at the empty seat beside the fish man as the jazz singer started to wail. Trembling, she began to ask him questions. Pipín purred. Who was this young beauty who seemed to know so much about him? Audrey glowed. He spoke of the sea as she had experienced it, a magical realm where a human might spring free from the prison of self. Somehow France came up, and he launched into a tirade about the arrogance of the French, then paused and asked Audrey what part of Mexico she was from.

"France," she said, smiling.

SUDDENLY, THE undertow had her. That's what Pipín did: He grabbed time and love and destiny and yanked them in his wake. Suddenly they were heading back to her hotel together, Pipín anxious to atone for his blunder. Suddenly they were in her bed.

Suddenly the blonde jazz singer was packing the next day and leaving Pipín's hotel suite in a huff. Suddenly she was on his boat a day later, kissing him after a training dive, when he bolted right back into the ocean—the safety diver whom he'd just met and hired, Massimo Berttoni, hadn't resurfaced after going down to retrieve the sled. Suddenly she was staring at death, handling it with more calm than anyone in his crew. Suddenly she was at the dead man's post, with Pipín's life in her hands: She was his new safety diver at 197 feet.

Suddenly she was on the phone, calling her parents in Mexico City to ask them to retrieve her furniture and dog and clothes and car from her apartment because she'd decided to drop out of college and fly to Miami to live with her thesis subject, and her shell-shocked parents were jumping on a plane to Cabo to see if she'd come down with typhoid fever again, or something worse, and when they arrived and asked this man Pipín what the mad rush was, he replied, "I don't live by a compass. I go with the wind. If I don't take her with me, it will be painful, but I know I won't come back for her. The magic is right here. Right now. You can't kill the magic and bring it back to life."

Then he popped a world-record 429-foot dive and they flew away together.

HOW LONG could they last before one of them came up for air? She'd never even had a boyfriend. He believed that he'd been selected to go on a quest by an undersea god.

"People have always told me that God lives in heaven," he wrote in a book. "Yet, as much as I have tried, I have never been able to see him. I have seen that other God, the one that lives down in the deepest blue of the submarine abyss, where I descend. . . . He gave me the mission of showing all humans how to discover their aquatic potential. . . . He gave me the skills to descend at ease into his realm of darkness, where he always shows his face as pure light."

It was one thing to take the plunge with such a man. Two wives and a slew of girlfriends had, but none had gone down far enough, and none had stayed under. He became disillusioned, or in need of someone else's touch to soothe his restless, lonely heart. His eye would stray. Once he awakened soaked in rubbing alcohol beside a girlfriend, her eyes ablaze as she held a lighter over him and screamed, "Who *is* she? Tell me now!"

Now it was Audrey waking up beside a man whose moods shifted faster than sky over ocean, a generous man who could make sudden friends—or enemies—for life. Who *had* to beat Italian rival Umberto Pelizzari's new record by 13 meters, *right now*, if Pelizzari had just beaten his by 12. A man who . . . wait a minute. Had she really seen what she thought she'd seen just before bedtime? Yes. A man who turned to his Santería gods for guidance, summoning them with honey and cigar smoke and herbs and branches and bones and scraps of coconut shell, and a funny sort of song?

She got out of bed at dawn and headed to the kitchen. Coffee for Pipín. Coffee and fruit for the little statue of one of his gods when Pipín wasn't around to make the offering. She accommodated his myth: the knight on the underwater god's mission. She could even turn a blind eye to his wandering eye.

Their hands compulsively touched when they walked or sat. They were each other turned inside out, two souls melding parts to produce a whole: I'll take us around the world. You'll see and do things beyond your dreams. I'll live in the tunnel. You'll order out for reality and a side of perspective. I'll exaggerate, tell the world that I achieved a record dive "with absolute self-control and an unyielding faith" thanks to a state of concentration in which "electric energy, magnetic energy and all the forces of nature converge to increase my biological capabilities." You'll cock an eyebrow, just enough. I'll make the cash flow. You'll keep the checkbook. I'll teach you to seize today. You'll remember my two promises yesterday and three appointments tomorrow. I'll dream up the world's deepest dive tank with a domed underwater disco where scuba dancers boogie in leaded, magnetized shoes. You'll find the shoemaker.

"She could find solutions just by looking in my eyes," Pipín would say. "I thought I'd go from girl to girl the rest of my life, because even the ones who were scuba divers had other priorities. Sooner or later the woman would ask, 'Why is your mind always *there*?' But not Audrey."

The magic kept coming. Three weeks after they fell in love, they were freediving with dolphins off the coast of Honduras in front of cameras for his new Mexican TV series, then with sea lions off the Galápagos and with humpback whales off the Dominican Republic. Well, at least *she* was. He watched in astonishment as the 45-ton whales cavorted with her in a watery waltz, then in vexation as they flinched from him—as if they sensed that she was the one who cried when shrimp died in the aquarium, the one who studied and sketched fish . . . and he was the one who speared them. She shed the air tank, bubbles and noise. She *became* the mermaid. Her drawings ripened. In one that she titled *Pleasure Shared*, she was naked, her hair fanning in the water, her back arched in abandon, her legs splayed beneath a shark.

A cloud hung over her enchantment, a gnawing fear: He feared nothing—not in the water. Standard diving protocol? Rules made for others. At any moment the man she loved could die. "I've seen world championship divers, and I've seen him," photographer and scuba diver Ron Everdij would say, "and they are not like him. It's like the difference between runners from Kenya and runners from the rest of the world. But one day he'll go wrong. He thinks he's invincible. He's like one of those people who's arrested for shoplifting and goes right back to the same store the next day."

Lying still in a swimming pool practicing apnea, the suspension of breathing, he could last more than seven minutes. But the pressure, both physical and mental, where he went—where World War II submarines would creak and groan—sliced that time in half. She watched him on their backyard patio on the waterway at the edge of Miami Beach as he prepared himself for this, pounding out stomach crunches and bench presses while he held his breath for one minute . . . two . . . 2:30 . . . and counted the contractions that rippled his diaphragm as his body screamed for air. He'd keep going—2:45 . . . 2:50—everything around him melting into gray soup, and it was only by the little trick he'd discovered, focusing on the fading backyard fence and the tall building beyond it and compelling them to return to their perpendicularity, that he could reach his record of 45 contractions, that he could hang on for just a few . . . ticks . . . more.

But sometimes, in the ocean, he miscalculated. He'd blacked out by descending too swiftly; or too slowly, when currents swept the cable off a vertical line; or too soon, before he'd recuperated from a previous dive. Sometimes his equipment malfunctioned. His cable had snapped. Many times his sled had gotten stuck, and once it had pile-driven him into knee-high mud 377 feet below. He'd been partially paralyzed for a half hour after he pinched his nostrils and blew so hard, trying to equalize, that air leaked into his brain. He'd died three times during No Limits dives, he said, convinced that Olokun, the Santería undersea god, had brought him back to life each time in a bath of white light.

He'd suffered so many decompression hits when he went under on scuba tanks that a neurologist had warned him never to touch a tank again. Audrey, watching him strap another one on anyway, wondered if she should take a knife and slash the hoses. He often wouldn't bother to use Trimix—the combination of nitrogen, helium and oxygen that scuba divers are cautioned to use in place of compressed air at depths greater than 125 feet—or to slow down for the two-or three-hour ascents sometimes necessary to avoid the bends. His elbow and leg would begin to itch when he surfaced, a sign that nitrogen bubbles were trapped in his veins or his bones and that one day the bones might begin to snap like pencils.

Keep going deeper, his friends warned him, and you'll end up in a coffin, Pipín, if you're lucky. A wheelchair, Pipín, if you're not. But he'd scoff, even as he neared 40 and the blackouts multiplied. Audrey would push away his panicking crew when he surfaced unconscious, open his airway and blow on the skin around his mouth to stimulate his reflex to breathe, Pipín, breathe! Then wait and pray and wonder what made this man keep gambling.

She had to go deeper. It was the only way to understand him. She had to kiss him goodbye, when Cuban authorities forbade him to return, and fly to his homeland alone to trace his life.

SHE HAD to stand on the cliff overhanging Matanzas Bay—his backyard— and picture Francisco Ferreras, poised here in front of the boys who stared and sneered at him, about to take his first risk. It was 1969. He was seven. The boy who had found it so difficult to walk because his metatarsals were malformed and his feet jutted inward, was about to start running. The child who was mute until he finally uttered "*pi-pin . . . pi-pin*"—no, not a word, but close enough to celebrate and to turn into his nickname for life—was about to leave them all speechless. The boy trapped inside his own body was about to spring free.

He peered down at the water. None of the kids gathered about him would dare this. But no one was there to stop him. Not his uncle, Dr. Panchín Guerra, who'd prescribed water therapy to trigger the boy's dormant motor skills and had been astounded when the child began to swim before he could walk. Not Haydée, the big-hipped black servant who was sure the Santería ritual she'd snuck the boy off to had done the trick, the throbbing drums and animal sacrifices that had summoned Olokun, the old African god of the undersea and of good health, to cure the child. Not Pipín's father, who'd never lived with him in the big walled estate on the cliff and who'd soon be divorced from Pipín's mother. Not the mother herself, who left the house to work in Cuba's agriculture ministry each morning before Pipín woke up and didn't return until after he fell asleep—seven days a week.

Pipín took a deep breath. Then the boy with the orthopedic shoes and eyeglasses and rasping asthma flew off the cliff and plunged into the sea. The other children scanned the water in astonishment, then fear: Where was he? Pipín was pulling off Part II of his magic act, having darted into an underwater cave he'd discovered earlier beneath the cliff.

Audrey entered the cave with her video camera. Here he'd sat, in a space as big as a living room with a foot of air to breathe between the ceiling and the water's surface, relishing the thought of them all up there panicking, ashamed of themselves for all the shame they'd made him feel. Here he'd sat, filling the cave with his imagination and loneliness. At peace for once. It was like being in the trap again, cut off from the world and scarcely able to move, only it was a beautiful trap because *he* had contrived it. A beautiful aloneness because he'd arranged it.

But it was such brief magic. Because soon after he dived and made the world go away, his world went away from him. The grandmother, uncle and aunts who'd helped raise him fled Fidel Castro's regime for Florida. The servants who mothered him and introduced him to the old African gods were dispersed. He was placed in a boarding school that specialized

108

in sports training so that he might pursue his proclivity for swimming. He returned to the underwater cave on weekends and in the summers, clutching a plastic bag of fruit so he could stay inside his lair longer and make loneliness lovelier still.

But he needed to enlarge his kingdom. He forged a mask by heating the rubber from Soviet boots and pressing two ovals of glass into it. He fashioned fins by cutting swaths from plastic boxes of frozen fish and binding them with screws filched from window frames. He rigged a speargun from a piece of pipe and elastic bands. He hardened his determination and deltoids by swimming laps for four hours a day at boarding school, where he was developing into one of Cuba's top junior swimmers, and in truth, just finding a way to exhaust his anxiety so he could sleep. By 13 his asthma and orthopedic shoes were gone, and so was his mother—she had moved to Mexico City for four years to serve as first secretary to the Cuban ambassador. Pipín's domain grew wider still.

Down he went after the big groupers and snappers lurking in the deep water. He learned to imitate their movements, to intuit their intentions, to stalk them in the dark caves they darted into to evade him. He became a shark. "For me, sharks aren't monsters, but partners," he'd say. "In my imagination I become one of them."

He emerged from the sea and tried to fit into the world of the two-legged land creatures. He scraped by in school until his final year, when he and his classmates were ordered to harvest sugarcane on a weekend when he'd planned another spearfishing expedition. *Why am I learning math or history?* he'd remember thinking. *The only history I want to know is my history. I go underwater to feel a pleasure greater than any that life on land has to offer me. It is better than sex.* He refused to join the harvest and was expelled.

His mother sobbed. The boy was trapped again. She was about to return to Cuba to become a university professor. His father was a judge. They'd both fought in the revolution and been decorated as heroes. How could their dropout son earn love and admiration? How could a spearfisherman be a hero? In the army, perhaps? He suffered a nervous breakdown and was discharged. In the working world, possibly? None of his jobs, diving for bosses who sent him down after sponge, lobsters and sunken treasure, lasted more than a year. In marriage, maybe? He took a dancer named Luisa into the underwater cave to make love to her for the first time, then married her at 19. It ended in a year and a half.

An Italian diving journalist on holiday in Havana saw how deep the 19-year-old could dive and hurried him to Cuban authorities, urging them to let Pipín travel overseas and break the world record. They yawned. They'd never heard of such a sport. For six years they yawned as Pipín pestered them. Then came his moment. Cuba, unveiling a seaside resort in Cayo Largo in 1987, invited a group of international underwater photojournalists to publicize it. Sure, why not let that crazy fish man entertain them?

He scurried about the resort, a charming nobody promising photographers the chance to document the deepest dive ever without the aid of apparatus. Here, at last, was a chance to show his parents and everyone else.

Damned if he didn't—67 meters, 220 feet!—and if the photojournalists didn't send dispatches around the world. He was on fire now, lusting for bigger, deeper, farther, more. He busted the world record again a year later with a 226-foot dive.

He knew his limit was his anxious heart, his teeming brain. He studied controlled breathing techniques with a Hindu yogi. When he consulted Buddhist monks they told him, *Learn to wait*. Learn to wait? Pipín? Suddenly, as news of his exploits traveled, he was on diving magazine covers. Suddenly a yacht ornament for Cuban generals and politicians on fishing trips. Suddenly signing a sponsorship deal with Europe's largest diving equipment company, marrying an Italian beauty, hosting an Italian TV travel show.

Suddenly, in 1991, chalking up a world-record 377-foot No Limits dive, the first ever televised live in Europe . . . but still sure that his mother was unimpressed. Suddenly watching his second marriage go up in smoke, then two of his high-placed friends in the Cuban military getting executed for drug trafficking. Suddenly sweating bullets because they were his two buffers in a regime that could turn on him at any moment for the six cars and three houses he'd finagled with his new fame and riches. Suddenly stepping onto a friend's private plane in the Bahamas in 1993 and severing one more connection—to his homeland, his parents, his separated wife and three-year-old daughter—and defecting to the U.S.

When Audrey had heard all the stories and visited all his old diving haunts, she flew back to him in Florida. Full of wonder that she'd been granted entrance into his world, the one he'd created against all odds. Full of wondering: for how long?

DEATH CREPT closer. It found them again in Cabo San Lucas, of all places, where Pipín and Audrey had returned to reclaim Pipín's world record, to dip once more in the water where magic, eight months earlier, had struck. Pepe's body surfaced instead.

This wasn't like losing Berttoni, a stranger added as a safety diver on the fly. Pepe had been Pipín's fun-loving pal since they were teenagers in Cuba, his crew chief, the safety diver at the bottom, the only one deeper than Audrey—the man who'd introduced her to the king.

Oh, God, if only Jacques Mayol and Enzo Maiorca could've lived with the limits. If only the Frenchman and the Italian hadn't devised weighted sleds sliding down cables to smash the depth barriers in the '60s and '70s, Pipín's quest could've remained simple and pure, and nobody would've had to die. He might never have known the adrenaline rush of No Limits, never reached depths that were perilous even to men on tanks, depths that required all that equipment that could break and all those safety divers who could die.

But what had killed Pepe? Pipín theorized that venom from a scorpion bite Pepe had suffered the day before, which hadn't seemed to affect him, somehow had been activated by the pressure on his body at 260 feet. But the whispers soon began: that Pipín was cutting corners, that both Pepe and Berttoni might have died because they descended to unsafe depths the way their leader routinely did, breathing from a tank of compressed air instead of Trimix.

Nightmares wracked Pipín. He knew this second death of a crew member would be turned against him. He'd just broken with yet another institution—freediving's mainstream sanctioning body, AIDA—because his rival Pelizzari was behind it and because of his disagreement over some of the safety procedures that AIDA requires for certification of record dives. Pipín had just formed the International Association of Freediving (IAFD) despite howls that it was a dangerous conflict of interest for a man to act as his own sanctioning authority on a record attempt. But Pipín had seen Pepe go that deep without Trimix plenty of times, so that couldn't have caused his death, he insisted, and besides, in Pipín's world a man died because God decided it was his time.

Pepe was cremated. Audrey and the crew turned to Pipín. Well? Was the dive on or off? What do you do when your buddy dies trying to help you set a record?

Pipín turned to Audrey. She was the person he loved and trusted most, so it only made sense to ask her: When he dived, would she go one rung deeper and take Pepe's place?

She would. She did. He set another world record. But it wasn't deep enough.

COULD AUDREY take the next step? Would she leave the safety crew and become a No Limits diver too? Pipín asked her that one day. After all, it was better than sex. She was better than the young woman he was training on the sled. Besides, didn't it seem safer to be the diver on the sled than the diver *saving* the diver on the sled?

She didn't think long. Sure, she'd try it. Not for his reasons. Not to be singular, not to be separate—there wasn't a competitive bone in her body. To connect. With him. To inhabit his world completely. Wasn't it all or nothing with this man? "It's very difficult," she would write on her website, "to live with someone that experiences sensations unknown by the world, sensations that can't be described or shared. I thought that if I could enter his underwater world, I could be closer to him."

She began to train. He began to order her food when they went out to dinner. She led Pipín to their backyard Jacuzzi in 1997 and astonished him by lasting five minutes and 50 seconds submerged—a half minute longer than the female static apnea world record. They headed to the Cayman Islands for her maiden voyage, but suddenly Pipín, ascending from a scuba dive just minutes after a No Limits training dive, was losing consciousness on the boat, hitting his head, vomiting and shaking from a violent seizure. She found herself on an airplane back to Miami, sitting in a hospital room watching him twitch and slur for three days, then rise and walk out against doctors' advice, saying it was time to fly back to the Caymans and make their dives. With Pipín every accident became a reason to continue, every death a debt that could be repaid only by carrying on—never a signal to reassess, to slow down.

Audrey nailed her 263-foot dive a few days later, and bingo, she was the French female record holder. She loved it. Everything went away on a No Limits dive. Your worries. The world. Even your body. "You forget you have one," she told a reporter for deeperblue.net, "and that is when you meet the other person who lives inside you, the one in control of everything: your mind." A year later, in 1998, she joined Pipín for a 378-foot tandem dive in Cabo San Lucas, and they were the deepest-diving duo ever. They married in '99. A glance, that was all they'd have to exchange in the water now, and each would know exactly what the other meant. She became the deepest female diver ever with a 412½-foot plunge off the Canary Islands in 2000, surviving an 18-second fright when her sled got stuck at the bottom and safety diver Pascal Bernabé helped free her. She encored with a 427-footer off Fort Lauderdale a year later, extending her women's record and making her the fifth-deepest diver, of either sex, ever.

A startling thing was happening in her relationship with Pipín. She was the diver squeezing six workouts into a week while he blew off three. The one who could withstand 90 diaphragm contractions to his 45, could rev her heart rate to 200 while his max was 160. Who was unflappable even when Pipín ambushed her during training dives, springing out of nowhere at 375 feet to snatch her and test her composure. Who could read Egyptian history 20 minutes before a record dive while he couldn't absorb a letter from his mother for the two weeks before one of his. "It made me feel ashamed," he admitted. "How could she do that? She has the stronger mind. A perfect mind. I took her as a student, and she became the teacher."

Then came the audacity. Tanya Streeter of the Cayman Islands unfurled a 525-footer in August 2002, nearly *100 feet* beyond Audrey's record dive. In the factionalized freediving universe, full of strife and ego, Streeter's record triggered more strife, more ego. AIDA anointed Streeter's dive the new world record for both sexes because she'd achieved it using AIDA's judging protocol and safety standards. Pipín's IAFD insisted, of course, that Pipín's dive of 531½ feet in 2000 remained the record. To reclaim the female world record, Audrey would have to creep perilously close to Pipín's 531½-foot IAFD record. Or . . . past it.

Imagine that. Audrey taking *Pipín's* record. Her eyebrows jumped when Carlos Serra, Pipín's IAFD vice president, teased her about it. Her eyes went wide. "Don't say that," she pleaded. "Don't let him hear that. Don't even *think* that."

WELL . . . could she? Would she? The outrage couldn't stand. Pipín turned to Audrey. Was she ready to go *that* deep?

She was 28. She wanted to have children with him, but she knew that when she did, she'd have to turn and head back up to the surface. She looked in his eyes. She was like an old-fashioned French wife who'd muck the barn and pluck the grapes beside her man. She understood that world records were the family crop, the product that attracted the sponsorships and media and enrollment in their freediving courses, the TV and movie opportunities that sent them on adventures across the seven seas. She nodded. She'd go deeper.

But how *much* deeper? How far will a woman follow a man?

Five-hundred twenty-eight feet, decided Pipín, 161 meters. That would be the target for Audrey's dive last October 12 off the Dominican Republic. Three feet more than Streeter's record. Three and a half feet *less* than Pipín's. Audrey nodded.

Pipín changed his mind. Why not 531½? Wouldn't it be fitting, with the cameras rolling for their next movie, *Ocean Women*, to have her equal the world-record dive he'd made for the *Ocean Men* cameras in Cozumel, Mexico, two years before? Audrey agreed.

No, wait, said Pipín. Make it 538 feet—164 meters. Audrey was stunned. He wanted her to *beat* his record. Maybe because, where he'd gone all his life to separate, he'd finally connected. Maybe this was his gift to her.

Scratch that. She might as well go for 544½, said Pipín. After all, they'd just arrived in the Dominican Republic, and she was nailing these depths in training so easily. After all, didn't every extra foot she went using his techniques—a woman with scant athletic background and just five years of freediving experience—jam another foot in the mouth of his critics and rivals?

Hold on. How about 551 feet? Maybe because she was so damned unthreatening. Maybe because he was certain he could dive deeper.

O.K., then, we'll make it 558, a nice, round 170 meters. That was the depth she reached on her final training dive—unofficially the deepest in history—and then climbed back into the boat looking fine, admitting only later to safety diver Matt Briseno that she felt "weird."

Well, then, enthused Pipín, let's go for 597 feet—182 meters—and no, that wouldn't create an even riskier gap in their already overstretched chain of safety divers, see, because Pipín could leave his supervising post at the surface, don scuba tanks and become the bottom diver at 597, and then, on his next dive, could score that nice fat number still looming: 600. Serra, in charge of the dive logistics, was aghast. "Do you want to dig a hole and go through the planet to China?" he cried.

Pipín turned to Audrey. She'd watched him do the riskiest things and said nothing, but the thought of her husband at so extreme a depth on scuba tanks, after everything doctors had warned, made her finally dig in. No, Pipín, she said. She'd protect him. She'd go 561 feet, 36 less than he wanted, but still the deepest a human being had ever gone. But he'd have to wait for her at the top.

BLACK FISTS clenched on the horizon that morning, then ripped across the sky hurling wind and thunder and lightning. They blew open the door to the closet in Pipín's mind where all the magic lives, and out stepped Changó, the Santería god of storms. This had to be a sign from Changó, Pipín thought, a command to cancel the dive. But 15 boats waited to take on spectators and reporters and cameramen for the *Ocean Women* movie. At mid-afternoon, when the storm relented, the dive was on.

Audrey read about the pharaohs as Pipín did the final equipment check, a duty he usually shared with his crew. But they'd angered him by placing two decoupling devices on the sled backward during training dives, so he shooed them away. He opened the valve to make sure there was air in the tank that would inflate the lift bag and bring her back up. He shut it when he heard the hiss of air, but he didn't check the pressure with a gauge.

He tied a strip of red cloth around her wrist. Changó's color. He peeled a banana and dropped the skin in the sea for Olokun.

She smiled and entered the water in a yellow-and-black wet suit. Gray skies. Slight chop, maybe a foot. She and Pipín had both dived in much worse. She ventilated as Serra barked the five-minute countdown. Then she took her final breath of air, and vanished.

"F---, f---, f---," Pipín began murmuring.

"What's wrong?" asked Serra, studying two watches.

"Why is she going so slow?" he demanded.

Serra felt the cable shudder. She'd struck bottom at 1:42 . . . 14 seconds *faster* than she took during her training dive three days before. "Relax," he said.

Now all Audrey had to do was pull the pin that released the ascent portion of the sled, open the valve on the air tank and hang on for dear life as it carried her back to air, applause and Pipín's embrace. She turned the valve to release the 3,000 pounds per square inch of air compressed inside the tank.

The bag didn't inflate. She didn't budge.

Again she turned the valve. The sled still didn't rise.

What was happening? Was she so narked she couldn't open the valve? Was she dazed from nitrogen narcosis, which every diver at such depths experiences but she perhaps more because she'd increased her dive depths dramatically? Or, as several involved with the dive later suspected, was there just not enough air in the tank?

A half minute had passed. An eternity at such depth. Oxygen dwindling. More than 200 pounds of pressure per square inch leaning on her body. Pascal Bernabé, the bottom safety diver, Audrey's dear friend, inserted his mouthpiece into the lift bag to add air. The sled began to lift . . . but not enough, not enough.

She remained 538 feet below. A minute since she'd hit bottom. Why? Why wouldn't she grab Bernabé's mouthpiece and breathe—*live*? Why wouldn't he thrust it between her lips?

Because neither was looking at a watch. Because she still appeared so calm. Because they'd unjammed the sled at the bottom and salvaged her record dive off the Canary Islands. Because she'd never taken air from a tank at such depth, and many experts believed that doing so would cause spasmodic coughing—and drowning—or make the lungs expand and explode on the ascent. Because, perhaps, she was too narked to realize the danger. Because, maybe, the first breath she took from Pascal's air supply would render this dive a failure, a disappointment to all those waiting above. Because, as soft as Audrey was with shrimp and whales and human beings, that was how hard she was on herself. A perfectionist. A soldier with a duty. And she'd told Pascal, more than once, that he was *not* to give her air unless she signaled for it. But, goddammit, Pipín would flog himself later, she would've taken air if it had been *him* holding the mouthpiece to her lips, *him* stationed at the bottom, the way he'd wanted.

Pascal dipped beneath the sled, pushed it and watched it finally creep upward. Upward into a vast stretch of unmanned ocean: 260 feet of it between her and the next safety diver. No Cedric Darolles at his old post—394 feet—where he'd been stationed on Pipín's and Audrey's recent dives. He was dead, perished the year before while cave-diving, and Pipín hadn't replaced him. It was there, three minutes and 50 seconds into the dive, that Audrey lost consciousness and drifted away from the cable.

Above, Pipín was already in a frenzy over the time elapsed, slinging on a scuba tank, diving. Below, Audrey sagged into Pascal's arms as he ascended beneath her. Pascal couldn't do what his heart screamed to do. Couldn't rush her to the top or he'd die from a massive decompression hit, and there'd be two death certificates for sure. His heart pounded. Panic could kill him too. Two minutes. That's how long a diver who lost consciousness underwater had to live.

He carried her up, rising twice as fast as a scuba diver should. It took a minute and 55 seconds to get her to 295 feet. There Pipín appeared in an explosion of bubbles. Pascal handed him his wife.

Pipín rose, taking another decompression hit himself, bloody foam pouring from Audrey's mouth. Eight minutes and 38 seconds after her last breath, he surfaced with her body. She still had a pulse! He clamped his mouth on hers and tried to fill her with his breath, then Serra and the eight-man rescue patrol that the IAFD had hired took over. Serra looked in her eyes. He knew that the pulse was a lie, that her brain was dead.

It was all a blur after that. The motorboat dash to shore, the hopeless race to the hotel infirmary and then to the hospital. Pipín sitting in the hotel lobby afterward, lost somewhere deep inside his motionless body, his face frighteningly composed. "He seemed like a man executing a plan he'd downloaded into his memory for just such an occasion," Paul Kotik, a deeperblue.net journalist and diver, would say. "When we parted, I didn't think I'd see him alive again."

THE FUNERAL procession motored a few miles east of Miami Beach, then surrounded Pipín's boat, *Olokun*. He slipped into the water with a beige marble urn and, with remarkable poise, poured Audrey's cinders into the sea. Then he went home and sobbed until days turned into weeks.

How does a man grieve while the world's screaming in his ears? One after another they came, the questions, rumors and charges of negligence howling on websites and chorused by journalists and AIDA officials: Where, Pipín, is the video of her dive, taken by the camera attached to the sled? He couldn't bring himself to go near the IAFD vault where it lay, let alone relinquish it. Why were there so few safety divers, Pipín? He couldn't stand and explain his fear of hiring and *risking* more of them. Why, Pipín, wasn't Audrey wearing a self-inflating wet suit that she could've activated to jettison herself to safety, as other No Limits divers used, or a harness-and-pulley system that could've cranked her up from above? He couldn't lift his chin and whisper his belief that all the safety systems have flaws, and who was to say that her mouth wouldn't open and her lungs fill with water as the pulley yanked her up, or that Audrey would've activated one of those self-inflating suits if she'd worn one, when she hadn't even reached for Pascal's mouthpiece? Why not appoint a neutral expert to pinpoint the causes and perhaps save a future diver's life, Pipín? Why no doctor or intubation tubes on site, Pipín? He couldn't express the inexpressible, how safety nets shrivel a Wallenda's heart. Why no deaths in other divers' No Limits record attempts, Pipín? What about Berttoni's and Pepe's deaths, wasn't there a pattern, and how does a man who doesn't even wear a safety belt in his car end up in charge of safety for the world's deepest dive, and, *pssst*, have you heard that he practices witchcraft? Or that wild one that his defection from Cuba may have been a ruse so he could serve Castro as a spy?

He couldn't eat. Twenty-two pounds melted away. He couldn't sleep. He couldn't work. He couldn't process the report from Kim McCoy—the oceanographer who provided the IAFD with computerized readings of its dives—that listed all the factors that might have contributed to the sled's malfunction: a cracked Teflon bushing; a pair of wings that were designed to stabilize a camera but that created a lateral force on the line;

a new cable and bottom weight that turned out to be more prone to create a pendulum effect on the cable; and the possibility that the air tank wasn't full.

Pipín filed a lawsuit against Ricardo Hernández, a former IAFD employee leading the chorus of charges, for infliction of emotional distress, invasion of privacy and defamation. Hernández filed a counterclaim, recently dismissed, alleging that Pipín had fired him unfairly two years ago and that this had sent him into a psychiatrist's care. Why, Pipín kept wondering, couldn't they all just say what Audrey's mother, Anne-Marie, did: that no one was to blame, that it was fate, and that the sea wanted her forever?

For once in his life, Pipín couldn't even go into the ocean. He knew with terrifying certainty that no woman—even one whom he turned to for comfort in his grief—would ever go that deep with him again.

When it became more than he could bear, he went to his Santería shrine and summoned Olokun. Couldn't he just end it all, he asked, and join her? The reply seemed pitiless to him: Why do you even ask, Pipín? You know that she died a white death, a natural one, and that if yours isn't white as well, you'll *never* join her.

He packed all the statues and amulets from the shrine into a bag, boarded his boat and traveled for four hours. He cast everything into 10,000 feet of water. He went home and lay on a table for four hours more while a tattoo artist inscribed the image of the half-naked woman inside the hammerhead shark on his calf.

He replaced Olokun with Audrey. She became the one he spoke to each day, the one he asked for blessing and guidance. She'll be down there, he's certain, when he makes his planned world-record dive in mid-July, at precisely the coordinates where nine months earlier he turned the green water gray with his wife's ashes. He'll attempt 558 feet, equaling the depth of her final training dive, which he declared the new IAFD world record after her death. It's a dive that he says he must make, one that frightens his friends and that helped convince IAFD vice president Carlos Serra to part ways with him early this month.

When it's all done, you'll have to decide which side of the water's surface to see the myth through, and who got the moral of the story right. Those who see the half-naked woman inside the hammerhead shark and say, "Of course, because that's where she lives now." Or those who see it and say, "Of course, she was devoured." Remember one thing: It was Audrey who drew the picture.

POSTSCRIPT: *On October 12, 2003, one year after Audrey Mestre's death, Pipín Ferreras dove to a depth of 170 meters to match his late wife's feat and honor her memory. Tanya Streeter's 160-meter dive remains the record for women since Audrey's dive was not acknowledged as valid by AIDA, which continues to govern the sport of freediving. (Ferreras' IADF ceased operations in '04.) Soon after this story was published, director James Cameron* (Titanic) *bought the film rights; he is planning to shoot the movie in 3-D.*

The Boys on the Bus

Three days after 9/11, the author sought a way to take the measure of
the impact sports can have upon us in a time of tragedy. Strange though it felt,
he took his son to a high school football game.

VERYTHING IN THE LITTLE TOWN CAME TO A HALT at dusk on the day America mourned. Five police cars, blinking blue as they wove in escort, sealed off traffic and froze pedestrians in their paths. Drivers peeled to the shoulder of the road and stopped, waved and craned their necks to glimpse the passing procession.

In Paris on that same day—September 14, 2001—the Métro had gone still so passengers could pray, and the bells of Notre Dame had tolled for an hour in memory of the dead. In Berlin 200,000 had gathered before the Brandenburg Gate to reflect at the place where the wall between

121

democracy and communism had stood. In Dublin commerce and drinking had both been called off, shops and pubs shut tight, and in England the Queen had broken off her holiday to return home and grieve the World Trade Center massacre. In America, where the mass murder had occurred, four busloads of kids were leaving Summerville, S.C., to play a high school football game.

I was in the fourth row, left side, lead bus. Weeks earlier I'd promised my 11-year-old son, Noah, that we'd play hooky last week and make the five-hour drive to Atlanta to watch the Braves and the Philadelphia Phillies decide a pennant race. A nightmare had intervened, so here we were instead.

It was an odd thing to do—to go to a game—on a day when you walked around wondering why the hell games mattered anymore. But I wanted to know what a game felt and smelled like at a moment like this, why people bothered playing and watching, and even more so, what it all smelled like to my son. Sports, thanks to me, had already taken firm grip of Noah's life, but now and then I'd get this uneasy feeling about where it all might be leading, a feeling I'd never spoken of with him. Now that the earth had shaken and the whole deck of cards had spilled on the floor, it made no sense to hide what I'd been holding.

Already the stink of sweat filled the bus, the smell of teenage boys looking inside themselves to see if what they would need, just an hour later, was there. The Green Wave of Summerville High was leaving its flag-festooned town and heading to its biggest game of the season, at Stratford High in nearby Goose Creek, against the team ranked No. 2 in the state. In two of the last three seasons, the winner of this game had gone on to win the state title.

Noah flipped and spun a football in his hands. That had been the first thing he'd thought of when I told him we were going to a ball game on the day of mourning. "Can we go on the field?" he asked. "Can we play catch?"

"Well, I . . . guess so," I'd said.

Hell, what had I expected? I'd flung him, back and forth, between two worlds. He'd played on a baseball team in Australia, where parents applauded and cooed, "Awwww, bad *luck*, mate," whenever a boy or girl on his team swung and missed by a foot . . . and he'd played on a traveling AAU baseball team in the U.S., where parents stormed the dugout and seethed at coaches for pulling their sons out of games so benchwarmers could have a chance. He'd lived for a year in an old fishing village in Spain, where adoring grandmothers stroked his head each day on their daily shopping strolls . . . and he'd practiced for a year under a coach who nailed him in the head with a basketball from 20 feet away when his attention lapsed.

As his dad, I'd assigned him to ladle cabbage to the homeless in soup kitchens, and as his coach, to break the press in the last second of one-point, double-overtime championship games. He'd lived out *my* ambivalence, spent some years thousands of miles removed from box scores and title chases, spent others high-fiving me over touchdowns and slam dunks, slurping down *SportsCenter* and sports pages first thing every morning along with cereal and milk. Only a month ago my wife and I had argued over whether Noah should play baseball on the travel team again this fall, only a month after his summer all-star tournament had ended; argued over how much competition was too much in the making of a kid. She'd won.

Now, with a kickoff scheduled to rise into the air at eight o'clock and join the smoke and human ashes riding in the wind, with sports and suffering suddenly teetering on the scales of a national debate over who we are, I too was craning for a glimpse. A sideways look to see which world's values had taken stronger hold of my son; to see what ruled in his heart when people were suffering; to see what I had wrought.

In whispers I asked the boy seated in front of me on the bus if our police escort was unusual, related to the tragedy and the national day of prayer. No, he murmured, it happened every time the Green Wave hit the road. I started there with Noah, on the edges of what I wanted to learn. "What do you think," I asked, "of 86 kids getting a police escort to play a high school game?"

His eyes squinched. "They don't even do this for big league players," he said. "Must be nothing to do here."

I gazed around the bus, wondering which boys really wanted to play and which had just been swept along. The pros had shut down. The colleges had fallen silent. Why not the high school kids?

I laid that question in the lap of a legend, the Summerville coach, who had won more football games than any other coach in history. I wanted Noah to hear the opinion of John McKissick, a 74-year-old grandfather who had stayed for 50 years at one school, where he'd won 483 games, 10 state titles and 25 conference championships. A man who'd gone shoeless growing up in a two-bedroom shack after his daddy went bankrupt during the Depression, and then found his calling in a town that once postponed Halloween because it fell on a game night, and molded the lives of 1,700 of its kids because he never cut a player. A man who would've dropped from the sky as a paratrooper in the 82nd Airborne during the invasion of Japan had two atomic bombs not dropped from the sky first.

Never in those five decades in Summerville had McKissick gone a week in autumn without coaching a football game, not even when a heart attack killed his father the day before a game. But hadn't he wondered, when even some of the townspeople started calling in and saying the game should be postponed, whether it was time, finally, to let people sit still, to think and to feel?

"No," he said. "I don't think these kids should be home watching TV. I think they've seen enough. To be honest, I don't think they'd be home watching it anyway if we didn't play. Look, everybody has mourned. We've had moments of silence, prayers, talked about it in school. I called the team together the day it happened and said, 'Keep the people who died in your prayers, but we can't let it interfere with our schoolwork and our goals here on the football field. We've got to not dwell on it. We've got to keep moving on.' "

He noticed the bump on Noah's football where our dog's teeth had broken the skin and let the bladder push through, and he got him a re-placement. "Kid on our team's daddy worked at the Pentagon," McKissick said. "Name's Ryan Snipes."

Noah was silent, unreadable. I went looking for Ryan, a sophomore tight end with big hands and heartful eyes. On the morning of the attacks Ryan had watched a classmate—a girl whose father had called her that morning on his way to a meeting in one of the World Trade Center towers—faint when she saw the towers implode. That shook him, hard. Suddenly flashing before him were pictures of the Pentagon in flames, the building where his dad, an Air Force lieutenant colonel, had meet-ings nearly every day. Everything inside Ryan, level by level, collapsed. He bolted for the classroom door, and then fell to tears in front of everyone in the school lobby the moment he saw his sister and mom. For the next three hours, every 30 seconds, they called five phone numbers: nothing.

"There aren't words for the emptiness I felt inside," Ryan said. "Finally around two o'clock my sister called again, and I heard her say, '*Dad*,' and I knew he was alive. I cried again. He'd gotten a call on his way to the Pentagon to turn back, just after the planes hit the World Trade Center."

Ryan's sister and mother persuaded him to swallow his embarrassment over the tears and to return to school that day for practice, and to play this week to celebrate life, to show the terrorists that Americans can't be cowed. However, the girl who'd fainted didn't return to school on Wednesday, Thursday, Friday, her empty seat filling the classroom with dread, and the locker room was quieter than it had ever been, and Ryan's sports heroes kept saying no, no way they'd play ball at a time like this.

Now game time was nearing, and the guilt was sawing away. "I don't know how I feel about playing this game," Ryan said. "Where I'd like to be right now is up there digging up the rubble. I think a lot of the guys haven't been sure how they felt about this. Then we decided yesterday, Let's win it for the people up there."

The buses rolled into the parking lot at Stratford High. Noah carried his ball as we followed the players out. From the opposite direction came the Stratford Knights, heading toward the field for calisthenics. The two squads passed each other in single file, inches apart. On the day of national unity, no two players exchanged a glance.

ME? I had my notions on the subject, but I hadn't said a word yet to Noah—I didn't want to stack the deck.

He'd never been in a football locker room. He'd never seen kids prowl and pace and pee before a game. Comp McCurry, the Green Wave's hard-muscled, hard-jawed young assistant coach, worked his way through the locker room, popping players with forearm shivers and chucks on the chin: "Woooooo! Ready to play a *ball* game! Ready to strap it *on*! Ready to bust some *chops*!" The boys strapped on their equipment and filed out in silent platoons—offense, defense, special teams—accompanied by McKissick's sergeants, steeling themselves one last time for what was about to come. I looked at Noah. No, 11 years old was too young. He couldn't be watching those kids and seeing what I was seeing, future soldiers being readied for an unimaginably treacherous war.

The stands were packed, 8,000 strong, wearing patriotic ribbons and waving flags. The bands from the two schools joined on the field and played *God Bless America*. Eyes filled with tears. Coach McKissick kept his team behind the stands, speaking softly to the players, fighting the tide. "Gonna do what we've done for 50 years," he said. "Nothing different. Get your mind on the football game."

The P.A. announcer began a tribute to those lost and those still searching for them. His voice crackled, then cracked, then choked with sobs. The flag was raised, and a minister said a prayer. I turned to Noah. "Have you prayed?" I asked as Stratford students sent balloons into the air.

"We had 15 minutes of silence at school today," he said.

"What happened during those 15 minutes?" I asked.

"I heard Sidra sniffling, so I think she was crying, and Laura Jett's mouth was moving, so I think she was praying."

"But you—what about you?"

"Yeah. I did. And I prayed in bed the other night for all the families."

"Was that the first time you've ever prayed—not at dinner with us, I mean, but on your own?"

"Uh . . . I guess."

"Might want to try that again."

"Yeah."

The metal stands beneath us began to shake from the stomping feet. The kickoff sailed through the night, and the crowd—ever on cue—roared. The Summerville offense quickly stalled. "Do you think we should go to war?" I asked Noah.

"No," he said. "I don't want to worry about getting bombed every night. I don't want to end up right dab in the middle of a war."

I loved that *dab*. I looked out as cheerleaders for the black-clad Knights cartwheeled and flipped before us, and somehow I saw my high horse. I couldn't resist climbing on. "You know," I said to Noah, "a lot of people say we should have games right away so we can get back to normal as soon as possible. But maybe we shouldn't be in such a hurry for normal. Maybe we should stop for a while and think about whether we could do better than that. What if we started spending, say, only a quarter of the time we spend on sports and did something good for some of those families we saw on TV?"

He said nothing for a while. Then he asked, "Is that called a reverse?"

I glanced at the field, where the Stratford quarterback had passed the ball to the wide receiver, who was passing it right back to the quarterback.

"No," I said. "That's a flea-flicker."

Stratford was leading 7–0 in the second quarter. I sat there watching fans cheer and groan, parents pass out burgers, tuba players blare the *Rocky* theme song. I had been to only one Summerville game in my life, so I couldn't quite gauge whether it was me or the game itself which lacked a certain charge. Then a Stratford kid fumbled, players dived for the bouncing ball . . . and the stadium went black.

Stone cold black, lights out, all four stanchions. A gasp went up. My heart clawed its way into my throat. A girl cried, "They're gonna bomb us!"

A teenager called, "What should we do?"

"Quiet!" men shouted. "*Quiet!*"

"Dad, look!" said Noah. "There's a plane up there!"

"It's O.K.," I said. All eyes were fixed on the blinking light in the sky. "It's just the electricity. The power went out."

On the field silhouettes stampeded here, then there, the players as startled as the crowd. "Dad," said Noah, "don't you think we should go?"

"No," I lied.

A few people began to exit. "Ladies and gentlemen!" the P.A. announcer called out. "Please limit your movements!"

The plane had nearly passed. "They wouldn't know about a little thing like a Summerville football game . . . would they?" Noah asked.

I hated that *they*. We sat through 12 minutes of silence and darkness during a football game on the day America mourned.

HE WANTED to play catch at halftime behind the stands, so we did, running down each other's spirals as a trumpeter on the field played taps. He wanted to eat funnel cake buried in sugar, so we did that, too, as we talked to the piccolo player whose 42-year-old dad spoke of reenlisting. She was scared and thought we shouldn't be at a football game.

We settled back into our seats and watched Stratford score on a one-yard burst to take a 14–0 lead. The crowd roared. I looked at Noah and stumbled around for words.

"So, what do you think about games?" I asked.

"Huh?"

"You know, what do they *mean* to you? I mean, when a game you're playing in is about to start, what's it feel like to you, how important is it to you . . . I mean, *really*?"

I waited. Had I gone too far, drilling him on the stop-and-go move under the driveway hoop, hitting him grounder after grounder in imaginary Shortstop Showdowns between Jeter and A-Rod? Had I pulled the rope back the other way often enough, hard enough? Then again, how far would my heart sink if he said, You know, Dad, winning, losing—I don't really give a hoot.

"I try my hardest to win games," Noah said. "I'll dive on any court for a ball except the one outside our school—it's just too hard. I don't like losing. I think about what I could've done better."

"And how about that championship game against Charleston Catholic, the double-overtime loss?"

"That bothered me awhile. I pretended it was that game a couple of days later when I was playing alone, and I made all kinds of baskets, and we killed 'em, and the announcer kept saying, 'Look at Noah Smith! He's going wild!' I didn't think about it much more after that. That's only one game. If I make the pros, I kinda think I won't remember that."

We rode back to Summerville with the Green Wave, another half hour of silence, after its 21–0 loss. Coach McKissick said his boys had looked confused out there, and that maybe events had made them lose focus. Ryan Snipes said his game face had gone to pieces during that pregame prayer and tribute. Coach McCurry exploded, stepping over bodies and shoulder pads in the bus to scream, "Nothing's damn funny!" at a couple of players who'd pulled down a window and exchanged giggles with a girl.

We left the bus and got into our car to head home. Now that it was over, I told Noah what I really thought: that there was nothing terrible, or even remotely disrespectful, about playing a game now or watching one. That most of the fans out there seemed to enjoy the chance to come together and show that they cared about their kids, their country and the families who'd lost so much. And that, God knows, no matter the individual price down the road, we needed folks right now who didn't dwell, who turned anguish into action, lickety-split.

But something, I said, was still off about that game. I'd played in and watched too many games not to know it. Because when games are right, they're like pulling a blanket over your head when you're a kid—suddenly the world goes away and nothing outside that little space even exists; it's delicious.

Yep, it's like playing a trick on yourself, and for it all to work right, it has to start with the players believing that the outcome *really* matters, then spread out over the crowd and the viewers at home and cover them too, get them screaming and jumping and throwing pillows at the screen. Only a few athletes, or maybe a handful of fans, who *aren't* losing themselves in the game—that's all it takes to start lifting the edge of the blanket, to start making everyone see that the game doesn't really mean a thing. So how can we possibly expect the pretense to hold up three days after a mass murder, and why would we even ask it to? But when it does work, I said, it's a thing of such beauty that I want him always to treasure the trick, on one condition: that some part of him, when he isn't playing in a game, knows it's just that—a trick. O.K., Noah? *Noah?*

I took my eyes off the road and sneaked a look in the backseat. It was nearly midnight on the national day of mourning, and the kid was fast asleep.

———◆———

POSTSCRIPT: *That 2001 season would prove to be one of only two losing seasons in John McKissick's career (the other was in 1957). McKissick, already the winningest football coach in history on any level, became the first to reach the 500-win milestone in 2003. His record today stands at 556-130-13; his teams have won 30 regional titles and 10 state championships. He started coaching in Summerville in 1952 and has still never missed a game.*

{ Part Two }

As Time Runs Out

*Dying of cancer, Jim Valvano fought for his life the
same way he coached basketball: by learning all he could,
talking up a storm and insisting on the last shot.*

HE ENTERED THE ARENA WITH HIS WIFE ON HIS arm and a container of holy water from Lourdes in his black leather bag. His back and hips and knees ached. That was the disease, they told him. His ears rang and his stomach turned and his hands and feet were dead. That, they said, was the cure. Each step he took brought a rattle from his bag. Twenty-four tablets of Advil were usually enough to get him through the day.

He braced himself. No doubt someone would approach him this evening, pump his hand and say it. Strangers were always writing it or saying it to him: "We're pulling for you, Vee! You can do it! Nobody thought you had a prayer against Houston in that national championship game in '83, and you pulled that off, right? Keep fighting, Vee. You can do it again."

No. Not in the same breath. Not in the same sentence, not in the same paragraph, not in the same magazine or book could the two be uttered: a basketball opponent and a cancer eating its way through the marrow and bone of his spine. A basketball opponent and death. *No.* In their fear of dying, people didn't make it larger than it was. They shrank it, they trivialized it. Vee versus metastatic adenocarcinoma. Vee versus Phi Slamma Jamma. Go get 'em, baby. Shock the world, Vee.

No. No correlation, baby, he longed to tell them sometimes. *None.*

The cameras, the reporters, the microphones awaited him inside the Civic Center in Tallahassee. A brand-new season. Iowa State at Florida State, 46-year-old Jimmy Valvano's first game back as an ESPN college basketball analyst since he had learned last summer that he most likely had a year to live.

He tried to quicken his pace. His left leg wouldn't let him. Four or five times each day he dabbed his finger in the holy water and made the sign of the cross on his forehead, his chest, his back, his hips and his knees. Then he poured a little more into his palm and rubbed the water deep into his hands and feet.

When he was coach at North Carolina State, Vee used to pause at this point, just as he entered the arena. Having delivered his pregame talk, he would leave the locker room on the lower level of Reynolds Coliseum in Raleigh, mount the steps that led to the court, and stand on the top one, still unseen by the crowd. For a moment he would not be an actor at the heart of the drama. He would be a spectator absorbing the immensity, the feeling of it all—the band blaring fight songs, the crowd roaring, the cheerleaders tumbling through the air, the players taking turns gliding to the glass for layups. And he would think, God, I am lucky. What do other people do when they go to work? Go to an office, sit at a desk? I get *this*!

Yes, here was Vee's gift, the gift of the select, to be in the swirl and at the very same moment above it, gazing down, assessing it, drinking in all of its absurdity and wonder. It enabled him to be the funniest and most fascinating postgame lounge act in sports; it enabled him to survive the scandal at North Carolina State that stripped him of his reputation and his job. Even during his most harrowing moments, part of Vee was always saying, "God, in a year this is going to make a great story." Exaggerate this detail just a little, repeat that one phrase four or five times, and it's going to have 'em howling. Even in the darkness after he had been forced to resign, he looked down at himself lying in bed and thought, Boy, that poor son of a bitch, he's really taking a pounding. But he'll be back. Give him time. He'll be fine.

That was what cancer had stolen. The fear and the pain and the grief swallowed a man, robbed him of detachment, riveted him to *himself.* "I can't do it," he said. "I can't separate from myself anymore."

He tightened his grip on the black leather bag and walked under the lights.

IT FLOODED through him when he walked onto a basketball court—the jump shots with crumpled paper cups he took as a little boy after every high school game his dad coached, the million three-man weaves, all the sweat and the squeaks and the passion so white-hot that twice during his career he had rocketed off the bench to scream . . . and blacked out . . . and five or six times every season the backside of his suit pants had gone *rrr-iii-p*! He wore Wolfpack red underwear just in case, but it didn't really matter. A guy could walk around in his underwear at home; Vee was at home. Maybe here, for two hours tonight, he could forget.

He looked up and saw a man striding toward him. It was the Florida State coach, Pat Kennedy, who had been Valvano's assistant at Iona College. Kennedy leaned toward Vee's ear and opened his mouth to speak. Those who had been in a bar at 1 a.m. when Vee was making people laugh so hard that they cried, those who had seen him grab the deejay's microphone at 2 a.m. and climb on a chair to sing Sinatra, those whose hotel doors he had rapped on at 3:30 a.m. to talk about life and whose lampshades he had dented with his head when their eyelids sagged—"Had to do something to wake you up! You weren't listening!"—they could not fathom that this was happening to him. Vee was a man with an electric cable crackling through his body; he might walk a couple of dozen laps around an arena after a big win to let off a little hiss, or wander the streets of a city until dawn after a loss. He was the kind of guy you wanted to cook dinner for or show your new house to, because that would make it the alltime greatest dinner, the alltime best house, terrific, absolutely *terrific*—and Vee *meant* it. And now Kennedy's mouth was opening just a few inches from Vee's ear, and there were a thousand thoughts and feelings scratching at each other to get out—"Every day with you was an exciting day. Every day you had 10 new ideas. Every day you left me with a smile on my face, saying, 'Boy, that Valvano's something else.' And you left me thinking I could do more with my life than I'd ever thought before. Certain people give life to other people. You did that for me"—but no words would come out of Kennedy's mouth. Instead he just kissed Vee.

This was what Valvano missed most after his coaching career ended in April 1990. Nobody kissed a TV analyst, nobody hugged him, nobody cried on his shoulder. Vee used to astonish the directors who hired him to give those dime-a-dozen, $50-a-pop guest speeches at their summer basketball camps in the Poconos back in the '70s. The directors would look back as they strolled to their offices after introducing him and see a guy in a floppy Beatle haircut pulling a white rat—a *real* white rat, gutted and stuffed by a taxidermist and mounted on a skateboard—toward the microphone and roaring to the kids, "What kind of a greeting is *that*? Look how you're sitting! I come all the way here and what do I get? A coupla hundred crotch shots? I'm supposed to stand up here and give a good speech staring at a coupla hundred sets of jewels? Whadda we have here, a bunch of *big-timers*? I want *rats*! Let's try it again. You only get out of life what you demand! I'm gonna come to the microphone all over again, and this time I want a standing O, and once I get it you can bet I'm going to give you the best damn speech I possibly can!" The camp directors would look back again and see a couple of hundred kids on their feet, cheering wildly. Look back a few minutes later and see them crying. Look again and see them carrying Valvano from basket to basket to cut down the nets and chanting, "VEE! VEE! VEE!" And for the rest of those camps, the directors and counselors would have to peer in every direction each time they opened a door or walked down a path, because Vee had convinced a few hundred kids to leap from behind walls and bushes in front of them, to sacrifice their bodies like True Rats, to shuffle in front of the big-timers and *take the charge*!

He didn't recruit kids to his college program; he swept them there. He walked into a prospect's home, and 15 minutes later he had rearranged the living-room furniture to demonstrate a defense, had Mom overplaying the easy chair, Dad on the lamp, Junior and his sister trapping the coffee table. Where the hell else was the kid going to go to school? In the 30 games Vee coached each season, the 100 speeches he eventually gave each year, the objective was the same: to make people leap, make them laugh, make them cry, make them dream, to *move* people. "Alive!" he would say. "That's what makes me feel *alive!*"

And then one day last spring he was playing golf on a course in the hills overlooking the Mediterranean in the north of Spain. He had weathered the scandal at N.C. State. He had won an ACE for excellence in cable-television sports analysis. He had turned down an offer to coach at Wichita State and signed contract extensions with ABC and ESPN. He had time, finally, for long dinners with his wife, for poetry readings and movies with his 12-, 20- and 23-year-old daughters. He had an assignment to do sideline commentary on a World League football game in Barcelona; he had a tee time on the course just north of the city. "How beautiful it was that day," he would remember. "How happy I was. . . . " And then he felt an ache in his testicles. That's how death comes. A pang in the crotch when a man's standing in the sun gazing across the green hills and the bluest goddam sea in the world, deciding between a three-wood and an iron.

He laughed at all the inevitable aching-testicle jokes; the doctor was almost sure it was just an infection or perhaps referred pain from the lower backache Vee had been feeling. He was still laughing while in the MRI tube last June at Duke University hospital, joking through the intercom with the nurses about the heavy-metal music they were pumping into his headphones as they scanned his spine to see if he had damaged a disk, when the radiologist glanced at the image appearing on his screen, and suddenly the laughter stopped and the nurses fell silent. And the dread, the sick dread began to spread through his stomach as the radiologist quietly said, "Come with me, Coach." And then: "Let me show you a picture of a healthy spine, Coach. . . . Now look at yours."

The vertebrae in his were black where the others were white. And the dread went up Vee's chest, wrapped around his ribs and his throat, but he squeezed out another joke: "You forgot to use the flash."

No laughter. "Coach, this is just how we see it in the textbook. . . . Coach, I'm 90 percent sure this is cancer."

The world spun, and he asked a dozen questions that couldn't be answered yet, but the look on the radiologist's face said this was bad, very bad. Vee walked into the waiting room and told his wife, Pam, and they held each other and cried and drove home, where his oldest daughter, Nicole, was helping his middle daughter, Jamie, with a Music 100 class project. They were banging on a piano key, beating a wooden spoon against a pot, a pencil against a wine bottle and two candlesticks against each other when the door opened and their dad said, "I've got cancer. I'm going to die. . . . I don't want to die. . . . I'm sorry. . . . I'm *sorry*."

IT WAS still incomprehensible five months later. His sockets were a little deeper, his olive skin wrapped a little more tightly around his skull, but the 35 pounds he had lost made his body seem fit, trim. His hair, against all medical logic, had survived massive chemotherapy. He lived in a land where people vanished when they became terminally ill. Most people who saw him walking through airports, stepping in front of cameras and cracking jokes about his plummeting weight—"Hey, I'm the quickest analyst in the country now. There's not an announcer who can go around me!"—assumed his cancer was in remission. It was not. "How you doin', Coach?" they would call.

What could he say? "Hangin' in there," he usually replied. "Hangin' in there."

The crowd at the Civic Center caught sight of him now. The Florida State band rose to its feet, waved a sign—Welcome Back, Baby!—and chanted, "JIMMY VEE! JIMMY VEE! JIMMY VEE!. . ."

It was a Friday night. On Monday morning, as he did every two weeks, he would walk into the basement of the oncology center at Duke and sit with a hundred people who stared into the nothingness, waiting hours for their turns. His name would be called and a nurse would say, "Veins or port?" and he would say, "Port," which meant that his veins had collapsed from being pierced by so many needles, and that the four vials the doctors needed today would have to be drawn from the lump over his left breast, where a plastic access valve had been surgically inserted. He would remove his shirt, and a nurse would swab the lump with disinfectant and squirt it with ethyl chloride to numb it, flush out the tube inserted inside his superior vena cava with saline solution, take his blood and send him back to the waiting room while the lab ran tests on the blood. He would wait another 45 minutes, murmuring something now and then to Pam or a word of encouragement to nearby patients; then he would go to the office of a doctor who tried to be cheerful but who saw 40 cancer patients a day; and then he would be sent to the third floor to lie down again and have Velban, a cell killer, pushed into his veins through the port in the hope that it would kill as many cancer cells as healthy cells. Finally he would limp out clutching Pam for support, his body bent as if beaten with a bat, and you could count on it, somebody would ask him for his autograph, and you could count on it, he would smile wanly and say, "Sure."

"... JIMMY VEE! JIMMY VEE! JIMMY VEE!" He put the headphones on and turned the sound up so he could hear the producer's cues over the ringing that was always in his ears now, and then he stepped onto the court to tape an introduction to the game. He could feel it now, surging up through the hardwood, into his deadened feet—the thump, thump, thump of basketballs as the two teams pounded through layup drills. Everything had a beat, a lovely chaos with an old, familiar rhythm. The players were grinning and slapping five with him, the fans were waving paper and pens at him, the band was blaring the theme song from *Rocky*, the cheerleaders were tumbling through the air, and Vee's right foot was tapping. In one breath he looked into the ESPN camera and told the audience how Iowa State would have to use its speed and *stick the jump shot* to win, whereas Florida State would have to *pound it inside*. In the next breath he turned to the boom mike and the interviewer on his right to answer her question about the cancer consuming his spine, and with the horn section and the backflips and the crowd's roar all around, he fell into that same easy metaphor and delivered it in that same hoarse, hyped voice. "I'm not happy to be *here*. I'm just happy to *be*! Even as we speak the good cells are going after the bad cells. You gotta encourage 'em. Good cells. . . . *Go get 'em!* That's what's going on right now!. . . *It's hoops time! Let's play some hoops!*"

"I'M HELPLESS! I make no decisions! I have no control! I'm totally at the mercy of the disease and the treatment! I'm not a dad! I'm not a husband! I'm a *freak*! I can't do anything! I just lie there and they stick needles into this lump in my chest and pour poison in my body, and I don't believe in it. I'm a *freak*!"

He couldn't cry *that* into a microphone to the million and a half people listening at home and watching in bars, but it was right there, at the back of his tongue, at the base of his brain, welling up and wanting to spill. It did, sometimes. There was no reason to hide it, no reason anymore to hide anything. There were days, now and then, that he passed huddled in his bathrobe in front of the television, flinching from the pain, curling up in sorrow and wondering how in God's name he would summon the strength again to make the quip that would put everyone around him at ease, to tell the world in that hoarse, hyped voice, *You gotta get it into the middle, it's the only way to beat a trap defense!* as if there were a hundred thousand more tomorrows. There were days when Jamie, who had taken off her junior year at N.C. State to help him through this horror, would shout, "Get up! Go talk to your doctor! Go see a priest! Don't just lie there! You've given up! Get up! Yell at somebody! Yell at *me*!"

"Can a doctor or a priest take the cancer out of my body?" he would ask.

"I don't know! I just want you to *do* something! Yell, fight, punch! Even if it's all for nothing. So we can say, 'There's *Dad*.'"

The old Dad, The Charge of the Light Brigade Dad, son of a man who had a booming voice and an ear-to-ear grin and a yellow-pad list of things that Vee's team needed to get right to work on . . . but didn't they understand? How could Vee allow himself to hope? If Vee liked a movie, he saw it five times. If Vee liked a song, he transcribed every word, memorized it, sang it 20 times a day and talked his kids into singing it with him a half dozen more times on the way to the beach. Vee couldn't throw half or three quarters of his heart into anything; he had to throw it all. Didn't they know how dangerous it was for a man like him to throw all of his heart into a hope as slender as this? Vee was a dreamer. Vee had no life insurance. A man whose lows were as low as his highs were high couldn't hope too hard, couldn't lean too far, because the next downturn in his condition or the next darting away of his doctor's eyes could send him whirling down a shaft from which he might never escape.

Besides, where were the hooks to hang his hopes on? Doctors couldn't even find the origin of his cancer—they were guessing the lungs, even though he had never smoked more than an occasional cigar. With his kind of cancer, there were no tumors to X-ray, no reliable way to chart the course of the disease. "You'll know when it's getting worse," they told him. "You'll know by the pain." So he would wake up each morning and ask himself the terrifying question: Is there more pain?

Get up! Yell! Fight! Punch! He tried. He refused to put on the gown when he checked into the hospital every sixth week for massive doses of chemotherapy. He refused to take the prescription pain pills. He talked to God out loud. He marched into the salon and ordered them to buzz off all of his hair—*he* would take it off, not the chemotherapy. The same way, in the last minute of a tie game when the other team had the ball, he flouted convention and ordered his players to foul and risk handing the opponents the game-winning free throw—*Vee* wanted the rock at the end, *Vee* wanted the last shot. He refused to sit there, cringing on defense, waiting for fate to happen to him.

But the joke was on him. The hair grew right back and never fell out. Every tactic in this new war came back at him turned upside down. Every stoking of his fever to live increased his horror of death. And he would remember that astonishing flood of emotional letters that dying people had written to him after N.C. State had shocked Houston nine years earlier, people thanking *him* for giving them a reason not to give up, and he would sit there, shaking his head. Could he explain all that during the next timeout? Could he let everyone know that he only had to see his three daughters walk in the house in order to cry now, that a TV commercial showing a dad accepting a bowl of cereal from his little girl, hugging her and saying, "I must be pretty special for you to bring me bran flakes," brings tears to his eyes because they're just so goddam happy and lucky?

Iowa State guard Justus Thigpen's jump shot was descending a good foot in front of the rim, a fine opportunity for Vee to say, as he had with a slow, stupefied shake of his head two days earlier at home, "*Justus Thigpen!* Can you believe it? Who knows how much time I have left, and I've been sitting here poring over *Justus Thigpen's stats* in the Iowa State basketball brochure. I'm sitting here reading, and I quote, that 'Justus Thigpen was twice selected Big Eight Player of the Week' and that 'he scored 11 points at Kansas and 17 points in ISU's overtime win on ESPN versus Colorado.' *What the hell am I doing?* The triviality of it just clobbers me. You get this sick and you say to yourself, 'Sports means nothing,' and that feels terrible. God, I devoted my whole *life* to it."

He might say *that* to a million and a half people. He *could* say that. He was a man who converted feelings to thoughts and thoughts to words with stunning ease—solid to liquid, liquid to gas; it was beautiful and terrible, both. Sometimes he would look at his daughters or his wife and say, "God . . . I'm going to miss you," and it would rip their hearts in half. What were the rules after you had dragged out of the doctor the fact that only a few patients with metastatic adenocarcinoma diagnosed in its late stages, like Vee's, lived more than two years, and most were gone within a year? Did you tell the people you loved all the things that were banging at the walls of your heart, or did you keep them locked inside to save your family the agony of hearing them? Nobody taught you how to do this; what were the rules?

Maybe it was time now for the TV camera to focus on his hands, the left one balled and the right one wrapped around it, desperately trying to squeeze some feeling into it as Bob Sura zinged in a 21-footer and Florida State's lead swelled to 50–31. Perhaps Vee should tell all the viewers and listeners, even if it wasn't what they had tuned in to hear: "I'm being deprived of my senses. I can hardly taste food anymore. I can't hear. I can't feel. My wife will have to button my shirt soon because I won't be able to feel the buttons between my fingers. It's got my feet and my hands and my ears . . . but it doesn't have my mind and my heart and my soul. And it's not *going* to. I'm going to fight this as long as I can. I'm going to keep doing what I love.

"I'm going to have to miss some games because of chemotherapy. I don't think you're going to see John Saunders in the studio saying, '*Live! From room 401 at Duke University Hospital, it's Jimmy Valvano!*' because I'm going to be at the sink throwing up. I don't want to be wheeled to the microphone to do games, but I *will*. I'll keep doing this until my mouth doesn't work, until my brain doesn't function."

Maybe he should tell them what he does some days at home in Cary, N.C., how he removes his shoes and walks barefoot in the grass. Just to feel. How he puts his hands around the trunks of the pine trees and closes his eyes. Just to *feel*.

HERE WAS a story he could tell. Goddam it, the Seminoles were up by 21 at halftime, let him tell it. It was the one about a 23-year-old coach at Johns Hopkins University who was on a bus ride home from Gettysburg,

Pa., with his players, exuberant over his squad's 3-0 start. A 23-year-old coach who had plotted his life on an index card: five years, high school head coach. Five years, small-college head coach. Five years, university assistant coach. Five years, small-university head coach. Ten years, big-time university head coach. A 23-year-old who didn't know he was going to compress the first 20 years of the plan into 13, who didn't realize he was going to have his dream, live his Pocono camp speech, cut the NCAA title nets at 37 . . . a 23-year-old who didn't know his life might already be half over. His players called him to the back of the bus. "Why is winning so important to you?" they asked. "We've never seen anything like it. You're irrational."

"Because the final score defines you," he said. "You lose; ergo, you're a loser. You win; ergo, you're a winner."

"No," the players insisted. "The participation is what matters, the constancy of effort. Trying your very best, regardless of whether you win or lose—that's what defines you."

It took 23 more years of living. It took a rampage in his office at home after a 39–36 N.C. State loss to Virginia in 1982, lamp busted, chairs toppled, papers and books shoved everywhere. It took charging through a locker-room door so hard that it knocked out the team doctor. It took the pregame talk of his life and the coaching jewel of his career, the '83 NCAA championship upset that helped rocket the Final Four onto the level of the World Series and the Super Bowl. It took a couple of dozen Christmases when his wife had to buy every gift and decorate every tree. It took bolting up from the mattress three or four times a night with his T-shirt soaked with sweat and his teeth rattling from the fever chills of chemotherapy and the terror of seeing himself die again and again in his dreams—yes, mostly it took *that* to know it in his gut, to say it: "They were right. The kids at Johns Hopkins were *right*. It's effort, not result. It's *trying*. God, what a great human being I could've been if I'd had this awareness back then. But how can you tell that to any coach who has a couple kids and a mortgage and 15,000 people in the stands who judge him only by wins and losses? Do you know, that 39–36 loss to Virginia was 10 years ago, but I could never let go of that game until I got sick. Now it doesn't bother me at all.

"But I can't sit here and swear I'd do everything differently. I wouldn't trade those years. Nobody had more fun than me. How many people do you know who've had their dream come true? You're looking at one. That was my creative period, my *run*, my burst of energy. . . . "

Start his own company, JTV Enterprises? *I can do that.* Write his own newspaper column, his own championship-season book? *I can do that.* Broadcast his own daily radio commentary, his own weekly call-in radio program and local TV show in Raleigh? *I can do that.* Sell the advertising time for his own radio and TV shows? *I can do that.* Commission an artist to paint an NCAA championship-game picture each year and sell the prints to boosters of the school that wins? *I can do that.* Commission a sculptor to produce life-sized figures of the greats of sport for teams to showcase outside their stadiums? *I can do that.* Write a cookbook? (He didn't know where the plastic bags for the kitchen trash can were.) *I can do that.* Make 10 Nike speeches, 20 alumni-club speeches, 25 to 50 speeches on the national lecture circuit and a dozen charity speeches a year? *I can do that.* Design and market individualized robes to sports teams that have female journalists in their locker rooms? *I can do that.* Appear on the Carson show, the Letterman show? *I can do that.* Host his own sports talk show on ESPN? *I can do that.* Take on the athletic director's job at N.C. State as well as coach basketball? Are you sure, Vee? *I can do that.*

This was not for glory, not for money. There was none of either in the AD's job, for God's sake. It came from a deeper, wider hunger, an existential tapeworm, a lust to live all the lives he could've lived, would've lived, should've lived, if it weren't for the fact that he had only one. A shake of the fist at Death long before it came knocking, a defiance of the worms.

Pam Valvano: "Girls! Dad's in the living room!"

Daughter: "Which channel?"

Vee: "Live! In person! Downstairs! I'm actually here!"

Home at 1 a.m. Wide-eyed in bed at two, mind still grinding, neurons suspicious, even back then, of sleep. *"Inside! Get the ball inside!"* A daughter standing in the hall in her pajamas, hearing him cry it out in his sleep. Up at 5 a.m. for the two meetings before the breakfast meeting. Rushing out of his campus office at 4 p.m. to catch a plane. Day after day, year after year. "A maniac," he said. "I was an absolute maniac, a terrible husband and father. Everybody in the stands went, 'Awwwwwww, isn't that cute?' when my little girl ran across the court in a cheerleader's outfit and hugged me before every home game, but for 23 years, *I wasn't home*. I figured I'd have 20 years in the big time, who knows, maybe win three national titles, then pack it in at 53 or 54, walk into the house one day, put on a sweater and announce: *'Here I am! Ozzie Nelson's here! I'm yours!'* I always saw myself as becoming the alltime-great grandfather. Leave the kids with me? No problem. Crapped his pants? Fine, I'll change him. Vomited? Wonderful, I'll clean him up. I was going to make it up to them, all the time I'd been away." His eyes welled. "God. . . . It sounds so silly now. . . .

"But I didn't feel guilt about it then. My thinking always was, I would make a life so exciting that my wife and kids would be thrilled just to be a part of it. But I remember one Father's Day when I happened to be home, and nobody had planned anything, nobody even mentioned it. How could they have planned anything? I'd probably never been home on Father's Day before. I might've been in Atlanta giving a Father's Day speech or in Chicago receiving a Father of the Year award, but you can bet I wasn't at home on Father's Day. Finally I asked them what we were going to do, and my daughter Jamie said, 'Dad, we spent all our lives being part of your life. When are you going to be part of *ours*?' It hit me like a punch in the stomach.

"But it went on and on, that insatiable desire to conquer the world. I was an arrogant son of a bitch. But it wasn't just arrogance. I kept thinking of those lines from *The Love Song of J. Alfred Prufrock*:

And indeed there will be time
To wonder, "Do I dare?" and, "Do I dare?"
Time to turn back and descend the stair, With a bald spot in the middle of my hair—
(They will say: 'How his hair is growing thin!')

"I *wanted* to dare. I wasn't afraid to show my bald spot, my vulnerability, by trying new things. I'd go to bed after watching TV on a Saturday night, and my mind would be saying, '*I* should be the host on *Saturday Night Live*. I can do that.' I look back now and I see the truth in the Icarus myth. You know the story about the boy who's so proud of his wings that he flies too close to the sun, and it melts the wax and he falls and dies? What enables us to achieve our greatness contains the seeds of our destruction.

"Every season I had bronchitis, bad colds; twice I had pneumonia. The night we won the NCAA, I was sick as a dog. I was the Mycin Man all season—erythromycin, clindamycin. I wouldn't rest. I'd just pop the antibiotics and keep going. Who knows? Maybe I put my body in a position to get this. I've been reading books about cancer. They say it often occurs if your immune system is lowered, and then you have a trauma. . . ."

Yes, a trauma. To hell with that basketball game; it was going to end just as it began, a Florida State blowout. Here was a man who lay awake every midnight, chewing on mortality—let him talk. Let him wonder out loud if a book published in 1989, and the 15 months of investigations and media barrage it set off, was his bullet . . . and then try *not* to wonder, try to shut that midnight whisper down and ignore the connection between cancer and personal trauma, because otherwise he would have to blame a few people—a writer, a local managing editor—for this nightmare he was living, and he would have to hate, and hatred and blame were the worst detours a man could take when he was locked in mortal combat to live. "I can't do that," Vee would say. "I've got to fill these days I have left with love and laughter and forgiveness. But I wonder. . . . "

Jan. 7, 1989, the first headlines. A book entitled *Personal Fouls*, by Peter Golenbock, was about to appear, accusing Valvano and his staff of fixing grades, hiding drug-test results from authorities, diverting millions of dollars from the alumni club to the players and paying the players off with automobiles. One publishing house rejected the book but another one bought it, and the hammer blows began in earnest, usually starting with the Raleigh *News and Observer* and then ringing throughout the country, banging at the core of who Vee was. He called press conferences, he dug up graduation statistics, he demanded hearings by the North Carolina State Board of Trustees. But the Icarus arc was now at work—his glibness becoming proof, to his critics, of his guile; his gargantuan appetite for life proof of his greed.

The NCAA investigation lasted eight months. In the end the investigators found no million-dollar diversions, no automobiles, no grade-fixing, no hidden drug tests. They found two punishable violations—players had sold complimentary tickets and complimentary sneakers—and the NCAA placed N.C. State on two years' probation, declaring it ineligible for the 1990 NCAA tournament. Dave Didion, the lead investigator, wrote Valvano a letter. "I wanted to let him know that he had cooperated with me more than any coach I had ever worked with," said Didion, "and that not everyone thought he was evil. I wanted to let him know that if I had a son who was a prospect, I would be proud to have him play for Jim Valvano. He wasn't the smart-ass egomaniac I'd anticipated. Yes, the graduation rate of his players was not good . . . but no one cared to look at the overall graduation rate at N.C. State. Yes, he probably shouldn't have recruited some of the kids he did. But if he hadn't, he'd have ended up playing against them and getting his brains beaten out by them, because everybody else wanted those *same* kids."

Then came the final blow: allegations of point-shaving a few years earlier that involved former N.C. State forward Charles Shackleford. No one believed Valvano had knowledge of it, and nothing would ever be proved, but the hammering had to stop. In April 1990 he was forced to resign. "The pain of that—having my mother, my brothers, my wife, my children reading the things that were written about me," he said. "I felt physical *pain*. There were things I should've done differently, but I knew I hadn't done anything *wrong*. The insinuation that I didn't care about the kids. . . . I *hated* that. To be lumped with coaches who cared only about winning and nothing about education. . . . I *hated* that. I majored in English, not P.E. I had two daughters on the dean's list. All but perhaps two of my players at Johns Hopkins, Bucknell and Iona graduated. I didn't change. I'll take responsibility, but that's different from blame. I didn't admit the kids to N.C. State who didn't graduate—our admissions office did. In hindsight it's easy to say who shouldn't have been recruited, but who knew beforehand? Sometimes kids from worse backgrounds, with worse high school grades, did better than kids from decent homes, with decent grades.

"Maybe I trusted the kids too much. The school wanted me to force education down their throats, and I wouldn't do it. They wanted me to say, 'You don't go to class, you don't play. I take away ball.' What does that tell a kid? That *ball* is more important than education! My approach was, If you don't study, you pay the consequences. You flunk out. I tried to excite them about learning. I had Dereck Whittenburg read *King Lear* and then go to the chalkboard and do a pregame talk on it. I wasn't one of those coaches telling them to learn but never reading a book myself. I *lived* it. They saw me reading Shakespeare on buses. They saw me trying things outside of sports all the time.

"I guess I was unrealistic to think I could change kids. I should've said to them, 'I love you, but I don't trust you yet. You have to do this and this your first two years here, and *then* I'll trust you.' And there's no way around it—I didn't have as much time to give them after I became athletic director. I tried to do too much. They couldn't just walk into my office at any time of the day, like before, and talk. It was a little less each year, especially for the 13th, 14th, 15th players. But each time, the change was imperceptible to me. It happens without your realizing it.

"And now I'm fighting to live, and the irony of having people think of me as a man who cared only about winning and athletics . . . it overwhelms me. I'm looking for a reason to hope, a reason to *live*, and the only thing that helps me do that is my education, my *mind*. If I survive this, or even if I just wage this battle well, it will be because of what I grasped from reading, from understanding the world and my place in it, from learning to ask the right questions and to grasp all the alternative treatments for this disease—from *academia*, not from athletics. People think a sports background helps you fight death. Are you kidding? Athletes and coaches are taught that they're special. You're *nobody* when you're a cancer patient. You're *nobody*.

"I want to help every cancer patient I can now. For some reason, people look to me for hope. I'm feeling half dead, and they're coming up to me in the hospital for *hope*. I don't know if I can handle that, but it's the only conceivable good that can come out of this. If the Clinton Administration wants someone to raise money for cancer research, I'm here. If I survive, I'm going to work with cancer patients one-on-one and help them find a way to hang on, like so many people are trying to do for me. *Half a million people* die of cancer every year in America, one out of every four of us will get it, and there's no moral outrage; we *accept* it. I'm all for AIDS funding and research, but how can the government give 10 times as much per AIDS patient as per cancer patient? Barbra Streisand isn't singing for cancer, Elizabeth Taylor isn't holding a celebrity bash for cancer, and yet every time I go into that cancer building at Duke, it's a packed house! If it means more doctors, more space, more money, we've *got* to get it, because millions of people are going to find out that this is one hell of a way to go."

The basketball game was nearly over now. Valvano's mind and tongue were still flying, the jokes still crackling, but a deep fatigue was coming over his body. He looked across the court and saw his wife speaking to a woman beside her, saw his wife smile. And he thought: It's so good to see her smile, but how many times have I seen her crying lately? What's going to happen to her? Will she be all right? He would take a deep swallow of air the next day as he remembered that moment, that look across the court at her as the coaches shouted and the players panted and the fans roared. "You see, I had it all planned for our 25th anniversary, last August 6. I was going to give her three gifts: the deed to four acres where she could build her dream house, a big diamond ring, and a nice trip, just the two of us on a beach. She'd lift me up when she heard it and I'd cut the nets, a standing O. . . . *Goddam*. What did she get instead? A sick husband in a hospital bed getting Mitomycin, Cisplatin and Velban dripped into him. She got to clean me up when I vomited. *That's* love. I'd told her, 'We're going to get old together, Pam.' Probably the nicest thing I'd ever said to her. 'We're going to get old together'. . . . *Goddam*. . . . *Goddam*."

The game ended, and then he did something he had never done before. He thanked the hundred fans who had gathered to wish him well, said no to the coaches who asked if he would like to go out . . . and went back to his hotel room with his wife. She fell asleep, and he lay there at 1 a.m., alone, hungry for food and wine, hungry for conversation he was missing, and the laughter. He ordered a pizza, stared at the TV and cried.

HE JUMPED from his seat one day not long ago. The backside of his pants didn't rip—they weren't that tight anymore. A paragraph had jumped into his eyes from a book he was reading. "That is why athletics are important," wrote a British sportswriter named Brian Glanville. "They demonstrate the scope of human possibility, which is unlimited. The inconceivable is conceived, and then it is accomplished."

"That's *it*!" cried Vee. "*That's* why we strive! That's the value of sports! All those games, they mean nothing—and they mean everything!" His fist clenched. He hadn't poured himself into emptiness for 23 years, he hadn't devoured Justus Thigpen's stats for nothing, he hadn't. The people who compared his upset of Houston to his fight against cancer were right!

"It's what I've got to do to stay alive," he said. "I've got to find the unlimited scope of human possibility within myself. I've got to conceive the inconceivable—then accomplish it! My mom's *convinced* I'm going to get better. My mom's always right!"

In early December, when the pain grew so fierce he had to call off a weekend of studio work for ESPN, he had a local shop print up 1,000 small cards. He had hundreds of people across the country calling him, writing him, encouraging him, but he needed more. VICTORIES it said on each card. "Valvano's Incredible Cancer Team of Really Important Extraordinary Stars."

"See?" he said. "I'm going to make a *team*. I'm going to give a card to everyone I meet as I go around the country doing games. On the back of each card are the requirements of my players. One, they have to say, 'Jimmy Vee, you will make it.' Two, they have to say it out loud—it's important to verbalize. They can call my office number and, if I'm not there, leave a message on my answering machine: *'Jimmy, don't give up!'* And three, they have to do something to improve their own health, whether it's mental, spiritual or physical.

"My own team—everybody can join. This is it, baby, my ultimate pre-game talk. I *need* this one, *gotta* have it. Gotta have so many people calling my answering machine each day that they can't get through. Gotta have people all over the country opening their windows and shouting it out: 'JIMMY VEEEEEE! DON'T GIVE UP!'"

———

POSTSCRIPT: *Jim Valvano would die four months after the publication of this story, on April 28, 1993, at Duke University Medical Center. "His last six months of life were incredible," said Duke coach Mike Krzyzewski. "He wanted everyone to attack this disease with passion." Since then, The V Foundation has raised more than $70 million and funded cancer research grants in 37 states. Over 100 "V Scholar" grants have been awarded to young researchers throughout the country.*

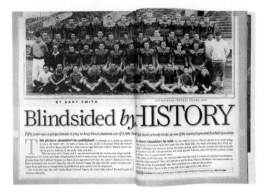

Blindsided by History

Fifty years ago, segregationists trying to keep black students out of Little Rock Central High left a team stranded with no school to play for—and broke up one of the country's greatest football dynasties.

THIS PICTURE SHOULDN'T BE PUBLISHED. IT BELONGS in a moldy scrapbook in some old man's attic. Its time is done. Its way of life is finished. Even the school these 42 white boys played for a half century ago did away with it. Took it down one day to paint a hallway in the early '90s, and then. . . .

What became of it? Some said it was stowed beneath the auditorium stage and destroyed in a fire. Some said that a black janitor threw it away along with four decades of other team photos from that hallway because no black faces appeared in them. No, others claimed, it was a black principal who decreed that the school's history began the day that all people became welcome there and that no image from its prehistoric past would ever be displayed.

Not even this one, the Little Rock Central Tigers of 1957. The year they were the best high school football team in America.

THIS STORY shouldn't be told. No one wants to hear it. They're all too busy celebrating another group at Central High that year—the nine black kids. Too busy planning their 50th anniversary, building their museum across the street, getting ready for the crowds and the network news reporters and the two Clintons, President Bill and Senator Hillary, who will fill the school's front yard on September 25 to commemorate *them.*

Besides, there's no one to tell it. Even the white boys who lived it have no desire to dredge it up again. It reeks of political incorrectness. It's sure to be misconstrued. They can't ask you to feel for them: They're Southern Caucasian males on the other side of 65, for goodness' sake. Born and bred not to feel for themselves.

Just 42 more of the white faces on the wrong side of the saga of the Little Rock 9.

THIS IS the photograph of today's team. This is the picture that everyone coming to the 50th anniversary wants to see. Forty-four of the 67 players are black. One's a Turk. One's the son of an Iranian. One's parents are from Nigeria. Another's father is Korean, his stepdad black, his mother white. Then there's the white country boy who hunts ducks at dawn on school days. All playing for a school that owns the second-most state football championships—32—of any school in the U.S.

These kids know the story of the Little Rock 9 by heart. They've seen the plaques honoring them in their school's entry, the benches dedicated to them out front, the statues of them on the state capitol lawn. They've seen films, read books and written reports about what the nine endured so that Central High's team picture could look the way it does today.

But those white boys in that vanished photo, their Tigers predecessors . . . who are they? What happened to them that fateful year and the even more wrenching one that followed? Today's team hasn't a clue.

WHAT IF Little Rock Central added a wrinkle to its 50th anniversary? Imagine if everyone in those two team pictures sat elbow to elbow at dinner in the school cafeteria and tried to understand what happened from both sides, what might be learned.

No, not Hollywood's or history's version. Not what happened to the heroes or the hatemongers, not the *black-and-white* version. The story of the gray, the people in between, the majority that ends up drifting toward one side or the other and determining history, often without even knowing why. The ones we need to understand most, because they're *us*—the kids we likely would've been had we grown up white in the '50s in the South—and because we, too, might drift when *our* moment comes. Just teenagers, so absorbed in their search for love and identity that they hadn't even begun to take stock of the injustices swirling around them, to understand the forces about to sweep them off their feet. Teenagers just hungry to feel part of a group, the one that gave their town its greatest pride: its mighty football team.

Sure, it would be awkward for everyone at first. It's a subject the old-timers barely talked about for years, and then only among themselves. Some haven't set foot on school grounds since everything splintered. But if they pulled up in front of Central High today, they'd shake their heads and feel like 17-year-olds again . . . because that grand old fortress looks just the way it did back then, when it was on postcards instead of the front page of *The New York Times*. Two *long* city blocks of edifice, seven stories of yellow brick and stone, 370 tons of steel, a 1927 castle gussied up in Art

Deco and Collegiate Gothic: *America's Most Beautiful High School.* That's what the American Institute of Architects crowned her.

The ol' boys would be anxious as they walked from their cars, the way the neighborhood's changed. Randy Rankin, the starting quarterback now, would assure them it's not that dire, but . . . well, yeah, three of his buddies have been jumped by local thugs after games, and not all at once.

Guess there's a price to be paid for change, one of the kids would say. To which Bill May and his old teammates might glance at each other, shake their heads and say, "Boys . . . you don't know the half of it. . . . "

BILL MAY blinked as he approached the school. Sawhorses . . . soldiers . . . cops . . . guns? At Little Rock Central, the lord and master of all high schools in Arkansas? One public high school, up till that year, for all the white kids in a town of 100,000, the same school most of their parents, aunts, uncles and grandparents had attended—a city suckled by the same behemoth. A greenhouse for National Merit scholars, future Ivy Leaguers and Hollywood hotshots, for baseball Hall of Famers Bill Dickey and Brooks Robinson, for more state titles in team sports than any other high school in the continental U.S., for track teams that went 15 years without a defeat . . . and, oh, my Lord, the gridiron. Bill May and his teammates didn't just dominate Arkansas football in the '50s—their second string could've done that. They took on the beasts of the South on Friday nights, beat the best that Texas, Tennessee, Louisiana and Kentucky could muster in front of crowds sometimes as big as the ones at the University of Arkansas.

But now the crowds were right in front of Central High, staring at 270 Arkansas National Guardsmen who ringed the building that first week of school in 1957, wondering whether those troops would let nine black kids become the first in the South to integrate a city school. Some of the soldiers had just graduated from Central High.

None of the Little Rock 9 showed up the first day, advised by school district officials to stay away. On the third day 15-year-old Elizabeth Eckford tried to crack the fortress, she alone figuring that those soldiers *had* to be there to uphold the 1954 Supreme Court ruling mandating an end to segregated schools. Wrong. Under orders from Governor Orval Faubus, the troops crossed their bayonets, closed ranks and turned her away.

Faubus wasn't *preventing integration*, he insisted. He was *preserving the peace*, he said, because "blood will run in the street" if blacks attended Central. The crowd surrounded the girl, spitting and yelling, "Lynch her. . . . Drag her over to this tree!" Lord knows how she got home that day.

Bill? Hell, the all-state tackle was just trying to make it through the moil for the team's 8 a.m. preclass skull session for the season opener, just a few days away, in the Tigers' bid for a sixth straight state championship. Bill was like most of his teammates: white kids who'd grown up so separate from African-Americans—even the wealthier players with black maids in their homes—that they were surprised to learn that any black kid would even *want* to go to their school. White kids were taught by elders that every human being was a child of God to be treated with respect, but don't touch the railing on the escalator at Blass Department Store because colored people had touched it.

Bill, at last, was wide awake. The superintendent of the school district, his dad's friend Virgil Blossom—under death threats for being the architect of the integration of Little Rock's schools—was sleeping in Bill's bedroom to throw his enemies off the trail. Good for Blossom, who had survived an assassination attempt a few months earlier, but not for Bill. Blossom snored.

Bill realized, too late, that he was approaching a police checkpoint, that students' cars were being searched and he'd never be able to explain that the brass knuckles and blackjacks in his trunk had been purchased by him and classmates on a lark during a school trip to New York City the previous spring, then left in his car and forgotten.

Just then, the Tigers' legendary coach, Wilson Matthews, appeared outside the school. "Leave them alone!" he barked at the police, motioning toward Bill and the teammates carpooling with him. "They're *my* boys!" No cop dared defy Wilson Matthews.

But Coach Matthews couldn't protect all his brood. Four blocks away Buford Blackwell—the affable 6' 4" defensive end—was crossing the 14th Street Overpass when the police flagged him down. From his car they pulled six screwdrivers, three claw hammers—he was doing carpentry for a neighbor—and a gun. It was only an air pistol, not even loaded with BBs, but that did it. Buford was spread-eagled, frisked and hauled off to the federal building, emerging with an FBI record.

The ol' boys, taking their seats in the cafeteria, would have the kids' attention now. What would Bill May tell them that he began learning that year about race in America? "If I was black," he'd say, "I'd have ended up a Black Panther."

SO . . . THE '57 team took the Little Rock 9's side? That's what today's team wants most to ask the old-timers. "They must've been the leaders in this school, the way we are now," says lineman Quadel Foreman. "Did they step up and be leaders or were they influenced by what other people did?"

Well, boys, it's . . . complicated. . . .

It was a Monday morning, three days after the '57 Tigers had pulverized Texarkana High of Texas 54–13, to run their record to 2–0 and their winning streak to 23. A federal judge had just ordered the National Guard removed so integration could proceed. The Little Rock 9, any moment now, would enter Central High for the first time. The crowd of segregationists outside, fed by out-of-staters swarming to the battle's front line, swelled to several thousand, sorely outnumbering the 150 cops. There was no air conditioning. The windows were open. The hate blew in. "Two-four-six-eight, we ain't gonna integrate!" they chanted. "Let's go home and get our shotguns!" one man cried.

Coach Matthews poked his head outside. A block or two away white men were beating and kicking a black reporter and chasing another down the street. Matthews reeled back inside, telling people that it looked like blacks outside were being killed. In enlightened Little Rock, of all places, where African-Americans had already been hired onto the police force and quietly allowed into the public library, parks and zoo. Tigers tackle Bubba Crist, trying to get into school, saw whites shatter the car window of two black construction workers with a shovel just before they were dragged out and beaten.

Maybe football would take the students' minds off the lunacy outside. The morning bulletin asked everyone to chorus 15 hurrahs to inspire the Black and Old Gold for that Friday's game against powerhouse Istrouma High of Baton Rouge—the last opponent to have beaten the Tigers, two years earlier, behind a Southern god and All-America named Billy Cannon. The horde outside, hearing those 15 roars and thinking that the Negroes had somehow sneaked in, went into a froth.

Moments later the nine *were* inside, smuggled in through a delivery entrance by police. Some white kids leaped out of windows and screamed, "They're in! The n------ are in!" The crowd surged, hurling itself at the police line. Rocks and bottles began flying at passing cars. Five more reporters and cameramen were attacked; hell, they looked like Yankees. Women and girls outside sobbed and begged all the white kids to walk out of school.

Coach Matthews used to vomit before every football game, sickened by the faintest whiff of losing. All at once, four days before his team's biggest challenge, he was on the verge of losing everything: winning streak, football team . . . maybe the whole school. Five weeks earlier, the day before two-a-days had begun, he'd gathered his Tigers in the empty bleachers, let it get real quiet, then said, "Boys, I want you each to go home tonight, get on your knees and give your soul to God . . . because tomorrow your goddam ass is mine." Now events were loosening his iron grip: What if one of his starters got tangled up in this and got expelled? His quarterback—future Razorbacks All-America Billy Moore—would fight a buzzsaw barehanded, and his teammates would follow him into the sawmill. His fullback, Steve Hathcote, was so wild he'd drill you with a 90-mph fastball in an American Legion game and scream, "Rub it and you're chickens---!" What about Central's 6' 4", 220-pound tackle, John Rath? His old man, a moderate on the school board, was already receiving threats at home from bigots.

The coach peered outside. White students were streaming out of school to the applause of the crowd. The black kids were getting bumped and berated in the halls. Matthews sent word through the building: All varsity football players were to leave their classes and report to him—*now*.

Matthews, an ol' country boy from Arkansas, was shrewd; he'd glimpsed the future. One day, he'd warned his team, "there'll be black boys here so tall they can stand flat-footed and piss in a wagon bed, and you white boys won't even be team managers." But for now the school district wasn't even allowing the Little Rock 9 to hum in the school's a cappella choir, let alone tackle a white boy in front of 12,000 people, so nothing good could come of this for him.

"Sit down," the ex-Marine ordered as his players filed into a classroom. "Don't look out the window and worry about what's going on outside. If

I hear of *any* of you getting involved in any of this, you're finished with football. You'll answer to me."

No coach on earth could make a player cry, crap and vomit all at once like Wilson Matthews could. Outside, the howling for the heads of the Little Rock 9 grew louder. Inside that classroom the Little Rock 42 sat in stone silence.

THAT SILENCE is what today's players need to hear about. They understand the outsiders' pain, the loneliness and fear that Minnijean Brown must've felt as she was about to enter her first English class that day 50 years ago. It's what occurs in the minds and hearts of the *insiders* that the kids need to grasp. It's Johnny Coggins whom they need to gather around, because if they don't understand the ambivalence that can take hold of even the good kids when the moment comes, they too one day might find themselves in quicksand. . . .

Johnny wasn't sequestered with the varsity that morning when Minnijean and the other eight black kids entered Central. He was a junior defensive end on the B team—not yet worthy of being summoned and supervised by Coach Matthews—sitting in Miss West's English class in a corner room nearest to the mob outside begging police to turn over just one of those Negroes, just one to be lynched as an example to the rest. He didn't agree with what they were screaming, he'd tell the kids today. On the contrary, he was discovering that day that he was a closet liberal, that he felt sick for those black kids, embarrassed for the whole human race. And still. . . .

The classroom door opened. Minnijean entered and took a seat in the row next to Johnny, leaving him between the segregationists outside and her. His heart felt as if it would bang its way out of his chest. Three boys stood, flung their books to the floor, screamed at Minnijean and walked out. Miss West, a liberal, stared daggers at them.

The crowd outside urged the rest of the class to leave. Minnijean's dead-ahead gaze and small smile never flickered. The silence grew inside the bedlam. Johnny's mind raced. What if one of those nutballs out there had a gun? What if they branded him as what he was—a sympathizer—for not walking out? One of his best friends turned to him. "Let's get out of here," the boy murmured.

It caught Johnny by surprise. His pal was a straight-A student. The kids who were walking out to protest integration weren't the high achievers or the jocks. Johnny got B's and was one of Miss West's pets. And *still.* . . .

What you need to understand, Johnny could tell the 2006 team, is how confusing the moment is, if you've never shone a light on your own shadows. Thunderclouds of anxiety, fleeting glimmers of rationalization: *Miss West can't teach with this mob outside. . . . We can't learn anything today anyway. . . . Nobody can blame you, not in this madness. . . . Gotta stick with your buddy. . . .*

Miss West stared in disbelief as Johnny and his friend rose. "Don't do it," she said.

They did it. They walked out of the room, out of the building. The segregationists cheered.

Johnny felt his legs begin to move faster and faster, hurrying to get away. Two hours later the crowd would be cheering even louder: The black kids were gone. The mob's assaults on the police line had grown so fierce by high noon that the cops had smuggled the Little Rock 9 out of Central High in fear for their lives.

Johnny, who dreaded facing Miss West again, wouldn't return to school for a week. He'd tell today's team what he's tried to teach his own children, about the importance of inspecting yourself and your values early and often so you're ready when the moment lays ambush. About finding himself, all these years later, going overboard to boom greetings to black strangers, and buying whatever it is that the black salesman at the front door's selling. About five decades of regret.

QUADEL FOREMAN needs to take a walk to the auditorium with Buddy Tackett. See, Quadel would get it when Buddy began explaining what it was like to be the fat kid whom the boys would taunt and the girls would look right past. He'd understand when Buddy spoke of his epiphany in junior high, howling and hoisting barbells and gulping protein shakes, converting angst into dominance, lard into iron, a garage into a forge. Turning into the most powerful kid at Central, the all-state lineman who could pile-drive the seven-man blocking sled the length of the field alone.

Quadel would understand, even though he was 50 years younger and black, because Buddy's story was his story. It was this room—Central's magnificent auditorium—where both of them yearned to reap the recognition of who they'd become. This theater where Central still holds its pep rallies, leaps and roars for its football team; this stage where Buddy and Quadel longed to be anointed The Man.

Buddy would point toward the seats, empty now, and remember sitting here, shaking his head that morning: September 25, 1957. It was two days after the Little Rock 9's attempt to integrate the school had ended in chaos. Two days before the big game against Baton Rouge Istrouma. Buddy's father had just dropped him off at school. They'd hesitated for a moment outside, blinking. There was a howitzer and a tank, machine guns mounted at the corners of the football stadium and on the school's roof. A helicopter churned overhead as a platoon raced up and down Park Street with fixed bayonets. *Sweet Jesus.* Overnight, President Eisenhower had sent 1,200 paratroopers from the Army's crack division, the famed Screaming Eagles of the 101st Airborne, to occupy the school and quell the mob.

Buddy's father had looked at him. "You think you ought to go in there?" he asked.

"If I don't," said Buddy, "Coach Matthews will be at our house this afternoon."

"Guess you better go in," his father said.

Nearly 700 students, in fear or in protest, *hadn't* gone in, a third of the student body missing at that morning's hastily called assembly. Fifty-seven hours before the Tigers' showdown, their auditorium was hushed, their stage empty.

The silence deepened as Maj. Gen. Edwin Walker and his swagger stick came down the aisle and mounted the stage. "You have nothing to fear from my soldiers, and no one will interfere with your coming, going or your peaceful pursuit of your studies," he declared. "However, I would be less than honest if I failed to tell you that I intend to use all means necessary to prevent any interference with the execution of your school board's plan."

General Walker meant business. Outside the school a segregationist who refused to disperse got his head bloodied by a Screaming Eagle's rifle butt. Moments after the assembly the Little Rock 9, sheathed by 20 paratroopers, did just what Quadel would reenact dozens of times a half century later, picturing white people screaming at him: walk up those steps and integrate Central forever.

When the phone call came to Central just before lunch, saying that the school would be blown up at noon and flushing the entire student body into the yard, nobody giggled or horseplayed the way they had when the National Guard was there. It was a whole new ball game now, Buddy would tell Quadel, and it was only beginning. Because soon his school would go from a battlefield to an empty building, its football team all that would remain of it, and then the team, too, would begin falling apart. . . .

Over nine black kids, he'd keep muttering, in a school of *two thousand.* Hell, no, he wasn't for integration any more than most of his team was, but for God's sake, if the adults had just stayed out of it, the kids would've accommodated the change. No one consulted them, even though it was *they* who would pay the price.

And no, Buddy knew, that price couldn't be stacked up against the one paid by those nine black kids, or their parents and grandparents, but if healing was everyone's goal, neither price should be forgotten.

Quadel would get his moment in that auditorium, the one he hungered for all those years when the kids called him Fatty. He'd be summoned to the microphone at a pep rally last fall, introduced as "the big man on campus" to a roof-raising roar and asked to make a speech.

Buddy never would. His eyes would blink hard as they took one last sweep of that auditorium. Then he'd drop his head and rub away his tears.

NOW THE kids would begin to unravel a mystery. Why do they hear so much from coach Bernie Cox about *Tiger Pride*—the two words that symbolize their glorious tradition, the two words they bark when they break their huddles, and the title of the book written by Bernie's son, Brian—but rarely see that tradition in the flesh? Now they'd begin to understand why so few of the old-timers return to reap and resow it.

It won't be easy for the old men to explain their absence. Most could drive to campus in the time it takes to get a haircut. They'd hesitate, fumble for words, until someone at last would say it: "It's just not the same school." Running the risk that that might be taken as racism, when yes, it may be, at least in part, but no, it's not what they mean. Running the risk that these kids are too young to understand that a man carries a snapshot in his head all his life of his school days, and what it's like to walk through a doorway and have that snapshot shredded. To suddenly confront a new one in the same setting, full of people who look and dress and talk so differently from him, a snapshot that only makes it harder for him to be sure that the one in his head, fast fading with age—*who he was*—ever even existed. . . .

The '57 Tigers walked out of their locker room after school on that history-making day, September 25, still snapping on chin straps and tucking jerseys into pants, and stared. Their practice field had been turned into a campground, helicopter landing pad and armored vehicle parking lot for the 101st Airborne. "How we gonna practice?" somebody asked.

Coach Matthews appeared, screaming at the Screaming Eagles as if they were . . . hell, as if they were *Tigers*. "Get these goddam things off this field now!" The players watched in wonder. The 101st *became* them, jumping to Matthews's command, clearing tents and moving jeeps to the end of the field. A helicopter levitated so fast that the players looked to see if it even had a pilot in it. "*That's* how we're gonna practice," somebody said. The Tigers began preparing for strapping Istrouma.

The helicopter, looking for a place to land, dodged the coach's flying clipboard and veered off like a spooked dragonfly. "Your sporting blood has turned to piss!" Matthews would howl if his players so much as glanced at the 101st. But guess who came to dinner that Friday night? A few minutes before kickoff the Screaming Eagles marched into the stadium, took seats at the top and began cheering for the Black and Old Gold.

Late in the fourth quarter, with Buddy imploring his teammates to hang on to their fragile 12–6 lead, Tigers all-state end Bill Hicks lined up a 31-yard field goal against the wind, toward goal posts that a day earlier had been antennae mounts for the 101st's radio communications . . . and hammered it through. Central's students jumped to their feet and traded fist pumps with the 101st. Their winning streak climbed to 24. The wall between them and their occupiers began to crumble.

BUT THOSE *other* outsiders? What about that wall? Here's what the kids today don't understand about the old-timers who didn't scale it: That team never shared an experience with those black kids. It never saw them

run or sweat on a field, joke or laugh or cheer. Most of the '57 Tigers didn't
share classes with them. They flattened themselves against the hallway
walls and watched the nine blitz by inside those six-man wedges formed
by the 101st between classes. They never glimpsed *themselves* in those
nine kids. Sure, they could have, if they'd been strong enough to step out
of the pack during lunch, ignore all the peer pressure, risk running afoul
of Coach Matthews's edict, chance revenge on their parents' businesses
or on themselves—like one white student who got threatened and had
his car vandalized for talking to a black senior named Ernest Green. How
many on today's team would be that strong? Step right up.

Now you might see Jerome Raynor, a black defensive back on the '06
team, clear his throat and admit that he failed to stop classmates from
mocking the one male on last year's jayvee cheerleading squad. Now Aaron Nichols, the black cornerback who was called "n------" and ostracized
by a roomful of white kids on his own first day in an English class at a
rural middle school just a few years ago, would confess, "If I was those
white guys back then, I'd have probably stayed away from the black kids.
Sometimes you just keep your mouth shut and stay out of trouble."

Ralph Brodie at last would speak. He was a starting defensive back
on the '57 team, the state champ in the high hurdles and president of
Central's student body . . . never dreaming then that he'd been elected to a
lifetime job. Never dreaming that three months of his 67th year would be
consumed by writing letters to the media, gathering first-person accounts,
petitioning the anniversary and museum planning commissions to let the
dinosaurs tell their side of integration.

"Listen," he'd tell today's team, "no one's saying the Little Rock 9
weren't heroes. They were. But there might not be a Little Rock 9 alive
if not for the vast majority of the students inside. We could be holding a
memorial for lives lost instead of a celebration if not for those students,
teachers, administrators and coaches in that building who conducted
themselves with dignity under tremendous pressure."

Take Coach Matthews, God rest his soul, dead five years now from
heart failure. How did he keep 42 players on the same track with all those
sparks and cinders flying around their heads? Starting with Ralph's own
head, roiling with anxiety when he was summoned to the principal's office one day that season, handed a telephone and told that a reporter

who worked for ABC wanted to speak to him, fella by the name of Mike Wallace. Ralph tiptoed through Wallace's land-mine questions, trying to convince him that his schoolmates weren't the pariahs being portrayed to the nation, but not inflame the pariahs amassed outside their front door.

WALLACE: Would you say the sentiment [among students] is mostly toward integration or segregation?

RALPH: We are going to have to have integration sometime, so we might as well have it now.

WALLACE: Would it make a big difference to you if you saw a white girl dating a Negro boy?

RALPH: I believe it would.

WALLACE: Why?

RALPH: I don't know. I just was brought up that way.

WALLACE: Do you think Negroes are equal in intelligence, and physically, to white people?

RALPH: If they have had the same benefits and advantages, I think they're equally as smart.

When the interview—which first appeared in the *New York Post*—was reprinted in the *Arkansas Democrat Gazette*, Ralph's relatives feared for his life, and Ralph turned to Little Rock's prosecuting attorney for protection when the media hounding continued. Who can say when the course of a life begins to turn? The boy who was class president every year from fourth grade on, the one whose peers were convinced he'd be governor one day and perhaps even president, would end up deciding to have nothing to do with public life.

Now Ralph could start pointing to his old teammates, turning first to center Joe Matthews—no relation to the coach—who had a police car parked outside his house at night because of threats against his father. That was Central's principal, Jess Matthews, who lost 20 pounds and turned to sleeping pills that year because of the stress.

Then point to big John Rath, the starting tackle whose dad's company was being boycotted because of the stance he'd taken on the school board in favor of integration and whose sister was being called a "n----- lover" and bumped in the halls at Central because she'd befriended one of the blacks.

Then point to Bill May, the lineman who—late for a test one day—ran from his locker carrying a big red plastic tube of pencils that soldiers mistook for a stick of dynamite, pursuing him into his class and marching him to the principal. Coach Matthews came on the run, accompanied soldiers in a search of Bill's locker and was appalled by the tobacco pipe that turned up . . . until Bill convinced him that it was only a prop in his role as an old man in the school play *Arsenic and Old Lace*.

How about the coaches themselves? Every bomb threat, Matthews and his staff had to search the school for explosives, sometimes in the dead of night. There were 46 that year. One of his young assistants, Lawrence Mobley—who'd planned a career as a high school teacher and coach— swallowed so much tension that he quit at the end of the school year. Good thing that another young assistant, Clyde Hart, wasn't spooked out of the business. Otherwise, Olympic gold medalists Michael Johnson and Jeremy Wariner, years later at Baylor, would never have had the world's best 400-meter coach.

Somehow the Tigers focused and poleaxed their next five opponents, ran the winning streak to 29 and then stunned the No. 1 team in Kentucky, Tilghman High of Paducah, with three first-quarter touchdown explosions by running back Bruce Fullerton. "The greatest high school football team I've ever seen," gasped Tilghman coach Ralph McRight after the 46–13 rout.

JUST BEFORE Thanksgiving the Screaming Eagles vanished, withdrawing to a nearby military base in case they were needed and turning over the job to the federalized National Guard. Bad news for the Little Rock 9. Many in the Guard, opposed to race-mixing, turned a blind eye to the abusers inside the school. Their numbers are disputed—perhaps 50 white students organized and coached by their parents, bent on breaking the spirits of those nine black kids, according to some; far more, easily in the hundreds, some of the Little Rock 9 insist. They got kicked, tripped, punched, spat on and shoved down stairs. One black girl had acid flung in her face and her head held under a hot shower. Minnijean Brown finally lost her cool in the cafeteria when a boy kicked a chair in front of her. She dumped a bowl of chili on his head, got suspended and, after another incident, expelled.

None of the reported incidents involved the football players. Yes, they could've done more to help the Little Rock 9; yes, some still regret it.

Backup running back Josh McHughes, a lawyer, still winces when he bumps into Elizabeth Eckford in the courthouse where she works as a probation officer, still remembers her as a scared 11th-grader hurtling down the halls clutching her books to her chest as if they were her only protection in the world, still wishes he could utter the words he wanted to but didn't: *It's going to be all right, Elizabeth.* Running back Ronnie Spann wishes he'd introduced himself to Carlotta Walls in biology instead of keeping his distance. "But the coach and my parents kept saying, 'Stay out of it,' and the kids who were friendly to blacks got ostracized," he'd tell today's team, "and I was a kid just trying to fit in. If I saw her now, I'd say I'm sorry I didn't hug you and hold your hand. If I could do it over, I'd be a friend."

What the '57 Tigers did was give their school one clean thing that soiled year, one refuge from the storm. They demolished Pine Bluff 33–0, stupefied Blytheville 53–12, then slapped a 40–7 Turkey Day exclamation point on rival North Little Rock and on the Streak: 33!

How good were they? Their first string punted once that season. Hicks, the amiable kicker and end, and Fullerton were named All-Americas, and *The Sporting News* chose Fullerton as the National Player of the Year. Twelve players became college starters, not including Fullerton, who bumped into a future NFL Hall of Famer named Lance Alworth at his position at Arkansas. Nine Tigers were named all-state. The National Sports News Service of Minnesota knighted them as the nation's No. 1 team, and 43 years later they'd be chosen by a scholastic sports magazine as one of the dozen best teams in the history of high school football.

At graduation, Hicks made one last contribution. Among a crowd including soldiers, police, national reporters and Martin Luther King Jr., the player spotted a kid with a package of eggs ticketed for Ernest Green when he walked across the stage to get his diploma, and Hicks forced a turnover that saved the school from one more front-page disaster.

But—remember?—this isn't the Hollywood version. This story can't end with the All-America saving the day, with the police dragging the villain away, with Green squeezing his sheepskin and exchanging a poignant nod with Dr. King, and the front door of Central High open, at last, to everyone.

Because that's when the front door shut to everyone.

THIS PICTURE should never have been made. It's a photo of an impossibility: the football team of a high school that didn't exist. It's the team picture of the '58 Tigers.

It would perplex today's team when Buddy pulled it out, because most have never heard the last part of the story. Yes, the '57 Tigers were proof of sport's capacity to insulate a young man from his world, to seal him in a bubble where he and his teammates could achieve perfection even as that world unraveled. But Buddy and the other juniors on that team, the ones who returned in '58, can teach the kids a deeper truth: The bubble's an illusion.

No, it's not a true team picture, the kids will notice. It's a collection of individual photos cobbled together. It's the best the Tigers could manage that unimaginable year.

Just before school began Governor Faubus got this big idea, the only way he could prevent a second year of integration. He closed Little Rock's public high schools—even the all-black one, Horace Mann—leaving nearly 4,000 kids to fend for themselves. So strong was the segregationists' fear of black people that he and the city's leaders were willing to damage their own children.

Wait a minute. . . . If you don't have a high school, it dawned on them, you can't have a high school football team. To preserve one sacred way of life—racial separation—they would have to sacrifice another: Friday night football. They'd have to shut down the best team in America and its 33-game winning streak.

Wait another minute. . . . Who *said* you can't have a high school football team just because you don't have a high school? Canceling football, Faubus decreed, would be "a cruel and unnecessary blow to the children." O.K., then, everyone agreed: Play ball!

Sure, Buddy would tell the current team, it seemed like a blast, at first. Everyone kept figuring that sanity and school would be back in session any day. Central's teachers began delivering classes on TV, but few players bothered to watch. Most did worksheets for two correspondence courses offered by the University of Arkansas, then went to practice in the shadows of their ghost school.

They won their first two games ugly, stretching the streak to 35. Then the noose tightened. Their friends began melting away, snatching the final vacancies at schools 20, 40, 60 miles away or moving to relatives' homes far away to salvage their school year. Pressure mounted on the players. How could they walk out on each other and the Streak? But how long could they hold out?

On the eve of the city's day of reckoning—a public referendum on integration and the fate of their high schools—the Tigers traveled to the nest of their nemesis: Istrouma of Baton Rouge. Buddy and his boys will never forget that suffocating night on that gumbo of a field, rain-soaked and reeking with chicken-manure fertilizer. The first series, quarterback Fallon Davis sloshed right and threw an interception that was returned for a touchdown. In that flash, it seemed, all that the Tigers had lost finally registered. Their unforgettable coach, Wilson Matthews, had left before the season to take an assistant's job at Arkansas. Their depth had been eroded by the opening of a second whites-only school, Hall High. Their support—the bonfires, the pep rallies, the 16 busloads of fans that trailed them on road trips—was gone too. Istrouma humiliated Central 42–0 to end the streak.

Players dropped to the locker room floor, sobbing. As the team slunk back into town the next day, the people of Little Rock were voting nearly 3 to 1 to keep their minds and high schools closed.

The exodus began the following week. Tackle Bubba Crist approached coach Gene Hall alone, determined not to break down. Playing at Central was the finest thing in his life, but he couldn't bear the thought of redoing his senior year. He landed at a hastily opened private school with no football team, his scholarship chances gone, and ended up in a cardboard-box plant for 37 years, tearing up both knees pushing palettes, suffering three crushed vertebrae when stacks of boxes crashed on him, and so full of regret that he'd leave his football letters to gather dust in a closet even after his wife had them framed.

"Bullet" Bob Shepherd, Central's starting left halfback, departed. Josh McHughes, the backup who'd had a track scholarship to LSU dangled in front of him, if he could pare a few tenths of a second off his high hurdles time, went too, tears streaming as he took one last look around the stadium. At Mabelvale, the school he transferred to 10 miles away, three football players surrounded him and told him that Central big shots weren't welcome on their team. His athletic life and track scholarship dreams were done.

The Tigers got gut-punched at home by Fort Smith 19–6—their first in-state loss in seven years. The exodus became a mad scramble, 26 players departing the next week, most of them too stunned or ashamed to bid farewell . . . just disappearing. The opposite of integration wasn't segregation. It was disintegration.

The diehards, led by Buddy and fullback Steve Hathcote, dug in and won their last four games with subs and B-teamers before shriveling crowds. Davis, the senior quarterback who'd transferred, forsaking the town's dream assignment, watched the Thanksgiving finale from the stands, crying his eyes out.

The Tigers jumped and screamed when they won on that bitter-cold Thanksgiving to finish 8-3-1. "Then it hit us," running back Jack McClain would tell the kids. "What do we do now? No school, no practice, no games. Can somebody answer me? Coach Matthews? God? Where do I fit in this world?"

THERE WOULD be a hush in that cafeteria now. Sixty-seven teenagers wondering if the answer to those questions could be read in the furrows on those old faces . . . or if it was better not to lift their eyes and look.

Four members of the '58 team—Buddy, Hathcote, Rath and guard Ken Zini—would receive scholarships to Arkansas and make the jump in the middle of their twisted senior year, but none would be prepared academically or emotionally, and none would last more than three semesters.

Many of the others never got high school diplomas and never knew how to explain that on résumés or job applications.

They'd wince for the rest of their lives when people asked the most ordinary question: *Where you from? What high school did you go to?* "To have people look at you when you told them," Bubba Crist would say, "like you were damn hatin' heathens. . . ."

The turning point would come in '59, when segregationists on the school board fired 44 teachers at the closed high schools for suspected sympathies with Negroes. At last Little Rock had had enough. It held another referendum and purged the school board segregationists, which led to the reopening of schools the following September and the readmittance of a handful of African-Americans. By then Faubus had been reelected to a third term—to be followed by a fourth, fifth and sixth—and had finished No. 10 in a national poll to determine the Most Admired Men in the World.

The absurdity of it all avalanched on Hathcote years later when one of his daughters came home from the military with a black husband and began handing him biracial grandbabies. "Integration was jammed down our throats," he'd tell today's team. "It would've happened anyway if they'd just let it happen." He'd pause. "Then again . . . maybe it wouldn't have."

WHAT WOULD the old-timers have thought if they'd been there when the 2006 team photo was snapped? If they'd heard the black cornerback telling the darker special-teamer that he's so damn black that he'd show up in the photo as just a number and a black dot, telling the Korean-American he looked like a Mexican, then begging the Iranian's son not to go terrorist and blow the whole roster up. If they'd heard the blacks busting on the white kids for being crackers, and the crackers replying, "Don't make us hang you."

If they'd seen kids named Jahon and Andochini and Kalif and Myron and DeArius and Jim and Batuhan all running the same bleacher steps that they had run a half century ago, and Kevin Nichols, the African-American ringleader of all the racial jesting, asking Patrick Conley, the white tight end with the 4.3 GPA, "What's the square root of these bleachers?" and Patrick cracking back that black kids might know that if they didn't sleep through classes, and everyone huffing and guffawing.

What would the old-timers think if they returned to this cafeteria at lunch and felt little racial tension in a school that's just more than half black, but watched the students separate by habit to eat with kids of their own color, as three football players—Quadel Foreman, Genesis Cole and Bryant Miller—shuttled between the two groups, trying to build a bridge.

How would they respond when white wide receiver Will Carson said, "I don't know how you *could* be any good at football without black people." Imagine the conversation that could trigger about stereotypes and assumptions, how they can build barriers or be turned into humor to tear barriers down. And how often, on both sides, they're dead wrong.

The old Tigers? They might assume that today's Central High—its neighborhood wracked by poverty and one of the state's highest violent crime rates—couldn't be one of America's elite academic institutions. But *Newsweek* last year rated it the 20th-best high school in America.

The new Tigers? They'd assume that the fastest and strongest guys in the room would be theirs. But Bruce Fullerton's 10 flat in the 100-yard dash and Buddy Tackett's 520-pound deadlift would smoke 'em all. They'd assume that Gen. Edwin Walker was an integrationist. But he was arrested for sedition four years later as the ringleader of riots attempting to prevent a black man, James Meredith, from entering the University of Mississippi. Why, they'd even assume that they'd be seeing the old Tigers here again on September 25, when the world shows up on their front lawn for the big anniversary. But wrong again. No, some of their predecessors would tell them as they bid farewell. Too many years of feeling stereotyped, ignored, forgotten and stigmatized.

This get-together would be it, the only chance for 67 teenagers to hear the story. The one about how a bunch of old white guys, best damn football team in the United States, got an inkling of how it feels to be black.

———◆———

POSTSCRIPT: *On September 25, 2007, thousands gathered at the steps of Little Rock Central High to celebrate the students who integrated the Arkansas school 50 years earlier. Each of the nine pioneers spoke of his experiences, in 1957 and since, to an audience that included more than 200 of their former classmates and a handful of players from Central's preintegrated football team.*

The Bird Fell to Earth

For one fairy-tale year, Mark Fidrych swept the game off its feet.
He was fresh, quirky and the king of baseball. What was left when the
fairy tale ended? Exactly 121 acres of farmland.

T 5:50 A.M. THE ALARM CLOCK RINGS, AND THE
dream he has started having recently—the one in
which he keeps throwing strike after strike after
strike; no crowd, no cameras, no reporters, just he
and his body back in that sweet sweaty rut—comes to an end. Sasha, his
ancient black mutt, lifts her grizzled face from the single bed they share
and blinks.

He pulls on his long johns, tattered jeans, boots, red flannel jacket
and the blue denim jacket with four rips on the right sleeve, then plops
an old brown hat on his head of tangled hair. There are three puncture

172

marks on his right shoulder, a little wariness in his brown eyes and the faintest footprints of crow around his eyes, but the face is still young and the dirty blond curls still fall around it.

Yella, the half St. Bernard, half collie evicted from the single bed because of overcrowding, shakes himself down and falls into line behind his master and Sasha. They shuffle quietly past the room of his sleeping parents. "You stay," he orders Sasha. It's too cold for the old mutt, and she doesn't fight the order.

Out the kitchen door they walk into the flat gray dawn, his boots crunching old snow and frozen manure, the late February chill sneaking in through each hole in his sleeve. Ten years ago, almost to this very day, on a sunny morning in Lakeland, Fla., Mark Fidrych entered the dream year. Today he enters his beat-up blue Chevy pickup with Yella, pulls up to the back door of a restaurant called The Grille and muscles two garbage cans full of pig slop onto the truck bed.

He drives the scraps back to his farm, where there are 20 pigs, 12 cows, three sheep, two goats, six chickens and six geese. One of the baby pigs is dead, likely smothered in the litter's crush for their mother's milk. Mark Fidrych lifts it by the back legs and stretches it out on a steel barrel. "It's no skin off my butt," he says. "I just haven't buried it yet."

Mark pours the slop into a feeding box, flecks of tomato sauce spattering his boots, and watches the pigs bite and shove each other to get to the food. "I'm in love with my land," he says. "I got it all from playing ball. It gives me prestige. Someone says, 'What you got?' I say, 'One hundred and twenty-one acres of nice land.'"

So . . . he's a farmer now? "No," he says. "I'm not a farmer."

IT'S 8 A.M. Mark has the sure thing in his hands, the surest thing since a baseball and glove. "When you have a chain saw in your hands, there's nothin' that can hurt you," he says. "A chain saw goes through anything."

After baseball deserted him for good, in June 1983, his friends would often find him sitting on a woodpile on his farm, staring deep into nothing. "It's over, it's over, it's over" kept rolling in his head. "Why me? Why *me*?" Sometimes that question rose in his throat as rage, rage against something too large for a man's bare hands. So he would yank the starter on the chain saw and send its teeth into the closest and tallest piece of life he could find, leaning into the cut until he felt the wicked satisfaction of the tree's groan and crash, saying to himself, "See ya. Chop it down. Next tree. See ya. Chop it down. . . .'"

Once a tree was felled, he would reduce it to 16-inch logs and then, still working frantically, drive the splitting maul through the core. But it wasn't enough. "Why me?" was a question of *being*, and he lived in a country that had no time for that. "What do you do now?"—the question of *doing*—was the one Americans always asked, and he didn't know how to answer that. All he knew was that he *wasn't* a farmer.

Two years ago Mark and two buddies formed a three-man team for a wood-chopping contest in their little town of Northboro, Mass., and he got to splitting so frenetically he drove the wedge through his friend's arm, chipping a piece off the bone near the elbow, and then split two more logs before he realized what he had done. The competition was canceled.

Some days Mark would leave his chain saw and splitting wedge behind, walk into the woods and scream. Just after the dream year, he had looked down at his hands and told a reporter, "I've got a trade now. These hands are vital. I can't pour cement with these hands." Since leaving baseball, those hands had poured cement for swimming pools, cleared lots for new houses, fed pigs and chopped wood. He sold a pig or cow now and then, or a piece of land that he bought when he was playing ball. A few times a year, someone pays him to speak at a banquet. For six months last year he was a traveling liquor salesman, but the money and the necktie were no good, so he quit. He doesn't need much, just enough for the $6,000 in taxes on his mostly wooded farm, with a little left over for hamburger and beer money. And an answer for "What do you do now?"

So he sips his beer and talks of plans—to buy a bulldozer, a car mechanic's garage, a gas station, a car wash, a limousine service, a trucking company, or maybe he would become a truck driver, a real estate developer. . . . "A hundred and fifty ideas going on at once," says Mark Philbin, a friend, "I'll say, 'Slow down, *Mahk*. What are you talking about?'"

Mark was a country boy and maybe chopping wood and pouring pig slop on his own 121-acre farm was more than he ever would have asked for if a dump truck full of fame hadn't pulled up to his life, buried him in it and then left, letting the wind blow it all away. But the dilemma won't go away. "Why do I need big money?" he asks. "I make 18 to 20 thousand a year. You got a thousand dollars, you got a thousand problems. I've always been small. I just want to stay small."

Then a Miller Lite commercial flickers across the TV screen and he flings the back of his hand at the set and growls, "I could be doing one of those goddamn things, too."

This morning he has two big scratches on his neck from hacking at the brush on his land, clearing it for the house he plans to build. He is 31 and it is time he no longer lived with his parents.

TEN A.M. "Maybe the dream is a vibration that I should try to pitch again. There weren't no outside things in the dream, no score, no outcome. Just me, pitching. Just me, playing." He's back in the truck now, heading to Mike's Donut Shoppe in Northboro to get coffee for the three men helping him clear his land; Sasha and Yella are panting in the back. In the truck his mind wanders. Hell, ever since the doc opened up the right shoulder last summer, sewed up the two tears in the rotator cuff and chiseled down the end of the bone sticking up under his armpit, the wing has felt good again. Once more he can open car doors and drink beer with his right hand. He no longer tosses and turns Sasha awake at three in the morning from the pain. "I know I could get a major league hitter out now," he says. "I *know* it."

Damn, maybe it could be 1976 all over again. Remember that?

On an April day in Oakland, Ralph Houk, then manager of the Tigers, signaled to the bullpen. On the run, still half unzipped, shoving his shirt and cup into place came a gangly kid with curly blond hair bouncing over his ears, entering his first major league game.

He dropped to his knees and smoothed out all the little holes the other pitcher had left on the mound, like a little kid in his sandbox, lost in an imaginary world. When his infielders or outfielders made a good play, he ran to them to shake their hands in the middle of an inning. He did knee bends and squats on the mound, and when he set himself to pitch, he held the ball in front of him and appeared to talk to it. Of course, he was actually talking to himself, focusing on his task, but in 1976, when a children's game was becoming overrun with attaché-carrying shortstops and talk of holdouts and strikes and agents' percentages, who cared about details like that?

"Never in my 37 years of baseball have I seen a player like him, and never will I again," says the Tigers' president, Jim Campbell. "My gosh, I don't know why we don't see more people like Mark Fidrych. He was what he was. All natural. So hyper, so uninhibited. A minute after he came into my office he'd have one cheek of his butt on the corner of my desk. Before you knew it, he'd by *lying* on my desk, his head resting in one hand, the other hand gesturing in the air."

"The best young pitcher I've ever had in my career," says Houk.

A 10th-round pick by the Tigers in the '74 draft, Mark had stayed in a tent his first few days of Rookie League ball until management talked him into a motel. His fastball and slider were as naturally hyper as he, but his control, for a wild kid, was confounding. A minor league manager, assessing Fidrych's tall, gawky body, his plume of hair and free spirit, nicknamed him the Bird after the *Sesame Street* character Big Bird. The night the Tigers told him he was going north with the big team in '76, he smuggled a girl over the fence of their Lakeland complex, lay down on the mound with her and celebrated.

His salary was $16,500, he had no agent, and the guy in the upper deck didn't need four beers to gaze down at Fidrych and imagine he saw himself. On June 28, before 50,000 fans at Tiger Stadium and a *Monday Night Baseball* national audience, Fidrych pitched a seven-hit, 5–1 victory over the Yankees. The camera kept hopping from him—in apparent dialogue with the ball—to a fan in a yellow bird costume frolicking through the stands, and twice after the game, Mark had to make curtain calls for the mob that chanted "Bird! Bird! Bird!" and wouldn't leave.

"Our family, the whole town, felt part of it," says his sister, Carol Ann. Her eyes look off. "We had the best times going to his games. Ahhhh, the *best* times. About once a month I still go back and look at a video of highlights of him pitching that year. He was the happiest I've ever seen him. On the video you can see it—his face *glowed*."

He became the second rookie in history to start an All-Star Game, went 19–9 on a next-to-last-place team, led all major league starters in ERA (2.34), was voted Man of the Year by the National Association of Professional Baseball Leagues, and single-handedly boosted Tigers attendance by more than 400,000. Bird T-shirts, buttons and records appeared, helicopters bearing greetings to the Bird circled the stadium, and a resolution was introduced in the Michigan state legislature demanding that the Tigers raise his pay. The Twins delayed a game for nearly half an hour to funnel the huge crowd into one of his games. The Angels, afraid to disappoint a packed house when Fidrych missed a start, put him in a cage in their stadium concourse to sign autographs. Men who had spent their lives trying to become polished and sophisticated fought for position to get the signature and shake the hand of a man who had remained spontaneous and natural.

Maybe if he could have kept it small, if he could have risen off his knees from the dirt, thrown the hyper fastball by the batter and gone home, it could have lasted longer than a year. Maybe, in a country that was expert at turning the natural into the stale, it was better that it didn't. The day after the Monday night game, a man from the William Morris Agency in Manhattan called and soon was lining up commercials and appearances. Soon Mark was hiding in the stadium until near midnight, then dashing for his car, zigzagging to avoid fans leaping onto the hood. The parking lot and hallway of his apartment became so jammed with people that he had to move to another complex in the suburbs with a 24-hour security patrol. "He'd call me and tell me reporters were calling his hotel room at midnight the night before he had to pitch, that people were banging on his hotel door all day," recalls Stephen Pinkus, the William Morris agent. "'They're driving me nuts,' he'd say. 'Why?' I'd say. 'Because you're a star and that's what happens.' He didn't understand. He was completely out of his league. All he wanted to do was drink beer and listen to rock music and have fun."

The Tigers asked him to get rid of his two motorcycles. When he accepted a Thunderbird from the Ford Motor Company, a Detroit columnist wrote that Fidrych had lost his innocence. *Rolling Stone* published a story chronicling his sex life. Every day, no matter whether he pitched or not, a troop of reporters asked him for every detail of things that he had done unconsciously, gnawed on each particular until it stopped seeming natural at all. "I never thought all that would be part of it," he says. "As soon as people started writing about it, talking about it so much, you *think* about it."

The daydream in the truck has lasted too long. He pulls onto his farm, surveys the growing piles of cut brush with pleasure and calls the workers to their coffee.

"Hey," one of them asks through the steam from his cup, "we were wondering, Mahk, back when you played, how fast could you throw a ball?"

"In the 90s."

"Nineties, huh?"

Mark's eyes shift. "How much more you think you'll get to today?"

LUNCHTIME. CHET'S Diner. Thank God the blowhard isn't here, the one always talking about how he wants to make Mahk a pitchah again. Because if the blowhard were here Mahk would have to disappear inside himself or out the door, suddenly remembering an appointment, as if Mahk were the kind of guy who made *appointments*. Then he couldn't have sat and watched that pretty little black-haired bundle of laughter and efficiency, the waitress at Chet's, the Greek man's daughter, Ann, whom he is going to marry in October.

"Need a Chetbuhgah, a supah Deluxe with no tomatoes and a bread setup, sweetie," she calls to her mother at the grill. "Need a bowl o' chowdah, Dad. How ya doin", guys? Watcha want today? Onion ring-a-lings and a rootin'-tootin' beer?. . . . Dad, I said chowdah, not chili. Quick, quick, like a bunny. No, Mothah, no tomatoes on that buhgah. I know, sweetie, isn't life hahd?"

A biochemistry major who graduated from Fairfield University and then decided she'd rather get up at 4:30 every morning and work the diner with her folks, a 30-year-old woman, smart and strong, who went to Algonquin High in Northboro with him but barely even knew him then and never saw him throw a baseball—that's who Mark Fidrych needed. For three months, in a little town rampant with gossip peddlers, where everyone knew Mark and everyone knew Ann, no one in town knew about Mark *and* Ann. Mark cloaked their relationship in secrecy. As if he knew what other eyes might do to something sacred. "It's my thrill, just her and me," he says. "People don't understand. It's better when it's a secret, when no one knows."

There was another reason for the secret, too. As soon as everyone knew, it became a commitment. Commitments scare Mark. He could sit on a woodpile for weeks, but when he decided to chop, he chopped every bloody limb, human or hickory, that got in his way. He gave so much of himself he couldn't shrug and walk away if the commitment splintered. So he sat on a barstool or the back of the truck and talked about 150 jobs he *might* do, or, before Ann, ogled the three girls in tight sweaters he *might* ask out. The first girl he'd ever fallen for had left him, then a 2½-year relationship in Detroit had ended when the woman wouldn't go with him to the minor leagues, or to Northboro. That left the women who recognized him at the bars. "Of course I felt women only liked me because of baseball," he says. "It made me wonder if it was worth giving myself to any woman again. It's hard to be confident about showing feelings.

"Ann doesn't *know* me, that's probably why we get along so well. You don't understand. I committed myself once. I committed to baseball. . . ."

ONE-THIRTY P.M. Mark is honking and helloing to the guys in the duck-bill caps, waving and joking with the old women coming out of the shops. "What's up, Joe? How ya doin", Steve?" Driving past Pierce's Sunoco, where he used to pump gas, past Murray's Package Store, where they still have the picture of him in his Tiger uniform, past the empty lot where the Cut Off bar used to be before it was condemned, where he and the boys locked themselves into the little bathroom for wrestling matches or had competitions to see who could slide the farthest down the bar on his backside. Little town. Good town. Quiet and simple.

He arrives back at his land and finds the two surveyors, the ones he's paying to plot a road to the site where he will build his new house, taking a break to find batteries for their headsets.

"So we can communicate through the forest," explains one.

"Hell, what's wrong with yellin' and screamin'?" asks Mark.

What a world. He had wanted to be a car mechanic, back in the days when if you heard a car cough, you knew it was either the plugs or points or carburetor. But now the engines are computerized and the mechanics hook up blinking machines to them as if they're coronary patients, and Mark doesn't have the heart for it anymore. He had dreamed of owning land, and suddenly, at 22, he had enough to buy a piece you could fit a couple dozen ballfields on, cash on the barrelhead—no loans or interest payments. He wanted to keep life simple. Then came tax time and the accountant looked at him as if he was a lost little boy: 121 acres of pine and birch and not a single stick of *shelter.*

Pinball used to be good, too. "Five balls for a quahtah, and it didn't take that many points to win a free game," he says. "Then it became three balls for a quahtah and you needed a million points. Then came Pac-Man and all that crap. Do good and you only get to put your initials next to your score. It ain't what it used to be. Nothin' in life matches up to anything."

God knows, he tried to keep it simple. He turned down the back-slapping jobs he could have had in Detroit and returned to the little town to stay near the dirt and wear torn jeans that showed his underwear. People marveled at the way he still rolled on the ground with dogs and kids. But then he had to shake himself off and get vertical, and the only place verticality had ever meant simplicity was on a hill of dirt, 60' 6" from a batter. "Baseball stayed the same," he says. "Three outs an inning, nine innings and the game's over. I remember Alleycat Johnson, a guy who was my teammate in the minor leagues, telling me, 'You know, Mahk, when you're on that mound, you're a master, a scientist. But when you walk off it, you're crazy; no one knows what you'll do. You've got a million-dollar arm and a 10-cent mind.' " He laughs, then pauses. "He was right. I've never found another place as comfortable as a mound. *Never.*"

The simple life was gone, and every time he returned to Detroit and the baggage handlers ran for his luggage and the Avis folks tried harder, he wondered if he should surrender to it, exploit it. He did promotional work for an auto-parts company long enough to get a bellyful of small talk and a pocketful of business cards, then moved on. He interviewed with a Detroit TV station last summer to do sports commentaries but lost interest when he realized he would have to move there. He did some color commentary for the Tigers' cable TV network in '84 and received no offer to continue working there. "He'd say *anything* on the air," recalls Bill Freehan, the ex-Tiger catcher who also did commentary for the network. "He'd yell, 'That pitch was a hooo-rah!' and the guy on the air with him would say, 'Huh?' He'd be talking when it was time to cut to a commercial, and the director would be tapping him on the shoulder, and Mark wouldn't understand what he wanted. But I love the guy."

He went to New York three times in 1984 to do casting tapes for Miller Lite, auditioning for a commercial in which he talked to a ball at a bar, and froze when the camera rolled and he had to read the cue card. Reading still troubles him. "I've boycotted books," he says. Finally, after 80 takes, he was told the commercial would run during the '84 World

Series. It never aired, and no one else called. The reason corporate America loved him when he pitched—he was natural, unsophisticated, *real*—was the same reason it shunned him when he couldn't pitch.

"Maybe if he'd lasted a few more years. . ." says Bob Wolff, his former agent. "I've been able to do a lot of things for a lot of athletes, but I've never come up with an answer for one when the people start asking. 'Who did you *used* to be?' "

"Hey, let's take a plane ride to Michigan," says Mark, kicking his boot at the snow. "They recognize you like it was yesterday. That's a plus in my atmosphere, right? Why didn't they just tell me I'm not good enough to do a commercial? What in hell's wrong with showing me cutting wood and drinking a Miller Lite or a Coke?"

He remembers that he doesn't want that anyway, that he opted for the simple, uncluttered life. "It's no skin off my butt," he says. Pinkus, Mark's agent at the height of his popularity, estimates that the dream year grossed his former client $125,000 in off-the-field money. If it had happened 10 years later, when the American marketing machine was greased and waxed?

"You say he's not working a regular job now?" says Pinkus. "Maybe I could make him a sports announcer or something, pull some strings. Honey, bring me Fidrych's phone number—excuse me, I was talking to my secretary. I have the most extensive Rolodex in the country, got Ronald Reagan's number when he was president of the Screen Actors Guild. What do you mean, it's not there? How could you not have Fidrych in my Rolodex?"

DUSK. WORK is done. Mark enters through the kitchen door, past the unused living room where the furniture is covered with sheets and all the plaques and trophies from his career rest in darkness. In the attic and cellar are cardboard boxes full of the stuffed birds that fans besieged him with in '76. Sometimes his dad, Paul, as assistant principal of an elementary school in Worcester who's nearing retirement, intercepts him just after he's showered off the farm dirt, just before he bolts out the door again.

"What did you do today, Mahk?"

"Nothin'. "

"Where you goin'?"

"Out."

"I'll ask him what he's going to do with his life, and he'll say, 'Don't worry about it,' but I do," says his father. "If I mention to him, 'Spring training opened today,' he'll just say, 'Yep.' He doesn't want to hear it from me."

It all started with Paul Fidrych, a superb athlete whose dream and thigh bone snapped one day when he was playing football in high school. Rather than talk of what he was or could have been, Paul spent hours hitting ground balls and popups, squatting like a catcher for his only son, quietly feeding the dream to him. He coached Mark's team in Little League and Babe Ruth, and during the hush when his son stood at the foul line in a high school basketball game, you could hear Paul Fidrych holler, "Concentrate, Mahk, *concentrate!*"

With a baseball in his hand, or a snowball or a rock, Mark could. In a classroom his mind roamed, his fingers and feet fidgeted, the words on the page blurred. He flunked first grade, then flunked second. A few friends taunted him, but most just moved on to the next grade and forgot him. Tall for his age, he towered over classmates two years younger, and when he dominated them at recess, it only made things worse. Patiently his dad tried to tutor him, but the words kept dancing and the boy knew he was disappointing everyone. He remembers his Aunt Nel, back then, telling him that he should go into the woods and scream if he felt real bad. He thought she was crazy back then.

Everyone in town thought Mark was just a wild, fun-loving, floppy-haired hyper kid when he'd do 360s in his sister's car on the frozen pond or lie on his back on a barroom dance floor and wriggle. "Sometimes," he says, "I'd think, 'Why live?' "

His father wanted him to go to college. Mark wanted to do oil changes at Pierce's Sunoco. For his dad, he would do almost anything. His first Scholastic Aptitude Test score was too low for college entrance, so he gave his ID card to a buddy who offered to pinch-hit for the second try. The difference was so dramatic that the SAT board notified him he was a cheater.

Suddenly, miraculously, came the call from the Detroit Tigers, and Mark didn't need the car on the pond to feel himself spin. "All of sudden I had guys behind me who could field; I just threw strikes and let the other team hit ground balls," he says. "All of a sudden people actually wanted to hear what *I* had to say!"

After two years in the minors, the dream year came. His father shuttled to and from Detroit to watch his boy pitch.

By the end of the year, Mark was asking a doctor for something to calm his nerves. "Next year I hope a kid comes along that does better than me," he said then. "Then they'll leave me alone."

A few months later, in March of '77, a fly ball arced toward him and Rusty Staub in the Lakeland outfield.

"You want this one, Rusty?"

"No, kid. You take it."

Exuberantly—how else?—he streaked beneath the towering fly ball. His left knee popped, tearing cartilage. He cried in his hospital bed as security guards kept overwrought fans away. SPORTS ILLUSTRATED decided not to run his picture on the cover of its baseball issue that year. "What kinda horsebleep's that?" he said. "So I got hurt. I ain't dead. I'll never talk to those bastards again. People using me, man. I'm sick of people using me."

Ten days after the returned from the disabled list, his right shoulder popped. He went 6-4 that season, plagued by arm pain, and the dream was gone. In his rage he broke the washer and dryer in the Tigers laundry room, then, stricken with remorse, fell to his knees and fixed them.

Nobody knew what caused the crippling pain, but many suspected it was Mark's overeagerness to be a star pitcher again, that he'd begun throwing too hard too soon after he had injured the knee.

Most of the next six years were spent in the minors. He tried doctors, osteopaths, chiropractors, hypnotists and psychologists. He gulped aspirin and anti-inflammation pills. Fans called and wrote in with miracle cures, suggesting that he stick the troubled arm into a swarm of bees or pack it in red Florida clay. An old man with arthritis-swollen knuckles drove to Northboro from New Jersey to give him some red gook that smelled like kerosene. All the old guy wanted was for Fidrych to sign a contract guaranteeing him 10% of his salary once Mark was healed. He signed the contract, but the stuff only made the shoulder stink as well as hurt.

One night in June 1983, a lonely man with a 2–5 record and a 9.68 ERA called his father from Norfolk, Va. "I'm done, Dad," Mark said. "They've let me go. Thanks for everything you've taught me, but I've got to get out of this game. I did it for you."

"I still think you've got it in you, Mahk," said his dad.

"No, Dad."

"Don't give up this easy. You've got to look in the mirror."

"Dad, I've been looking in the mirror for the last six years."

Sometimes, when Paul Fidrych is watching a ball game these days, he still feels the emotion rising up into his larynx. "I wish he would try it again," he says. "I find myself wondering how far he could have gone. I don't want that question in his mind, the way it's always been in mine since I broke my leg. I think he could do it; he has the desire. Did you see him cut wood today?

"Once in a while he'll be sitting here watching a game and he'll say, 'I had 29 major league victories, that's not too bad,' and I'll say, 'Yeah, Mahk, that's not too bad.' But you know something? Jim Palmer stole the Cy Young Award from Mahk that year. He stole it. The Gold Glove, too—Mahk had *no* errors.

"Listen, I'm going to give you a name: *Charles Grogan.* He's got the same determination Mahk used to have, never gets tired of practicing. He's big and strong, same way Mahk used to be. He's only eight years old. He's my grandson."

EIGHT P.M. A deep quiet grips the little town. Inside a bar Mark begins to methodically drink beer and to weigh his options.

Maybe settling down and getting married to Ann will help. "This commitment will last," he says. "You can be married and have a sore arm, right? But what if the Kansas City Royals call tomorrow and say they need a pitching coach? I still got it in my blood."

Maybe Mark should try to pitch again. "My arm has felt fine since the surgery. The doc finding all those things wrong inside was the best relief of my life. Now I know my problems weren't in my head. I haven't thrown a baseball since, only a snowball. Maybe that dream means I should just play in the Stan Musial League around here and see how it feels. I won't count baseball out. I won't."

Maybe Mark shouldn't try to pitch again. "I'd lose a full five months of my life getting in shape. I don't want to be that dedicated again. What if I say I'll play in the Musical League and I can't make it to a game or enough guys don't show up to play? I can't screw around in life anymore."

Maybe Mark should have children. "The best thing I loved about playing ball was seeing a little kid's happy face. Yeah, I want kids. But sometimes I feel I wouldn't want to bring a kid into this world. The poor kid. . . . It was so hard for me."

He rises to leave. "Ten years," he says. "It's hard to believe. I got no regrets. I'd do it like that all again. You know, I still get fan mail. I wait a week before I answer it, so it builds up. It sounds crazy but it makes me feel more important. Please, just end this story by saying thank you to the people. Thank you to our society."

He walks out of the bar It's 11 p.m. Early for a 21-year-old icon, late for a 31-year-old pig farmer.

POSTSCRIPT: *Mark Fidrych wears the same long, blond hair and still lives in the same farmhouse in Northboro, Mass., with his wife, Ann, and daughter, Jessica. There's a standing offer at nearby Worcester State to become the team's pitching coach (it's the alma mater of his father and his daughter), but Fidrych says he's strictly a "5-to-whenever" guy these days, driving his 10-wheeler in the early morning and maintaining his farm, where he's now having vegetables planted. He's still listed in the local phone book.*

Running for Their Lives

Thanks to a selfless coach, the sons of Mexican migrants in a dirt-poor California town turned their backs on drugs and gangs and built an athletic dynasty. So how could he leave them? And what would they do without him?

THERE WAS SILENCE WHEN THE FOOTRACE ENDED. Then Ayon threw his arms around the coach's wife and cried, "Why did God do this? I don't know why God did this!" and the boys in red and white each staggered off alone to cry.

They had failed the most successful coach in California schoolboy history. They'd failed the elders who'd walked at their heels to the starting line, reminding them that they had to win the state championship for Mr. White. They'd fallen apart on the old man's last day as a coach, they'd spit on his dynasty and ministry both. *Sixth place.*

Mr. White's wife went to dry their tears. But then she and the elders began crying too, and it was hopeless. No high school sports program in California had ever done what theirs had—won nine state titles—but it had been this team's duty to send Mr. White into the sunset with the untouchable number, the fitting number, the perfect number: 10.

One by one, that autumn day a year and a half ago, the Mexican-American boys awaited their chance to speak to the white man alone. To say, "I'm sorry, Blanco. I'm sorry for letting you down."

Except one.

EIGHT MONTHS passed. Evening fell on the heat-slugged little town. Laundry sagged from plastic lines like skin from the brown dogs' ribs. Workers, home from a long day of picking grapes, sat inside their stucco box houses as if stoned by the sun. Chickens in their front yards gave up pecking at the bare earth. Not a peep came through the doors of El Cha Cha Cha.

Wait. Something just stirred on the southwest edge of town. A plume of dust, out in the almond groves. A herd of brown boys kicking up powder on a dirt road.

A bicycle nipped at their heels. It accelerated if they slackened and made them raise dust again. It moved up onto their flank to protect them against the farm dogs' fangs. It dropped back to round up stragglers. Jim White thought he had passed the torch to his faithful assistant, Amador Ayon, thought he had retired and begun to fade away. But his town and his wife and his gut hadn't let him, so here he was at 62, weeks before the 2003–04 school year and cross-country season began, sheepdogging his flock through 100° heat, chasing state title number 10. Again.

He rose from the seat of the bike and pumped harder, exchanging nods and words as he passed Julio and Baltazar and Octavio and Steven, both Tonys and both Juans, all the boys who'd hoped with all their hearts that the sun wouldn't set on them, that the town's patriarch wouldn't retire during their four years at McFarland High . . . that they wouldn't end up sitting inside those stucco box houses at night for the rest of their lives, dazed by fieldwork and sun.

What were the odds that Ayon or anyone else could take over and keep this magic dust cloud moving? What were the odds that in the annals of California high school sports—all the years chocked with big-city phenoms and rugged valley boys and wealthy suburban programs—the greatest dynasty would be produced by a band of 5½-foot Mexican-Americans at a little high school in a town with no traffic light or movie theater, one of the poorest communities in America? That year after year a blue-eyed man on a bicycle could compel another bunch of teenage campesinos to run eight miles across the fields and orchards where they'd already worked all day harvesting oranges and grapes and almonds and peaches and plums? Every evening? In their *off*-season?

Mr. White tucked his bike behind the front-runner, the fastest one, the unlikeliest leader he'd ever had. The boy who wished that Mr. White had just packed up and left to live his last years in his cabin an hour away in the Sierra Mountains, as he'd planned.

The man and the boy kept pumping their knees. They were both striving for more than number 10, both straining against all the invisible strings that bound them to McFarland. Both struggling to find their way out.

Mr. White drew closer. "Good work, Javi," he murmured.

Javier Medina didn't lift his eyes. He turned his shoulder to his town's legend.

IT DIDN'T seem like a hard town to leave. Most people left before realizing they'd ever entered, barreling through the Central Valley three hours north of Los Angeles along Highway 99, a strip of asphalt that separated McFarland's poor West Side from its poorer East Side. The white descendants of the Dust Bowl refugees who had founded the town had no trouble abandoning it in the 1960s and '70s to Mexican immigrants weary of wandering from town to town, crop to crop. McFarland's movie theater became a mortuary, its newspaper was long gone, and all the bars but El Cha Cha Cha were boarded up. The town had two places to go to jail and nine places to go to eat. The population was 9,600 if you didn't count a couple of thousand illegals and the 1,100 behind bars. McFarland was renowned chiefly for its high incidence of cancer, which had afflicted one of Mr. White's nephews and more than 20 other children between the mid-'70s and mid-'90s and scared visiting teams into bringing their own water.

Mr. White loved McFarland.

He arrived in 1964 fresh from college in L.A., took a fifth-grade teaching job and jumped in with both feet, making sure his yard, too, had chickens and rabbits scratching at it. He wanted to get to know people. He wanted small. He came from a family of missionaries but had fallen in love with sports: Here was his chance to merge duty with passion. He began coaching every school and rec team he could, basketball and baseball and football and track, and when little boys knocked on his front door asking if he'd come out to play tag or ball, he'd say *sure*.

So what if the town turned brown before his very eyes? In college he'd chosen a roommate who was half Mexican, half Native American. So what if Mr. White had never been a runner? The local runts he wanted to coach in cross-country hadn't a prayer on a basketball court or a football field— endurance and slow-twitch muscles were their genetic gifts—and for all his compassion, he needed to win. So what if he had to wait 17 years to get a coaching job at the high school? He'd grown up in a dozen houses in Stockton, moving as swiftly as his father could build a new one and sell the old, and he longed for roots the same way that the weary migrants around him did. Four decades after Jim and Cheryl White arrived in McFarland, the town would be 99.9% Mexican, and that—as their three long-since-departed daughters like to say—was only because Mr. and Mrs. White stayed.

Blanco, his runners often called him. English was their second language, one that bedeviled them in the classroom and kept most of them out of college. Most went to the fields when they reached puberty, stooping and snipping, climbing and crawling and duckwalking through irrigation puddles to supplement their parents' pitiful wages. No one could figure it out, how the runners with the shortest legs and the grimmest lives began winning everything once Blanco took over their program, in 1980. He'd joke that it was the town's notorious water or the beans that McFarland's mamas served. He persuaded the boys that it was the "voodoo juice" oil he'd give them before races to rub on their aching backs and legs, the cleansing teas and the shakes full of complex carbohydrates and the gel capsules full of vitamin E and bee pollen that he'd dole out. But the secret was his vast investment of time and heart.

He'd grip the rawhide hands of the boys' fathers and look in their eyes, convince them that something beyond food, clothing and shelter mattered, that this silly Anglo notion of high school athletics had meaning. He'd fetch their sons in a battered '59 pickup that had been a forest ranger's truck, two lucky lads up front drinking in his stories and 16 crammed in the back where they could keep an eye on the road through the rotting floorboards. He'd haul them into the foothills to run the orange groves. He'd take them to collect old bottles or newspapers, to sell tamales, to hoe cotton fields—*Mexican golf*, the locals called it—raising funds so they could compete all across California.

He'd take them where their own fathers hadn't the energy or money to take them—bowling lanes and Putt-Putt courses and movie theaters in Bakersfield, a half hour away—and farther, much farther, to do things many Mexican boys in McFarland had never done. To set eyes on the ocean, to stay in a hotel, to sleep under a white man's roof and sing *Ging Gang Goolie* on a 12-hour road trip. To camp at Yosemite and run five miles at sunrise to fish for trout at a lake, then run five back to cook it and roast marshmallows over a fire. To fly in an airplane, as the program grew, to run in New York City and Charlotte, even Germany and China. To see that the flat farmland starting at the edge of town didn't go forever, needn't swallow them if they could just master themselves, just do the simplest, hardest thing: lay one sneaker in front of the other again and again.

He never had a son. He had hundreds of sons. He'd take his runners to the doctor, visit their mothers in hospitals and their brothers in jails. He'd help them study, drive them to college, pay their tuition, feed and clothe them, go to court with them and to the wall for them even when, long after graduation, they strayed off the path. "I need you to come back and run with us, buddy," he'd tell fleshy 25-year-olds through prison bars. Cheryl, who'd grown up watching her mother, a minister's wife, do such things for her husband's Church of Christ congregations, showered the boys with homemade cookies and hugs, heart-to-heart lunches and handwritten notes signed "Mrs. Coach." Mr. White, following the calling of his cousins and uncles, had served as a minister in his church in McFarland; his sister and an uncle had served missions overseas: He knew no other way to run a team.

He rarely raised his voice. He'd stumbled upon the sorcerer's stone of coaching: Give so much of yourself that your boys can't bear to let you down. They won the first state cross-country championship held in California, in 1987, and their town gussied them up in foam antlers and had them pull Mr. White through the streets, scrunched in a red Flyer wagon and wearing a Santa hat. They won 22 of 24 league titles and 15 sectional championships, beating schools with enrollments seven times as large as theirs. The first 15 years that California held championships, they won nine, all in Divisions III and IV, but some years they likely would've taken the whole tamale against the megaschools in Divisions I and II as well, if only they'd gotten the chance. They became McFarland's treasure, their ranks swelling each year as graduates circled back to push them and chide them and mentor them, to chorus Mr. White's wisdom to the next wave. They became so much like a family that one day even Javier Medina decided that he wanted in.

Something takes a part of me.
Something lost and never seen.
Every time I start to believe,
Something's raped and taken from me.

JAVIER LAY in his bedroom, listening to Korn howl the lyrics to *Freak on a Leash*. He was in eighth grade. It was 1999. He was teetering. His sister, Corina, had already tumbled into drugs and darkness, tattooing her wrists with SURENAS LOCAS—Crazy Southerners, the female subset of a McFarland gang. Their father kept vanishing, into jail for half a year for hitting Corina, or God knows where for months on end after drinking and raging and being thrown out of the house by Javi's mother.

Javi cranked the music—*Sometimes I cannot take this place/Sometimes it's my life I can't taste/Sometimes I cannot feel my face*—and put on his game face. It wasn't easy. His eyelashes were too long, his eyes too soulful, his stack of books too high for punkhood. He yanked on his blue Korn T-shirt, grabbed the notebook that he'd driven a screw into and headed to school, late again.

He had tried to honor his favorite anarchy-rock band by ducking into the locker room during Mr. White's gym class at McFarland Middle School and sandpapering KORN onto the brand-new lockers. It had nearly gotten him expelled and—as he tried to talk his way out of it—into perhaps deeper trouble still. *"I'm going to run for Mr. White one day,"* he'd blurted to the startled vice principal, one of White's assistant coaches and former runners, David Diaz.

Even Mr. White snorted when he heard that one. *Javi?* The smart aleck who'd flunked Mr. White's phys-ed class because he refused to suit up, suddenly grunting out 10 half-mile repeats straight uphill at a 2:45 clip? *Yeah, right.* The sulker with the 0.9 grade-point average in seventh grade, the school's Snail Award winner for most days tardy, setting his alarm clock for 6 a.m. to run along the irrigation canals? *Sure.* The younger brother of Salvador Jr., who had smart-mouthed and drag-assed his way through high school while running for Blanco just a few years before? Mr. White's life's work was retrieval, salvage, salvation and so, of course, he'd give Javi a shot, but. . . .

Javi went home, lay in bed and, for the third time, read *Banner in the Sky*, a book about a fatherless boy who climbs a mountain that no one believed could be climbed. Javi went outside as darkness fell and lay in the back of his father's pickup truck, staring at the sky while his dad sat in a plastic chair nearby and drank beer in silence.

They couldn't talk. Salvador Sr. spoke Spanish, insistent on remaining Mexican. Javi spoke English, determined to be American. Each was too stubborn to speak the words he knew in the other's tongue. When Salvador, a third-grade dropout who didn't read or write, saw his son disappear behind another book, he'd bark, "Go out and play! You'll hurt your eyes!" He had smuggled himself into the U.S. twice as a teenager, the first time beneath the hood of a pickup truck, the second, for keeps, in a footrace with the border patrol, one of 25 desperate men who darted across the desert. Only two had made it. He believed in work, not words, but he wouldn't let Javi work with him in the grape or rose fields, denied him his share of McFarland's bitter drink. "You're too soft," Salvador said. On summer mornings Javi would watch his older brother and the other boys in town climb into pickups and head off for the fields with their fathers; then he'd return to his books and his bedroom.

Salvador crushed his beer can and rattled it into the bucket of empties. Before the *snap* of the day's first pop-top, he'd vacuum and mop the house and wash every dirty dish, and when he went on errands he couldn't pass a stranger stranded on the road without stopping to help. That was the man Javi loved. Some days he would hide his father's beers in a kitchen cabinet. Others, he was so hungry for approval that he'd be the first to his feet to fetch Dad another cold one. Korn was correct: Life was pathetic.

Salvador sipped and stabbed a callused finger at the stars. "Los Siete Osos," he murmured. The Seven Bears. Javi nodded. Salvador pointed and murmured again. "El Camino de San Diego." The Road to San Diego—the swath of stars that Mexicans on foot followed at night on their way to San Diego, America, hope. Javi nodded again. Those constellations, these moments beneath the night sky, were what he and his father had. When adults asked what he'd like to be when he grew up, Javi had begun to say the most astonishing thing for a McFarland boy: an astronomer.

But how could he reach the stars from a town like his? Just one man there had stretched that far: the tall, handsome white man bicycling down the road, herding his family every single day. Something about Mr. White's steadiness, his resolute pursuit of the highest goals, struck Javi even as he defied the man in gym class. Maybe, too, it was the twinkle in Blanco's eyes as he mangled Spanish, the silly dances he'd do and the pranks he'd play, smuggling cookies into a teacher's purse and then clucking in disbelief over her gluttony, or crooning "Jose can you see . . . any bedbugs on me?" to every Jose in town. Somehow, Blanco was both a remorseless taskmaster and a big, goofy kid—and one of the few gringo teachers who didn't commute from Bakersfield, who'd lived among McFarland's Mexicans for nearly four decades, showing them the surest way out of town . . . but never taking it.

Javi showed up one day at a rec department cross-country practice directed by one of Mr. White's former runners, a proving ground for prospects. *I'm going to show Mr. White something he won't believe*, Javi told himself. He gasped and quit running and had to walk to the finish. But he came back for the next practice and the next, and by the end of eighth grade—*too soft, huh?*—he had run faster than anyone believed a boy with a chip on his shoulder could: a 4:55 mile!

He joined the fleet trying to stay in front of Mr. White's front tire. He muttered an obscenity during a team outing, and Mrs. White walked him off alone and said, "Oh, no, no, no, not in this family." He apologized, and his life began to fall into a groove. "Running bolts my head on," he'd explain. "I know who I am by running. It puts me into reality, so I don't float off into space. I forget my problems. I say, 'I run for McFarland,' and people are like, 'Wowww!' Deep down I want people to think of me as part of something, even though I pretend that none of that matters. Jeez, man, without this program, I'd have no personality, I'd be . . . nothing."

He made his first true friends, a brotherhood of sweat and pain with runners Juan Gonzalez and Steven Cavazos. He loved bumping fists before and after each practice with his teammates and all of Mr. White's former runners, *los veteranos* who still trained with the team and became a battalion of big brothers to Javi. He loved arriving at meets on the bus and watching the other schools' runners' heads swivel and their eyes cloud and lips move: *McFarland's here.* He loved closing ranks for the team prayer and feeling his stomach knot at the sight of taller, wealthier boys on the starting line. "They're all white," a new kid on the team would sometimes say, and Mr. White would reply, "Yep . . . and they're all bigger. But I guarantee you they aren't as tough and don't work as hard as you do. Let's go take them down."

Mr. White was right. State title number 8 came in Javi's freshman year, when he ran with the frosh-soph team. *Omniscient* wasn't a word he'd toss around with the guys, but that was the word, he decided, for Mr. White. Just follow him, Javi told himself, and good things will happen. He followed Mr. White across the country, felt the thunder of Niagara Falls on a running trip, looked down on a cloud from atop the Golden Gate Bridge, saw water at Lake Tahoe that was bluer than any in a dream . . . and began to fix his eyes on college *somewhere else.* He scratched his way to No. 5 varsity runner in his sophomore year on a team that, midway through the season, clawed all the way to the No. 1 ranking in the nation among small schools and to No. 4 overall. Anyone who came to the races could see that Javi wasn't too soft to work in the fields, could see his grit as he rubbed out opponents in the last quarter mile . . . anyone at all. But his father never came.

"Oh, how your father brags of your achievements to his relatives," Javi's mother, Sylvia, would tell her son. But never a word from Salvador to Javi, even when his sophomore season ended with the ultimate ascent, up the ladder with his teammates as their names were painted in white letters on the ninth black silhouette of California on the school gym's outer wall, the display that opponents gaped at when they visited cross-country's Mecca.

Of course, the Snail still crept in late for some practices, skipped some and moped through others. Javi still was a boy missing something, one who could get lost searching for it in the spaces inside his head. He remembered to get his eyebrow and ear pierced and his hair dyed blond, but he forgot to bring his running gear to a meet. An excellent idea, he thought it was, to sign the Whites' guest book JAVI BAD A** in gangsta graffiti bubble lettering. Then he had to Wite-Out the words to remove the red from Mr. and Mrs. White's eyes. That was Javi. Ten years from now, a *veterano* wondered aloud, would Javi be in astrophysics . . . or in jail?

Mr. White was the weight that could tip the balance. Javi would do almost anything to please that man. He'd set up tables and sell concessions at rec department races to raise funds for the McFarland program, slice fruit for the peewee runners and act as their rabbit to improve their times. His grade-point average rocketed to 3.5 his first semester in high school, then to 4.0, then 4.17. He affixed the watch Mr. White gave him to his bedroom wall—he couldn't risk wearing it on his wrist. He taped Mr. White's photograph amid the pictures of planets that orbited his room.

One day late in his sophomore year, the planets moved, the solar system shifted. Javi heard the rumor: *Mr. White's leaving.*

HOW DO you leave a place where you've taught and coached and loved for 38 years? How do you tell a couple of dozen Mexican boys that it's time to give your children's children what you didn't have time to give your own children: *you.* How do you tell teenagers what you owe your wife after four decades of flying out the door at dawn and trudging back in as she falls asleep? How do you explain to field hands' sons that you've worked so many years that your annual retirement pay would total 96% of what you'd get if you kept working . . . that you're human, not a saint?

You don't. You don't explain. You don't call a team meeting and make a big wet fuss over this being your last year and how much they've all meant to you. Not when you're Mr. White, and your life leans on actions rather than words. Not when the words might stick in your throat. You just take aside your trusty disciple Ayon and tell him that you're going to start pulling back and letting him emerge as the leader during this transition year, because that's your goal: to pass the torch without extinguishing the flame.

The rumor festered. The family gathered, as always, at Mr. White's home for their evening runs that summer of 2002. Javi peered at the dark windows of Blanco's weather-beaten stucco box house. Where was he? Off in Texas or Long Beach visiting his daughters, Ayon would say. Off at his new cabin up in the mountains, building the wraparound deck of his wife's dreams. He'll be back to coach this year, don't worry about what happens after that, and c'mon, now, guys, let's pick it up.

Javi slogged toward the almond groves. Who had sat all the boys down beneath the orange trees and, in the dulcet voice of a pastor, reminded them over and over how important it was, every day, to show up? Who had said he'd always be there for them?

Every time I start to believe. . . .

Somehow it didn't seem so urgent anymore to throw one foot in front of the other. Somehow, as summer ground on and no one knew when to expect the coach, it no longer seemed imperative to show up. Mr. White would act as if nothing was wrong, no big deal, when he did appear, full of pleasantries and wisecracks—as unaware of the effect on Javi of his looming departure, it seemed, as Javi's dad had appeared to be all those times he'd left.

But Javi couldn't confront Mr. White any more than he could his father, and so he began to do things that seemed to have nothing to do with the hurt. He began staying up late, emptying a few beer cans of his own and drifting into practice late because he was walking a girl home from school, kissing off Mr. White's age-old warning that nothing would pull a butterfly back to the caterpillar pile faster than a girlfriend. He didn't need Mr. White's voodoo juice before races anymore. He'd hear the other runners beg Mr. White to change his mind about retiring, but Javi wouldn't do it. *If someone wants to leave,* he kept thinking, *then I don't need him.* It wasn't easy being the one who saw through the armor of the town's white knight. But Javi had gone it alone before, and dammit, his second father wasn't going to lay a finger on the wound left by his first.

The Whites felt him slipping through their fingers but kept giving him another chance. They were old pros at this, at rescuing runners who'd dropped out or impregnated girlfriends or slept on plastic lounge chairs because their parents couldn't afford a bed. But Javi was different from the other lost boys, more intelligent, more sensitive, more perplexing . . . always just out of Mr. White's reach. His long eyelashes would flutter and his face contort for a half minute before he'd reply to the simplest query, agonizing over how much to drop his guard.

Mrs. White took him out to lunch for one of her heart-to-hearts, but only one heart was put on the table. Mr. White went to Javi's house to talk to Javi's father but couldn't penetrate the beer and language barriers. He tried teasing Javi back into the fold, then tightening the screws. "Look, everyone, we have a new kid running with us today," he'd say when Javi showed up after a few days' absence. "Got your brain on today, Javi?" None of it worked, none of it could, because Javi was waiting for the man to show his feelings, not his needle.

More than for their town or their school, the boys had always run for Mr. White, a tie so strong that it bordered on dependency. Now that rope began to unravel. The team split into cliques. The boys yo-yoed. One day they would speed up, at *los veteranos'* insistence: It was Blanco's final year! The next they'd crawl: It was Blanco's final year. Yet by sheer force of habit McFarland ran well enough, as the state championships approached, to be favored to win number 10—and a fourth straight crown.

Javi, who had become the team's No. 2 runner, could see it in *los veteranos'* eyes: He'd be marked in his town forever if he failed. It jabbed at his sleep like the bedsprings coming through his mattress. The day before the state meet, Mr. White opened *The Bakersfield Californian*'s sports page and shuddered. *What?*

"We realize that second place is just not going to happen," said Javi in the article. "We're going to win, and that's it. We're not competing against other teams. We're competing against ourselves and trying to get a personal record." Javi had turned his terror inside out.

Ayon pulled the boy aside, aghast. "No McFarland runner," he growled, "has ever been as blunt as you." Silence filled the team van on the ride to Fresno that gloomy Saturday. Thirty former McFarland runners awaited the boys at Woodward Park, reminding them of their obligation to Blanco even as they braced at the starting line. The gun sounded, and the alumni took off as if it were their race, crunching through the dead leaves outside the ropes to keep a bead on the boys.

It was too much cargo to bear. Javi crossed the line in 16:41, 23 seconds slower than his best time on the five-kilometer course he'd run so many times. McFarland's top five runners ran their worst races of the year, and the team's sixth-place finish was its worst ever in a state meet. The boys were still weeping into their mashed potatoes at a buffet an hour later, still sobbing when they stumbled out of the van back in McFarland. Javi went straight to his bedroom and wouldn't come out.

The boys trudged into the team banquet two months later as if they weren't good enough for the tuxedos Mr. White had rented for them.

Blanco apologized to the town, took the blame for what happened and couldn't beat his tears to the end of his farewell speech. Javi didn't cry, as his mother and the others did. Javi never saw Mr. White give his speech. He'd turned his chair to face the other way.

SIXTH PLACE sat in Mr. White's gut like a pit from one of his backyard nectarines. Retirement tasted like the pesticide on a summer breeze. Instead of pride over all the migrants' sons he'd transformed into teachers and administrators and coaches, uneasiness settled over him as he gazed at the mementos of his coaching career. All his life he'd played to win, even if it meant bumping the Ping-Pong table in mid-rally, pinning down an opponent's arm as he went up for a rebound or wreaking havoc as a flag football coach by instructing one of his players to almost leave the field during a mass substitution, then streak up the sideline unnoticed to snag a touchdown pass.

What, he kept asking himself, had gone so wrong on his final day? Forty-two years earlier his varsity basketball coach had burned him at Magic Valley Christian College in Idaho, banishing him to the jayvee for his defiance of a decree that students attend no other church but the one on campus. He'd *never* do such a thing when he became a coach, he'd vowed—he'd bend over backward to be fair to his kids. But maybe, in his final year, he'd violated his golden rule. Maybe he'd cheated his runners by his absences from summer practice, the furnace in which his teams were always forged.

His wife smelled his uneasiness, and she wasn't so sure that she was ready to retire as Mrs. Coach. Cheryl approached the school board president, Linda Genel, and told her that she'd had a dream in which her husband got the thing he'd been giving boys for decades—a second chance. The idea caught fire with the school board, and a contract was cobbled together that would permit Mr. White to receive his retirement pay yet be kept on as a full-time substitute gym teacher at the middle school for one more semester, so he could sing his swan song again with the boys of McFarland High. Mr. White agreed. All the runners seemed thrilled.

Except one.

Javi spiraled down . . . down . . . down. It was so easy, in a town plagued by gang violence and drug problems, to end up with your mug on a pickle jar on the counter at the Chevron station, soliciting donations to pay your burial expenses. But when the gunfire hit Javi's family last spring, it was his 22-year-old cousin, Ruben Juarez Jr., who died, and it was Ruben himself who pulled the trigger rather than surrender to police and face a third conviction that likely would've sent him to prison for life. Javi froze. He had grown up playing tag in the dark with Ruben. He stopped eating and studying, cut classes and track practices, piled up detentions and flunked history. He shut himself in his bedroom and let the confusion in his house howl around him.

"Go see Mr. White," begged his mother.

"I can't," muttered Javi.

"Why not?" asked his brother, Salvador.

"He doesn't care about us anymore," said Javi.

He entered a 5K road race in June and, before Mr. White's disbelieving eyes, crawled to the finish in 21 minutes. This was his next leader, his fastest returning senior, the one that Blanco's season of redemption would hinge on? Maybe, Mr. White and *los veteranos* began to suspect, working the fields—which Javi had never done—was more important than any of them had realized. Maybe the fields were what had burned the *will* into their runners all those years, and there was just no way this boy who read books could ever muster it. "Not bad, Javi, only five girls beat you," Mr. White fumed after the race. "Were you waiting for somebody, or just counting the flowers? What's a McFarland runner doing back there? You need to step it up. You need to wake up."

Ayon could see it coming, another slap to his hero's face, and could bear it no more. He invited Javi to a Chinese restaurant, waited until he lifted his fork over his beef and broccoli, and then cut loose, freezing that fork in midair for five minutes. "If you can't cut it, I don't care if you're a senior!" Ayon hissed. "You won't be on this team! What happened last year can't happen again. You've got to be a leader!"

Who's to say just when or why a boy begins to become a man? Maybe the death of his cousin finally cried out its counterpoint to Javi: *Don't waste your life. It's too precious.* Javi made a promise to God that he wouldn't waste it. Maybe it was seeing Mr. White show up on July 1 for the summer's first evening run, and every night after that, and the words Mr. White spoke to him after one evening run. "I know how you felt last year," he said. "But I'm going to be here for you this year, every day. I'm going to give everything I've got, and I'm hoping you're going to give everything too." Javi still harbored doubts, still wondered if Mr. White was returning out of obligation rather than desire. But he stopped brooding and decided to give the coach that second chance, becoming resolute in his evening training, adding six-mile runs three mornings a week, hitting the weights in the afternoons and running in a wet vest in the pool. He wrote down his teammates' phone numbers to make sure they'd show up too.

Mr. White assessed his squad: a young one, teeming with promising freshmen and sophomores but lacking a single junior and crying out for leadership from the three seniors—Javi, Steven and Juan, introverts all. A state title? A tall task.

"We're going to low-key everything," declared Mr. White. "I want to enter the state meet under cover."

"We're not going to talk about doing it for Mr. White this year," Javi said. "We'll just see what happens." But privately he set three lofty goals: a sub-16-minute 5K; a top 10 state ranking for McFarland among all schools, regardless of size; and state championship number 10.

Two days before the season's first meet, gunfire erupted again, and two of Mr. White's former runners dropped. Jose Velasco, a pal of Javi's brother, died in a drive-by gang murder, and Jose's brother Aurelio survived a bullet in the neck. The Whites went to the Velascos' house on the double, still distraught over the stabbing death of another former runner just weeks earlier. Javi felt as if he were going to throw up. At night he stayed home, warned by his brother that retaliation was in the air and that more bullets might soon be too.

Three weeks later, at the Bell-Jeff Invitational in L.A., Javi led his team to a sweeping 2-3-7-8-10-11 finish as McFarland thrashed 58 schools—33 of them from higher divisions—to gain the No. 2 overall ranking in the state. Their cover was blown. They were in the headlines.

Then came trouble. Freshman phenom Julio Olvera fell hard for a girl, tumbled all the way into the caterpillar pile, then inflamed a nerve in his hip and ended up having to run for a month in a swimming pool. Juan Gonzalez hurt his knee and was finished, for all intents and purposes, for the season. Now McFarland was down to two seniors and a slew of raw freshmen and sophomores. Ninth-grader Baltazar Topete, the No. 5 varsity runner, informed Mr. White that he'd be retiring when Mr. White did because all this pain was pointless without him, and Cheryl kept asking, "Are you sure you want to leave, Jim? Are you sure you're ready?" until the old coach, too, began to wonder whether the torch could ever be passed.

Javi, too, had begun feeling the gravitational pull of a poor Mexican-American town. None of Javi's senior friends spoke of moving on, as if the next phase were a betrayal. "Go to college wherever you want," his father said when he learned that Javi was applying to UCLA, UC Santa Barbara, UC San Diego and San Diego State. "We just won't visit you." It was a leathery Mexican fieldworker's way of saying, "I'm going to miss you, it hurts to think of you going away," but how was Javi, for all the reading he did, ever to read that deep between the lines?

Somehow everything was connected. Somehow McFarland's pack mentality and Javi's own fear of pulling away clutched at him even when it was time to leave everyone behind in a meet. Week after week he led his team across the finish line, but his times remained a half minute slower than his goal. "Kindergarten times," he snorted. "I'm holding back, running *with* people and not grinding them up. I'm looking for someone to go with, like Steve or Juan, someone I *know*."

And yet, barely realizing it, he'd begun imploring his teammates with the same words that Mr. White had once used on him: He was becoming a leader. Mr. White saw it one day in practice when he instructed his boys to cover a 4½-mile steep uphill climb in 33:30. "No, we're not gonna run 33:30 like Mr. White said, we're gonna run it in 31:30," he heard Javi tell them, and then he watched Javi stay with the trailers, talk them through their pain and sheepdog every one of them home in 31:30. "He's just a different kid this year," Mr. White told people. "He's fantastic. He doesn't have that sad face anymore. He's talking, encouraging all the other kids and working his butt off."

The town bid its formal farewell to Mr. White at midseason. It draped banners for each of the championship years over the hoods of nine shiny new pickup trucks, filled them with runners, past and present, and enthroned Mr. and Mrs. White in a red Porsche at the front of the procession, waving regally while horns honked as if every virgin in town had just been married off. Then everyone sat down to celebrate a life, and Mr. White knew in his bones that he had to leave, this time for good.

In the second-to-last meet of the year, Javi's breakthrough race came at last, a blazing 16:07. "I actually believed in myself," he marveled. "It's peculiar. The fastest race I've ever run felt the easiest."

But there was no time to revel. Every day, every race, was little more than a prelude to what really mattered, the state championships two days after Thanksgiving. Mr. White's Last Day: Take 2.

WORD WENT out to the vets. Don't spook the boys this time. Don't even mention that it's Coach's adios. No need even to show up in Fresno, matter of fact. Mum's the word, men. No Churchill from Blanco. Just another stroll in the park.

The old Javi reared his head. He showed up for McFarland's final practice a half hour late, well after stretching time, when team meetings were held and the leader might be expected to talk from the heart.

He slept in his mother's bed on the eve of the race, a night of freedom from his bedsprings, but still he tossed and turned for hours. A 16:01 or better would place him among the top 10 runners in McFarland's storied history and might pull the freshmen and the sophomores into the 16:30-to-16:45 range required to topple their more experienced foes. A loss, and Javi might go down as the runner who smothered *both* of Mr. White's last hurrahs. It wouldn't be easy, not with the team's leading freshman, Olvera, barely recovered from his hip injury, and not with Carmel and Oak Park, the other two favorites in Division IV, coming in loaded with seniors.

Mr. White and his boys each dropped to one knee and prayed, the runners' white shorts and singlets stark against their brown skin and against Woodward Park's blaze of autumn oranges and yellows and reds. They all locked arms, and their eyes began to mist—exactly what Mr. White had been determined to avoid—as Juan Gonzalez stammered out how much he loved them all and how sorry he was that, because of his knee, he couldn't go to war with them. They walked to the starting line, where 184 other boys in other colors waited to take them down. Javi looked back. There, for the first time, stood his father.

The boys tapped fists. Mr. White and Ayon watched in silence. The gun sounded, and the two men hurried through the mass of spectators and across the creek to catch the boys at the first mile marker. Javi flew by it in 4:52, among the top 10, and his six teammates all managed 5:07

or better . . . not bad, not bad. Blanco's eyes clouded at the second mile marker—they'd bogged down too much in the hills!—then he bolted toward the finish to rally the final kick of his coaching life.

Six runners funneled through the chute, then Javi—he'd done his job, or near enough, with a 16:10 and seventh place, the second-fastest 5K of his life. He whirled at the finish line and squinted, waiting to glimpse the next flash of white breaking from the tree line. . .and waiting. . .and waiting, hope vanishing with every tick of the clock. Finally, at 16:51, they began to arrive, each nearly a half minute too slow, gasping their apologies to Javi.

He reeled away, no time to think, and wrapped his arms around his father and pulled him to his chest.

NO ONE cried after Mr. White's last race. Blanco wouldn't let them, moving from runner to runner to let each one know that third place, behind Carmel and Oak Park, was no disgrace. "You couldn't do it all," he told Javi.

Javi looked up at his coach in a mournful daze. "Are you doing O.K., Mr. White?"

"I'm doing fine, Javi."

It was all over, and now Javi entered no-man's-land, waiting to see if his dream of studying astronomy and running in college would come true. Waiting to find out if he'd really do it, really walk away and reach the other side of the almonds and oranges and grapes, or if this season was the peak of his life, as it had been for so many other runners, and now he'd struggle the way they had when there was no Mr. White to run for.

No, he sensed. A boy couldn't *walk* away from McFarland, he had to run, and so he got up the next morning and ran six miles, and a few days later he upped it to eight, sometimes even 10, as if the season had never ended. "If I don't stop," he said, "I'll keep going."

The team's last night together came at their banquet seven weeks ago. Javi wouldn't go to the podium, just couldn't do it, to express the team's feelings about Mr. White, leaving that to Juan. But Javi hung on every sentence from Mr. White, and when tears streamed down the coach's cheeks and he croaked, "I felt like I deserted the boys a little last year," the words went inside Javi and melted one more layer of ice.

"It felt like a victory, no, not a victory . . . a breakthrough," Javi said.

"Something more than 'good job,' because we've heard plenty of 'good jobs.' Something from his heart. I know I should've been more understanding of him. I know I lost a relationship with a good man. And so as I was leaving I told him ... uh ... 'I just *hope* you won't be a stranger and I won't be a stranger. I hope I see you more often,' and Mr. White said, 'Yeah,' and ... and it's not anything big, but I gave him a hug. I know it sounds like something small, but I'd never done it before, and for me it felt *big*. Maybe it wasn't as big for him as it was for me, but I ... I was just trying to tell him something."

Mr. White got it. He walked away feeling wonderful about Javi and the deep shelf of talent he was leaving behind, vowing to the boys that he'd be back to watch them run, then drying his eyes and heading for his mountain cabin with Mrs. Coach.

And Javi? He lies in bed at night now staring at the planets on the wall, wondering if he'll ever sort the whole thing out. He had reached none of his three goals—not the state title, not the top 10 ranking, not the sub-16 5K—but his final season had given him something else, fruits he hadn't even thought to reach for. In those last two races he'd finally learned to run without the McFarland pack: He'd become a racer. And up on his wall hung that hug with his father, a picture splashed across five columns of *The Bakersfield Californian* that brought tears to his dad's eyes and kept bringing him back into Javi's room to peer at it in the moonlight while his son slept. And in Javi's heart hung that other hug, with that other man, that moment when at last he didn't run.

———

POSTSCRIPT: *After graduating from McFarland in 2004, Javier Medina enrolled at San Diego City College for three years before being accepted to UC San Diego, where he is studying sociology. Now a junior, Medina no longer races competitively, but continues to run 5Ks for fun. "I try to keep in touch with [Jim White], but we don't see each other as much as I'd like," he says. White now spends most of his time in the mountains, but often visits his old school. In '07, the team placed third at the state championship, its best finish since White retired.*

Crime and Punishment

Crime and Punishment

*After high school hoops star Richie Parker was convicted of
sexual abuse, a moral firestorm ignited everywhere he turned. Some
tried to save him, some to savage him—and all were scarred.*

ERE IS A MAN. BARELY A MAN; HE JUST RAN
out of adolescence. He stands alone, 2,000 miles
from home, beside a swimming pool, in a stucco-
walled apartment complex, in a city built on an
American desert.

*Seton Hall chancellor Thomas R. Peterson buckled under to intense pressure
from media and alumni yesterday when he denied admission to star basketball recruit and admitted sex felon Richie Parker.*
—NEW YORK POST, January 24, 1995

It's too hot to run. But he must run. He strips to his trunks. He steps into the pool.

The University of Utah ceased its recruiting of former Manhattan Center basketball star Richie Parker in light of a barrage of media criticism and pressure from the university president regarding Parker's sexual abuse conviction.

—NEW YORK NEWSDAY, May 6, 1995

His hands ball up. His left elbow draws back, pushing against the water. Slowly his foot begins to rise from the floor of the pool.

George Washington University officials informed high school basketball star Richie Parker yesterday they "regrettably" would stop recruiting him and blamed "unbalanced publicity" for a wave of criticism that hit the school for pursuing the youth, who had pleaded guilty to a sexual assault.

—THE WASHINGTON POST, June 30, 1995

His foot gradually descends to the bottom of the pool. His other foot begins to push off. His shoulders tighten. The water pushes back.

Richie Parker will never wear a UTEP basketball uniform. UTEP has bowed out of its recruitment of the controversial basketball player, athletic director John Thompson announced Friday.

—EL PASO HERALD-POST, February 24, 1996

His knee slowly lifts again. His arms silently pump.

USC on Wednesday terminated its recruitment of former New York City All-America point guard Richie Parker, a convicted sex offender. The decision came after . . . two days of sometimes heated exchanges among athletic department personnel.

—ORANGE COUNTY REGISTER, March 28, 1996

He climbs out finally and pants for air, in the desert that once was the bottom of an ocean.

HERE IS a periodic table. It's the one you would see near the blackboard in any high school chemistry class, a listing of the 109 elements according to atomic number. Why is it being inflicted on you here, in a sports magazine? *Patience.* Remember, this is a story about higher education.

Near the lower lefthand corner of the chart is an element named cesium. Among its own—the metals surrounding it in the chart, such as sodium and potassium—cesium is a quiet, unassuming element. But because it has just one electron on its outer shell, one electron aching to leap to any atom that is lacking a full outer shell of electrons, cesium is a bomb in a suitcase when it leaves its neighborhood. On contact with oxygen, cesium will cause an explosion. Introduce it to chlorine, fluorine, iodine or bromine and look out! Almost everywhere it goes, trying to rid itself of the baggage of that one electron, another eruption occurs, and only those who understand what cannot be seen can make any sense of it at all.

HERE IS an assistant principal. She works at Manhattan Center, the East Harlem high school Richie Parker once attended. Teenagers deposit their leather jackets in Ellen Scheinbach's closet in the morning for safekeeping, come to her at lunchtime for oatmeal cookies and advice. The phone's constantly ringing, teachers are always poking in their heads. "A lunatic asylum!" she calls her office, ambling about with her spectacles dangling from a neck chain. But now there's silence, and it's Richie's mother, Rosita, shuffling on her bad knees, clutching her envelope of articles clipped from the *New York Post* and the *Daily News*, extending them toward the assistant principal and asking her to explain.

Ellen Scheinbach is an authority figure, one of the few Rosita knows. Surely she can explain how *all this* could result from that one day in this building, in January 1994, when Rosita's 6'5" son, a junior then—a well-liked boy known for his silence, his gentle nature and his skill on a basketball court—was walking through these halls, having gone to the nurse's office with a sprained ankle and having found the nurse not there, was returning to class when he paused . . . and turned. And headed toward the bottom of a stairwell in the back of the school, where he and a schoolmate, Leslie Francis, soon compelled a 16-year-old freshman girl to perform oral sex on them. And how 15 minutes later, the girl came running up the stairwell, sobbing, and soon thereafter Richie and the other boy were being led away in handcuffs. And how from that moment on, virtually everywhere Richie would turn to rid himself of the baggage of those 15 minutes, another explosion would occur. How careers would be smashed, men fired, dreams destroyed. How some relationships would splinter and others almost spontaneously be fused. How secrets would burst from hidden places, and rage and fear would tremble in the air behind her lean, quiet son. The assistant principal can explain all this to Rosita, can't she?

Ellen throws up her arms. The incongruity of it all still confounds her. Richie Parker? Richie didn't drink. Richie didn't curse. Richie didn't get into arguments or fights; he had never even gotten detention. She knew lots of kids who would play peek-a-boo with a toddler in the bleachers for a few minutes, but Richie was the only one she knew who would do it for an hour. The only time she had ever seen him exert his will—to *force* any issue—was on a basketball court, and even there he did it so softly, so smoothly, that she would be startled to learn at the end of a game that he had scored 35 points. He would be rated one of America's top 50 high school seniors in 1995, a notch or two below Georgia Tech signee Stephon Marbury in New York's schoolboy hierarchy.

Two investigations—one conducted by a George Washington University lawyer and another by the lawyer of the stairwell victim, not to mention the searchlight sweep of Richie's life by the media—failed to turn up a single thread that would indicate that those 15 minutes in the stairwell were part of a larger pattern. Richie himself had insisted on his innocence at first, but eventually he pleaded guilty when the charges were lowered from first-degree sodomy to first-degree sexual abuse in January 1995. His sentence was five years of probation. So now Rosita's standing on the other side of Ellen's desk, holding a half-dozen full-back-page pictures of her son under screaming SEX FELON headlines, asking her what the world has come to that one rotten act by a 17-year-old could take on such monstrous proportions and why Seton Hall has just reneged on its promise of a scholarship for Richie as long as he didn't get a prison sentence. And it's only the beginning, because now the great American morality play is ready to hit the road, with actors and actresses all across the land raring to perform their roles, eager to savage or salvage the teenager from 110th Street in Manhattan—often knowing nothing more of him than his name. Ellen keeps shaking her head and blinking. Sports, having some-how become the realm in which Americans derive their strongest sense of community, has become the stage where all the great moral issues are played out, often rough and ugly, right alongside the games.

Ellen had tried to protect Richie from that. She had tried to smuggle him out when the media surrounded her school. She sat beside him at games when he could no longer play, to shield him from the media's popping cameras and questions. She went to Seton Hall and told administrators that she would trust Richie with her daughter, if she had one. But it was hopeless. In the same way that cesium needs to rid itself of that one dangling electron on its outer shell, Richie needed to take his sin to a university, to one of America's last "pure" places, and have it absolved so he could find his way to the promised land, the NBA. In the same way that fluorine longs for that extra electron to complete itself, the universities and their coaches were drawn to the basketball player who could enhance their profile, increase their alumni contributions and TV revenues. And the mutual attraction would keep causing explosions, hurling Richie and yet another university far apart, and Rosita would keep returning to Ellen, her eyes filling with tears. Hasn't her son, she would ask, done everything demanded of him?

Yes, Rosita, yes, he fulfilled the requirements of the criminal justice system and of the out-of-court settlement of the victim's civil lawsuit. He had met monthly with his probation officer, met regularly with a counselor, made both a private and a public apology to the victim, an acknowledgment that regardless of the details of the incident, he had done something profoundly wrong in that stairwell. He had promised to speak out against sexual abuse and to make financial restitution to the victim with a percentage of any money he might generate one day in the NBA. He had earned A's and B's at Manhattan Outreach Center, the school he was sent to in the wake of the court ruling, met NCAA qualifications on his fourth try with an SAT score of 830 and enrolled at Mesa (Ariz.) Community College, which refused to let him play ball but allowed him to be a student. And, yes, both the victim and her lawyer had requested that the country's media and universities let him move on. "He's rare among people who've committed a sexual offense," says Michael Feldman of Jacoby & Meyers, the victim's attorney. "He admitted that he did something wrong and committed to help the victim. How does it assist women to refuse him an opportunity now?"

"We believe Richie is truly sorry," the girl's father had told the *Daily News*. "We're religious people who believe in redemption. We don't believe in third chances. We do believe in second chances."

So how can Ellen explain to the 49-year-old woman with the envelope full of news clippings that the second chance, the fresh start, the comeback, the stuff of magazine covers and made-for-television movies, the mother's milk that immigrant America was nursed on and cannot—to its everlasting credit and eternal confusion—seem to wean itself from, has been denied to her son?

"What can I do?" Ellen cries. "I can't get the reporter from the *New York Post* fired. I can't speak to women's groups who are saying he shouldn't have the right to go to college and play basketball. What is a women's group, anyway? I know plenty of women, but what's a women's group? I can't call [Georgetown coach] John Thompson and tell him to give Richie a chance—you think he's going to listen to some little old Jewish lady? So I'm just left with this horrible frustration. It's like trying to comfort the survivor of a plane wreck when Rosita comes here. There's nothing I can do.

"He was 17 when this happened. For 15 minutes of rotten judgment, he's been crucified! These women's groups are talking about O.J. Simpson and Mike Tyson, and they're using Richie's name. When teachers here heard what he was accused of, they said, 'Are you kidding?' This is a kid who always tried to fade into the background, who wouldn't push back if you pushed him. Even when he wanted something, he'd just stand there and wait till you *asked* what he wanted. Look, I don't know what happened in that stairwell, but if he did it, he must've had a brain lesion. This kid is not a threat.

"If he were white, would this story have been written this way? But no, he fit the perfect stereotype. He has no money, and he's a black male teenager, so they could have a field day. What do people want—for him to fail, so he's out on a street corner? Are they saying you can never redeem yourself? If he wanted to be a doctor instead of a basketball player, would they say, 'You can't take biochemistry class'? Basketball is his talent, and while he's on probation he's entitled to play that the same way he'd be entitled to be a musician or an artist. Everyone thinks the NCAA is so macho. I've never seen so many wimpy men in my life."

Once, just once in the 2½ years of watching everything around Richie go to pieces, has Ellen feared that he might go to pieces too. She had never seen him cry, never heard him blame anyone else, never sensed a chip on his shoulder. But when it was clear that the board of education was about to suspend him from Manhattan Center in the middle of his senior season and that the media swirl was sucking down his teammates too, he came to her office with his mother and read his letter of resignation from the team. When he finished, he finally broke down and clutched his mother. "If not for you," he sobbed to her, "I don't think I could make it."

In the end, Ellen decides, perhaps there isn't much she can do to help Rosita, but there's something Rosita has done to help her. "I've learned a lot from her," says Ellen. "I've learned that no matter how frustrated and upset you get, you just keep turning to your kid and saying, 'I love you, and no matter what happens, there's one place for you that's safe.' When my son has a problem now I just try to hug him and say, 'Whatever decision you make I'll stand by you.' Because *it works*. I've seen it work. It saved Richie Parker."

HERE IS a copy editor on the sports desk of a major city newspaper. She's smart, and she's funny, and if an office push-up contest or footrace suddenly breaks out, hopefully after deadline, she's the one you want to put your money on. Of course, because she's a woman, the sensitive stories go to Jill Agostino for editing. Anguish? That's a Jill piece. Morality issue? Absolutely Agostino. Not that it's ever actually stated in a sports department that men are bereft in those areas. It's just sort of understood.

So she gets the Richie Parker stories to polish for *Newsday*. And as she's scanning the words on her computer screen in early 1995, she begins to feel something tightening inside her. It's the old uneasiness, the one she dreads, the one she has no time for here, now, as the clock hands dig toward deadline; the one she might try to run into the ground tomorrow when she's doing her five miles, or scrub away in the quiet of her Long Island apartment, or stow away and convert to fuel someday, something to help flog herself through an extra hour of work when she has to prove her worth to some sexist idiot who dismisses her as a token woman in a man's world, a newspaper sports desk. But not now. Not here. No way.

She begins to sense it here and there between the lines—the implication that Parker is being treated unfairly—and her uneasiness starts to turn to quiet anger. She doesn't sleep much that night, doesn't feel like eating the next day. Another Parker story comes her way a few evenings later, then there's an afternoon drive to work listening to radio talk-show callers chew the issue to death, some of them actually sticking up for the kid, and her quiet anger curdles into a rage that no one knows, no one sees.

The writers like Jill. She's not one of those editors who must tinker with a story to justify their existence. One *Newsday* reporter writes an article that comes right out and says Parker is a good kid who made a mistake and deserves a second chance, and he calls Jill as she's editing it, cheerfully asking her how she likes his piece. There's silence on the phone. And then it erupts from her, something she has never even been able to tell her family.

"I've been raped," says Jill. "I don't agree with you."

"Oh, I didn't. . . . Jill, I'm sorry," he says.

She feels like a jerk for making the reporter feel like a jerk, but it's too late now, the anger's out on the table, and it's not finished. Mistake? How can anyone call it that? Leaving your headlights on or forgetting your keys, *that's* a mistake—not humiliating a woman the way Jill had been nearly nine years earlier, at age 22, by a man on a boat on Queechy Lake in upstate New York. She goes into her boss's office, seething at a society where a man like Mike Tyson can walk out of jail a few years after raping a woman and be greeted by a thunderous roar and a paycheck worth millions of dollars, and TV commentators can blather on about all that *Tyson* has been through, as if the perpetrator was the victim and the real victim was yesterday's oatmeal. "I want to write a column," she tells her boss. "People need to know what it's like for the victim. I was raped."

His jaw drops. Well . . . uh . . . sure, Jill, but. . . .

She barely sleeps that night. Her husband, Michael, says that if she's sure she wants to do this, he's behind her. She's sure. She sits on the couch the next day with a red pen, a blue pen and a notepad. The red ink is for *her* pain—the italicized sections interspersed in the column that recount that night on the lake where she swam as a little girl: *"I wanted to throw up every time I smelled the mixture of Grand Marnier and tobacco smoke on his breath as he held me down...."* The blue ink is for Richie Parker: "How often do you think Parker will think about this incident once he's on a college basketball court? For the victim, not a day will go by without that memory.... Parker's punishment should last until his victim is able to walk alone up the street, or through a parking lot, or down a dimly lit hallway and feel safe. Until the nightmares cease. Until a day goes by and she doesn't think about the horrible things these boys made her do. But it won't."

What are you doing? a voice inside her asks when she has finished writing. To her, this is not an act of courage, as some would take it. To her, this is Jill Agostino publicly admitting her most private pain just on the chance that it will make some men begin to comprehend how it feels to be violated, how it eats into a woman's life forever, how it can make her hold her breath when a stranger steps into an empty elevator with her, make her want to run when a man rolls down his car window and asks her for directions, make her stare into a mirror some days and hate her body because somehow it betrayed her.

She can't surrender to the urge to crumple up the notepad paper, because if she does, the man in the boat wins again, and she can't let him keep winning. He has won too many times, at night when she sits up rigid in bed from nightmares she can never quite recollect—only raw terror and the faint echo of all the world's laughter. He won every time she bought another size 8 blouse for a size 4 body, every time she froze when a colleague she didn't know well threw an arm around her shoulder, every time she couldn't sleep and had to caffeinate and will herself through the next day so that no one, except perhaps her husband, would ever dream that she was anything but the sharp, competitive woman that the world always sees.

Now comes the next agony. She can't let her family find out in a newspaper story. She must call her mother and father and brother and sister and tell them about the rape and why she buried it. She must listen to her mother cry and feel guilty for not protecting her daughter from something she couldn't possibly have protected her from. A few days later the story appears. Seven hundred and fifty thousand readers learn Jill's secret, and countless thousands more—including old boyfriends, old co-workers, old roommates—come across it in the newspapers across the country that run the story. Some of her colleagues are moved to tears by her column. Some confess to her their own buried stories of rape.

The eddies never seem to end. Radio talk shows call her to be a guest and ask her about her rape, and she has to keep reliving the worst moment of her life. The victim's lawyer calls to compliment her story and asks her if she would testify in his client's civil lawsuit against Parker. When that's settled out of court, he asks if she'd consider doing that in another lawsuit in which the jury needs to feel the long ripple of a rape, and she says yes, because how can she refuse to help someone who has endured what she has or allow so many people to keep insinuating that it's the violated woman who is to blame? SPORTS ILLUSTRATED calls a year later and asks to interview her, and she has to worry how that will affect the way her colleagues at her new workplace, *The New York Times*, will look at her, worry that *this* is who she is now to people, this is *all* she is. Each new episode will mean another week of barely eating, barely sleeping, a few more nightmares and 10 or 15 extra miles of running, but she can't back down. She has never met Richie Parker and no doubt never will, but Jill Agostino is paying for his crime, oh, yes, she's paying.

HERE IS an assistant coach from the University of Utah. Once Donny Daniels, too, was a black teenager from a crowded city who lived to play basketball. And so even though he is the 40-year-old father of three, including two daughters, on this spring day in 1995, he is walking into his past when he walks into the Parkers' apartment. He finds Richie just as quiet and respectful as all his sources vowed. He sits in the living room with the 108 basketball trophies that take Rosita hours to dust. He looks into the kitchen where she cooks pots and pans full of baked chicken, ziti, collard greens, banana pudding and sweet-potato pies on Sundays and has half the neighborhood into her house, just like it used to be when she was growing up in North Carolina. He gazes around the home where Rosita and Richie's ever-so-quiet father, Richard, and Richie's two older sisters, Monica and Tanya, who have both attended college, eat and tease each other and laugh.

Donny talks to Rosita, who for years telephoned after Richie to make sure he had gone where he said he was going, who tried to seal her son from all the bad choices blowing around outside the window. No, Donny can't see her running a half-dozen times to the emergency room with high blood pressure at each twist her son's story takes; can't see her bent in half with chest pains six months after Richie's arrest, paramedics rushing through that front door and clamping an oxygen mask over her mouth, driving an IV needle into her arm, pushing a nitroglycerine pill under her tongue, trying to stave off the heart attack or stroke that's on the verge of occurring as her son watches, even more scared than he was on that long night when he lay awake smelling urine in a New York City jail. He can't see her lying in the hospital, realizing that if she doesn't stop letting the newspaper stories affect her so deeply, they're going to kill her. But listening to the mother and the son, he can feel it.

And it's all that feeling that Donny lets out when the *New York Post* reporter gets a tip and calls him a few days later to ask, "How can Utah consider rewarding a sex felon with a scholarship?" All that feeling from a man who senses that his and his university's integrity is being assaulted. Of course, he has never walked into the *victim's* house and felt what a heart might feel there. "There are two victims here," he tells the reporter. "He doesn't evaporate into the atmosphere. He's not a piece of dirt. He has feelings and emotions. . . . They both made a mistake; they shouldn't have been there. But everyone's worried about the girl. What about him?. . . You don't see her name or picture, but Richie Parker is plastered all over. . . . She probably will get a doctorate and marry a successful guy and live in the Hamptons. . . . Will he ever be able to forget it?. . . Who's hurt more for life?"

Imagine the explosion this quote causes back in Salt Lake City, the ripping apart of molecules. Imagine how rapidly the college president and athletic director must run from that quote, how swiftly Richie's chance to attend Utah vaporizes, how many columns are written citing Richie as the prime example of America's coddling of athletes and Neanderthal treatment of women. Imagine how tightly doors shut to discuss what must be done with Donny.

He is luckier than others will be. He is placed on probation for a year and ordered to attend sensitivity training sessions with a director from the Women's Resource Center on campus. He gets a second chance.

A year later, when a writer from SI calls, Donny says he was wrong for saying what he did but wishes to say nothing more, and his boss, coach Rick Majerus, the most affable of men, seals his lips as well. Better to fence off the area and let the pieces lie where they fell, to be covered by the sediment of time.

HERE IS a university president. Here is the picture of Teddy Roosevelt on his office wall. Which is which? Who's who? Mustache. Spectacles. Hair combed back. Eyes atwinkle. Robust body. Bent for bold action. Oh, so *that's* how you tell the two of them apart: Stephen Trachtenberg's the better politician.

He's the man who transformed the University of Hartford and George Washington, the one who gives big-idea speeches and writes ethics essays for books, magazines and newspapers. He knows something about everything. Even chemistry.

Yes, he's going to do it. He's going to give this Parker kid another chance, and he's going to satisfy the alumni and faculty and the women's groups and the media and the talk-show callers, and even the victim. He's going to introduce cesium to fluorine, and—*eureka!*—nothing's going to go *ka-boom!*

And why not? He's a master at problem-solving, a genius at persuasion. "He has a tremendous capacity to anticipate a whole variety of outcomes and the implications of those outcomes," says George Washington vice president Bob Chernak, "and then calculate how to move an issue toward the most favorable one. He's always three steps ahead of you. He's thinking of ideas in his sleep."

Stephen inherited a university with a profound identity crisis, not to mention a 1–27 basketball team, in 1988. In the wake of his brainstorms, applications have nearly doubled, contributions have soared, average SAT scores have rocketed, and the hoops team has become an NCAA tournament fixture. A new challenge? Bully! A fray? Fine! He would wade right into it and convince people he was right, the way he did during the student sit-ins at Boston University back in the '60s as a bearded associate dean, persuading protesters not to risk a violent confrontation with police. He has built up a tall pile of chips at George Washington, and he's willing to ante up for Richie Parker.

Sure, he's eager to help his basketball team, but it's also something else. Sure, he's the son of one hell of a Brooklyn life insurance salesman, but he's also the son of a social activist, a mother who sent him to summer camps with black kids and wanted him to become a doctor who would treat the poor, not to mention the grandson of a Ukrainian Jew who fled to America for a second chance. His record of helping kids out of deep holes is long. At Hartford he gave a scholarship to a young man with an eighth-grade education who had been convicted on drug-dealing and burglary charges. That man, John Richters—who played no sport—went on to graduate summa cum laude and get a Ph.D. in psychology and now works as a program chief at the National Institutes of Health in the study of chronically antisocial children.

A young deer—that's the image that forms in the university president's head when Richie enters his office in May 1995. Barely audible, Richie expresses contrition and an earnest desire to attend George Washington, and he's so hopeful that he buys a school hat and T-shirt. All the questions march through Stephen's head as Richie walks out of his office. Is it a college's job to mete out more punishment than the legal system does? Perhaps not, but isn't it a university president's job to make sure that a parent doesn't send an 18-year-old daughter to live in a dorm room next door to a sex offender? What if it were *his* daughter? If a sex felon shouldn't get a basketball scholarship, what about an academic scholarship? What about a thief, a mugger, an embezzler? A custodian or a waiter can return to his normal life after the legal system passes judgment, but a gifted basketball player cannot? Pro sports are fine for felons to play, but not college athletics? What kind of message does it send out when a sex offender gets a scholarship? When you remove the emotion from the question . . . but maybe you *shouldn't* remove the emotion from the question. All this confusion, does it signal a society lost in the wilderness . . . or one finally mature enough to look at questions it has always shut its eyes to? His mind gnaws at the bone, at every last bit of gristle. Beneath it all, he can sense what's going on, the vague feeling people are beginning to have that their love of sports—the sense of escape and belonging that they provide—is doubling back on them like some hidden undertow, pulling them all out to sea. It's not the ripest time for redemption.

But he takes a deep breath and begins constructing a master plan. He sends a university lawyer, a woman, to New York City to compile a mas-

sive dossier on Richie. If she finds any smudge, besides the stairwell incident, George Washington can retreat—but he keeps checking with her,
and she doesn't. Shrewder still, he decides that *he* won't decide Richie's
fate; he'll leave that to a blue-ribbon committee, one that he structures
as if he were a supplicant at a Hindu shrine, bowing to a dozen different gods, to every possible political correctness: seven blacks and eight
whites, seven females and eight males, including a professor of law, an
assistant chief of police, a minister, a campus chaplain, an academic coordinator, a faculty clinical psychologist, a director of multicultural student
services, a superintendent of schools, two judges, two trustees and three
students. "A Noah's Ark committee," he calls it. If the menagerie chooses
to accept Richie, Stephen will have him redshirted for a year, ease him
into campus life, save him from the jackals waiting at enemy arenas. And
then, as the frosting on the cake, even before the committee makes its recommendation on Richie, he offers the victim, a valedictorian of her junior
high class, a scholarship when she graduates from high school. A university lawyer warns him that one won't look pretty in a tabloid headline, but
Stephen is determined. Win-win for everyone, right?

Do you recall Chernobyl? It all begins to rain down on Stephen Trachtenberg: the *New York Post* reporter, radioactive telephone calls, faxes and letters, scalding editorials, icy questions from the board of trustees, student
petitions and condemnation from the faculty senate. Stephen, the father of
George Washington University, is being called immoral, a fool, a calculat-
ing liar. Even his wife, Francine, in his corner all the way, warns him that
he has underestimated what he's up against, that, politically speaking, he
has made the wrong call. He's losing sleep. It's usurping his entire day and
all of his night. The story moves to *The Washington Post*'s front page—*that's*
trouble. If only he could buy enough time for his plan to incubate, for the
score of Richie's last SAT test to arrive and the Noah's Ark committee to
see the results of the nearly complete investigation, but no, Stephen looks
to one flank, then the other and sees a remarkable alliance closing in on
him. The feminists *and* conservatives, "the forces of the left and the forces
of the right," he says, "coming together like the teeth of a vise." Eight years
of working 12-hour days to build George Washington's image is being frittered away, and image is money. And he can't even try to persuade the
public that he's right—the NCAA gag rule preventing school officials from

discussing a recruit has stripped him of his greatest gift. Could he even lose his job over this, if the teeth keep closing? Could he?

One by one, those in his inner circle who admire the risk he has taken, or have simply indulged it, urge him to halt, even as his investigator's reports on Richie keep coming in, convincing him more than ever that it's right to go on. Finally it's just Stephen out there, hanging onto Richie by his fingernails as everything around them shakes. At last, he has to let go. Stephen looks at himself in the mirror. It's not Teddy he sees. It's not the man who could persuade almost anyone of anything. "I gave Richie Parker a moment of hope," he says, the light going out of his eyes, "and then I took it away."

HERE IS the victim. No, here the victim is not. She has never emerged from the shadows of that stairwell. She will not emerge now. Of her you shall only know this: For months after the incident she endured nightmares and telephoned threats from people who blamed her. She is an excellent student, but her grades dipped, and the taunts from schoolmates forced her to transfer from one high school, then another. She undergoes therapy. As she gets ready for her senior year, her family will not even reveal the borough where her current school is located.

She hopes to become a doctor. Her father is a social worker who deals with abused children, her mother a hospital nurse. Six years ago they and their daughter left Ghana and came to America, looking for another chance.

HERE IS a number. Such a nice, plump number. Say it: *500*. Let them scoff at Dave Possinger, let them cringe at his intensity, let them ask him, like wise guys, to total up the traffic lights in the towns where he has coached, but this would be proof he could clutch all the way to the coffin: *500*. One more win is all he needs. One more.

And no, this won't be 500 by dint of sheer endurance, a box turtle's milestone. Eighteen years is all it took Dave, an astonishing average of 28 victories a year. He is the best coach you never heard of, a 52-year-old man marooned in the bush country of NAIA and junior college basketball by bad luck and an old whiff of scandal. But it's summer, and the 1995–96 season is just a few months away, and on opening night his Sullivan

County (N.Y.) Community College team will no doubt pulverize Dutchess C.C. as it does every year, and he will join that invisible club: *500*.

He has envisioned the moment all summer, even as the man he has just chosen as his assistant coach, Charles Harris, has begun to grow intrigued by the never-ending newspaper accounts of a kid in New York City named Richie Parker. Richie is the last thing on Dave's mind. Dave has just coached his team to the national junior college Division III championship and is loaded to repeat in 1995–96, and he has no reason to think that Richie will end up with him in the bush country, at a low-level community college. Start making contacts and see what's out there, especially for the year after this, is all he has asked of Harris, a likable 40-year-old black man who Dave is sure will make a superb recruiter.

Everywhere Dave goes that summer, even on his vacation in the Philippines, he imagines the magical night that is coming: The limousine his girlfriend is renting to take him to the game. The official hoisting of the national-championship banner, his second in four years at the junior college in Loch Sheldrake, N.Y. Former players converging to congratulate him, a capacity crowd rising to recognize him. The plaque, the ringing speeches, the commemorative T-shirts, the late-night dinner for 100 in the Italian restaurant. "It dominated my thoughts every day," Dave recalls. "Even in places in the Philippines where there was no running water, no electricity, I'd see kids playing basketball and I'd think about 500. It would stand for all the years, all the kids, all the hard work." It would stand for his nine seasons at a New York NAIA school named St. Thomas Aquinas, where his 295–49 record helped make the program the country's winningest of the 1980s, on *any* level—yes, Dean Smith at North Carolina was second to Dave Possinger. It would stand for his four-year run of 133–5 at Sullivan County and ease the pain from the '89 scandal that forced him out after one year at Western Carolina, his one shot as an NCAA Division I coach, even though it was his assistant, not him, who was cited for minor recruiting violations. Perhaps 500 wouldn't mean quite so much if he had a wife and children, but no, it's just him and his basset hound Free Throw, and 500 stands for his life.

A few hours drive south, at a showcase game for unrecruited players, his soon-to-be-named assistant Harris is watching the one obvious jewel on the floor, Richie Parker. It's crazy, thinks Harris, who remembers inmates from the local prison taking classes from Sullivan County when he was enrolled there in the 1970s. "Everyone has something in their closet they're not proud of," Harris says, "and everyone deserves a second chance." A long shot, but what a coup if he could offer the kid the second chance that the four-year colleges wouldn't.

Harris gets clearance, he says later, from Sullivan County's athletic director, Mike McGuire, to have Richie apply to the school—not as a scholarship student but as any normal student would. Searching for a way to contact Richie, Harris calls the *New York Post* reporter. It's like the mouse asking the cat for directions to the cheese.

McGuire says now that if he heard the name Richie Parker, it didn't register. And that he definitely never gave Harris permission—even though Harris had been unofficially approved to go on contract in two months and had already invested countless hours and a few hundred dollars from his own pocket on phone calls and recruiting trips—to present himself to a *New York Post* reporter as a Sullivan County assistant coach and declare that Sullivan County was "committed to working" with Richie Parker.

You know what happens next. You know about the reporter's call to the president, asking if he knows that Sullivan County is recruiting a sex felon. You know about the next day's headlines, the ducking for cover. Richie, of course, will never play at Sullivan County. Harris's fate will hang in the balance for a few months while the school wrings its hands. In October, after he has spent weeks monitoring the players in study hall and working at practices without pay, hoping for the best, Harris is told he won't be hired.

Harris, with head-coaching dreams of his own, is crushed. Dave, who feels responsible for Harris, is devastated. There have been other slights from his superiors at Sullivan County, he feels, but to do this to a well-meaning man trying to give a kid a second chance—how can he go on working there and live with himself? But then, how can he walk out on his team two weeks before the season opener and deprive himself of the Holy Grail: *500?*

Simple, Dave's friends tell him. Win the opener, then quit. What a scene it would be, the man of the hour strolling to the microphone, saying, "Ladies and gentlemen, thank you. *I quit!*" But Dave's conscience won't let him do it. "If I start something," he tells his friends, "I have to finish it."

Five days before the opener, he quits. He can't sleep. A few days later he smirks and tells a reporter, "Your job is to tell me why I shouldn't jump off a building." His team goes on to win the national championship again. Without him.

His record hangs there, rolling around the rim—499 wins and 116 losses—but athletic directors look right past him, searching for a younger man. Eight months later he still hasn't even received an interview. He takes a job as a regional director for National Scouting Report, a service designed to help high school kids get—what else?—college scholarships. "But there's still a claw in the back of my throat," he says, "a claw telling me, 'You are a basketball coach.' "

A week after he quits, Dave goes to his dresser drawer. He opens it and stares at what he purchased in the Philippines a few months earlier, and he makes a decision. Damn the math, they can't take it from him. It's there now, glittering in 18-carat gold from a chain around his neck: *500.*

HERE IS the girlfriend of the boy who has pleaded guilty to sexual abuse. She's tall and lean, a beautiful girl whose demeanor is so composed that everyone always assumes she's older than she really is, until that day when people are running to her in the hall, telling her to come quickly, something terrible has happened, and Richie's in the principal's office talking so helter-skelter that none of it makes sense, and the police are on their way, and she's nearly in hysterics.

He's the schoolmate Jaywana Bradley fell in love with in 10th grade, the one who taught her to play basketball so well that by her senior year she will be named by the *Daily News* as one of the best schoolgirl players in Manhattan. Who knew, perhaps they would go off together to trumpets, the king and queen of Manhattan hoops moving on, hand in hand, to set up court on a college campus. . .until this.

But what, exactly, is this? Jaywana keeps finding herself in bed, crying, wondering. People keep asking her, "You gonna leave Richie?" Some call her a fool if she sticks with him, and a few boys walk right up to her and say, "Why you going out with a rapist?"

She can't quite answer that. Maybe it's because her mother and father believe in Richie, her dad accompanying the Parkers to court hearings. Maybe it's just sitting there in the Parker apartment all those evenings, playing spades with the family and watching TV, feeling that relentless presence of Rosita—like a rock, a magnetic rock. Listening to Rosita talk about the past, telling how her father died when she was one, how her mother died of diabetic complications when she was 13, how her twin sister stepped in front of a car and was killed when they were five, leaving Rosita clutching the sleeve of the coat with which she had tried to yank back her twin. Maybe Jaywana, just like Richie, just keeps absorbing Rosita's relentless message: "Make your life what it's meant to be, and don't let anyone or anything stop you."

Maybe it's two young people pulling closer and closer together the more that forces try to drive them apart. Maybe she's a sucker for that playful, silly Richie, the side he only shows close family and friends. And maybe it comes from holding him, wiping away his tears the way she does when George Washington closes the door on him and she ends up getting the big-time basketball scholarship to Massachusetts that was supposed to be his.

He goes off to Mesa, to the junior college that decides not to let him play basketball, and she goes off to UMass, and they don't see each other for a long while. He has time to sort out what's essential, what he needs, *now*, sooner than he ever dreamed. When they come home for Christmas, he asks her to come over, calls her to his room and asks her to close her eyes. When she opens them, he's on his knee, asking her to marry him, and she says yes. And later, when she asks him when, he says, "As soon as we're done college."

More and more now, Jaywana finds herself daydreaming of a future. There is no city or people there, just her and Richie in a house surrounded by land and trees as far as the eye can see, a place where no one can touch them. Why the two of them against all odds? She can't explain. "I don't know what made me stick through it with him," she says. "All I know is that nothing anybody can ever say or do can pull me apart from him."

HERE IS death. Now, wait a minute—no one is going to be foolish enough to blame Richie Parker's 15 minutes in the stairwell or the administration of Mesa Community College or even the media for the death of a coach's father, but every event in life is chained to the next, and how do you ever separate the links?

This was supposed to be the year that Rob Standifer gave his father, Bob, a gift—perhaps the last one—in exchange for the gift his father had given him. All Rob's life his dad had awakened at 3 a.m. and reported to work three hours early at a construction company, logging 12- to 14-hour shifts. It didn't matter how badly his dad felt, with his bad back, his diabetes or his weak heart. Work made his father feel good, and his father had a knack of passing that feeling all around. The lesson Rob took into his bones was the old American one: Outwork everyone and you'll succeed in life.

And it seemed true. As a kid Rob was always the first one on the basketball court as a point of pride, shooting 1,000 shots a day, and sure enough, he found himself playing for the Mesa Community College team that nearly won the junior college title in 1987, finishing third in the national tournament in Hutchinson, Kans. He worked for nothing as a high school assistant and then for next to nothing for five years as an assistant at Mesa, and he was rewarded with the head-coaching job two years ago. He was only 27, but his dream, to coach a major-college team, was no longer quite so far away.

The pantry was bare his rookie year, but Mesa went 15–15. Then, doing it his dad's way—his typical off-season day ran from 7 a.m. to 10 at night—he ran the summer league, organized a computerized scouting system, cultivated his high school coaching contacts, recruited at hours when other coaches relaxed, pushed his players through an exhaustive weightlifting program and then nurtured them at night with so many phone calls that his friends called him Ma Bell. He was single and on fire. "I could be a maniac," says Rob, "and I was."

The pantry filled fast. Twice in the summer league in 1995 his players whipped a team with four former Arizona State starters on it, and Rob's target was clear. He was going to take his father and his team back to Hutchinson and this time win the whole damn thing.

Richie? He would sure make things easier. Rob had seen him play in the annual summer tournament at Arizona State, which Richie's New York City club team, Riverside Church, traveled to each year. Just like all the other coaches, Rob was struck by the distance between Richie and the world's image of Richie. Just like all the other coaches, he got that same feeling in the pit of his stomach when he saw a talented high school player—if you didn't get him dunking *for* you, he might soon be dunking *on* you. Besides, Rob knew Ernie Lorch, the Riverside director, and already had taken a few of Lorch's kids at Mesa. And so Rob, too, was drawn in. Mesa would be Richie's safety net, the faraway junior college where he could go to heal himself and play ball if all the Division I scholarship offers went up in smoke.

And because there was so much smoke, and Richie kept hoping and waiting for the next Division I chance, his decision to go to Mesa occurred at the last minute, just a few days before the start of school last August. And because Richie waited, Rob had to wait, and by the time he found out Richie was coming, there was no chance for cool heads to sit and debate this and perhaps construct a plan. Rob told the story of Richie Parker to three women—his mother, his girlfriend and his girlfriend's mother, and they all agreed with him. "What Richie did was flat wrong," Rob says, "but are you going to be part of the problem or part of the solution?" And he insists—*are you crazy?*—that of course he notified his superiors, two of them, about Richie and his baggage.

But the Mesa athletic director, Allen Benedict, says he was told nothing of Richie's past, that all he got was a 9 p.m. call from Rob telling him that a great player was coming from New York. The next morning, while Richie was at 30,000 feet heading west across the heart of America, the junior college president was on the phone with Benedict, saying, "Why did a reporter from the *New York Post* just call me . . . and who is Richie Parker?" And then the National Organization for Women was checking in, and cameras were peering inside the gym for a peek at Richie, and a TV truck was pulling up to Benedict's house. "Whether you do something wrong or not isn't the point sometimes," says Benedict. "It's the perception."

Rob was called in to a meeting less than two weeks before the first practice and forced to quit. Richie called Rob, nearly in tears at what he had wrought.

As for Richie, he could stay, but he couldn't play basketball. College athletics, Mesa president Larry Christiansen reasoned, are like a driver's license—a privilege, not a right. What the westward journey and the open spaces had done for so many others, they couldn't do for Richie Parker.

Richie had to decide, then and there, what was most important in his life. He chose to stay at Mesa, take courses and learn who he was without a basketball. He would work the shot clock at games, like one of those earnest guys in glasses that no one ever notices, and by the end of the year the administrators at Mesa would all say good things about him.

Rob had to tell his father the terrible news. He knew his dad was on the edge of the cliff—doctors had said that if not for the zest that Bob derived from his work, his heart would've likely given way three or four years before—so the son tried to shrug and keep his face a blank, so he wouldn't give his father that nudge. Bob was devastated, but as with all his other pain, he tried to keep it inside. He was bewildered, too. The ethic he had passed on to his only child—outwork everyone and you'll succeed—had failed, been displaced, it seemed, by a new one: Image is everything.

Rob didn't eat for three days after that, unless you count the antacid medication. He wouldn't even show his girlfriend, Danelle Scuzzaro, how badly this hurt.

On the fourth day after he was let go, he picked up a diamond ring at the jeweler's and took Danelle to dinner. Afterward, he dropped to his knee—cesium is the damnedest thing—and asked her to marry him. She said yes, and thank god.

Two weeks later, at 5:15 a.m., he got the call from his mother. His father's heart had stopped, at the age of 61. It might well have happened then anyway. "What happened to me didn't kill him," says Rob, "but it didn't help."

There was only one thing to be said for the timing. All the tears Rob had held back after losing his job could finally come out, and they did . . . again . . . and again . . . and again. . . .

WAIT A moment. What about the reporter from the *New York Post*—isn't he here too? Sure, just a moment, he's still on the telephone. Gosh, look at him, just a kid, wouldn't even pass for 25. Just started at the *Post*, covering high school sports, when suddenly—*whoa!*—he has his teeth into the story of his life, and his incisors are wonderful.

Look at Barry Baum rolling out of bed in his Manhattan apartment and running, literally, to the newsstand at the corner of 79th and Broadway to check if the *Daily News* has scooped him on the Parker story. That has actually happened before, so Barry knows that sinking feeling. See him getting that 10 a.m. call from his editor, groggily picking up the phone—a medic on call in a tabloid war. "So what's goin' on with Parker today?" his editor demands. And Barry says, "I'll let you know," then shakes off the cobwebs and begins working the phones, looking for a tip. He loves this part, the detective work. And the most amazing thing keeps occurring. Because there's such an innocent charm about Barry, people *want* to help him.

Some high school scout or basketball junkie with his ear to the streets keeps slipping him the name of the next university showing interest in Richie, and then Barry plays his role, just as the university administrators and the coaches and the women's groups and the loved ones do. He becomes the Bunsen burner, the heat that agitates the cesium and fluorine molecules into rapid movement, more-violent collision. He leaps to call the university president and the campus women's center to ask that 64-megaton question—"How do you feel about your school recruiting a sex felon?"—and if they say they don't know who Richie Parker is, so they can't comment, he faxes them a pile of his Parker stories, and suddenly they have a comment. And all at once the coach and the athletic director are being called onto the president's carpet, or what's left of it, and then there's a follow-up exclusive story to write when they all abandon Richie, and there's no time to consider all the layers, all the moral nuances, because the editor's on the phone barking, "O.K., hurry, rewrite that for the second edition!"—just like in the movies. And then street vendors are snaking between the cars bottlenecked at the bridges and tunnels leading into the city the next morning, catching drivers' eyes with thick SEX FELON headlines, and every person who contributes his 50 cents confirms the *Post* editor's instincts and becomes another link in the chain.

"There were nights when I couldn't sleep, an adrenaline I had for a long time," says Barry. "I'd lie in bed, realizing I'd come to New York and made an impact on one of the biggest stories of the year."

Hadn't his editor at the *Post* told him, "We're going to put your name in lights," when he hired Barry in August 1994? Wasn't that music to his ears? Even as a little kid in Brooklyn Heights, he had dreamed of busting back-page stories for the New York tabloids. At 15 he talked his way into becoming the Knicks ball boy by rat-tat-tatting 10 letters to the team trainer, and then parlayed that job into his own cable-TV show in Manhattan, *Courtside with Barry Baum*, by convincing the station of the wonderful access to big-name Knicks that a precocious 16-year-old ball boy had. He appeared on the televised dating show *Love Connection* three times, and when one of his dates sniffed about Barry's making the wrong turn on their evening out, he brought down the house by sniffing back, "Get a load of Miss Rand McNally, never made a wrong turn in her life!"

And then suddenly the kid who grew up calling *New York Post* and *Daily News* columnists with kudos and beg-to-differs is being lauded for his own back-page *Post* scoops on New York radio talk shows, being asked to appear on the all-sports station, WFAN, and invited to speak at a journalism symposium at Madison Square Garden with a poster board full of his Parker stories. Adrenaline, yes, but anguish, too, stuff you don't talk about when you're a guest on WFAN. Because the nasty phone calls to Barry's desk have begun, people hissing, "Leave Richie Parker alone!"

Then, when he's a guest on a radio talk show one day, a caller says, "Don't you see what you're doing? This is a black kid who comes from nowhere, and you're a white guy who probably comes from a lot of money." Barry blinks. "It hits me," he says. "That's true. I've always had everything, and I'd never even thought of the race factor." New York City high school coaches, his contacts, start saying, "C'mon, Barry, back off. What are you trying to prove?" Even his own father, Bruce, finally says, "Leave him alone already, Barry," and that stings.

"That even someone who knew me that well wouldn't realize that I'm just trying to do my job. . . . " he says. "I mean, don't give me credit for keeping Richie Parker out of college, but don't blame me for it either. And the more people tell me to *stop* reporting a story, the more it means it *is* a story, right? But I keep wondering about Richie. All that time, I couldn't talk to him because his lawyer wouldn't let me, so I couldn't feel him. Finally they let me. You know, it changes things once you talk to him. Before that he was an object, and it was easy to write, 'Richie Parker, sex felon,' because I didn't know him. He was the predator and the girl was the victim, right? I talked to him at a Rucker League game last August, and he actually smiled at me. A smile is a big thing.

"Look, I've never had a problem with Richie playing college basketball. It's not the colleges' job to punish him further. He should be allowed to play—but not without students and their parents being notified, maybe by a letter from the university administration. You know, like Megan's Law, notifying people that a sex felon is in their neighborhood. It's funny. It's like *I've* become Megan's Law for these universities. I'm the one who tells them he's coming. It was amazing how quickly it played out with Oral Roberts. I reported that the school was interested, the story breaks across the country, the TV reporters arrive on campus—and the school announces it has already pulled out! It was like the fire trucks coming, and there's no fire, the local residents have already put it out. These universities have no backbone! Every university president I talk to, except for maybe Stephen Trachtenberg, it's like talking to the same guy. Every one of them says, 'I can't believe my coach did this and that isn't what we stand for and blah-blah-blah. I'm convinced there's only one college president in the United States: He just keeps changing his name!'"

One major-college coach, off the record, asks Barry what will happen if he takes the risk on Richie. What's Barry supposed to do, lie? He tells the truth, the coach says thank you and backs off, and—*poof!*—the chance is gone, the chemical reaction begun and finished before anyone ever even smelled it occurring. And it begins to dawn on Barry: "Somehow, I'm in this story. I'm not just the observer. People are making decisions based on my reporting. There I am, 25 years old and playing the part of deciding if this kid's going to get into college or not, and maybe, if he's good enough, even into the NBA. I have no agenda or angle at all, but he'd probably be playing now if I hadn't called Utah or GW or. . . .

"So where is the line? I've never been taught that line. I keep wondering, Am I doing the right thing? But I shouldn't have to make that choice. I started compiling a list in my mind of all the people whose lives I've affected, the people who have gotten fired, all the universities. And it tears me apart, because the last thing I want to do is hurt anyone. But I know if I stop reporting it and the *Daily News* gets the story, which you know they will, then my editor will call me and say, 'What's goin' on with Parker? What happened? Where are the words?' and what am I going to say? I can't win. So people blame me. It's like *I* was the one in the stairwell."

He stares off at the wall, catches his breath. "And it's not over yet," Barry says. "It's not over until I find out where Richie Parker's going."

ONE DAY about a month ago Richie Parker stepped into an airplane in Arizona. The plane rose, and he looked through the window one last time at the desert and flew back across America, with no idea what would happen next. "I've learned I can survive without basketball," he said last

229

month. "I've learned how the real world is and that I'm stronger than I knew I was. There's less fear now. I know myself more. I trust people less, but that doesn't make me sad. Just more aware of things. I can still live a good life." And he said a lot more, but it would be improper to let him do it here, for it might mislead the reader into thinking this was a story about Richie Parker.

This land is vast, and it contains so many kinds of people, and that is its grace. Two weeks ago Gale Stevens Haynes, the 45-year-old provost of the Brooklyn campus of Long Island University—and the black mother of three teenage daughters—offered Richie Parker a basketball scholarship to her Division I school. She didn't pull the offer back when the *New York Post* reporter found out, and Richie accepted it. When asked why she did it, she said, "Unless there's an island that I don't know about, where we send people forever who have done something wrong, then we have to provide pathways for these people so they can rejoin society. If we don't, it can only explode. It can only explode in *all* of our faces."

POSTSCRIPT: *After collecting the fifth-most career points in Long Island University history, Richie Parker graduated in 2000 with a degree in sociology. In his freshman season, LIU earned an NCAA tournament berth and Parker gained praise for his conduct both on and off the court. He now works as the assistant director of student activities at LIU and speaks to troubled youth as a part of the Stay Strong Foundation. While Parker never made it to the NBA, he has played in Europe, South America, the ABA and the USBL. The 32-year-old says he has one "ultimate goal": to coach at LIU and give back to his alma mater.*

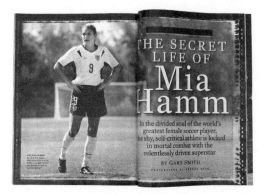

The Secret Life of Mia Hamm

*In the divided soul of the world's greatest female soccer player, the
woman driven to dominate was locked in mortal combat with the one dying
to disappear. Really, she'd be happier if you didn't read this story.*

HERE WAS SHE? SHE'D BEEN RIGHT IN
front of his camera when he'd started gunning
the motor drive. Dammit, the photographer
was sure of it.

He blinked at the images on his laptop. Only 48 hours remained before
90,000 people would jam the Rose Bowl—to watch women play soccer,
for crying out loud. How was it possible, firing 3½ frames every second?
Somehow, on the brink of the 1999 World Cup final against China, when

Robert Hanashiro had gathered the team for a front-page picture in *USA Today* and gotten all the faces of American women's soccer smiling . . . *the* face of American soccer was nowhere to be seen. *Poof.* The greatest goal scorer in the history of international soccer. Vanished.

Where in the world was Mia Hamm?

DON'T READ this story. For Mia's sake. Don't read it or even look at her picture. It might take too long. Then she'd feel like a burden. You might get to know her. Then she'd have to agonize over what you think.

She'll be disappearing soon anyway. For good. She's got one more year, the woman who launched millions of girls across thousands of fields. Two final engagements on the world stage. The first begins this weekend, in the World Cup, which is back on U.S. soil because of the SARS epidemic in China. The second occurs in Athens, at next summer's Olympics. In between she'll marry one of the best players in Major League Baseball, but there's no way you'll see that.

Perhaps, in spite of her, we'll see her place in history—the first female team-sport superstar—and finally understand how many more complications lay in her path than in those blazed by the women icons of the solo sports, the Babes and Billie Jeans, the Wilmas and Chrissies and Peggys who preceded her.

It's tricky business, being anointed queen amid a circle of female peers, having to dismantle the throne even as you sit on it. Maybe she can pull it off here too. Maybe she can fill 24 pages without being seen. Maybe at the end of them you still won't know what makes a woman ignite and extinguish herself all at once.

HOW WILL this story start?" Mia asks. She's nervous about it already. "Will it begin, 'I was born a poor black child. . . . ?' "

No. But close. She was baptized as a middle-income black couple's godchild. With a pair of misshapen feet and sharply bowed legs soon to be wrapped in casts, then in orthotic shoes connected by a steel bar. In a small African-American Catholic church in Selma, Ala., because her fighter-pilot father wanted to taste what life was like for blacks in a segregated Southern town and had already bailed out of the white Catholic church with the shallow social conscience. Just a few feet from the church garage where Mia's ballerina mother taught black girls how to pirouette because she'd seen a black man in a civil rights march carrying a crucifix with a sign on it saying, HE DIED FOR US TOO.

Pretty please, Mia begs you. Bail out on this story before it gets too tangled. Because just when you're coming to grips with Selma, and with a dad who goes from strafing Vietcong from an F-100 to weekend retreats with his wife among rural 'Bama blacks organized by the Taize brothers— antiwar and antimaterialist Christians dedicated to sharing their lives with victims of violence, poverty and racial oppression—you'll be flung from town to town, country to country, all the places our heroine moves to and vanishes from. All the places where neighbors and teammates look up one day and ask, "Where is she? Where's Mia Hamm?"

She's in Florence today. That's Italy. She's two. Banging down the Hamms's long apartment hallway, delighted with the percussion of her new Italian hightops on the hard floor. She's the Hamms's third straight daughter. It's her third home, her family having moved from Selma to Monterey, Calif., for a half year so that Air Force captain Bill Hamm could learn Italian there, and then on to Florence on a two-year grant for overseas graduate study designed to improve understanding between U.S. military officers and their foreign counterparts.

Clomp, clomp, clomp. Mia has bolted out of those leg casts and orthotic shoes as if they were jail, and she hasn't stopped bolting since, except for those astonishing two weeks when she sat on the potty, as still as Buddha, surrounded by books she'd piled up in her determination to meet Mom's challenge: Mia could go to school with her two older sisters only if she was out of diapers. She did it. Turbo potty training, the awed Hamms called it. Now the family's taking its proud housebroken runt to the park. "*Andiamo!*" Mia keeps hooting, bursting ahead of them all to the next Florence street corner. "Let's go!"

She's flying down a sliding board in her purple dress and white lace tights—every detail in the formaldehyde of family lore—when she sees her first soccer ball, en route from an Italian man's foot to his five-year-old son. It's the sport her father has begun to watch on weekends, bicycling to the stadium and falling in love with the throng and the drama and the way one man with a ball on his foot can bring a city to its feet.

In one *whoosh* Mia shoots down the sliding board, leaps a puddle and flies across the grass, intercepting the ball and kicking it again and again until the five-year-old boy loses interest and the marveling Italian papa takes up the game with her for nearly half an hour.

Bad accent. Bad clothes. Bad haircut. Those are Mia's first words at age 31 when she's asked what comes to mind as she looks at a picture of herself at a desk as a little girl.

All innocence and exuberance. Nothing can touch her. Those are Mia's words when it's a picture of her as a little girl playing ball.

A FUNNY thing happens. Mia's standing on the fringe of a pack of boys in Wichita Falls, Texas, cooking in the sun and in her own self-consciousness. *What'll people think of you?* It's the question her mother asks whenever the Hamm girls—four of them now—are out of line. It's 1977. It's Mia's fourth town in her five-year life, and in each new place she has to worry about what a whole new set of people will think of her, and she gets this feeling in her gut as if she's going to vomit, this sick feeling that she's not going to fit in.

She doesn't want to play dress-up or dolls with girls, or wear tutus and dance *The Nutcracker* like her mother. Doesn't matter how many times Stephanie Hamm explains to folks that she's nicknamed her third daughter, Mariel, after a dancer with whom she studied, Mia Slavenska. Nor how many times Mom coos that Mia has the body and athleticism and pixie face to play every gamine in every ballet ever choreographed. Mia had burst into tears and stormed out of her second dance class, recoiling from a life surrounded by mirrors, a life surrounded by Mia.

She wants to do what guys do—make friends and forget about herself by playin' ball—but she can't because she's too shy and shrimpy, and the boys might hoot her off the block. Can't because her skin's so thin that if they do, this powder keg of emotion inside her might detonate right in front of everyone. Can't, most of all, because she's . . . a girl.

Suddenly this frail, dark-haired eight-year-old boy with a trace of the Orient in his eyes and skin glides into the group and begins to speak quietly to the leader. And somehow, at the end of it all, the boys break into two teams, and the Thai-American boy waves her into his huddle. He's her ticket in. He's her brand-new brother, Garrett. One of them, at least. The other one's half African-American and half Puerto Rican, a newborn named Martin. The Hamms—weary after four daughters of trying to produce a son—have done the most remarkable thing: adopted two different-colored ones.

Garrett scrawls a play in the dirt. The boys nod. He's a born leader, like Mia's dad. Mia grins. It's funny how vulnerable, how separate she felt a few minutes ago over there on the sidewalk, and how connected she feels to everyone around her now, how safe, on a team. Amazing how so many strangers just turned into pals.

She's got cover now, a big bro she can draft behind on her bike every day when they race off to play ball, one who'll choose her for his side and tout her as his "secret weapon." One she can watch and try to imitate, from his sidearm pitching motion to his shrug over everything except the important stuff—like whether *that kid just stepped out of bounds . . . or did not!* One who can fade right, looking, looking, and launch a spiral to that little mop of brown hair that no one notices, no one even sees, darting deep . . . touchdown, Mia!

YOU'RE STILL reading? Cut Mia a break. Skim this part. She's 12. Thick hair still shorn as short as a boy's. She has moved to San Antonio for three years and just moved back to Wichita Falls. She's about to walk off a soccer field where she just drilled four goals and assisted on two others, just torched a team of boys, half the spectators never realizing that the dominant player's packing a pair of X chromosomes. She's about to leave the rectangle, to cross the white stripe, the dividing line between two worlds. On this side it's O.K. to spill everything boiling inside her, O.K. to erupt, explode, dominate, celebrate, to be better than someone else. On the other. . . .

She heads to the bathroom. She's got to be careful. She's always the new kid in the 'hood, always starting out in a hole, always playing so hard just to feel worthy of being one of the guys, to disappear by blending in. Playing so hard that she keeps standing out, too far out, her hunger and talent carrying her clean past her objective. Now the game's over and she must start shrinking again, fast. Now she feels the opponents' parents' eyes on her, hears them wondering why the star player's waiting in line outside the *girls'* restroom, and her cheeks are flushing red and her tongue's getting tied and someone's telling her, *Hey, the boys' room is over there!*

Dad, who has just refereed three games at the same complex, gives her a one-arm hug, hands her two bucks—50 cents a goal—and climbs in the Pumpkin, the orange camper the Hamms brought back from Italy and put a quarter-zillion miles on. He's a rare cat. A Democrat fighter pilot. A lieutenant colonel who, years later, will plant an AMERICANS FOR PEACE poster in his front yard amid the early drumbeats of war on Iraq. A perfect ref because he's so stoic and rational, but put him in the stands at one of his kids' games, and look out! He rides refs and opponents so hard that he gets the heave-ho from an official in one of Mia's games and a middle finger from one of the players in another. Mia has seen the one thing that brings out the tendons in the stoic's neck. Mia knows how much winning matters.

They pull away from the soccer fields. Dad glimpses Mia's face in the rearview mirror. She sees where they're heading: the Maternity Cottage. She sees her Saturday going up in smoke. She's turning purple. Here it comes. . . .

Fifteen minutes ago, this eruption of feeling went into a steal and a sprint and a 20-yard *zzzzt* that the goalie never saw—into explosions that made you hold your breath each time she touched the ball. Now there's no ball and no field. How does a dad handle a furnace with so much potential to create magic—or meltdown? Bill cringes, helpless, never quite sure. He has tried sympathy, bedroom banishment, flinging a flip-flop at her, everything except the remedy his eldest daughter, Tiffany, tried once when Mia went over the edge: lashing her to the couch with pantyhose. The family couldn't guess what might set her off. It might be a teasing remark about the hand-me-down sweater she wears on Alternate Dress Day. It could be the skirt Mom tries to funnel her into for holidays and photos, or her failed attempt to slink out of the family picture, or that damn wing of hair flapping off the left side of her head on school picture days. Or, worst of all, losing at something cataclysmic like Old Maid or Uno or knee football in the hallway.

She quits when she smells defeat coming, because if she waits until it arrives, she'll tear herself to shreds. Her face will contort, her eyes gush, her nose stream, and then the worst thing of all will happen: Everyone will stare at the self-conscious girl. Her one hope is to twist embarrassment into anger—to scream, punch, topple the board game or hurl her sister Lovdy's cookie batter on the floor or threaten to smash Lovdy's collection of porcelain miniature horses into a thousand pieces. To have something else disintegrate instead of her.

The Curse, she'd call her raging emotions. All the Hamm girls have it, genetic dynamite straight from Mom, but none has it more than Mia. *I'm sorry*, she keeps saying when the dust settles. *I'm so sorry.* She'll have to spend her life guarding that furnace door. God, it seems so much simpler just to be a boy on a ball field, where you can turn humiliation into a header, fury into a breakaway. Where you get a bonus, as well, a piece of what Garrett's getting so much of: Dad's attention.

The Pumpkin rumbles up in front of the Maternity Cottage. Mia stops heaving, rubs away her tears, hangs her head and resigns herself to whiplash, this wrenching between worlds with such different rules, values . . . and equipment.

Out come the brooms, mops, buckets, scrub brushes, paintbrushes, sandpaper, rakes, shovels, clippers. Out comes Stephanie Hamm, still stunning at 40, lush dark hair flowing over her shoulders. She's a rare cat. A prospective nun who became a ballerina. The eldest of 11 children, daughter of an Air Force pilot who grew up, like Mia, bouncing from town to town, determined to exhaust her love for dance and fulfill her mother's wish that one of her children become a nun or priest, dedicated to following her Aunt Margaret into a convent. Until, at 15, she met Bill Hamm and fell hard.

Somehow, the nun and the ballerina inside her both survived the fall. Six children to raise, a home to pack in cardboard boxes and a new town to learn every few years: They aren't alibi enough for her conscience, aren't freedom from all those expectations. She sees her children off to school, spends the day on the phone or running around town gathering funds, food and clothing for another church campaign or community cause, making the house shine because what if someone comes to the door—*what'll people think?*—as she's preparing dinner, then rattling off instructions to Bill when he returns from the base and racing off to the theater to choreograph a recital or to perform, off to the dance studio to take or give lessons. She can't say no. She's too kind. If it's Wednesday during Lent, they'll eat peanut soup or potato meal or unseasoned rice and lentils, the blander the better, so the Hammies can learn what it's like to spoon down the grub that African children do, so they can swallow the family's prevailing ethic: *You're no better than anyone else. We're all equals in a community, all responsible for one another.* She hurries back at 10 p.m., brainstorming the church rummage sale that her children will captain that weekend, her eyes sweeping the floor to make sure the dinner crumbs were swept, because if not, they'll be in a pile on a plate at the offender's place at the table in the morning when the Hamms show up for their bowls of seven-grain gruel. Stephanie is the prettiest and trimmest, the most competent, selfless and giving mother a girl could have, but it's not enough. She doubts all of it. Every one of her *mosts* should be even more. If someone like that doesn't measure up, how can her daughters begin to think that they do?

It all crests one day when Mia's mom finds herself in a hospital bed. She's a fervent Catholic, ripping herself to pieces because she's just suffered a third-month miscarriage of a baby that, God forgive her, she secretly dreaded having, that she never should've conceived because four daughters and two recently adopted sons and a half-dozen charitable causes and a dancing career have left her feeling as if she's got nothing, God forgive her, left to give. A doctor enters the room and begins to gently chastise the woman on the next bed, scolding her about the abortion she's just undergone and the failure to be responsible about birth control, and the words pierce Stephanie's ripe conscience as if they were arrows targeted for her.

Suddenly Mia's mother is in charge of the Maternity Cottage, a Wichita Falls shelter for unmarried mothers who've been a little lax about birth control as well. Suddenly the Hamms are buying and gutting a dilapidated four-bedroom house, renovating it, maintaining the property, fund-raising to keep it afloat and inviting the spillover into their own home. Suddenly there are pregnant, unhappy strangers and their toddlers occupying what's left of Mia's mom's time and attention, not to mention her family's dinner table and the television set when Mia's favorite show is on. And no matter how much Mia respects her mother's golden heart and her father's generous spirit, she's a 12-year-old kid, for goodness' sake, who just wants to go home after a soccer game, wolf down a half-dozen chocolate-chip cookies that no Ethiopian kid'll ever lay eyes on, and play two-on-two hoops with the three guys on the next block. Instead she picks up a paint scraper and starts chipping away at the misery of the world.

OH, BOY. Here comes a grenade, rolling straight toward the Hamm house: a TV truck. Word's spread about this cute little 13-year-old gal on Notre Dame's junior high football team. That's worth both the six and 10 o'clock news, for sure, in North Texas in 1985.

Sure, her mom said, when Mia asked if she could play on the football team. Go for it, Mia. There's so much encouragement in this house. So much *Reach for the stars, girl!* But it's all beginning to grow confusing, sometimes even inside the white stripes. Guys who used to be fine about Mia's playing ball, after they saw she had the goods, aren't so fond of the idea now that the testosterone's kicking in and she's still beating them deep on fly patterns. Some have started singling her out, ridiculing her, steamrollering her. She doesn't sob inside the lines, though. You can't do that if you want to play with boys. Nobody bites her bottom lip better than Mia Hamm.

Play on girls' teams? She tried that once. She's just not like other girls. Some of her teammates layered on eye liner and mascara to play soccer. Some looked at boys *during* games. A few so resented her dominance that they stopped passing her the ball. She'd get it anyway, but how are you supposed to feel knocking some lipsticked center half off the ball and banging home your fourth of the day? She felt apologetic. She felt like the kid always raising her hand in class with the right answer, and so she pulled back sometimes, disappearing right in the middle of games.

The TV truck's nearly here. Mia's in her bedroom sobbing. Her mom's calling, *Hey, Mia, you better pull it together fast. What'll people think?* But she's flattened. Lovdy, avenging some previous sisterly atrocity, has just lowered the boom, the Hamm hammer, the clan's heaviest guilt mallet. "You think you're better than everyone else, don't you, Mia? Just because you're gonna be on TV, you think you're pretty hot. Well, you're arrogant." Mia? Mia hasn't puffed or crowed in her life, but ohmygod, if that's what people might think. . . .

She's a Hamm. She does the right thing. She exits her room when the doorbell rings, and tries to be polite. She gives the microphone and camera a few monosyllables, so no one can possibly think that she thinks she's hot stuff. The family gathers around the TV that night when her big moment comes. Where in the world is Mia Hamm? Holed up in her room.

LET HER stay there. She'll loathe this section of the story, about what a phenomenal soccer player she turns into, and how a small girl from a small town gets discovered. It's full of compliments, which are almost as painful to Mia as insults.

She's 14. It's 1986. She tries out for the North Texas Olympic Development girls' team 150 miles away in Dallas, and when the players split up for a scrimmage and a defender belts one skyward to clear it out of her end, every coach jotting notes on a clipboard stops and stares. Some little bitty gal bolts into the path of that clearing pass, wheels and drills it before it ever hits the ground, a 35-yard rocket volley into the upper right-hand corner of the net. Whoever she is, she's on the team . . . and six months later she's jumped to the *women's* team.

The team travels to Metairie, La., to play in a regional tournament. Her coach, John Cossaboon, alerts Anson Dorrance that there's a player he needs to look at.

Dorrance is 35, but already he's the lord of U.S. women's soccer. Already he's coached North Carolina to three national titles and been named coach of the U.S. national women's team. "Don't tell me which one she is," he tells Cossaboon. It's his way of testing the supposed phenom, and himself. She should *appear* to him on her own.

Dorrance watches the first minute of the first game and heads straight to Cossaboon. He nods toward the littlest one, the youngest one, the streak of light. The one who knifes right at a defender, knocks the ball a yard past her and then beats her to it, rubbing her out in a footrace. "That's her, right?" Dorrance says.

"No," deadpans Cossaboon. "You got it wrong."

Dorrance blinks, then shakes his head. Nice try, pal. She's *his*. Just like that. On his national team at 15 and—a few years later—on his college team the minute she finds her way out of high school. She shows up at that first national camp with a mullet haircut and a deer-in-the-headlights stare . . . and comes home on fire. She can't stop babbling at the dinner table: How marvelous Michelle and April are, how wonderful Kristine and Wendy and Joy. Women who knock *her* off the ball after she knocks *them* off the ball. Vicious competitors. A whole community. They *exist*. Females just like her.

Well, not exactly like her. Lots of them wear skirts now and then, even makeup. Women she can study, women she can draft behind when they go to a restaurant or mall, women who can introduce her to sides of herself she's never met. Good Lord, in just a few years they'll have her standing in a fitting room, trying on a bikini!

Look at her, this new person in the mirror. Not bad. Legs not half so bowed as she thought. But she could lose her so easily: One mediocre tournament could make her vanish. It's not enough, the hour and a half of dribbling and shooting drills she does alone at school on summer mornings, chasing down every shot on a netless goal in the Texas heat. Mia needs to get her first pair of running shoes and go for miles. She needs to pack up and move, for the seventh time, to some place where the competition will force her game to grow. Alone this time. That's how badly she needs to be with those girls she's just discovered.

It scares the hell out of her, walking out of tiny Notre Dame High in Wichita Falls and her class of 35 in February of her sophomore year, with her basketball teammates fighting to recapture the state championship that she'd led them to as a freshman. She clamps back her emotions, says goodbye to her family and friends, and she's gone.

She walks into a school, Lake Braddock, with more than 5,000 students. Sick to her stomach. Silent. It's in Burke, Va., a soccer hotbed, where she'll live with a man she barely knows, her aunt's brother-in-law. There's no Garrett anymore to give her cover. He's back in Wichita Falls, still trying to come to terms with the diagnosis that doctors gave him two years before: aplastic anemia, a bone marrow disorder that's still, in the 1980s, usually fatal.

If she were a boy, she wouldn't have to agonize over joining a new team, because boys understand that sports create hierarchies and that the ball will go to the dominant player the moment he asserts himself. But girls have to assess you first; they have to decide they like you before they let you fit in. How can Mia—with no time to chat because she's cramming in extra courses in order to graduate a year early and start at North Carolina, and missing entire weeks of practice because she's off training with the best women in the world—pull this one off amid a pack of teenage girls who have played together for years?

Like this: By shrinking in team meetings and schlepping the team's gear. By taking the team's worst ball for individual drills and feeding all the girls the most wonderful passes and compliments. By making it clear to the coach, Carolyn Rice, that she's only to praise Mia fleetingly, furtively, amid kudos for the other girls. By erasing herself as she imposes herself and carries Lake Braddock to the state championship.

She returns from her first trip overseas with the national team bubbling with things to tell her family—what she's just seen and done in China, and the new world opening before her. But what awaits her are two coffins, a pair of funerals and a family lost in grief. Her mother's dad and brother have gone down together in a Cessna.

It's almost as if fate's conspiring to hammer home her life's theme, in case she forgets it for an instant: It's not about you, Mia Hamm.

"YOU'VE GOT the potential, Mia. You can be the best soccer player in the world. But do you know what it takes? It's a decision you make. You can't make it halfway. You have to make it in your heart and mind, completely. You don't make the decision slowly. It's like turning on a light switch."

Mia and Anson Dorrance sit in darkness in his office. She's never met anyone like this. A man handing her a hall pass from guilt, from 19 years of conditioning about what a female owes everyone around her. A man offering her an environment, both at Chapel Hill and on the national team, where it's O.K. for women to be sisters off the field and cutthroats on it. Where you step on the foot of an opponent shadowing you too closely; where the results of every day's drills are posted to show who's Top Gun in each and who's breathing down her neck; where losers of intrasquad scrimmages must bend over in front of the goal and clutch their ankles so winners can blast 20-yard bullets at their butts. Where Mia finally feels it's safe to start growing out her hair.

Mia's parents have moved back to Italy, where Bill is a U.S. Air Force attaché, but first her mother has sent Dorrance a long letter attempting to explain in advance in case her daughter's emotions run amok. Dorrance shrugs it off. He's never had a player like Mia, who can't eat or talk at the team's pregame buffet. Who goes off alone before a game, cutting through imaginary opponents, dancing with the ball like a ballerina, then paces the sideline inside her own private tunnel. Then, before the big games, bolts to the toilet or nearest trash can and vomits. Bile. There's nothing in her to vomit. Then brings the crowd to its feet, chanting, "Mia! Mia!"

when her foot touches the ball. Then flogs herself at halftime if she hasn't scored—*Dammit, I suck, I'm worthless, the world's ending*—as if she's about to become the outcast, the stranger over on the sidewalk the next time teams are chosen; as if she owes her girls a pair of goals to prove she belongs, must dominate to feel like an equal. Then she does what's so hard for her to do outside the rectangle: exposes her soul, lets go, explodes, slams two into the back of the net and fist-pumps or slides or bull-rushes the stands, not in celebration of Mia but in release from the pressure she keeps heaping upon herself. You *have* to take responsibility for the community. You *have* to be perfect. But you're no better than anyone else.

Dorrance doesn't want to resolve this tension inside her. He wants it to flow like molten metal on a hundred soccer fields across the globe. He wants the furnace at full blast; he'll live with the collateral damage when Mia's anxiety over losing or not scoring sends the blaze the wrong way.

"Please tell Mia to stop yelling at me!" Tar Heels teammates ask captain Angela Kelly as they race upfield.

"It's all right, Hammer!" Angela calls to Mia.

"But we're playing lousy!" Mia shouts.

"Sure, you can tell them to step it up, but not so mean, Hammer!"

Let them work it out, Dorrance figures. Let Tony DiCicco, who replaces him in 1994 as coach of the national team, pick up the pieces and the chairs after Mia hisses "Shut up!" at him during a game in France, then gets in a screaming match with him at halftime and starts knocking over seats in the locker room.

Dorrance will live with first-stage meltdown. It's stage two that's more worrisome. That's when Mia, sometimes because she's pulled back her game for fear of doing too much and upsetting her teammates, loses her rhythm and confidence and grows so frustrated at not living up to her own standards that her whole body sags. She can't run away when failure's coming, as she used to as a child, but her heart and soul do. She stops chasing balls. "Take her out!" captain Carla Overbeck shouts at the coach when that happens.

Dorrance has players around Mia, like Kelly and Overbeck, who can act as a firewall. He builds the sisterhood strong enough to heal the wounds. He knows Mia will feel so awful the next day that she'll mend the fences. It's worth it, all of it, because this is the player he's been searching for ever since he became a coach, one who catches fire each time the flint of her values is struck: You're doing this for 19 teammates, Mia. For American soccer. For millions of girls you can inspire. You can give by taking, Mia.

But now he wants her to take the next step—to choose athletic immortality, to give and take more. Mia's silent. He's asking something of her that happens only on the other side of the stripe: spontaneity, a light-switch decision, a go-for-broker.

It's 1991. Title IX, mandating equal opportunities for women in collegiate sports, has just begun to bear fruit. Sometimes only a few hundred people show up to watch the U.S. team play: There's no such thing as a female spectator team sport. Mia and her teammates do their own laundry, carry their own gear, sometimes drive their team vans. There's so little interest in their games that they send faxes to inform friends in the U.S. of how they're doing in the inaugural '91 World Cup and return from China with the championship to a welcoming party of three. They function in darkness.

"It's a decision, Mia," Dorrance says quietly in the darkness, "that you make like *that.*" His hand strikes the switch. Light floods the room. She hasn't said a word, but Dorrance's drama works. She decides she's going for it. Never dreaming how much light she'll cast, and how much of her the light will expose.

DOES THE face launch the movement? Or does the movement launch the face? At some point the two entwine, and no one can say. At some point little girls begin roaming the team's hotel hallways, looking for Mia, and after she poses for a picture and begins to walk away, they say, our whole team's waiting outside for you, can you come? At some point they begin falling asleep with her face on their walls and ceilings, the last image on their retinas each day, this woman who convinces them, without uttering a word, that it's O.K. to sweat, seethe, leap, let go. They begin writing her letters, wearing her ponytail and number 9 jersey to her games and shrieking, "Mia! Mia!" at the same pitch and frenzy as starving baby birds.

At some point she agrees, in spite of all her misgivings, to do the Letterman show and the Pert Plus commercial and the Barbie doll and the

Gatorade and the Nike sneakers, because people she trusts persuade her that doing so will liberate even more girls who stand on the sidewalk as teams are chosen. Convince more girls that anything's possible, even the new soccer-playing Barbie doll.

The movement needs the face because the face, no longer a pixie tomboy's, offers the femininity, the beauty and the naked passion that the sport and the camera need. The face needs the movement because it offers the sense of mission, the justification for all those solitary three-a-day workouts, that a Hamm needs. Where else can the lenses go when the U.S. women's team wins the 1996 Olympic gold medal on U.S. soil in front of 76,489 fans but to the burning hazel eyes of the team's leading scorer, the woman who led UNC to four national titles? She becomes, according to surveys, the most recognized and appealing female athlete in America, and the fourth-most-admired one, behind Michael Jordan, Tiger Woods and Lance Armstrong. One of the select few whose first name suffices. One of PEOPLE's 50 Most Beautiful People. Nike names its largest building after her, and people she's never laid eyes on begin saying, "If you need me, I'll be in Mia at 3:30 today." The shyest one becomes the anointed one.

Sometimes it's beautiful. When she knows a public moment's coming, when she has agreed to it and prepared herself, she might still pace and fret, but when the lights turn on, so does the performer. She's eloquent, gracious, funny. People walk away dazzled by Mia.

Other times it's painful. She's walking off the practice field. A pack of reporters she didn't expect walks right past all her teammates and surrounds her. They're asking her the question that paralyzes her: What's it like to be the best woman player in the world? They're creating more responsibility, more expectations. They're asking her to put herself first. She can't do it.

"Ask me that question when I can dominate on both offense and defense like [teammate] Kristine Lilly does," she replies. "Ask me when I can head a ball like Tisha Venturini, defend as well as Joy Fawcett, play an all-around game like Julie Foudy." It's how she feels. It's a way of disappearing. It's both.

The reporters roll their eyes. A pack of fans gathers around the pack of reporters. Mothers and daughters begging for autographs. *Mia! Meeee-*

aaaaaa! Over here! A hundred baby birds to feed, and the mother bird must choose which ones. The team bus revs. The media want more, much more, but she has no quick answers: They all require so much thought. Her mates are waiting. They're the ones she wants to be with. They're why she works out eight hours a day—to be good enough just to be part of them.

The vise tightens around the woman who makes all those girls feel so free. It's all on her face. Everything's being squeezed through layers and folds of intellect and feeling, being measured once, measured twice. What'll people think? What'll her teammates think if she keeps standing here, separate, consenting to all this attention? So she *must* say no. But what'll the reporters and fans think if she spurns them, and what about her responsibility to women's soccer? So she *can't* say no. But she's determined to have boundaries. No matter how much she loves her mother, she's not going to *be* her, she's not going to live her life by other people's expectations. So she *must* say no.

Yes or no, a strange thing happens. There's so much heat inside her, people sometimes walk away thinking that Mia's cold.

She's not built for celebrity. She can't play the game—any game—lightly, can't make breezy chitchat with strangers while all that's grinding inside her; she can't fake it. She's too busy trying to decide what's the right thing to do, too caught in her own crossfire, too wary of what lurks just below it. When a girl rises in a roomful of eight-to 14-year-olds in Sydney and asks Mia what her main goal in life is, she replies, "Not to embarrass myself." She's kidding. Sort of. Maybe.

She finds her way into the corner or the foyer at receptions and cocktail parties, or onto the floor to play with somebody's child. She lowers a ball-cap brim over her lowered eyes on the street. "I'm sure I miss some things about the world," she tells people, "but I can tell you a lot about my shoes."

That's what the world misses about her, what teammates who've known her for years cherish: her wicked sarcasm, her honesty, her vulnerability, days when her guard comes down and she's positively giddy. They get her dead-on Noo Yawk and Brit and Aussie accents, her impersonations, her rocking *Rocky Top* on karaoke nights. They get long notes so heartfelt that some keep them and read them before every game. They get her on their doorstep after a five-hour flight when their parents die. They get a teammate whose eyes well up in compassion when they're feeling down and need to talk, one who crisscrosses headbands over her nose in commiseration when they suffer a fracture and have to wear a face guard. They get her hauling the equipment bag out of the bus when they're trudging to their hotel rooms at midnight. Doing all the community work. They get appearances in her commercials, they get cash, because she takes less and insists that they be included. Newcomers keep their distance at first, wary of her moods, but by their third year on the team they love her: They've seen so much goodness unfold.

The U.S. team becomes sisters, more than any team of men ever became brothers, because their star will have it no other way. They yank her onto elevators when the autograph stalkers become too much. They pretend to be her to throw the hounds off her scent. They help her disappear.

They're there for her when darkness falls. A doctor walks into the waiting room at the National Institutes of Health in Bethesda, Md., in 1996 and tells Mia, her mother and her brother Garrett that there's only one chance left for him, a Hail Mary bone-marrow transplant. She reels out of that room, punishing herself for every day she chased a ball across the world and forgot about her family. Two months after the transplant in 1997, his immune system fails, his left arm goes numb, and a fungal infection attacks his brain. She feels the full power of her parents' hearts, gratitude that they opened up to a boy born in Bangkok 28 years before, as the family encircles his bed. She looks at her siblings, red eye to red eye, and realizes that all the old explosions are meaningless now, and that she will never again go months without calling them.

She takes a long, hard look at stardom, too. It has never seemed more foolish. She's never wanted more to vanish. Then she looks again. Her choice in the matter is fading, just like her brother. She'll never embrace celebrity, but now she's got to grip its hand. Because she's found her higher calling, her purpose, here on this bed: to reach even deeper on the field, and off it too, to play like Bill Hamm's daughter so she can give like Stephanie Hamm's. To use fame to channel hundreds of thousands of dollars into the Mia Hamm Foundation, to provide athletic opportunities for girls and funds to people desperate for bone-marrow transplants. To write letters to inspire sick children, to visit them and take them to arcades.

She watches her brother's breath hitch, his eyes open for an instant. "Ohhh, Garrett," she calls. And then he's gone: the boy who first brought her in from the sideline, and now won't let her go back.

NOW PLACE the ball on a white dot 12 yards from the goal. Fix the eyes of 90,185 people on it, the most ever to watch a women's competition, and lock the gaze of 40 million more on it on television. Turn up the heat: 105° on the field, players dizzy from dehydration. Turn it up higher: World Cup final, 0–0, U.S. and China deadlocked after 90 minutes of regulation and two 15-minute overtimes. And higher: birth of a women's professional league possibly riding on the five penalty kicks each team will take from the white dot on the floor of the Rose Bowl to break the tie.

Call Mia Hamm's name. Put her on the spot. She can't possibly disappear, not in front of 40,090,185 people—can she?

Holy smoke! She's *trying* to. She's telling assistant coach Lauren Gregg that she doesn't want to take one of the five penalty kicks. "Why isn't Mac taking one?" she asks, referring to teammate Shannon MacMillan. "Mac should be taking one."

"Mia, you're taking one," says Gregg.

"Why?" asks Mia.

Why? Her agent's fielding, and refusing, 15 requests a day for interviews and appearances and photo shoots of the best female player in the world as the U.S. women's team becomes the sizzle story of 1999. She's in a Gatorade commercial going one-on-one with Michael Jordan in a variety of sports as *Anything You Can Do, I Can Do Better* jingles in the background. It's crunch time. It's when superstars demand the ball. They have no conscience. They're sharks.

In a skybox sits Bill Clinton, pulled so near the edge of his seat by this game that he has nearly fallen out of it. On the sideline stands Robert Hanashiro, discovering that his front-page *USA Today* Mia-less team photo isn't the failure he feared. "Nice photo," people at the Rose Bowl tell him. "It's fitting. That's Mia." In the stands, flown here from Japan by the U.S. military at President Clinton's request, is Mia's husband, Christiaan Corry.

Wait a minute. Mia's *married*? Absolutely. Well, sort of. To a quiet, intense young man she met in a class at UNC and wedded at 22. His intensity and easy wit remind her of her father's, and his career choice—he becomes a Marine helicopter pilot—does too. What she miscalculates is how much energy and time marriage takes, how little she has left for it when her soccer devours so much. She and Christiaan are so busy following their dreams that they're rarely on the same continent, let alone the same bed. So her marriage often seems invisible, too, and she makes sure it is to the world, pleading with reporters who write about her to steer clear of it.

A hush falls over the Rose Bowl in anticipation of the shootout. Mia's teammates wrap themselves in iced towels and pour water over their heads, but it's too late for Mia, the white dot has set all her combustibles aflame. Doesn't matter that just a few months before, she became, at 27, the leading international scorer in soccer history, male or female; that she left Pelé in the dust 34 goals ago. Doesn't count that her defense and passing have improved so relentlessly that she no longer needs to score to alter a game, and that opponents double-team her, freeing her pals to score. Mia scored two goals early in the World Cup tournament, then ran dry, and the questions have begun again, reporters digging up those stats about her dearth of offense in major tournaments, spinning their cute little MIA puns and tying her in so many knots over failing to meet so many people's expectations that it becomes harder and harder for her to explode. An eight-game drought just a few months ago brought her into Tony DiCicco's office in tears. Do you know how scary it is to be Mia Hamm and not feel like playing soccer?

If she misses the kick that decides this World Cup, she'll have to live inside those flames until her final breath. Her penalty kicks in practice have been shaky. *Oh, no.* What if the coach thinks he *has* to choose her because she's supposedly the star? She has to let him know he's not obligated. *Oh, no.* A hierarchy's being created here, a threat to sisterhood and equality and all the potato meal that ever stuck to the roof of her mouth, a thing loathsome enough when it's being foisted on the team by outsiders—the media or a sneaker corporation or a soccer federation presenting awards—but unbearable when it's the coach doing it, the family's father figure. She has to show her teammates that she doesn't feel entitled to one of these five kicks. *Oh, no.* What if she protests too much and they think she doesn't want to contribute, that she fears the responsibility, that she's foisting it on somebody else? Trust me. You don't want to be *in Mia* at 3:51 PDT on July 10, 1999.

Mia fails. She can't airbrush herself out of the biggest moment of her career. She is chosen to kick fourth for the Americans. They're up 3-2—the third Chinese attempt was punched away by U.S. goalkeeper Briana Scurry—when Mia approaches the white dot. If she scores, the Chinese are against the wall. She places the ball on the dot, pushes a strand of hair from her face. She will remember nothing from then until the ball strikes the net, and the Rose Bowl explodes.

She screams, but her face never relaxes, never smiles, her eyes still burning and her jaw clenched as she races back to her teammates. She is not a woman celebrating. She's a woman howling *I beat you, goddammit,* at all her fear and doubt.

She passes out in the locker room an hour and a half after the game, awakens on a table with IV tubes in her arms and spends the rest of the night in her hotel room, vomiting bile, going hot and cold, unable to speak or even open her eyes, they burn so much. Fried as much by months of anxiety over the World Cup as by the blazing sun over the Rose Bowl.

At the jubilant team party at the hotel that night, everyone asks the same question that people asked at Mia's prom, at her school sports banquet, on her high school team picture day, and at 11:30 p.m. when her college teammates hit the Chapel Hill bars to celebrate another championship: Where's Mia Hamm?

HOW MUCH do they pay you to write a story?" she asks. "Maybe I could pay you that much not to write it." She's joking. Sort of. Maybe.

Goodness, we're on the 20th page of a story that she hoped to God, if it *had* to be written at all, wouldn't last more than four. So let's not linger on the depressing loss to Norway in the 2000 Olympic final or the two goals Mia is limited to in the tournament. Let's skip past the new league kicking off in 2001, the Women's United Soccer Association, thanks to Mia and her national teammates' agreeing to play for peanuts. Let's zip past the burden placed on her, as the only household name, to sell her new team, the Washington Freedom, and the WUSA itself—and the feeling that she's doing too much . . . but never enough.

Let's hurry past the shoulder problem and knee surgery that hamper her during her first two seasons with the Freedom, and all the losing that miserable first summer, when the sisterhood disperses and leaves her surrounded by strangers again: the new kid who still finds it so hard to fit in. When she's named the Freedom's captain and discovers once more, as she did in her senior year at UNC, that she's not cut out for it. When she barks at players who don't know her well enough to say, "Oh, that's just Mia," the way her USA mates do; when she's too intense for teammates cowed by a captain running sprints with her own stopwatch; when she's just not sure enough that everyone wants to hear what she has to say.

Let's even jump past the turnaround, the second year with the Freedom, when she relinquishes the captaincy and plays mostly the second halves of games as she recovers from her knee injury, and still hushes the whispers that she's past her prime by leading the league in assists, tying for the lead in points and taking her team to the title game before finally losing. Let's triple-jump past the divorce in 2001—*yes, please*, croaks Mia—when marriage by e-mail finally collapses. Past all the sleepless and headache-racked nights holed up in her bedroom, haunted by her failure to keep a vow made in front of her family and friends.

Let's run straight to joy—unfettered, uncluttered, unmeasured. Let's fly to Nomar.

ON THE white dot, of all places. That's where they meet. At a promotional event in 1998 at Harvard, where she and Nomar end up in a shootout, five kicks each, to entertain the fans. He makes three. She makes four.

"Thanks for throwing it," Mia says.

"I had to let you win," Nomar replies.

Nine months later, during the most painful patch of her career. That's when they really talk for the first time, during her eight-game slump in early '99. She's so desperate that she digs up the phone number he gave her and begs his forgiveness for bothering him. "I'm struggling right now," she says. "Do you have any ideas? What do you do when you're in a slump?"

"I pick out something small," he says. "Something I can control, something I can manage. And I just focus on that."

"O.K.," she says.

"Are you winning?" he asks.

"Yeah."

"Are you playing well, outside of your scoring?"

"Well . . . yeah."

"Then you've got to just enjoy the game. You've got to stop worrying."

She tries that for a change. And not long afterward, on a give-and-go with Foudy against Japan, she scores and races to midfield, screaming to Julie, "Can you get a f---ing 500-pound gorilla off my back?" When Julie pretends to grab the beast and fling it away, she cries, "Thank you!" and swoons to the ground.

Just don't spoil it. Don't ask what Nomar's last name is. That's part of his allure, that he's one of a select few athletes whose first name suffices, a star big and bright enough to eclipse her—a cover for the cover girl. God, it's a relief when slack-jawed strangers approach and walk right past her, to him. Lord, it's a lesson to see how much easier he is with fame, comfortable enough to set boundaries and live by them without anguish, to give freely without feeling threatened when it's time to, and to say no thank you when it's not. A man she can study, a man she can draft behind when they go to a restaurant or mall, a man who can introduce her to sides of herself she has never met . . . and to her oldest self, the nine-year-old whose best buddies were ballplayin' guys.

He's a freak on fitness and perfecting technique, just as she is. They spend seven-hour days together for six weeks during the winters of 2002 and '03 at Athletes' Performance, a fitness and biomechanics center in Tempe, Ariz., where they hone every muscle and movement that they use in their games, Mia even perfecting how her feet touch the ground when she runs. She doesn't need that when she's with Nomar, of course. Her feet don't touch it.

Happy-go-lucky, playful, carefree, a real goofball . . . her friends use words like those to describe Mia these days. Why, she even wears skirts and flowing dresses at the drop of a ball cap. She's begun to paint abstract shapes, sharing a canvas and colors with Nomar on one of them. She glows when she's with him, teammates marvel. It's so wonderful that neither one wants to talk about it. And on the soccer field she's sounder of body and mind than she ever was, a better all-around player.

He flies her to the Caribbean last Thanksgiving, gets down on one knee and asks her to marry him. For once in her life, Mia answers a question without having to think.

"I WANT to enjoy this World Cup and Olympics. That's what I want to do with my last year. I'm learning to realize this is awesome, that the positives so outweigh the negatives or the pressures. It's a waste of energy and emotion to focus on what you can't control, to brood over each play. It's not the message I want to give to the younger players.

"I'm trying to make relationships my first priority. In the end the medals never say, 'I love you.' They tarnish and collect dust. People tried to tell me that before. You can read it in books and hear it on *Oprah* and say, 'Oh, yeah.' But it has to be in your gut, and I guess it wasn't. Your perception is your reality. I'm starting to trust myself."

Yes, let's let Mia talk for a change, before she hangs it up next August along with most of the other women at the heart of the sisterhood who've been playing together since the late '80s. Mia, Julie, Joy, Kristine and Brandi Chastain are already planning reunions at which they'll gather and laugh over all the silly things they did. Like the time that everyone misinterpreted, when a teammate yanked Mia's shorts up to her chest just as that photographer was snapping that front-page picture for *USA Today*, and she felt laughter coming on so hard that she had to duck behind a teammate.

Mia actually seems to be relishing the prospect of retirement, something no one could've imagined of her two years ago. To be looking forward to making little Nomars, to sitting in a backyard with her siblings and parents and watching all the Hamm grandchildren play touch football for as long as a Hamm can bear to sit and watch.

Of course, that's when she's not worrying about getting cut from the U.S. team any moment now, or writhing over what you think about every word in this story. Remember, she's just starting to trust herself. Just starting a long trip.

Let's let her savor the WUSA championship she helped lead her team to last month, even though the league into which she poured so much of herself folded three weeks later. Let's let her get married in private after the World Cup and then vanish with the balloons and the doves and the fireworks at the closing ceremonies next summer in Athens. She's spun enough gold, forged enough steel in that furnace. Let's remember her as the bridge, the one all the ponytailed phenoms are climbing across to leave behind the 20th century, when so many women had to feel apologetic about going for it all, in order to reach the 21st, when they'll all be standing on the white dot waiting for the ball, and the photo op, and the commercial.

She's 31. It's time. Sometimes you've got to disappear before you can really see yourself.

POSTSCRIPT: *Today Mia Hamm lives in Manhattan Beach, Calif. Married to Los Angeles Dodgers third baseman Nomar Garciaparra in November 2003, Hamm gave birth to twin girls, Ava and Grace, on March 27, 2007, almost three years after leading the U.S. to a gold medal at the Olympic Games in Athens. In her final game, a friendly match against Mexico in December '04, she had two assists and wore the name "Garciaparra" on her back for the second half. In '07, the newly formed Women's Professional Soccer League, set to begin competition in April '09, iconized her as the figure in its official logo.*

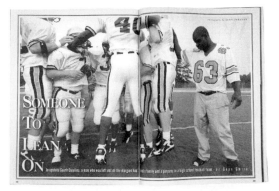

Someone to Lean On

In upstate South Carolina, a black boy left out on the fringe was invited inside the lines by a white coach. Four decades later, he's a football star and his town's biggest celebrity—and still in 11th grade.

E BEGIN WAY OVER THERE, OUT ON THE margin. We begin with a dirty, disheveled 18-year-old boy roaring down a hill on a grocery cart, screaming like a banshee, holding a transistor radio to his ear. No one ever plays with him, for he can barely speak and never understands the rules. He can't read or write a word. He needs to be put away in some kind of institution, people keep telling his mother, because anything, anything at all, can happen out there on the margin. There's already a gully over his left eye from the time he stepped in front of a car as a five-year-old and nearly died from the impact. There are teeth missing from the day he swerved in front of a car while riding his grocery cart, and there's a scar on his thigh from the day he was playing with a packet of tiny sticks and suddenly everything around him was ablaze. There is something, as well, that you can't see, except sometimes in his eyes: fear. Fear of people. Once some kids told him to pull the lever on the fire-alarm box and then watched him being led away to jail. Another time he was seized by a group of boys who yanked down his pants and painted his buttocks with paint thinner, burning him nearly as badly as the blazing sticks had.

All of which might explain why his grocery cart keeps taking him to a football field at McCants Junior High in Anderson, S.C. It's autumn 1964. Everything on that grid is so different from life out on the margin. All the boys wear the same neat, clean clothing and move to assigned places at the bark of a one-word command. There are units and sub-units, and everyone knows precisely where he belongs. From a safe distance, the boy watches T.L. Hanna High School's junior varsity team practice on the McCants field and mutely absorbs it all.

One day the players hear noises and look over. The boy on the margin is commanding his own team, one that only he can see, through a series of calisthenics and drills, doing his best to mimic the coaches' body language, signals and commands. The players giggle; it's a distraction, to be sure. The young coach, whose future hinges on his ability to maintain discipline and precision on that grid, turns and looks too.

The choices that make or unmake a life are so small. "Come over here, boy," calls the coach.

WHEN WE speak of the power of sports today, it's always in terms of their grip on the national marketplace, their headlock on the American psyche. It's so easy to forget all about their other power. . . .

Radio turned 50 two months ago, but you might not have read about it. He bounded through the corridors of T.L. Hanna High collecting his birthday gifts, waving and slapping fives and hugging kids and wiggling his rear end as the students chanted, "Go, Radio, you got it!" It took the whole bed of head football coach Harold Jones's pickup truck to get all the gifts home, just as it has on the other birthdays and the Christmases that Radio has celebrated at the school for the last 32 years.

No, he never made it to an institution. He became one instead. Just before his last birthday, folks in Anderson were remarking on all the speckles of white on his head and in his whiskers. "When Radio dies, it'll be the biggest funeral in the history of Anderson," said Herb Phillips, an assistant football coach at Hanna. "It'll be like a senator's or a governor's funeral."

"Gonna be *sad* sad, like losing a family member," said Terry Honeycutt, another football assistant.

"He's the best-known figure in high school football in upstate South Carolina," said former Hanna coach Jim Fraser.

"He *is* T.L. Hanna—it's that simple," said Coach Jones, who for three decades has kept Radio under his wing.

In many countries where towns have plazas and cafes and bars and butcher shops all within a few blocks of people's homes, there is no margin. There are places for those with defects, impediments and afflictions to mingle with their neighbors, to be taken care of and teased, to feel part of something larger. They become local characters, not freaks. Somehow in America those places have vanished or never existed, and people like Radio end up in homes behind walls, living with strangers who are just like them, or mumbling through the streets of large cities, ragged and gaunt.

But there remains one rarely noticed place where they can still belong, a niche no sociologist figured on—after all, isn't sports where people turn to watch the strong chew up and spit out the weak? But something about high school athletics is still human enough to accommodate people whose minds work at different speeds and angles, and so you can find these people on the sidelines or in the bleachers all across the U.S., lighting up as they exchange greetings with the regulars. Why, in just the small circle of schools against which Hanna competes, there is one-eyed and slow-witted Lonnie McGee racing onto the field with the football team at Greer High each Friday night, and before him there was Housecat, whose mission in life, until he died not so long ago, was to chase down every foul ball and home run hit at Greer games, even if he had to barge into someone's home to do so, and hurry that ball right back to the umpire. There is Marlee Gambrell, born with heart and hearing and vision defects, hooting "Don't worry 'bout it!" in the darkest moments at Belton-Honea Path High. And up until recently, there was wild-eyed Doris, taking care of the water bottles and ringing that half-ton bell on the sidelines at Easley High. Thrilled, every one of them, to take on the title—team manager—that most teenagers smirk at.

But none of them has been more loved, or more legendary, than Radio. He holds more high school varsity letters than any other man in history, having received one each from the Hanna football, basketball and track teams every year for the past three decades and filed them all carefully between his box spring and his mattress. Who else can lay claim to having missed just one week of high school in the past 10 years? Only once, and long ago, did Radio make the mistake of saying he was in the 12th grade, and then he was consumed by terror when the coaches told him that meant he would be graduating soon. Ever since then he has nodded wisely and declaimed loudly to one and all, *"I be in 'lebenf grade,"* always reaching out a hand to touch his listener when he speaks, always seeking assurance that he still belongs and that everything is O.K.

He awakens each morning before six and, being unable to tell time, has to be restrained by his older brother or by his brother's wife from making an immediate beeline for the bus stop. Radio is the first of the 15 kids at the stop to bound onto bus No. 9 and the first to bound off it in front of T.L. Hanna High. He bops in and out of classes all day, taking copious notes—an unrelenting series of loops—and glowing at the end of each marking period when he receives his report card just like everyone else. A mesh sack full of footballs slung over his shoulder, he bounds onto the practice field after school, and the players, like their fathers before them, rub his head as if he were a pet retriever and laugh as he commences his gibber-jabber commands, gobbledygook pep talks and flapdoodle defensive signals.

"Dat yo' man, boy! Don' you unnerstan' dat? Dat yo' man! Don' you worry 'bout yo' man! You got to git dat kwahback! Ain' dat right?"

"Right, Radio."

"Huh?"

"You're right, Radio."

"What? Huh?"

Oh, yes, sometimes Radio can drive them up a wall and across the ceiling. But it's all worth it, every maddening and bewildering moment of it, when practice ends and all the coaches sit in a circle around Radio in their office, competing to see who can recount the latest or most vintage Radio anecdote, knowing that he will bark out some four-word proclamation that will make the moment even richer. Each sentence Radio speaks is a victory for them, because they know it is the love and attention they have been showering on him for decades that has given the mute boy a voice. Maybe Coach Jones will tell the story about the time back in the mid-'80s, when he was also T.L. Hanna's track coach, that he took Radio to the all-day Trojan Relays at Northwestern High in Rock Hill, S.C., and wondered for hours what had become of Radio . . . finally finding out upon returning to the team bus at the end of the meet. There lay Radio in the front seat, doubled in pain, sweating bullets . . . and there lay the cooler, bereft of all 30 roast-beef sandwiches, not to mention a dozen sodas, that Coach Jones had packed for the kids. *"Dem sammiches good!"* Radio still yelps a decade later. Which no doubt leads into the tale of the time Radio lifted the entire canister of cheese at a school cafeteria salad bar and dumped a foot-high pile of grated cheddar on his lettuce—*"Cheese go good wid salad!"* Which brings up the time Radio was so fixated on the hot dog he was carrying before a game at Greenwood High that when he slipped on the wet grass, rather than release his cargo and use his hand to break the fall, he salvaged the frankfurter and landed on his wrist, fracturing it. Radio sat in the mud and polished off his hot dog and *then* burst into tears.

No name for Radio's defect has ever been pronounced, as far as anyone knows. It is no doubt genetic, because he shares it with his father, whom he has rarely seen since his first few years of life, and with Cool Rock, the brother two years his junior who shares Radio's bedroom. Cool Rock still can't be understood when he tries to speak. But then, Cool Rock was never adopted by a team.

Even when James Robert Kennedy was a little boy, everywhere he went, his radio went too, until folks finally had no choice but to make Radio his name. From the radio came a human voice, the only one he could count on to speak to him when his mother, Janie Mae Greenlee, left for long hours to clean and cook at the local hospital or schools. Now and then the boy would even lift his radio to his lips and talk back to it.

He attended a school for the learning disabled for a few months one year, but it didn't take. Back then he couldn't use a fork or pedal a bike, and because cruelty runs downhill, it wasn't a good idea for a cat or a dog to approach him. "What's my name?" Jones asked as he and his fellow jayvee coach, Dennis Patterson, began luring Radio closer and closer with bottles of soda that autumn of '64. "Do you remember what I told you yesterday?"

"*Woomifflcojowu.*"

"Try again. You can have this whole bottle if you can say it. *Coach . . . Jones.*"

What made Coach Jones invite the wild boy with the missing teeth to come to a game, to help carry the watercoolers and then hop into Harold's pickup truck for a ride home? Why would a coach work so hard at discipline and deployment and then let loose a pinball on his chess board? After all, everyone knew Coach Jones to be a strict and quiet man who virtually never showed emotion or affection. No one knew that when he was a kid growing up in Anderson, he was the one who would fight anyone who picked on the delicate boy who lived across the street, and he was the one who, when working at his grandfather's theater, would slip a retarded man in the door for free and put a box of popcorn in his hands.

And so, before you knew it, Radio was going everywhere Coach Jones and his jayvee team went, and Radio's halftime show was gaining renown. Radio would charge onto the field and bend down like a center, screeching those preposterous signals, hike the ball to himself and dipsy-doodle all around. Finding no one open except himself, Radio would flip the ball to Radio and then, to the crowd's roar, boogie-woogie all the way to pay dirt.

In no time, Coach Jones was inviting Radio to school on game days, handing him sneakers, a T-shirt and shorts so he could take gym class with the other kids. Soon Radio was following the kids into health class, history and social studies. Sure, it probably broke some law, and no doubt it exposed the school to all manner of liability. But one glare from Coach Jones was all it took to keep Radio in line, one threat that he would be banished from the team if he misbehaved. The principal had little choice but to accept Radio as part of the school. "The kids would kill me if I ever got rid of him," says current principal Mike Sams. They loved the frantic hip-hop way he ran in phys-ed class until that sorry day four years ago when he tore a hamstring and scrabbled around the gym floor like a crab, sobbing, *"I wan' my mama!"* They loved the way he rubbed his furrowed face and sighed *"Whoooo!"* as he took history tests, as if in deep consternation over the complexity of the questions, and then painstakingly filled in each blank with the same set of loops.

Soon Radio was wolfing down breakfast and two lunches a day in the cafeteria, then cleaning up the tables in his long yellow rubber gloves and running errands for teachers all over the school. Soon he was jump-starting dull assemblies and sluggish pep rallies, erupting out of his seat to do one of those shimmy-shuffle-shakedowns that got the whole student body to bopping and bellowing. It only got better when Radio was inducted into Hanna's Naval Junior ROTC unit, and he began wearing a full military uniform each Wednesday. What a sight he was in crisp dress whites and blues and merit ribbons, racing into special-ed class and pulling out his Crayolas for 10 or 15 minutes of coloring, then bolting out the door and up a stairway, two steps at a time, to monitor the halls—*"Where you goin', boy? Don' wun! No wunnin' in da hall! Hi, honey! I like you!"* After a few minutes of that, standing fully erect and with his eyes open, he'd often fall dead asleep. If his schedule simply didn't permit a snooze, he could always—in the midst of a violent six-on-six drill later that day at football practice—sprawl out on a tackling dummy and doze like a baby.

It was all too wonderful to confine to autumn, and soon Radio was the manager of the basketball and track teams as well. How could Coach Jones resist when Radio put on that basset hound face at track meets and begged to run too? And so, even though Coach Jones was in charge of a juggernaut, a team that would win 10 state titles between 1970 and '92, he would take the opposing coach aside and ask if Radio could enter the slow heats of the 100-, 200- and 400-meter dashes. Wearing spikes and shorts and a singlet just like everyone else, Radio would blast out of the starting blocks, blazing when he was in front of the stands and then slowing to a walk, or stopping altogether to pull up his socks, once he reached the curve and there was no attention to bask in. "What happened on that curve, Radio?" the coaches would kid him later. "Did the gorilla jump on your back?" It was at times such as those—when Radio's eyes might suddenly cloud with fear, and he would ask, *"Where dat go-wi-wa hide? Behind dem trees?"*—that everyone would be reminded of how frightening a place the world could be for Radio, and how close an eye they would have to keep on him.

Coach Jones took Radio to the doctor every year, monitored Radio's diet when his blood-pressure readings and cholesterol count went through the roof, and made sure his medical and dental bills were paid. "Radio," says assistant coach Honeycutt, "would be dead by now if not for Coach Jones." The players who lived in Radio's neighborhood kept at bay the bullies who used to target him, and a half-dozen players might each deliver a hamburger and an order of fries to Radio on game day, each unaware that Radio was squirreling the food away in his backpack, each proudly believing that his offering was the only one. One day, when Radio's invariably empty billfold was stolen at school, the players all but formed vigilante squads, and the coaches hastily bought Radio a new wallet for fear that a student might be found dangling from a ventilation duct. Even in the fourth quarter of a tense game, when a player was bent-in-half tired and cringing from a coach's screams for blowing a coverage, and Radio would get right in his face and reenact the entire tirade, or demand out of the clear blue to know his shoe size, the player's tolerance would hold. "O.K., Radio, O.K.," the Hanna kids would say, and a few seconds later, Radio would have them giggling.

Just once, 22 years ago, did Radio miss a game. It was not long after Coach Jones and Radio had gotten their promotions to the varsity, but being only an assistant coach then, Jones could only swallow his Adam's apple when Fraser, the head coach, decided the bus was too crowded for Radio to make the road trip to Northwestern High. Fraser slipped Radio a five to ease his conscience, but the sight of that slump-shouldered man standing alone in the school parking lot, tears rolling down his cheeks, would haunt the coach forever, as would the 27–20 loss that followed. "He'll be the first one on the bus from here on out," Fraser vowed that night, and when the T.L. Hanna Yellow Jackets, with Radio leading them onto the field, rolled all the way to the state final that year, Radio's position was forever secure.

From then on rain was the only thing that Radio had to fear on game day. Each wet Friday he would scramble out the school's back door every few minutes, mournfully holding out his palm to feel the air, then rushing back to Coach Jones to confirm, for the 28th time, *"Gonna 'top wainin', wight, Co' Jone'?"* And when God smiled, and the rain clouds ran away, Radio bloomed.

Imagine, just for a moment, that you could go to a football game one day and play every role, be everyone in the whole stadium. That's what Radio did every game. Gumming and gnawing another freshly mooched fried-chicken drumstick, he would start out as the official greeter, holding open the Hanna program to make sure all arriving fans saw his photograph and hoisting up his pants legs to make sure everyone got a gander at his new pair of shoes—*"Wook at my Weeboks!"*—along with his socks, one white and one black. Then, dropping one drumstick and seizing another, he would commandeer the bass drum as the Hanna band made its knee-pumping entrance, quickly double back to wolf down a free hot dog and then scurry up to the press box to become the radio color commentator, barking over the WAIM airwaves, *"We gon' beat dey butt!"* All at once it would occur to Radio that he was also Hanna's coach, and he'd bolt down onto the field to yelp stretching instructions to the team during warmups—*"You roll dat neck, boy!"*—and then back to the bleachers to scarf some free popcorn and sign his autograph, loop-de-loop.

For the next two hours, to the ricochet of impulse, he would be the band director leading the touchdown celebration tune, the pom-pom-shaking cheerleader, the team trainer kneading cramps from players' calves, the 15-year-old flirt tossing popcorn at the cheerleaders' bare legs, the drum majorette in the halftime show, the fanatic racing up and down the sidelines with a giant Hanna flag, the water boy rushing squeeze bottles—empty, as often as not—onto the field during timeouts, and the coach arm-waggling defensive signals at the offensive line . . . all to the steady background bleating, from white-haired alumni and kids alike, of "Raaaadiooooooo! Hey, Raaaadiooooooo, come over here!"

His legend radiated from the school throughout the town. At the annual Anderson Christmas parade, the local cable television crew could not get enough of Radio marching the loosey-goosiest goose step in martial history, wearing his Santa Claus hat and shaking a fistful of sleigh bells—especially that Yule when his beltless pants slid to his ankles. He no longer had to pay to eat anything or walk to go anywhere in Anderson—there was always a free meal or a free ride. In the history of long shots, was there ever one longer than the possibility that a man such as he would be known and loved wherever he went? And if there was room in the program for Radio, then who *couldn't* be included, who *wasn't* welcome to join the community at its largest weekly gatherings? That was the message that Radio's presence sent to all those who felt a little odd, a little different.

The fans from the surrounding towns embraced him over the years as well, and one day when an assistant coach took him to a Clemson football game, it finally became clear what Hanna High had wrought. Honking and waving and cries of "Radio!" accompanied the two men the entire bumper-to-bumper trip, and no man has ever tailgated upon as many tails as Radio did that day.

But when darkness fell on Christmas Eve each year, just one car crunched onto the gravel in front of Radio's house. The curtain on the front window would rustle, for that's where Radio always awaited Coach Jones. The coach would hand Radio the wrapped gifts he had bought or collected from donors: shoes, socks, shirts, belts and, of course, another radio, for each year Radio's curiosity about who spoke to him from inside the little black box was more than the little black box could bear.

Fierce was Radio's loyalty in return. Fists pummeling, he would leap on the back of an assistant coach who pretended to sneak cases of soda from Coach Jones's truck, and he would materialize like a bad dream before the eyes of any referee who argued with Coach Jones. The one time in his career Coach Jones was ejected from a game, Radio screamed, *"You ass!"* at the ejecting referee so often, and with such precise diction, that he got the heave-ho, too.

Coach Jones was wonderful at hiding his exasperation with Radio, which might have been why he had to sip buttermilk during games to soothe his burning stomach. Who knew how many times a poignant silence during one of his pregame orations had been blown to smithereens by a shriek from Radio, and yet all Coach Jones would do was throw an arm around Radio's shoulder and roll his eyes toward heaven. Maybe that explained something. There was no one, outside of his five grandchildren or his wife, whom the coach would touch like that. He was the no-nonsense guy with bare gray cinder block office walls, but unlike most people, he hadn't completely done away with his other self, that loose and long-buried child. It was always right there at his elbow, rocking from foot to foot.

One August day two years ago, a few weeks before school opened, Coach Jones got a phone call. Radio's mother had died of heart failure in the middle of the night, and Radio was out of his head with grief. He had smashed two holes in a wall of his house, and the police had been called to restrain him. Surely, now that his mama was gone, he would finally have to go into a home.

Coach Jones had always worried about what would happen to Radio the day he retired or the day Radio's mother died. He knew his assistants loved Radio as much as he did, but still. . . . He marshaled his staff and collected a big tray of food that day and headed to Radio's house. One by one the coaches hugged Radio and cried with him. If he could just hold on until football practice started again, and if Radio's older brother, Walter Turner—the only one of Janie Mae Greenlee's three sons who wasn't born with the defect—and Walter's wife, Pat, could take care of Radio in the evenings, when the school day was done, then Hanna and Coach Jones and his staff would handle the rest. And that's just what has happened.

Summers, though, are still the most difficult time for Radio. Should a traveler ever get lost in upstate South Carolina some July or August day and find himself wandering near the railroad tracks in Anderson and happen to notice an old boarded-up school with a FOR SALE sign planted in the weeds out front, he ought to take a little look at the abandoned McCants Junior High football field just behind it. He might just see a man with sprinkles of white hair gesturing wildly at thin air, screaming, *"All wight, tomowwow's Thuhsday, dat's a light day! You wear yo' shorts an' T-shirts, no pads, an' be on da fiel' at four o'cwock on da nose, you got dat, boys?"*

Just smile and wave. It's only Radio, living the dream.

———

POSTSCRIPT: *Radio, now 61, still attends school at T.L. Hanna every day, despite the fame and attention he received after his story became a movie in 2003. "Radio loved [the premiere in Anderson, S.C.]," says Harold Jones, who retired in 1999. "Riding around in the limousines, he just loved it." A week later, though, a power box in Radio's room blew a fuse and started a fire. No one was injured—he woke up his two brothers and sister-in-law in time to evacuate the house—but the family lost everything. The community and movie studio responded, raising enough money to buy the family a new home.*

{ Part Three }

Shadow of a Nation

There was something deadly in the Crow tribe's quest for glory in a high school basketball gym. Along came a kid named Jonathan Takes Enemy, who was supposed to change all that.

> *"I have not told you half that happened when I was young. I can think back and tell you much more of war and horse stealing. But when the buffalo went away the hearts of my people fell to the ground, and they could not lift them up again. After this nothing happened. There was little singing anywhere."*
> —PLENTY COUPS, *Chief of the Crows,* 1930

INGING. DID YOU HEAR IT? THERE WAS SINGING IN the land once more that day. How could you not call the Crows a still-mighty tribe if you saw them on the move that afternoon? How could your heart not leave

269

the ground if you were one of those Indian boys leading them across the Valley of the Big Horn?

It was March 24, 1983, a day of thin clouds and pale sun in southern Montana. A bus slowed as it reached the crest of a hill, and from there, for the first time, the boys inside it could see everything. Fender to fender stretched the caravan of cars behind them, seven miles, eight—they had made the asphalt go away! Through the sage and the buffalo grass they swept, over buttes and boulder-filled gullies, as in the long-ago days when their scouts had spotted buffalo and their village had packed up its lodge poles and tepee skins, lashed them to the dogs and migrated in pursuit of the herd.

But what they pursued now was a high school basketball team, 12 teenagers on their way to Billings to play in the state tournament. The boys stared through their windows at the caravan. There was bone quiet in the bus. It was as if, all at once, the boys had sensed the size of this moment. . .and what awaited each of them once this moment was done.

In one seat, his nose pressed to the window, was one of Hardin High's starting guards, Everette Walks, a boy with unnaturally large hands who had never known his father. In a few weeks he would drop out of school, then cirrhosis would begin to lay waste his mother. He would wind up pushing a mop at 2 a.m. in a restaurant on the Crow reservation.

In another seat sat one of the forwards, an astounding leaper named Miles Fighter. He too had grown up with no father, and recently his mother had died of cirrhosis. In just a few years, he would be unemployed and drinking heavily.

Not far away sat the other starting guard, Jo Jo Pretty Paint, a brilliant long-range shooter, a dedicated kid—just a few minutes before a game at Miles City, his coach had found him alone, crouched, shuffling, covering an invisible opponent in the locker room shower. In two years Pretty Paint would go out drinking one evening, get into a car and career over an embankment. He would go to his grave with a photograph of himself in his uniform, clutching a basketball.

Hunched nearby, all knees and elbows and shoulders, was Darren Big Medicine, the easygoing center. Sixteen months after Pretty Paint's death, he would leave a party after a night of drinking, fall asleep as he sped along a reservation road, drive into a ditch and die.

And then there was Takes Enemy. . . .

WEEPING. DID you hear it? There was weeping in the land that day. Sobs for those missing from that glorious caravan, those decaying in the reservation dust, for Dale Spotted and Star Not Afraid and Darrell Hill and Tim Falls Down, Crow stars of the past dead of cirrhosis and suicide and knife-stabbing and a liquor-fogged car wreck. Sobs for the slow deaths occurring every night a mile from Jonathan Takes Enemy's high school, where an entire squad of jump shooters and dunkers and power forwards from the past could be found huddling against the chill and sprawled upon the sidewalks outside the bars on the south side of Hardin. Jonathan's predecessors. Jonathan's path-beaters. "Good Lord!" cries Mickey Kern, the computer-science teacher and former basketball scorekeeper at Hardin High. "How many have we lost? How *many*?"

But Takes Enemy—he would be the one who escaped, wouldn't he? That was what the white coaches and teachers and administrators at his school kept telling him. His mind was sharp, his skill immense; the destiny of all those others needn't be his. Brigham Young wanted him. Oregon State and Arizona State had sent letters. O.J. Simpson would shake his hand in New York City and present him with a crystal cup for being named Montana's Outstanding Athlete of 1984. He was 6' 2", he could twirl 360 degrees in the air and dunk, he could shoot from distance. He loved to take a rebound with one hand and bring it to his other palm with a resounding *slap*, make a right-angle cut on the dribble at a velocity that ripped the court wide open, then thread it with a blind running pass, an orange blur straight from the unconscious. "Watching him play," says Janine Pease-Windy Boy, the president of Little Big Horn College, the junior college on the Crow reservation, "was like watching clean water flow across rocks."

Young Indian boys formed trails behind him, wearing big buttons with his picture on their little chests. They ran onto the court and formed a corridor for him and his teammates to trot through during pregame introductions, they touched his hands and arms, they pretended to *be* him. The coaches had to lock the gym doors to start practice. Girls lifted their pens to the bathroom walls: "I was with Jonathan Takes Enemy last night," they wrote. "I'm going to have Jonathan Takes Enemy's baby." He was a junior in high school. Already he was the father of two. Already he drank too much. Already his sister Sharolyn was dead of cirrhosis. Sometimes

271

he walked alone in the night, shaking and sobbing. He was the newest hero of the tribe that loved basketball too much.

Takes Enemy felt the bus wheels rolling beneath him. The sun arced through the Montana sky. The circle was the symbol of never-ending life to the Crows—they saw it revealed in the shape and movement of the sun and moon, in the path of the eagle, in the contours of their tepees and the whorl of their dances. As long as the people kept faith with the circle, they believed, their tribe would endure. Jonathan settled back in his seat. Sometimes it seemed as if his life were handcuffed to a wheel, fated to take him up . . . and over . . . and down. . . .

Somewhere behind him on the highway, his first cousin would soon be getting off his job on the reservation's road crew and joining the exodus to the ball game in Billings—*the* legendary Crow player, some people said; the best player, *period*, in Montana high school history, said others. The one who ignited his tribe's passion for high school basketball back in the 1950s and seemed to start this dark cycle of great players arising and vanishing: Larry Pretty Weasel. The one whose drinking helped drive him out of Rocky Mountain College in Billings and back to the reservation in '58, just a few days before the NAIA's weekly bulletin arrived proclaiming him the best field-goal percentage shooter in the country.

Horns honked in the caravan behind Takes Enemy, passengers waved. In the long-ago days before white men had brought their horses or guns or cars or liquor, his people had chased buffalo in this same direction, across these same valleys, stampeding them over cliffs near the land where Billings would one day arise. This same creature whose skull the Crows would mount on a pole and make the centerpiece of their religious Sun Dance . . . they would drive over the edge of the cliff and then scramble down to devour.

The bus ascended another hill. Takes Enemy looked back at his people one more time.

ONE WINTER night in 1989, the custodian at Lodge Grass High on the Crow reservation forgot to flick off a switch. When the team bus pulled into the parking lot after a road game nearly four hours away, the lights above six of the 17 outdoor baskets that surround the school were still burning. It was 2 a.m. It was snowing. Two games of five-on-five were being played.

Somehow, in the mindless way that rivers sculpt valleys and shame shapes history, the Montana Indians' purest howl against a hundred years of repression and pain had become . . . high school basketball. Yes, the Crows' 8,300 people were racked by alcoholism and poverty, 75% of them were unemployed, the attrition rate for those who went to college was 95%, and their homeland, through cheating, broken treaties and sellouts, had dwindled from the 38.8 million acres guaranteed them by the U.S. government in 1851 to the present-day 1.1 million—*however*, just let them lace on sneakers and lay their hands on a basketball. Though Indians constituted but 7% of Montana's population, their schools would win 10 Class A, B and C state high school basketball titles between 1980 and '90.

To the north and northwest of the Crow reservation lay the reservations of the Blackfeet, Sioux, Flathead, Assiniboine, Gros Ventre, Chippewa, Cree, Salish, Kootenai and Pen D'Oreilles; to the east lay the Cheyenne. These tribes too loved to run and shoot and jump. At tournament time in Montana, Indian teams were known to streak onto the floor for layup drills in war headdress, their fans to shake arenas with chants and war cries and pounding drums as their boys raced up and down the floor at speeds few white teams could sustain. Old women wrapped in blankets were known to pound the bleachers in unison with their canes, to lose their cool and swing the canes at the calves of enemy players; a few, back in the 1940s, even jabbed opponents with hat pins as the boys ran up the sidelines.

Their children spent their days shooting at crooked rims and rotting wooden backboards. Their young men drove for days to reach Indian tournaments all across America and came home to strut the dusty streets in the sheeny jackets they had won there.

Of all the perplexing games that the white man had brought with him—frantic races for diplomas and dollar bills and development—here was the one that the lean, quick men on the reservations could instinctively play. Here was a way to bring pride back to their hollow chests and vacant eyes, some physical means, at last, for poor and undereducated men to reattain the status they once had gained through hunting and battle. Crow men had never taken up the craftwork, weaving or metallurgy that males in other tribes had. They were warriors, meat eaters, nomads whose prestige and self-esteem had come almost entirely from fulfilling an intricate set of requirements—called "counting coup"—while capturing enemy horses or waging battle. A man could count coup by touching an enemy, by seizing a bow or a gun in a hand-to-hand encounter, by capturing a horse in a hostile camp or by leading a successful raid. Only by counting coup, some say, could a man marry before the age of 25; only by counting coup in all four categories could he become a chief. A woman attained honor by the number of scalps and the war booty captured by her man, tokens of which she brandished when she danced.

And then the white men hunted the buffalo nearly to extinction and banned intertribal warfare. "It castrated the Crow male," says Ben Pease, a tribal elder who played basketball for Hardin High in the 1940s. "It created a vacuum. Something had to take war's place, some way had to be found to count coups. It was basketball."

Old Crow rituals had warm blood and fresh drama again. Some players tucked tiny medicine bundles—little pouches that might contain tobacco seeds or small pieces of bone or feather—inside their socks or tied them to their jerseys, the way warriors once had tied them to their braids before entering battle. Some burned cedar and prayed before big games. The same drum cadence and honor songs used 200 years ago to celebrate the seizing of a dozen horses or the killing of three Sioux now reverberated through gymnasiums and community halls at the capture of a basketball trophy.

But no Indian has ever played in the NBA. Only one, Don Wetzel of the Blackfeet, ever came off a Montana reservation to play for an NCAA Division I team—the University of Montana from 1967 to '71. Trophy cases in the lobbies of Indian schools throughout the state are filled with gleaming silver . . . and with black-bordered dedications to the dead. This is not the Crows' tragedy alone.

Every now and then, a lesser player left the Crow reservation and quietly, with no scholarship or fanfare, got his degree. But as best as anyone can figure, since 1970 only one prominent Crow player, Luke Spotted Bear, has received a college scholarship and graduated—from Mary College in Bismarck, N.Dak.—and Spotted Bear often felt that his people held this *against* him. "Some of them say I'm too good for them now," he says. "If possible, they don't want to be around me."

College recruiters stopped coming to the reservation, opportunities disappeared. The game that was a highway into mainstream America for black men . . . was a cul-de-sac for red ones. Something happened to their heroes when the drum beats died, when the war whoops faded, when the faces in the audience were not like theirs. Something in the Crows' love for basketball was toxic.

Along came a nice, shy boy named Jonathan Takes Enemy. All he was supposed to do was change all that.

HIS PEOPLE understood his significance. They sent him off to do battle with all the spiritual might they could muster. Before big games a medicine man would receive a cigarette from the Takes Enemy family, take it outside their house just in front of the Little Big Horn River in the town of Crow Agency, light it and pray to the Great Spirit for Jonathan.

Once, the medicine man wafted cedar smoke and an eagle feather over the gold chain that Takes Enemy carried with him to games for good luck. He warned Takes Enemy not to shake his opponents' hands before a game, so they could not drain away his power. All these steps were meant to protect Jonathan from harm, but he couldn't quite trust them. How could he escape the reservation and take up the solitary quest for success in the white world if he let himself think in the old way? How could he escape the dark fate of Spotted and Not Afraid and Falls Down if he believed that a man's destiny hung upon a puff of smoke in the wind?

When members of the tribe invited players on Jonathan's team to join them in sweat baths before the division and state tournaments, in order to purify their bodies and spirits in the ritual way their ancestors had before battle, Jonathan had refused; it was simply too hot in the sweat lodge. Jonathan's coach at Hardin, George Pfeifer—in his first year of coaching Indians and curious about their rituals—consented to do it. On a 20° day on the banks of the Little Big Horn, a powdery snow falling from the sky, the short, stout white man followed the example of eight Crow men and stripped off his clothes. "Go in, Brother George," directed one of them. Brother George got on his knees and crawled behind them into a low, dome-shaped shelter made of bent willows and covered by blankets. Inside, it was so dark that Brother George could not see the hand he held up in front of his face.

Someone poured a dipper of water over sandstones that had been heated in a bonfire for hours. Steam erupted from the rocks, hissed up and filled the sweat lodge with heat more intense than any sauna's. Sitting cheek to cheek, the men put a switch in Brother George's hand, expecting him to beat himself upon the back and legs to make it even hotter. In the darkness, he heard the others thwacking themselves, groaning and praying for his team in the Crow tongue. He gave up all pretense, flopped onto the floor and cupped his hands around his mouth to find a gulp of cooler air.

A half hour passed like this. A couple of dozen more dippers of water were poured onto the scalded rocks. At last the sweat-soaked men crawled out into the frigid daylight and promptly leapt into the icy river. Brother George's legs refused. He stood there, trembling with cold, about to be sick for three days.

"'You're not going to dive in the river, Brother George?" one cried.

"No way."

"That's all right, Brother George. No goddam magic in that."

BUT HERE was the difference: In a few weeks Pfeifer would laugh and tell anecdotes about the day that he left his world and entered another. Jonathan could not. Sometimes he felt the suspicious eyes of whites upon him, felt his tongue turn to stone, his English jumble, when he tried to express to them his feelings. He had but to utter that name to white ears—Takes Enemy—to feel his own ears begin to turn red.

All day and night as he grew up, the television had been on in his home, floating images into his head of white men who drove long cars and lived in wide houses, of Indians who were slow-witted and savage and usually, by the movie's end, dead. One day, when he was in junior high, he saw a movie about Custer's Last Stand. He couldn't help himself; in his stomach he felt thrilled when the Indians rolled over the hills and slaughtered every white man. It bewildered him, a few years later, to learn that it was the Sioux and Cheyenne who had slain Custer's troops—that several Crow scouts had ridden *with* Custer. Everything was muddy, nothing ran clean. It was whites who made him speak English most of the day when he entered first grade, rather than the Crow language he had grown up speaking; whites who hung a dead coyote from the outside mirror of Plenty Coups High School's team bus; whites who sang "One little, two little, three little Indians" at his brothers when they played away games in high school. And yet it was Hardin's white athletic director and assistant principal, Kim Anderson, who sometimes drove far out of his way to make sure Jonathan made it to school in the morning; white teachers who offered him encouragement and hope when he passed them in the halls.

Sometimes he would bicycle up the steep incline to the Custer Battlefield, a mile and a half from his home, to sit alone near the markers that showed where each of the white men had fallen, and to stare off into the distance. From here the world stretched out and waited for him to touch it; from here he could see land and a life beyond the reservation. In the daydream he often had here, it would be *he* who was walking from the wide house to the long car, *he* waving a cheery goodbye to his wife and kids, *he* driving off down the well-paved road to the well-paid job, *he* acting out the cliched American dream he saw on the TV screen. What choice had he? There no longer existed an Indian success cliché to dream of.

An hour or two later he would fly back down the hillside from the battlefield, barely needing to touch his pedals, determined to make the dream come true. It was only when the long hill ran out, when he labored back into his town, that the heaviness returned to his legs.

One evening a few months after his senior season, in which he averaged 28 points a game and shattered a Montana record by scoring 123 points in three state tournament games, his mother, Dorothy, held a "giveaway" in his honor. She was suffering from diabetes, which in a few years would force the amputation of her right leg below the knee and lash her to a kidney dialysis machine three days each week, yet she was determined to thank God and her tribe for the greatness of her son. Jonathan, her seventh surviving child—two had died shortly after birth—had been born with a crooked face and a too-large nose, and so in her hospital bed Dorothy had lifted the infant above her eyes and turned all her fears for him over to God. "Here, Lord," she whispered, "raise him up, he's all yours." The Lord's day-care center turned out to be a basketball court; from the age of three, all Jonathan did was dribble and shoot. On dry, frigid days he would play for so long that the ball would chafe away his skin, and he would come home at dusk with bloody fingers for his mother to bandage. Dorothy's eyes still shone when she stared at the Mother's Day card he had drawn in crayon for her in second grade: three yellow flowers in a blue vase, a snowcapped mountain beneath the sun—and a man slam-dunking a basketball. And just look how the boy had turned out, with a face straight and well proportioned, a body long and strong, a name that the wind had carried across the Big Horn and Wolf mountains, had whispered into the ears of the Cheyenne and Sioux, even laid upon the tongues of the pale skins. If only the boy's eyes would leave his shoes. If only the boy would stop stumbling home at 4 a.m. with the same stink on his breath as her husband, Lacey. . . .

In the giveaway ceremony, Jonathan's exploits were to be celebrated in the same manner in which Crows once commemorated a successful raid. Besides all the cousins and uncles and aunts and nephews and nieces who gathered, Jonathan's other "family," his clan, was there. There are 10 clans in the Crow tribe, some consisting of as many as a thousand members; at birth one automatically became a member of the same clan as one's mother. First Jonathan was to dance in a circle as singers sang his honor song, then he was to stand to the side as an "announcer" gave an account of his deeds, and finally he was to give away packages that consisted of four gifts to his clan uncles and aunts. It's a lovely ritual, one in which the hero, in a reversal of the white man's custom, showers his community with gifts in gratitude for the support and prayers that enabled him to succeed. Jonathan's family, just barely getting by on his father's meager salary as a custodian in the reservation hospital, couldn't possibly afford all these gifts, but in keeping with tradition his relatives had contributed so that the giveaway could take place.

Jonathan dreaded the stares that would be drawn to him if he wore the ceremonial Indian clothing, but he couldn't bear to disappoint his people. Slowly he pulled on the ribbon shirt, the buckskin vest, the colorful beaded armband and the war bonnet. They felt so odd upon him; he felt like no warrior at all. The first horse he had ever ridden had flung him from its back; the first bullet he had ever fired at an animal had slain a dirt clod far from its target. One of his great-great-grandfathers, known simply as Fly, had been a powerful warrior, a possessor of six wives. Another, Red Bear, had been a medicine man so potent that he simply had to fill his peace pipe and hold it toward the sun and all the tobacco in it would burn. Their home had been the river-fed valleys and shimmering plains, their roof the sky, their walls the snow-topped mountains a week's walk away. Jonathan? His home was a cramped three-bedroom box in which as many as 15 siblings and cousins often vied for sleeping space, sometimes on the floor beneath the kitchen table or even in the driveway, in the backseat of a car. Jonathan's bed, until he was seven, was a mattress jammed between the beds of his mom and dad.

With his family and his clan trailing behind him, he lowered his eyes and led them into the Little Big Horn College building for the giveaway. Rather than tokens of scalps or war booty captured from the enemy, Dorothy wore a huge orange shawl with large black letters stitched upon it that listed his coups: JONATHAN TAKES ENEMY, STATE CLASS A MVP, ALL-STATE 1ST TEAM, ALL-CONFERENCE 1984, CONVERSE BASKETBALL ALL-AMERICA HONORABLE MENTION, HERTZ AWARD, ATHLETE OF THE YEAR. Beneath were sewn four white stars; four is the Crows' sacred number. Jonathan was supposed to lead the assembly in a dance, but his feet could not quite bring themselves to do it. Almost imperceptibly he shifted his weight from one foot to the other, leading everyone around the room again and again in a plodding circle as the big drum pounded and the 11 singers in the center lifted their voices to his glory—and reminded him of his obligation to those around him.

Outstanding man
Look all around you
Nothing lasts forever
Look all around you
Share your talent and knowledge

SHARE WHAT? All he had to divvy up, it sometimes seemed, were self-doubt and pain. One day in ninth grade, at the end of basketball practice, his family had come to the school and told him that his sister had died at the age of 24, after years of hard drinking. He turned to the wall and broke down. Just a few weeks later his girlfriend told him she was pregnant. Terrified, he dropped out of school for the rest of the year, hid from his teachers on the streets, sometimes even hid from his own family—and reached for the same poison as his sister had.

He knew the danger he was wooing. The night he learned he had made the varsity, a rare honor for a freshman, he and a few friends went out in a pickup truck to drink beer. A tribal police car pulled up to the truck. Alcohol was banned on the reservation, but Crow police-men sometimes looked the other way. "Go home," this cop ordered the teenagers, but the kid at the wheel panicked, jammed the accelerator and roared away. Suddenly, Takes Enemy, a boy who was afraid even on a sled, found himself hurtling down a curving country road at 100 mph, four police cars with flashing lights and howling sirens just behind him. One came screaming up beside the truck, trying to slip by and box the teenagers in. Instead of letting it pass, Jonathan's friend lurched into the other lane to cut the car off. The pickup truck skidded off the road, toppled onto its roof and into a ditch. Takes Enemy limped out, some-how with just a badly bruised hip.

He vowed not to drink again. He remembered how uneasy he had been as a child, awakening on the mattress between his parents' beds to see the silhouette of his father stagger into the room. Even in an alcoholic haze, his father was a gentle man, but, still, that silhouette was not Dad—it was a *stranger*. Then, too, there was what alcohol had done to his cousin, the legend, Pretty Weasel. So many fans thronged gymnasiums to watch Pretty Weasel play for Hardin High that his team had to crawl through windows to get to its locker room. He could shoot jump shots with either hand, fake so deftly that he put defenders on their pants and, at 5' 10", outjump players a half-foot taller. It was almost, an opponent would muse years later, "as if you were playing against a kind of enchanted person." Pretty Weasel's younger brother Lamonte got drunk and died in a car accident. Then Pretty Weasel partied his way out of a four-year college scholarship and onto a reservation road crew.

But Jonathan couldn't keep his vow. He felt as if he were locked up in a tiny room inside his body, and it was only when he was playing basket-ball or drinking that he could break out of it. The first time he was drunk had been in seventh grade at Crow Fair, the week-long celebration every August when the field on the edge of his town became the tepee capital of the world. Hundreds of tepees were erected, and Native Americans from far away came to dance and drink and sing with his people deep into the night. Jonathan slipped the bootlegger $4 for a half-pint of whiskey, poured it down—and out poured the talking, laughing Jonathan he had always yearned to be. His mother came and found him at the fair at 3 a.m. Dorothy, a sweet, passive woman dedicated to the Pentecostal Church, began yelling that he would end up just like his father . . . but that was all. In many homes across the reservation . . . that was all.

His sophomore year he moved in with his girlfriend and her parents, to help her bring up their baby daughter. Four months after his girlfriend delivered, she had news for him. She was pregnant again. His whole life seemed hopeless, his daydream of escaping snuffed out. Was it his fault? No matter how hard Jonathan thought about it, he could never be sure. So many things had happened to his people that *were* beyond their control, it had become almost impossible to identify those that were *not*. He watched three brothers go to college and quickly drop out. He watched all three of them take turns with the bottle.

There were no movie theaters or bowling alleys or malls on the reservation. When it became too dark too see the rim on the courts behind the elementary school, Jonathan and his friends would drive up and down the main street of Crow Agency—from JR's Smokehouse to the irrigation supply yard and back again—seeing the same people, the same mange-eaten dogs and rust-eaten cars, until the monotony numbed them. Then someone would say, "Let's go drinking." It was a ritual that had become a display of solidarity and shared values among his tribe, so much so that to say no was to mark oneself as an alien. None of the teenagers had enough money to buy liquor, but all of them had Indian wealth—relatives. Uncles and aunts, cousins and grandparents are as close to most Crows as parents and siblings are to a white child; a boy can walk into five or six houses without knocking, open the refrigerator without asking, eat without cleaning up the crumbs. Jonathan and his friends would each ask a relative or two for a buck, and all of the sharing and family closeness in which the Crows pride themselves would boomerang. Each kid would come up with three or four dollars to pitch into the pot, and off they'd go to the liquor stores that waited for them just beyond the reservation borders. It wouldn't take long to see someone they knew who was of drinking age—the boys were related by blood or clan, it seemed, to *everyone*. They whisked their beer or whiskey back onto the reservation, where the statutes against juveniles drinking were less severe, and began gulping it as if it were a race to see who could forget his life first.

Jonathan's absences from school mounted. That was how he responded to trouble. He disappeared. His parents wanted him to get an education, but to make the house quiet for two hours each night and insist that he study, to pull him out of his bed when the school bus was rolling up the road—no, they couldn't quite do that. Each of them had dropped out after the ninth grade, but there was more to it than that. Almost every Crow parent had a close relative who had been forcibly taken from his home by white government agents in the early 1900s and sent off to a faraway boarding school, where his hair was shorn, his Indian clothes and name were taken away, and he was beaten for speaking his own language. How many Indians could chase an education without feeling an old pang in their bones?

On intelligence alone, Takes Enemy had made the honor roll in junior high, but now he fell behind in class and was too ashamed to ask the white teachers for help. He lost his eligibility for the first half-dozen games of both his sophomore and junior seasons, regained it after each Christmas and started dropping in 25 or 30 points with a dozen assists a game, leading his teammates flying up and down the floor. His coaches called it Blur Ball. His people called it Indian Ball. And his brothers, three of whom had also been stars at Hardin High, would whip the crowd to wildness, reaching back into imaginary quivers on their backs, loading their make-believe bows and zinging invisible arrows at the other teams; vibrating their hands over their mouths to make the high, shrill *wooo-wooo* battle cry that once froze frontiersmen's hearts; shouting themselves hoarse, making Takes Enemy feel as if he could simply lift up his legs and let his people's ecstasy wash him up and down the hardwood.

He scored 49 points in a state tournament game his senior year and was named the tournament's MVP. The outside walls of his house literally vanished, swathed in posters of congratulation from his fans. "A great major college prospect," said then BYU coach Ladell Andersen.

Do it, teachers urged him. Do it so they could once more believe in what they were doing, do it so *all* the Crow children whose eyes were on him could see how it was done. "Just *one*," they kept saying to him. "If just one great basketball player from here could make the break and succeed, it could change *everything*. College recruiters would start coming here, other kids would follow your example. You can be the one, Jonathan. You can be the breakthrough."

He was flown to BYU. He stared at the 26,000 white faces strolling across campus. He stood at the top of the basketball arena and looked down, his eyes growing wider and wider, the court growing tinier and farther away. He had never heard of anyone like himself playing in a place like this; he couldn't even fathom it. "He said almost nothing the whole time," recalls Andersen. "I asked him a few questions. He was nodding his head yes when he should have been shaking it no."

The stack of letters from universities grew at his home. Jonathan never replied. His senior year was ending, his sun descending toward the hills. In the long-ago days a Crow hero could go on doing what he did until an arrow or a bullet found him, then let the breeze carry off his soul to the Other Side Camp. But in the 20th century the hero's bullet was high school graduation—and then he had to go on living. "Where are you going to college?" people asked Jonathan everywhere he went. "He'll be home by Thanksgiving," they told each other. "Like crabs in a bucket, that's how we are," says Dell Fritzler, the coach at Plenty Coups High. "Whoever tries to get out, we yank him back down." Even Jonathan's own Indian name—bestowed upon him during his senior season after it had come to the medicine man in a dream—tugged downward at the boy. Iiwaaiale-tasaask, he was called. Does Not Put Himself Above Others. Go off to college? That would Definitely Put Himself Above Others. No, white people couldn't understand this; Jonathan himself could barely grasp the code: It was O.K. for an Indian to clench his teeth and compete as part of a team, especially an Indian team. But to do it alone, to remove yourself from the dozen people in your living room at midnight and go sit over a chemistry or algebra book—in many families, that tainted you. Look at him, they'd say. He's trying to be a white man.

Jonathan's head spun. Like most Crows, he'd been brought up not to make autonomous decisions but to take his cues from his immediate family, his extended family, his clan and his tribe. If *they* hadn't decided whether to assimilate into the white man's world or to recoil from it—how could he? And then, his two little children—he couldn't just walk away from them. The small living room he grew up in, with its 65 photographs of family members on the wall—a warm, happy place that the people in those pictures would flow into with no invitation, sit around sipping coffee and exchanging the sly puns and double entendres that his people excelled at, talking until there was nothing left to talk about and then talking some more—he couldn't just leave that behind. "Why?" he remembers wondering. "Why do I have to do it the white man's way to be a success in this world?" Why did all the human wealth he had gathered in his life, all the close friends and relatives, count for nothing when he crossed the reservation borders; why did material wealth seem to be the only gauge? And then his eyes and whys would turn the other way: "Why am I so important to my people? Why do I have to carry the hopes of the Crows?" All he had really wanted to do, ever since taking apart a stereo in the 10th grade and staring in wonder at all the pieces inside, was to go to a vocational school and learn electronics. But no, the herd was rolling, the people were waving and shouting him on, his legs were pulling him closer and closer to the ledge. He drank to close his eyes to it. One night at a school dance an administrator found out he was drunk. The next day he was ordered to take a chemical-dependency class.

Where were the people in his tribe who had lived through this? Why weren't they at Takes Enemy's door? Myron Falls Down, a prolific scorer for a Crow independent team in the 1970s, heard the rumors and wondered if he should do something. Six years earlier it had come to Falls Down like thunder through a hangover: That the addiction sucking the life from him and his people went beyond the beer they drank at night after playing ball, beyond the pills some ingested and the weed they puffed, beyond the Aqua Velva and Lysol and fingernail-polish remover some of them swilled; that *basketball*, the way the Crows were using it, had become a drug too. One morning in 1979, at the age of 27, he stood up from the bed where he slept every night with his ball. He went to the two glass-enclosed cases in the living room where his 50 trophies were displayed, and he began throwing them into cardboard boxes. "What are you doing?" cried his mother. She and his nieces raced to unscrew the little figurines from their wooden bases before he could sweep all of them away. He grabbed the five jackets he had won in tournaments, loaded them and his trophies into his car, drove to the dumpster on the edge of Lodge Grass and heaved them all in. He would never take another drink or drug after that day. He would never play, or go to see, another basketball game—not even, 10 years later, the junior high school games of his 13-year-old son. "If there was a connection between education and basketball on this reservation, there would be nothing wrong with basketball," says Falls Down, now a tribal health administrator. "But right now there is none. Basketball is an escape from reality for us. But I never did speak to Jonathan. I felt he or his family would have approached me if they wanted to hear my message."

Pretty Weasel—where was he? The man named Montana's Outstanding Athlete 27 years before Takes Enemy, the one recruited by the University of Utah, Texas A&M and Seattle University, the cousin caught in this same crossfire eight years before Jonathan was born. Relatives and friends had sat at Takes Enemy's dinner table to spill their guts and offer counsel, but the man who with one look or word might have given Jonathan a glimpse at the ledger, at the remorse and relief in the soul of a man who has walked away from his greatness, had signaled nothing. Pretty Weasel stood in the shadows at basketball games, refused invitations to giveaways, belittled his own legend. "Never saw myself play," he'd say. "Can't picture myself being able to play with those black boys. . . . But I don't give advice. "

Graduation day came. Jonathan still hadn't decided. Barely, just barely, he got his diploma. As the teachers watched him carry it across the stage, Anderson, the assistant principal, turned and said, "I hope we're not looking at the first day of the end of his life."

When the dance is over, sweetheart,
I will take you home in my one-eyed Ford.

THAT SLOPPY man with the red-rimmed eyes and the puffy face, taller than the others. . . .

That whiskered man with the slurred speech and the thick belly and the slumped shoulders, standing on the riverbank near Two Leggins Bridge . . . that's him. That's Jonathan Takes Enemy.

It's 1989. It's 3 a.m. When the bars close in Hardin, Jonathan and his friends often come here to sing and laugh and drink and dance until the sun comes up. At dawn somebody often hits somebody, and somebody's brother or cousin jumps in to help, and there's a whole pile of them in the dirt. And then they go home to sleep. There's no work for most of them to do.

But the sky's still dark, they all still feel good. They're singing "49" songs, native chants interspersed with English lyrics, sad-happy tunes

285

to the beat of a drum. Takes Enemy still can't bring himself to dance or sing, but he's thumping out the drumbeat on a car hood. "Way-la-hey-ley, way-la-hey-ley . . . ya-hey-oh-way-la-hey . . . " his companions croon. "When the dance is over, sweetheart, I will take you home in my one-eyed Ford."

The dance is over. It ended four years ago, as soon as it began. Six games into Jonathan's freshman season at Sheridan College, the Wyoming school whose scholarship offer he grabbed at the last minute because it was just an hour's drive from home, he quit. It's all still a blur to him: Hiding from everyone when it was time to leave home. Reporting to college two days late and only because Anderson found him and took him there. Being stopped in the yard as he left, asked by his teary-eyed mother, "Are you *sure* you want to go, Jonathan? They aren't *forcing* you?" Trying to go from a world where it's disrespectful to look someone in the eye into one where it's disrespectful *not* to. Sitting alone in his dorm room for days, walking alone to the cafeteria, eating alone. Telling none of the white people about his fear and loneliness. Being guided by no one through the bewildering transition from reservation to white world. Knowing before his first game that something was wrong, because he had done something he could never do the night before a high school game—sleep. Knowing that the feeling he had had at Hardin—that he was on a mission, playing for his people—was gone. Returning to the reservation three straight weekends and not coming back in time for Monday practice. Two weekends later, not coming back at all. Walking away from the No. 1–ranked junior college team in the nation . . . but whose nation, *whose*?

"Crawled back under the blanket," said the whites. They've seen Indians do it so often that they have a cliché for it. "Every Indian that leaves has a rubber band attached to his back," says Jonathan's brother James. The Crows have seen their people do it so often that they only shrug. In some strange way, by going away to college and then by quitting, too, Takes Enemy has managed to fulfill *everyone's* expectations.

Somewhere, perhaps upon the hilltop at Custer Battlefield, his daydream still exists. More and more, he bicycles back there, as if in search of it. After all, he is only 24, he tells himself, his life is just beginning—or already half over, according to Crow life-expectancy charts.

His pockets are empty. He bums beer money from his dad, who has stayed clean since entering an alcohol rehabilitation program recently. No one will hire Jonathan. No one will buy him drinks at the bars in Hardin the way they did when he was in high school. Sometimes he walks out of the bars and onto the streets, sees a teacher from the school driving by and slinks into the shadows. He's not a bum, he's *not*. Twice he has been thrown into the reservation jail for drinking, lain on the floor all night in a cell with 30 other drunk men, listened to them moan and retch.

He has gained more than 20 pounds. He still plays ball, lumbering up the floor in Indian tournaments held across the state and the country. After games the team goes drinking—and sometimes, even right before them. He signs up for courses at the reservation's junior college; some he completes, some he doesn't. He has a new girlfriend, Trudi Big Hair, and two more children, Jonathan and Tashina. The four of them sleep in a small room at his parents' house, and no one ever hints that it's time he moved out. Sometimes in the morning the children jump on him in bed and shout, exploding his hangovers. He drifts back to sleep until noon, goes to a class or two, kills a few hours staring at the TV or picking up his welfare check, plays pickup basketball with his friends until dark . . . and then often starts all over again. Each time he drinks, Trudi etches an X on the calendar. Day by day, Jonathan watches his life get crossed out.

Once or twice he has gone to see his old school play. He doesn't go inside. He watches from a half-open door. It's not his court anymore, not his domain. A new hero has arisen, a boy at Lodge Grass High named Elvis Old Bull. Old Bull takes his team to state titles in '88, '89 and '90, is named tournament MVP all three years, notices kids beginning to dress and cut their hair like he does, hears himself called a major college prospect. He has a child, but isn't married; he skips school too much; he drinks too much; his eyes are haunted. Sometimes Jonathan feels as if there is something he could tell the boy. But he doesn't. And the sun arcs across the Montana sky, and the eagle wheels, and the circle remains unbroken.

AUTUMN 1990. The sun drops behind the Big Horn Mountains. An orange 1980 Mustang turns onto the highway and bears north across the reservation, toward Billings. There is no caravan behind him. Takes Enemy goes alone.

His face is clean-shaven, his clothes are neat, his cheekbones have bloomed again. He is 25, but he looks like that boy in those high school pictures once more. All summer he has jumped rope, slipping into his backyard to do it at midnight when no one on the reservation could see.

He presses the accelerator. He has made just a short visit home today; he cannot dally. He needs to get off the reservation by nightfall and back to his apartment in Billings, to Trudi and little Jonathan and Tashina, back to his new life as a student and a basketball player at Rocky Mountain College. Because when the darkness comes and his friends come. . . . "To do this," he says, "I can't be near them. I miss them. But I have to be alone." He hasn't had a drink in months.

"It's my decision to go to college this time," Jonathan says. "I finally realized that I was running out of time. It's not that the reservation is a bad place. There are many good people there. But it's just not a place where you can become what you want to become. It's not a place where you can achieve your dreams."

Last spring he convinced Luke Gerber, the coach at Hardin High, that he was serious. Gerber called Jeff Malby, the coach at Rocky Mountain College, and Malby remembered how the clean water had once flowed across the rocks. He offered Takes Enemy a scholarship to the liberal arts college in Billings, with 810 students. So far, it fits Jonathan just right.

He passes the reservation border, glances into his rearview mirror. He knows that some people back there are now calling him an "apple"—red on the outside, white on the inside. He knows what he is leaving behind, what he is losing. Knows it in the morning when he passes his new neighbors in Billings and they just barely nod. Knows it when it's midnight and he and Trudi are buried in textbooks, and the apartment is silent. "It's just too quiet here," he'll say. "We're so isolated." And when he lies in bed at night and thinks of his sick mother, he knows it then, too.

His eyes move back to the windshield. Ahead of him, over the rolling hills, across the sage and buffalo grass, he can just make out the soft electric glow of Billings. He's starting to get an idea of what lies this way. He's passing all four of his classes. He's averaging 19.8 points and 4.6 assists for his new team. He's just getting his bearings, but his coaches say that he'll soon establish himself as the best player in Montana and that he's destined to be an NAIA All-America before he's done.

Everything's still so new to him. Paying his own rent each month from the grant money allotted to him by the tribe and the Bureau of Indian Affairs, paying electric bills, buying his own food. Studying until 1 a.m., making sure that Trudi gets off to Eastern Montana College in the morning, that his kids get off to day care and preschool, living in the white man's world, in a hurry, on a schedule.

He wants to go back to the reservation someday and help kids to take the risk, to see both the beauty and the danger of the circle. But he may never live there again. He rolls down his car window. He listens to the air. There is no singing in the land. There is only a quiet, sad-happy song inside a young man's heart.

POSTSCRIPT: *Jonathan Takes Enemy attended Rocky Mountain College, but never graduated; he stayed for two years before leaving the school and basketball behind, moving to his wife's reservation in Zillah, Wash. Film studios have called to inquire about making a movie about him, but he has shown no desire to speak to anyone outside his small personal circle—reporters included. Every few years, though, Jonathan Takes Enemy will appear in the stands at a basketball game, at Hardin High School or Rocky Mountain College. The crowds always notice. "He's the same as he was before," says Hardin coach Luke Gerber. "In Montana people still know his name. He's still a legend."*

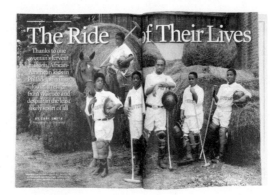

The Ride of Their Lives

Thanks to one woman's fervent mission, poor African-American kids in Philadelphia found a refuge from violence and despair in the unlikeliest sport of all, the rich man's game of polo.

THEY TOOK NO NOTICE, AT FIRST, OF THE $500 BLACK Taurus and the dented pickup with the rusted trailer rumbling out of the rolling green distance. Not the ladies in flowered hats chatting in the big white party tent, nor the sportsmen gathering their helmets and whips. Not the tanned elderly men tethered to tiny purebred dogs, nor the white-jacketed waiters preparing pâté and tumblers of vodka, crushed ice and pink lemonade.

Faintly, at first, came the *boom-cha-boom-boom . . . boom-cha-boom-boom.* The $500 black Taurus and the dented pickup turned off the country road and cut through pastures framed by white fences—rolling thunder drawing nearer and louder until even the party boys on the picnic blankets near the playing field turned to see what was coming.

The rap music stopped. The two vehicles halted. Out tumbled a couple of black teenagers wearing 'do-rags, cornrows and gold stud earrings, a swarm of small black children, four yelping dogs, four hand-me-down horses, two iguanas, a boa constrictor . . . and a white woman.

The black kids sprayed in all directions, the horses clattered off the trailer and the dogs darted among them all. The white woman rubbed out a cigarette, raised two fingers to her mouth and emitted a whistle that froze every creature in her caravan. "Get your boots and whites on!" she barked. "Where's the hose, where are the buckets?. . . Son of a biscuit-eater, who's tacking this horse? . . . Tuck your shirts in! . . . Freakin' *ragtag*!"

The spectators peered from behind their sunglasses as if watching a cloud of flies land upon a bowl of whipped cream.

America's only black polo team took the field.

THE WHITE WOMAN

THE UMPIRE rolled a wooden ball among them, and suddenly a posse of black kids from Philadelphia's worst streets, wielding mallets and riding 1,000-pound beasts, were going hell-bent-for-leather against a team of white millionaires.

There must've been at least one good reason why the white woman was obligated to advise opposing polo clubs before she arrived that her players were African-Americans. It just never occurred to her. Lezlie Hiner simply showed up with her kids, organized them with that foghorn bark and that ear-shredding whistle, relaxed them with a wisecrack and that laugh, that crusty eruption of who-gives-a-rat's-ass merriment over the mischief she was making in the world. "Play the man, not the ball!" she bellowed as her players roared past, 'do-rags flapping in the wind. "Push, push, don't be a wuss! Get the lead outta your ass!"

Don't be a wuss? Get the lead outta your ass? How did it come to this? How did a white woman end up yelling that to a tattooed, bearded, cornrowed, 6' 1", 220-pound black teenager named Lonnie Fields, from a neighborhood called the Bottom, who actually had two lead bullets in his ass?

THE BIG IDEA

SHE WORE no makeup, no jewelry, no skirt or dress and no coloring on the gray strands in her loosely tied hair. She never mentioned her past or her private life. Some people in polo circles assumed that she came from wealth and lived in luxury. But almost no one had a clue where in hell she and her big idea came from.

She was pulling away from a barn just outside Philly where she boarded her horse 14 years ago, late and in a hurry as always, when she saw a poor black kid in the rearview mirror, the blacksmith's apprentice, yearning to go with her on a trail ride. She had a weakness for strays. Her relatives in Pennsylvania would play "Guess Who Lez Is Bringing to Dinner" each Thanksgiving, then watch the front door and hold their breath: Orphaned mutts. Three-legged cats. Hitchhiking roadies. Oh, yeah, remember the Peruvian jockey?

She took the black kid under her wing for four years, watched his grades improve and his personality bloom as she taught him all about horses. The art gallery she owned went under, then she drifted into sales at her father's record-storage company, loathed that cubicle life and got axed for insubordination by her old man's vice president. Perfect timing. She'd just gotten the big idea. What if she started a nonprofit organization that let her hang out all day with horses *and* the kids in America's rearview mirror? What if she could use a dozen castoff thoroughbreds as carrots to lure inner-city children into a life of discipline and responsibility?

In 1994, at 37, she hatched Work to Ride at the Chamounix Equestrian Center—a fancy name for an old barn in Fairmount Park where Philadelphia's mounted police had once stabled their horses. She moved into the barn on a $1-a-year lease and took on 20 kids, many of them juvenile delinquents whom the city gladly dumped in her lap, and set them to work mucking stalls, pitchforking hay and feeding and bathing horses each day in exchange for riding lessons, weekend road trips, five-hour trail rides . . . and love. She had some notion of how to handle ponies and punks: Thirteen years as a racetrack hotwalker, groom and assistant trainer along with four years as a psych major at the University of South Carolina had seen to that.

The idea was divine. The kids were hellish. One reported to Chamounix with a gun. Another, avenging a horse bite, scampered up to the hayloft and flung a fire extinguisher at the gelding. A half-dozen got a bang out of winging manure pies at one another.

One by one, the initial Work-to-Riders scrammed or got the boot. One stuck: Jose Perez, a silent, good-natured 13-year-old petty thief and graffiti artist from a North Philly hood called the Badlands. Joining him, forming the core group that would last, was Lonnie, then a hulking 12-year-old who had flunked third grade, flung his math book at his fifth-grade teacher and been banished to reform camps for two summers before he drifted over to the stables one day from the nearby Pop Warner football field; his nine-year-old brother, Chris Perren, who loved Lonnie more than football and followed him to the barn; and Richard Prather, a dyslexic 15-year-old with 12 siblings and a frazzled reading tutor who delivered him to Lez.

Lez would shove a mongrel or two off the round table in her bare cinder-block office and sit the newcomers down to write a 300-word essay explaining why they wished to join her cavalry. By the time they were done mispunctuating the last run-on sentence and pledging to maintain a C average in school, they'd been inducted into the childless white woman's ragtag family and been branded by her forevermore as "one o' *my* kids."

Two years passed. The carrot worked. The powerless boys so dearly loved gaining power over half-ton beasts that they'd endure all the mucking and math classes. Lonnie even began to surrender his machismo because it just didn't work on a horse. They all learned to trot, then to gallop, then to *fly.*

But little by little the boys grew restless with half-day trail rides, equitation lessons and horse shows at Devon. Girl stuff. They wanted to hook, steal, slash, bump, bash. They wanted to play some *ball.*

They'd all tagged along to watch Lez play polo on weekends. They'd all begun borrowing mallets and playing polo on bicycles outside the barn. Now three black kids from the ghetto and a brown boy with a rap sheet and a Puerto Rican accent were looking at Lez, wanting to know why they couldn't play the sport of kings.

Nine hundred ninety-nine out of 1,000 40-year-old Caucasian females in the U.S., according to doctors, would have said to the four boys, "Are you freakin' nuts?" But then, 999 out of 1,000 40-year-old Caucasian females in the U.S. wouldn't have mud-wrestled for a $25 bar tab in Lugoff, S.C., 15 years earlier, either.

"Sure you can!" Lez replied to the boys, doling out mallets and leading them outside to see how much they'd swallow. The first few bites—that's all it took for her to realize that she'd stumbled upon the fattest, crunchiest carrot of all.

When she was reasonably sure it was reasonably safe to loose them on a playing field with stockbrokers and socialites, she loaded the boys, their secondhand mallets and the mares into her truck and trailer and headed off, three years before the turn of the millennium, to see just how much America could digest.

THE ACID REFLUX

SURE, THE members of the Bucks County Polo Club knew the four boys. Nice kids, well worth the 20 bucks that the polo players paid them to hotwalk their ponies when Lez brought them along to watch her play. So nobody paid the boys much notice during the two-day polo clinic until the end, when it was time to play a match. Then Lez headed onto the field to play a chukker . . . with Richard on a pony at her side.

A chukker lasts seven minutes. A match lasts six chukkers. Four players on a side. Lez heard members grumbling. True, her boys weren't members of the Bucks County Polo Club, but this clinic was open to the public, and other nonmembers were playing in the informal match. She felt it building, the anger that had gotten her axed from her job for insubordination. But remember, she was a role model now.

The chukker ended. Richard left the field. Lez sent Chris in to take his place. A club member in her 50s with a Boston accent trotted her pony toward Lez. "Other people need to play in this match too," she announced.

Lez snarled and flung her mallet to the ground. The lady snapped at her, peeled away, then came back. Lez grabbed the woman's mallet and yanked. The woman yanked back. "You don't want the kids to play, and you're a f-----' bigot!" Lez screamed. Holy cow! Two women at a polo match were about to fight!

Lonnie rushed to Lez's side, cursing the lady on the horse. Chris, Richard and Jose pulled Lez away.

The boys looked at one another in awe. White woman was for real. White woman had their backs. They knew two things that minute: They were going to play polo. They were Lez's kids for life.

THE DEEPER AGENDA

THERE WERE so many new things her boys would need to learn if they were serious about polo. Pâté and goat cheese, for starters. Stuffed mushrooms served on silver trays under the party tents when the matches ended, for another.

"Whazzat?" Chris would say.

"Dunno," Lonnie would reply.

"You try it first."

"*You.*"

"No, *you.*"

Lez had to get crackin'. She and her gang had left the Bucks County Polo Club in a huff and joined Cowtown, a folksy New Jersey polo club run by a broad-minded man named Donny Aikens. The boys played four matches a month across the mid-Atlantic states during summers as teammates of Cowtown's white adult players, then played on their own Work to Ride team in three-man indoor polo matches against private high school teams along the Eastern seaboard from fall to spring. And groped their way through a parallel universe of Brandywines and Strasburgs where their kind only bathed horses, shoed hooves and served the brie.

"But what *is* brie, Lez?"

"Eat it, you'll like it! Take a no-thank-you bite, and if you really hate it, discreetly spit it into your napkin. . . . Elbows off the table!. . . Hats off your heads!. . . Napkins in your laps!. . . Son of a biscuit-eater, don't eat the whole bucket of shrimp!"

All this would come from the side of this Mother Goose's mouth as she maneuvered her gaggle of black geese through the white party tents after matches, her foghorn dialed down 75 decibels to protect her posse's pride, her reminders to chew with their mouths closed murmured in a Spanish phrase they knew: *¡Cierra la boca!*

She took them to restaurants for dress rehearsals. Schooled them on salad forks and butter knives, *yes ma'ams* and *no sirs*, burps and biscotti. Cleaned up their vocabulary by pulling out a bottle of dish detergent each time they cursed, popping the cap and squirting their medicine into their mouths, a punishment so frequent that some boys could blow better bubbles with Palmolive than with Bazooka. Lonnie, Chris, Richard and Jose matured quickly under Lez's tutelage, but her jayvee squad was buck-wild, and yes, calamity occurred. Brothers Jabarr and Kareem Ross-er plundered postmatch platters of crab legs so completely that it took the breath away from the entire buffet line. Glasses shattered. China chipped. Flower-hatted women gasped.

There were two ways to tame wild horses. Breaking them was the swift-er way. Gentling them took longer, but in the end they could look you in the eye. Lez gentled her horses *and* her kids. Set boundaries and, when the kids crossed them, barked louder than her 145-pound Great Dane with one brown eye and one blue . . . but never put a thumb on their spirits.

Lonnie could bring his boa constrictor to matches in a pillowcase, Richard his iguana in a harness. They could say *We be* or *Who was you wit*? if they wished. They'd just lose a quarter each time off the $5 a week she pledged to pay them. They could pull up to a polo club booming Wu-Tang or Biggie Smalls from the monster speakers rigged into the trunk of Lonnie's Taurus and plop their helmets atop their 'do-rags and brim-backward ball caps, no sweat.

What did white people think the first time a tattooed, bearded, corn-rowed, 6' 1", 220-pound black teenager approached their polo field? "You here to work?" they'd ask Lonnie hopefully.

"We're here to *ride*," he'd reply.

What did Lonnie think? "Damn, you people got some change. You people livin' like we *dreamin'*. Yeah, yeah, I see you lookin' at me, thinkin', *Dude's a monster, looks like he's got issues,* and I'm lookin' back at you, too. I'd break the silence by hollerin', 'Hey, how you doin'?' Then I'd show them who I was, as a person and on the field."

On the ride to a new polo field Lez would prepare them for the stares and whispers, direct them to stow away any anger until the ride home. Once she arrived, single-mindedness was her weapon. She proceeded as if there were no opposing forces, focused so resolutely on her kids that she blew right by the stares. She didn't care what anyone thought. The deeper agenda wasn't to change white people. It was to change her kids. To make them see, by going *here*, that they could go *anywhere*.

Well, almost anywhere. One day in February 1998, just a block from his house in a West Philly neighborhood called the Bottom, Lonnie stood up for his brother Chris during an argument with a neighborhood kid. The kid vanished, but his 67-year-old stepfather appeared in a station wagon and got out of it with a gun. Lonnie and Chris bolted. Lonnie tripped and paid for it, a bullet ripping through his rectum, bladder and intestines, leaving him on a colostomy bag and unable to walk for two months, nearly ending his 15-year-old life.

The white woman shook. The white woman cried. The deeper agenda was no longer to change her kids' lives. It was to save them.

THE CROSSOVER

IT WASN'T easy for a coach, never knowing who'd be available each game. Chris, out for tardiness. Jose, out for car theft. Lonnie, out with bullet holes.

Players too young, horses too old: They got clobbered those first few years, tattooed to the tune of 25–2, 27–5, 38–3. They couldn't negotiate polo's sudden stops and turnarounds, didn't quite grasp the rules and nuances of team play, had to overcome the fear of swinging a mallet at a small ball with one hand while hanging on to 30 mph of galloping horse with the other. Chris flew off his mount three times in a minute and a half at the University of Virginia in Charlottesville. Worst of all were the shellackings by those smug, crew-cut cadets at Valley Forge Military Academy, the Work-to-Riders' cultural as well as geographic rivals, just a 20-minute drive from Philadelphia. The cadets bristled when the boys left their equipment, baggy pants and shirts scattered across the academy's spit-shined stables—and made them pay for it, every time, on the field.

Just wait, Lonnie vowed to his teammates. One day we'll bring down those rich military brats. Lez's boys got *serious*. They stood on milk crates to practice striking the ball with their long, crooked mallets. They stood on Philly street corners on summer days, baking in their polo outfits, asking for donations so they could afford the military academy's fee to practice once a week in a real polo arena, the *cadets'* arena, instead of on the old weed-choked Pop Warner football field near the barn.

They'd snarl at one another when some bevy of preppies from a $30,000-a-year boarding school—*girls!*—began flaying them during a winter interscholastic match in an indoor arena. They'd resort to cowboy polo, bumping and slamming or playing the ball instead of the opponent, ignoring Lez's shrieks and two-fingered whistles. Lonnie thumped one girl into the railing so hard that she screamed, "F--- you!" three times. Richard banged a young lady off the ball and discovered she wasn't a lady. "You're trying to kill me!" she howled. "I'll teach you, you bitch!" Funny. The white folks didn't have to gargle with Palmolive.

On the other side of the ledger, Lez's boys introduced two new moves to a 2,000-year-old sport that dated to Asian nomadic warriors—the crossover dribble and the shake 'n' bake—and one revolutionary way to elicit a pass from a teammate: *Yo, yo, yo, over here!* They loved the game so much that they didn't question Lez's sanity when she packed up her winless team and began driving south one April day in 1999.

Six hours later they were at the national interscholastic tournament in Charlottesville, Va. The cadets from Valley Forge were there. The other four teams looked at the Work-to-Riders from the corners of their eyes, and then, the minute they were out of earshot, freaked. Who were they? What were they? *Why* were they?

Of course they were *allowed* to play. The scarcity of scholastic polo teams meant that none had to win its way into the nationals. On the eve of the tournament, when the teams gathered for a break-the-iceberg dinner at the Boar's Head Inn, a 160-pound cadet from Valley Forge gazed across the table at Lonnie. "If *my* hair ever got nappy," he announced, "I'd shoot myself."

For one terrible moment, as everyone mulled the cultural as well as physical inadvisability of that remark, no one spoke. Lonnie tasted his embarrassment, felt his rage building . . . and clamped his teeth. He'd show those damn cadets on the field.

The Work-to-Riders got demolished by 20 goals in the first game and 17 in the next, sent packing without getting to play Valley Forge. Just wait, vowed Lonnie. One day. . . .

The extra practice at the military academy paid off. Within two years the Work-to-Riders were winning as often as they lost, and Lez's whistle now pierced the air to celebrate their triumphs as well as curb their anarchy. Other teams smelled the boys' dedication. Plenty of polo people— men such as the new Valley Forge Military Academy coach, Ted Torrey, and Lancaster Polo Club president Bob Lawson—were salt-of-the-earth sorts who welcomed the pepper of the earth to their sport, inviting Lez's kids to their fields and into their homes for overnight stays. The boys luxuriated in king-sized beds. They peered into closets that dwarfed their bedrooms at home. They rode in fox hunts and steeplechases, mingled with DuPonts and Weymouths.

The cadets kept beating them, but by margins slimmer and slimmer. The two teams began to congregate before and after matches, to take pointers from each other, to bust one another's chops. And would you look at that? Sergeant First Class Chuck Grant . . . playing polo in a 'do-rag!

THE REFUGE

A BLACK kid could keep it from his friends and loved ones for only so long. Sooner or later they'd find out that he was spending his Saturday nights holed up in some unmarried white woman's three-bedroom gray stone house in Northwest Philly . . . studying videotapes of last week's polo match.

Lonnie, exasperated when his friends thought he was playing water polo, dug up a Ralph Lauren shirt and stabbed his finger at the logo. "That's a *sport*?" they asked. No one from their families or neighborhoods, except for Lonnie's and Chris's mother, Sarah, ventured into the parallel universe to see the boys play.

Somehow, the less everyone else knew, the better. Chamounix became the boys' secret garden, three acres of wooded hills and fields surrounded by thousands of acres of Fairmount Park. Sparrows and roosters flapped through the barn. A rope swing dangled from a nearby tree. A creek gurgled past. The boys would rise early every summer morning and cross the crumbling pavement on foot, by bike, by bus. Their barn chores came first, and the cosmic lesson that a man must deal with the dung before he gallops to glory. Then they were free to play polo or tag or Capture the Flag on horseback, to chase frogs and butterflies, to turn trash-can lids into sleds when the winter snows came. Only when November stripped the sycamores and maples of their leaves could the crowns of the skyscrapers be seen. Only when the boys stood in stillness could the expressway's hum be heard. Right there, in the heart of the big city, they could be Huck Finns.

But at dusk they had to leave the safe place . . . and go home. Lonnie and Chris would start walking. The first mile was fine, all grass and trees. Then they'd reach the corner of Belmont and Parkside, the end of Fairmount Park. "That first step into hell," Lonnie called it. "Gunshots, prostitutes, sirens, ambulances, crackheads. Your head would be back on a swivel."

Lonnie's swivel was never swift enough. A block from his house, six months after he'd been shot and just as he was about to get back in the saddle again, he walked past a man whose knife was busy making a jack-o'-lantern of another man's head. The victim, his lip hanging off, pulled out a gun, and Lonnie ran for it again—too late. The bullet tore through the slasher's shoulder and into Lonnie's bad-luck backside.

THE LITTLE BLACK GIRL ON THE LITTLE BLACK PONY

SHADOWS DEEPENED beneath Lez's brown eyes. Duty began devouring all 18 waking hours of the day and all seven days of the week. Her friends warned her that she was grinding herself to dust.

She took the most troubled boys into her home to live for months at a time. She paid their families' bills. She paid Jose's tuition to a charter school to distance him from the crack dealers at his old school. She mucked and pitchforked in the morning, spent afternoons in the office contacting anyone who might donate to the cause or help arrange an exodus from the Bottom or the Badlands for her brood, then headed to school to pick up the first- and second-graders, the next generation of Work-to-Riders. At night she helped them study for math tests and build papier-mâché volcanoes for science, then drove them to their doorsteps, rolling into neighborhoods that would curdle a cop's blood.

Vacation? Three or four days a year, when her closet and drawers were empty, she'd tunnel into that underwear avalanche in the corner of her bedroom, haul it all to the basement laundry and call that an off day. Paycheck? She lived small, took virtually no salary and survived on the rapidly dwindling inheritance left by her dad, who died the year Work to Ride was born.

She got more than that nest egg from her old man. She got the freedom to middle-finger a middle-class life. He was a humdinger of a dad, the kind who'd buy his four daughters air rifles for Christmas so they could blast each other with Ping-Pong balls, who'd fly downstairs with a towel tied around his neck for a cape, flinging movie tickets and crowing, "Guess what? We're all gonna see *Superman* together!" He learned to fly without a cape in his 40s, after he and Lez's mother divorced, and he began using his Cessna to take low-income patients to faraway hospitals that specialized in treating certain injuries and diseases. Sure, his 16-year-old tomboy, Lez, living in the suburb of Willingboro, N.J., could get a horse and a job pumping gas to pay its boarding expenses, then live out of cardboard boxes and shovel crap at racetracks after she graduated from high school. Why not? Before she was born, he'd wanted her to be a boy anyway.

Lez took Dad's cue, followed her heart—too bumpy and zigzaggy a trail to bring along anything more than an occasional boyfriend, she'd long ago decided. Funny, the tricks life plays. Dad ended up with four girls. Lez ended up with nine boys. She *had* to find a girl to join the family, she decided in 2001, and the minute she saw that little 12-year-old ride by the barn on a little black pony, that tomboy with the scar curling across her left cheek, Lez knew *she* was the one. But the girl vanished before Lez could corner her, so for six months Lez searched for her, asking the black riders on Fairmount Park's trails and friends who lived in the nearby neighborhoods to put out the word: Find the little black girl on the little black pony.

Then one day, there she was, walking into the barn with a group of kids in an after-school program called HOPE Family Center. In? Damn right Mecca Liles-Harris wanted in. In no time she was sitting at the round table in Lez's cinder-block office, writing her galloping 300-word essay requesting admission: *I know how I will feel out on that field running to hit the ball air flying in my face. When I came to your last polo game just watching little Bee play I wanted to play as I was saying in my head look at him go so fast.*

Bee was Jabarr Rosser, the 10-year-old phenom Lez had incubated and hatched. A comical sight, with a helmet two sizes too big bouncing on his head, legs too short to reach his stirrups, a mallet twice as long as he was dragging at his side . . . suddenly poking the ball away from an adult, flying after it as if he were Velcroed to his horse, hoisting that long hammer to 12 o'clock high and letting the head drop with a clock hand's perfect sweep, rocketing the ball into the goal even before the *Aw, isn't he cute?* look had drained from the faces of his 40ish foes. Killer Bee, the astonished adults christened him.

Spectators began chanting, "Bee! Bee! Bee!" when the little varmint picked another pocket and pelted another pea. Horse owners shouted, "Lemme have that kid!" to Lez, and to be honest, sometimes she wanted to croak back, "You can have him!" He shattered her windshield playing polo on foot, put a couple of dozen dents in her truck and then one in her forehead. His grades went down the toilet, and his mouth did, too; his record 20 expletives on a weekend road trip left him literally foaming at the mouth.

Lez bounced him out of the program, the sweetest bounce a kid from the Bottom ever got. She put him on a plane in 2002, a 12-year-old flying off to live with Lez's pal Sissy Jones in Burleson, Texas, at the U.S. Polo Association's central regional youth training center. He soon became the youngest player chosen to the regional all-star team and got a promise of a polo scholarship to perennial power Texas A&M if he maintained a B average.

Lonnie, Chris, Richard and Jose had grown too old to play interscholastic polo. Mecca was the one Lez needed to replace Killer Bee. She was tough enough to play tackle football with the boys, sharp enough to clean 'em all out rolling dice or pitching quarters, feisty enough to bloody a lip when push came to shove. She took to her new sport as if she were Prince Charles's daughter; in no time she was a starter on the team.

It was Mecca, when the boys were rampaging through Lez's house during a weekend sleepover, who'd call them to task and captain the cleanup. It was Mecca, when Lez was barking up a tree trying to organize a half-dozen doughnut-crazed urchins for a road trip, who'd remember to pack the ponies' Pelham bits and leg wraps. She won the Best Comedian, Best Actress, Most Athletic, Most Courageous and Miss Citizenship awards in her eighth-grade class, got into Saul High School of Agricultural Sciences on Lez's recommendation because she wanted to become a veterinarian as well as polo's first African-American female pro . . . and go ahead, give the white woman a squirt of her own Palmolive if you must, but F---, Lez murmurs when she lies awake in bed at night, if only Mecca had taken that scholarship offered by that private school in California, if only she had fled. . . .

THE WHITE CARRIAGE

DARKNESS HAD already reached the Bottom. A million things remained to be done after dropping Mecca off at her house following polo practice that day last October, so Lez was in a hurry. It wouldn't have made any difference if she'd waited and watched the girl walk all the way to her front door. She's almost sure of that.

The phone call came to the barn a day and a half later. Lez screamed and cried and banged her fist on her desk, then jumped into her SUV and raced to Mecca's house to see for herself. The place was taped off, crawling with cops. Mecca, her mother, Sheila—a nurse's aide in a nursing home—and her mother's boyfriend, Daryl Bynum, had all been shot in the head not long after Lez had dropped the girl off, then thrown in a pile in the basement, their dinner still on the table.

The rest of that day is still like a dream to Lez, and maybe it'll stay that way if she just keeps busy enough. The Work to Ride family gathered in the barn to cry and talk and eat and cry some more. Richard tried to muck his way through it, moving from stall to stall with his pitchfork until he found himself beside Beuda, Mecca's horse, and then he broke down. Chris wept and begged Lez, "You've *got* to get these kids out of Philly." Two of the youngest Work-to-Riders, Bee's little brother Kareem and Lonnie's little brother John-John, were haunted by nightmares that the murderers were chasing them, too. Lonnie walked around Mecca's neighborhood wanting to grab everyone he saw—to question them or to hurt them, he wasn't sure which—before he finally gave up and sighed, "At least she don't gotta live in this f------up-ass world no more."

Theories buzzed through West Philly. The style of the killings reeked of a drug-related execution, some said. Others babbled rumors of a winning lottery ticket that had lured the murderers to the house, or of a case of mistaken identity, or of a jealous ex-lover wreaking revenge. But when the police showed up with questions, there were only shrugs and silence.

A half-assed activist. That's what Lez called her former self, the 25-year-old college student showing up at Rainbow Coalition meetings and holding up anti-Reagan signs at rallies. Now she was walking West Philly streets where there were no rainbows or coalitions, only poor black people as far as the eye could see, and holding a different sort of sign, a poster offering a $6,000 reward for information about a 14-year-old girl's murder. Wishing to God she'd begged, borrowed or stolen the money to put Mecca and her mom on a plane three months earlier when the Thacher School in Ojai, Calif., offered Mecca the $32,000-a-year polo scholarship, because maybe if the girl had visited the place, she'd have overcome her reticence about moving so far away . . . and lived.

A white horse-drawn carriage took Mecca's white coffin in the procession from the funeral home to the church. Her riderless polo pony walked behind the coffin, bearing Mecca's helmet and her boots turned backward, and the Work-to-Riders followed on horseback and on foot. They were joined by three teenage girls—polo opponents from the posh Garrison Forest School on the outskirts of Baltimore, who'd driven two hours and brought $600 they'd raised for a scholarship in Mecca's memory—and a dozen members of Pennsylvania and New Jersey polo clubs getting their first look at the Bottom.

The cool weather came. Lez worked the stalls in the mornings, just her and the animals and the NPR voice from the radio hanging from a nail, and she told everybody she was O.K. Then in the afternoons, when school let out and the kids returned to the barn, one of them would burst into tears, and Lez would go to pieces.

THE BOTTOM LINE

THE VIENNESE bronze statues and the gargantuan winged horses stared down at her. The sound of her footsteps echoed off the Italian marble floors and died in the recesses of the massive granite building. Lez entered the Fairmount Park Commission headquarters. The joint gave her the creeps.

Her landlords, the people who'd given Work to Ride its $1-a-year lease 10 years earlier, smiled and nodded and asked her to be seated at their long mahogany conference table, then cleared their throats. They weren't there to talk about the girl who'd been buried five weeks before, or to reward Lez for all she'd done so that more Meccas wouldn't be carried off in blue body bags. They were there to evict Lez from the barn.

She'd failed to hold up her end of the agreement, they said. Money that should've been spent fixing the barn's roof and plumbing had been spent taking kids and horses to polo clubs up and down the East Coast. A program that had been expected to bring in hundreds of children a year for riding lessons and camps hadn't materialized because she'd devoted so much time to nine or 10 poor kids in a rich man's sport. The commission was under budget pressure from the city. Work to Ride would ride into the sunset come July 4, 2004.

Lez's heart felt as if it were pounding its way out of her chest. Sure, everything that the park commission officials were saying might, in a literal sense, be true, but. . . .

Now her heart was pounding up in her throat. Sure, she had started out thinking she would take in more children, but. . . .

Now it was pounding in her ears. Sure, she'd *love* to have enough money and manpower to fix the roof and the bathroom and the lives of hundreds of kids, but. . . .

Her mouth opened. The officials' heads snapped back as she shouted and stormed out of the room.

There was no more crying over Mecca after that. Lez kept balling up all her grief, compressing it into anger and letting it fly.

A firestorm. That's what suddenly engulfed the park commission. Lez set her computer and phone lines blazing, pushed every button she could think of, called in every chit. The pashas of polo began hounding the park commission with calls to plead Lez's case. A U.S. congressman, a city councilman, a TV anchorwoman all did likewise, and then the rest of the Philly media caught wind of the story and bared their teeth, too.

An uneasy truce was reached. Lez would live up to her pledges, get the roof repaired, the plumbing and wiring fixed, the barn painted. She'd somehow raise more funds to hire more staff to start more programs to bring more children into the barn. She'd sharpen her administrative skills, start spending just as much time doing paperwork as papier-mâché volcanoes. Work to Ride got another one-year lease on life.

THE OTHER BOTTOM LINE

OCTOBER 9 will be Recognition Day at Valley Forge Military Academy. It's the day when the plebes at the school's adjunct college are honored for having survived the six weeks of push-ups and sit-ups and running and marching and spit-shining that prove they're ready to endure the discipline and responsibility ahead.

Lez will lead her brood into the stands at the parade grounds, and she'll look around at all that's been won and lost in a program that's hanging on for dear life. At her elbow will be Killer Bee, who couldn't follow the rules at the Texas polo ranch, blew his chance and got sent home over the summer. And Bee's 11-year-old brother, Kareem, who took Mecca's place on the team and helped lead it to its first victory over the academy, just a few months ago. And Kareem's twin sister, Kareema, who saw how fast and far a girl could go and decided that she wants to do what Mecca left undone. All of them peering at the cadets in their tight black pants, gray jackets, black hats and white gloves, marching toward them to the beat of the band's drums and horns.

It'll be so damn freaky seeing them in those uniforms, but when Richard and Chris march by—both of them on full rides to the $30,000-a-year college—everybody had better put his white gloves over his ears, because a sound unlike any other in the school's 76 years of existence will shatter the air.

Not to worry. In no time the black cadets' white mother will run out of breath, yank her two fingers out of her mouth and hurry back to work and to her next project. Don't you know? Lonnie couldn't get a full ride . . . but he's dying to be a cadet too.

———

POSTSCRIPT: *The Work to Ride program has since doubled in size under the care of Lezlie Hiner and now fields two polo teams—one for boys and one for girls. Richard Prather is studying criminal justice and Spanish at New Mexico State. Lonnie Fields and Jose Perez both completed the program and now work in Philadelphia. Jabarr Rosser (Killer Bee) was dismissed from the program for missing school, but his brother Kareem enrolled at the Valley Forge Military Academy in 2006 and went on to captain the school's polo team in his second year. In the fall of '08, four students from the Work to Ride program were attending Valley Forge.*

Coming Into Focus

The most striking transformation in modern sports—from callow prodigy to thoughtful champion, from punk to philanthropist—occurred right in front of our eyes. Could we trust the metamorphosis of Andre Agassi?

OU KNEW THE END WAS NEAR. THE SCREEN WOULD soon go black and leave you in the dark, wondering what the hell you'd just seen.

One Andre, two Andres, three Andres, four. Five Andres, six Andres, seven Andres, more. Has any athlete ever changed as much as Andre Agassi?

Sure, Tiger Woods changed his swing, Michael Jordan changed his sport. But who changes *himself*? Why would a man bother when he has the American dream by the throat? Metamorphosis is the rarest achievement in sports.

George Foreman did it, went from sullen menace to grinning Buddha. But Foreman had to go away to pull it off, hibernate from the limelight for a decade from his sport. Agassi never left.

All those years you'd watched him change, rebel becoming humanitarian, showman becoming machine, style becoming essence. But something about all those images of him—there were just too many, too different, too quick—made you keep waiting. To trust the change. Something about TV and Madison Avenue and celebrity made you suspicious of anything you saw on a screen.

"He's changed as much as anyone I've ever seen," vouched Jim Courier, a four-time Grand Slam singles champion who'd known Andre since they were teenagers.

"It's almost like an atonement," said Patrick McEnroe, the U.S. Davis Cup captain.

"He decided to be a grown-up," said commentator Mary Carillo. "He didn't have to do that. He had all the money and fame. He didn't have to become a great champion, either. But he did both. Now you really feel there's a soul in that guy."

When you asked them how and why that occurred, they said, Well, he married a good woman, he had kids, he grew up. But plenty of athletes do those things. Those answers were like all those images of Andre: They made you think you knew what happened to the man when you didn't have a clue. You'd have to see it with your own eyes, up close.

YOU WERE 50 feet away, watching him talk to the media after winning easily in the first round at the 2005 U.S. Open. Years ago, after a victory, he said, *I'm as happy as a fag in a submarine.* Years ago he growled at an audience in his home state, Nevada, for cheering an opponent's shot. Now, asked why he'd felt nervous in a first-rounder at age 35, he said, *Because everyone here took a day out of their lives to come watch me play.*

Did he feel badly for his opponent as he destroyed him? *No,* he said, *you don't cheat anybody out of their experience, whatever it is. I promise you, it's all part of what makes you who you are down the road. And if a match is getting blown out one way or the other, you've got to learn from it and you've got to understand it for what it is. I've been on the other side of that. I wouldn't want to cheat anybody out of that experience.*

You smelled it there, a whiff of what you were seeking: the seeker. But you'd have to go closer.

YOU WERE following him down a school hallway a month later. Andre was showing Robin Williams and members of Earth, Wind & Fire the academy that he built in the middle of the most destitute neighborhood in Las Vegas. It's a charter school, mostly poor black kids. He was explaining why learning levels here had made leaps so striking that the academy's middle school was the only one among 328 public schools in its county that's received an "exemplary" rating.

He took us to the room where Cirque du Soleil performers taught the kids acrobatics. Past the art class where a French painter who trained with Picasso taught them the use of color and space. He led us into a kindergarten class where, like a five-year-old himself, he burst forward so eagerly to tell everyone about the academy's innovations that he knocked over half of an edifice of blocks that the class had built, then dropped to his knees in such haste and remorse to rebuild it that he knocked over the rest.

You followed him down the gleaming hallways, thinking, *Man, he got it, he really got the big picture,* and wondering what the world would be like if a couple of superstars in each city did this. But his annual fund-raising gala for the school was scheduled for that weekend, and he was too busy to sit and explain how he got here, or let you get any closer.

TWO FEET away. Flying in a private jet two months later with Andre and his wife, Steffi Graf, on their way to play an exhibition arranged by a company that they endorse, Genworth Financial, in order to raise money for its youth charity work and Andre's charter school. Flying across a country in which celebrity means never having to ask a question—and damned if he wasn't asking you a zillion of them. Almost as many as you asked him. With eyes unlike any you'd seen in an athlete: curious, aglow.

But something was unsettling him. He kept wanting to know what *aspect* of his life you wanted to write about—to whittle down the big picture—and you kept explaining that it was the whole shebang you were after, how and why he traveled all the way from who he was to who he is.

Doubt fanned all over that full moon of a face. But suddenly he asked, *Do you have time to come to our house for a steak dinner? If it's not the best steak you've ever eaten,* he said, *then I've failed.*

IT WAS four inches thick, prime dry-aged loin, express-mailed from California in an ice pack, marinated for 16 hours and now searing over charcoal and water-soaked wood chips on a backyard grill, all of which he'd painstakingly researched. The flame was caramelizing a coating of port wine, kosher salt, sugar and a palette of seasonings that he wouldn't reveal because it was the fruit of six years' seeking—launched when Steffi, eager to meet his friends, innocently uttered the words, *Let's have a barbecue*—and because if he told you, then his steak soon might find itself in a tie with yours as the best you've ever eaten. You were sipping a peach-raspberry margarita that was the product of the same exhaustive quest. And it was true. They were both the best.

You watched him, during brief breaks from his cooking, play with his four-year-old son, Jaden, with the intensity of a man living his second childhood—no, his *first.* Andre was three when his father began tugging open the bedroom curtains in the morning, tugging on his toes, tugging off his blanket, tugging him onto the tennis court *before* he ate breakfast so he could become what his dad already was telling other people he would be: the No. 1 tennis player in the world.

You were sitting in front of a fire after dinner, looking around a house without a single trophy, plaque or tennis picture, without a nanny, maid or cook, asking him how he came to see the big picture, how he *got it* . . . and he started shaking his head no, saying that he hadn't got it, that he still couldn't see the big picture. *I can't see anything objectively or in context,* he said. *I wish I could. It drives me crazy. It causes a lot of problems. Show me a drop of water, and I'm fine. I'll learn everything about it. But don't show me the ocean. Don't show me the whole forest. Every time I try to see the big picture, I'm finished, I'm lost. . . .*

Wow. The seer was telling you he couldn't see. The seeker was telling you that the only way to see the forest was to go even closer, inside it, and take it tree by tree. Then he remembered this game, introduced by his first wife, back in an earlier life. . . .

YOU'RE ABOUT to enter a forest, says the beautiful woman. What does it look like?

It's dense, says Andre. *It's deep. There's no trail. No one has been here before. I have to find my own way.*

You come upon a key, she says. *What does it look like? What do you do with it?*

It's rusty, he says. *It's one of those big, old-fashioned keys. Normally I'd be curious, but in this case I feel no reason to find what it opens because it's obviously been used many times and what it opens has already been explored.*

Following her prompts, he comes upon a cup in the forest ... then a bear ... a wall ... and a body of water, describing each one and his reaction as he sees it in his mind's eye. It intrigues him, this game called A Walk in the Woods. But what does it mean?

His depiction of the forest as difficult and dense, Brooke Shields explains, reveals how he sees life. That rings true. The key symbolizes education, and since Andre is an eighth-grade dropout who learns through experience rather than books, his reaction to the key makes sense as well.

His eyes kindle. The game conjures the path-blazing life he wants to lead, self-discovery around every corner. Whenever that life comes to a pause, he grows so uneasy that he's willing to take wrong turns and even go backward.

Like marrying the beautiful woman.

Like leaving her in such haste that night: January 26, 1999.

He has just arrived in Los Angeles after a 13-hour flight from Australia, taken her to dinner and confirmed what he knows in his bones: It's over. It's nearing midnight, he hasn't slept in a day and a half, but he grabs some clothes, a bag of coffee beans and his margarita blender, heaves everything into the backseat of his big, white '76 El Dorado, Lilly, and heads hell-bent for his hometown, Las Vegas.

What do words mean? What's COMMITMENT? What's REAL? Tears stream down his cheeks as he rips at himself. The traffic, as he climbs the San Bernardino Mountains, slows to a crawl.

The cars around him begin to peel off in search of motels. But he needs motion. When he proposed to Brooke 2½ years earlier, he thought, *I'm asking her to marry me, and I could just as easily be breaking up with her.*

But he's a glutton for experience, for what lies beyond the next bend, and so, like tonight, he ignored the omens and shoved on.

O.K. So he's wrong again. Snow has shut the mountain pass. He turns Lilly around and begins creeping back, pulling off and being turned away at one crowded motel after another. It all begins to feel like a dream . . . or like his life. He's nearing 30, marriage shot, another Grand Slam title opportunity in Australia frittered away, his forward-then-backward career appearing ready to perish far short of the glory that his teenage fame and forehand promised.

A 12th motel sends him away. Now he's driven an hour and a half the wrong way, toward the life he just left. Wind batters his car. His mind swims with fatigue. Brooke's Walk in the Woods? It's just a Sunday stroll in the park compared with A Journey Through Andre's Forest.

He rises from a strange bed in a cheap motel somewhere between L.A. and the San Bernardino Mountains. What does he see in the mirror?

Eyes, wide as a child's, that he used to frame with eyeliner and mascara. Lips that pray before each meal and curse chair umpires. The face of a man who yearns to change, to find something rock-solid and reliable in himself that won't change.

He climbs back into his car. Which way now? His art goes to hell when he pursues love. His love goes to hell when he pursues his art. It's raining. He's crying. He heads back toward Vegas, toward an empty house.

His coach, Brad Gilbert, shows up a few weeks later. Andre tells him that his marriage is over. The television's on. As Andre clicks from one channel to the next, a vision fills the screen. The holy grail.

Tall. Willowy. Killer legs. Kind eyes. Private eyes. Resolute.

Steffi Graf's serving in the semifinals at Indian Wells, Calif.

"You need to meet *her*," says Brad.

Andre's eyes lift, full of futile hope. "I already tried that," he sighs. "A long time ago. . . . "

IT'S 1992. He's 22. He comes upon a field of grass. What does it look like? Faded green, bordered by white lime, surrounded by vintage wooden seats. *Intimate.*

Sacred. That's what everyone else calls Centre Court at Wimbledon.

To Andre it's stuffy, a place he avoided for three years. His fluorescent clothes, black hightops and denim shorts were forbidden by traditionalists there, the rebel complained, and besides, he needed the rest.

But this year he needs the grass. Somehow he has become his sport's richest and most famous player without doing one little thing: winning when it really mattered. It's his sixth year on the tour. He has never won a Grand Slam singles title. Credibility. That's what the sacred meadow offers.

And maybe her.

From the time he first laid eyes on Steffi, his soul knew. She *is* what he *isn't*. She has what he needs. At the French Open a few weeks earlier, he finally took a deep breath, gathered all his courage ... and asked his manager to ask her manager if they could meet.

"Meet her?" said Steffi's manager. "In regard to what?"

"Just to talk," said Andre's manager. "You know, he's not some wild rebel like they make him out to be. He's really a good, clean kid, very religious, in fact, born again."

Steffi's manager told Steffi that Andre wanted to talk to her about religion. Steffi told her manager to tell Andre's manager to tell Andre, No, thanks.

Her reply, reaching him just before Wimbledon begins, jolts him. They can't even talk? He's that unworthy?

He has one shot left. The male and female singles winners traditionally dance together at the Champions Ball at the end of the tournament. If they both win. . . .

Steffi mauls everyone for the 11th of her 22 majors. *Thump-thump.* . . .

One day later Andre survives 37 Goran Ivanisevic aces to win the men's championship in five sets—his first Slam title! He sags to his knees, drops to his back and sobs. *Thump-thump, thump-thump.* . . . On to the ball! His stomach tightens. He doesn't know how to dance! He can't wait to dance!

He arrives and stares. Swept-back hair, short white dress, plunging neckline.. . . . That's *Steffi Graf*? A Wimbledon member sidles up to him. *When*, asks Andre, *is the dance?*

Sorry, old chum, he's told, that's been scrapped.

The rebel blinks. What about tradition?

He can't squeak out a word to Steffi when the photographers put them elbow to elbow and pop flashes in his eyes. He flies home to Vegas, throws a party, gets drunk, gets sick, takes off his clothes and ends up on his lawn, staring at the stars, as naked as. . . .

THE DAY he was born. He opens his eyes. What does he see?

Fuzzy. Green. A ball. Dangling from a string attached to a racket hanging from the ceiling over his crib. Above it a man, moving the string, trying to compel the newborn's eyes to follow the ball.

Another ball. A balloon half filled with water, flying from the man's hand toward Andre's high chair a year later. The racket taped to Andre's hand—a Ping-Pong paddle split in half to make it lighter—smacks the balloon across the kitchen. *Fifteen-love*, crows the man.

Then another ball. A bladder extracted from a volleyball so it's light enough for a baby to whack with a sawed-off tennis racket, chase it in his walker, then whack it again and again.

Those eyes. They're what convince the man, at a Ping-Pong tournament one day, that his two-year-old will be rare. Every head in the audience shifts back and forth to follow the action, except Andre's. His eyes alone flash, affixed to that ball.

As soon as the boy can walk, his father—a short, stocky Iranian with a thick accent and thinning hair—takes him to the Tropicana Hotel's two tennis courts, which the immigrant grooms in exchange for their use. Emmanuel Agassi swooned for the sport as a 13-year-old in Tehran, coming upon it one day on a dirt court behind the American Mission Church. Sure, said the American and British soldiers who played there, the little street fighter could play if he would be their ball boy and groundskeeper. The game and the big Americans entranced him, transported him far away from the one-room home, too cramped even for a table, where he, his parents and four siblings ate on a dirt floor and shared, along with 35 others crammed into the compound, one hole in the ground—their toilet.

He fought his way out with his fists, all the way to the 1948 and '52 Olympics as a boxer for Iran, but when he arrived in the U.S. at age 22 with a couple of bucks, a couple of words of English and a new first name—Mike—he didn't choose his Olympic sport, the immigrants' sport, as his ticket into the big tent. He chose tennis. All his life he had been an outsider, a Christian Armenian in a Muslim Persian city. In his new land he was going to walk his yet-to-be-born children right up to the elite and hit 'em where they lived, where they played—in their country clubs.

He settled in Vegas and set to work. His eldest child, Rita, had the gift, but she hit puberty and hit the road, middle finger raised to her old man's relentless tennis regimen as she ran off with, of all people, tennis legend Pancho Gonzalez. His next child, Phillip, didn't quite have the foot speed or audacity that it took to play with the pros. His third, Tami, bumped her ceiling playing at Texas A&M.

That left Andre. Last child. Last chance.

Meet the future Number 1 tennis player in the world! Mike crows as he takes his four-year-old around the casino showroom where he serves as a host.

He builds a tennis court in his backyard. Andre enters a tunnel. As long as he remains inside it and never comes up to see the big picture—how vast the world is, how rife with challengers, how monstrous the odds stacked against him—he can go about the task of fulfilling his father's vision.

Dad plucks him from school a half hour early to get him on the court before Mike leaves for his night job at the casino. Weekends and summer days, Mike wakes up on a few hours' sleep and herds Andre onto the court where the 32 garbage cans await—each filled with 300 balls—along with the 11 machines that Dad has custom-welded to spit balls with different spins from different angles, one every two to three seconds . . . for the *first* of Andre's three-a-day workouts. Thousands of balls struck each day, 365 days a year, including Christmas and the day after a surgeon reattaches the piece of finger sliced off by a kid's blade when the 10-year-old Andre goes ice skating, which, dammit, he never should've done. Day off to heal? Kid can rip a forehand with a cast on his left hand. Don't pull the racket that far back, son—shorter the backswing, bigger the pop, like a boxer's straight right. C'mon, step inside the baseline, hit the ball early, *crush* it—lower, deeper, closer, farther, more topspin, *more*—go for broke on every shot!

Now Andre's hands are as fast as those phenomenal eyes, so swift that 20 years later he will enter a cage with a pitching machine set to throw

90-mph fastballs and hit them with a bat while *running toward* the machine. But what about the fire that he'll need to dominate the world, the desperation that drove Mike to the Olympics and America? There are four bedrooms and two bathrooms in his house, plumbing, electricity—and no Muslim bullies in sight. Well, then, Mike will be the bully. Mike will be the fire. Mike will snarl at Andre when his game goes sour during junior tournaments in Utah, Nevada and California. Mike will bring a hammer to a tennis match and bang on the railing in disgust. Mike will scream at officials and get thrown off the grounds. Mike will drive home, obsessing over each shot no matter how good it was because it could've been *better*. That's when Andre *wins*, which is virtually always. When he loses. . . .

He races off the court and hides behind a tree at age nine, sobbing in anticipation of the fire, after he drops the deciding tiebreaker in the final of the 12-and-under nationals. Runner-up trophies get left on the table at awards ceremonies or heaved in the trash.

What's a kid to do? Appeal to Mom? She's a peach, but tennis issues she leaves to her husband. Confront Dad? Sure, Andre is scared to, but it's more complicated than that. He loves his dad. Dad goes to war if anyone tries to take advantage of his son, gives Andre all his soul and heart, and his heart is as big as all Persia. In the middle of the night, if a friend has lost his job, Mike will go shopping and leave a heap of groceries on the friend's front step. He'll tip five bucks on a 50-cent cup of coffee, give people cars, nurse injured birds back to health, hard-boil eggs for them to sit on, end up with a half-dozen pigeons living in his house. But Andre can't, for the life of him, figure out why a game means so much to this man, why it feels as if it's *his* responsibility to keep his father and his father's home happy.

Puberty lurks. Mike grows anxious. He knows there's no player in Vegas good enough to compel his kid to keep improving. He knows, after his experience with his first daughter, that fathers and teenagers and tennis courts with 32 bins of balls are Vesuvius waiting to happen. Something has to give. Someone has to go.

THE BOY halts and looks around. He's 13. He's alone in the depths of the forest. He comes upon a training ground, an academy for young warriors.

What does it look like? What does he do?

Twenty-two acres. Forty-two tennis courts. One hundred eighty teen-agers, but only the select. A leathery ex-paratrooper in charge. Twenty-five hundred miles from home. Andre's heartsick. He had agreed to come. He felt he had no choice.

It's only for eight weeks, he tells himself. That's all his dad can afford, two months' tuition on the half scholarship that Andre's been offered to attend the Bollettieri Academy in Bradenton, Fla. Tennis boot camp. That's what it was called in the *60 Minutes* segment that introduced his father to it. Fifty-six days. Andre can last that long.

It rains one day, two weeks after his arrival. Andre's summoned to the indoor court to play in front of Nick Bollettieri for the first time. Ten minutes is all it takes. Nick calls Andre to his office and calls Mike in Vegas.

"Take your check back," says Nick. "He's here for free."

That's it. Gone, his friends. Gone, his mother's touch. Gone, his bed-room, his childhood and any normal teenage life. It's tennis, condition-ing and school from 6 a.m. to lights-out, then dreams of dog eat dog.

Nick anoints Andre top dog. He has never seen a kid hit the ball so clean and early and hard. He has never seen such eyes. "I became hyp-notized with those eyes," recalls Bollettieri. "I felt the depth. But there was also a question in those eyes: What am I doing here? I think Andre was frightened."

Terrified. But he's the coolest, most charismatic kid in camp; he can't tell anyone he's lost. He turns his fear and loneliness inside out, into hard, hip anger aimed at—no, not at the one who sent him here, not his father. At Nick. Rebellion by proxy.

Andre breaks curfews, drinks Jack Daniel's, berates opponents, smash-es balls at their teeth, smashes rackets, trashes linesmen. He gets a Mo-hawk haircut, grows it out, dyes it red, dyes it orange, draws crosses on his face with eyeliner, grows an inch-long pinkie fingernail, paints it red, paints it black . . . and takes the court at a televised Florida tournament in pink lipstick and ripped denim jeans. He'll do what his father—whose aversion to homosexuality is rooted in lurid tales he had heard as a boy in Tehran—wants him to do: play world-class tennis. But in a way that'll make his father cringe.

Only a few see beneath the bluff, see Andre's loneliness on Thanksgiving Day when nearly all the other kids can afford to fly home. He finds suckers to play for 40 bucks a match, sells clothes given to him by sports-apparel companies and buys an airline ticket home, unbeknownst to his parents. Just to stay at the home of his best friend, Perry Rogers, to sit in class with him, mingle in the halls, talk about the big dance—just to smell a normal life. Then fly back.

He can't bring himself to say, "Please, Dad, let me come home, for good." He knows the game would pass him by, knows how much his dad has sacrificed, knows he can't turn his back on the immigrant's American dream. What he *doesn't* know frightens him more: What becomes of Andre without tennis? Dammit, how did this happen? He *resents* tennis. He'd never chosen it. How dare it wash him so far away from home?

Then, after Andre's been at the academy a year, it gets scarier. He goes numb. Dead inside. Indifferent. Nick explodes, tells him to pack up, it's over. Andre stares at him and says what he can't say to his dad: "What difference does it make, Nick? Have you ever stopped for one second to feel what it feels like for a kid to leave his home, travel across the country and do this?"

Something in the boy's deadness makes the ex-paratrooper pause ... then soften. "What would it take to make it better?" Nick asks.

"Leaving here," says Andre, "and turning pro."

HE STAGGERS out of a stadium in Washington, D.C. He's 17. He can't bear this. He's just found God in a flurry of prayer meetings. He's just been born again. So why, if he's found the way, does he keep losing it in the third set? Why does he always feel that God is so angry at him? Why does he keep having that dream in which he's a child, walking down the hall toward his bedroom door in that long-ago far-away home when his path is cut off by a terrifying creature?

He stops and looks around. He's in the woods. He reels through Rock Creek Park, just outside the tennis center, then comes upon a pack of homeless men. He opens his bag and hands them every one of his rackets. He's quitting tennis, done with this gypsy life in a crummy rental car. It's time to find Andre.

He returns to his hotel and informs his brother, Phil, who travels with him. "So what are you going to do?" asks Phil.

Well, he does have that high school diploma, the one he scored via correspondence courses and *big* help from his mother after he dropped out. That qualifies him to . . . uh . . . hey, couldn't he give tennis lessons for $50 a pop?

The phone rings. A player has just backed out of an exhibition in Winston-Salem, N.C. It's $2,500 if Andre just shows up. It would take 50 tennis lessons to make that much, he calculates. He's back in the crummy rental car, barreling down the path that isn't his.

SUDDENLY IT opens wide. All that losing has shredded all those expectations for the long-haired hotshot out of Nick's academy. Suddenly he's got something to prove to himself instead of something to live up to: He's got *purpose*. He wins six tournaments in 1988 and rockets, at age 18, to No. 3 in the world. He still guns for white lines and glory on every shot, but he's just two steps from becoming what his father *told* everyone he'd be before he could tie his shoes, when. . . .

The question drops like a snake from a tree.

Are you playing tennis for you . . . or for someone else's image of you? Number 1 in the world—did you *sign* up for that?

His thoughts, during matches, start darting here and there, a flock of startled birds. He falls behind, overwhelmed by the mind flutter, and does the one thing that would cut Dad's heart deepest: goes numb, caves in, folds, accepts losing. Big strokes, small heart, the lads in the locker room start whispering.

Then the oddest thing of all occurs. He comes upon the pot of gold. Millions in endorsement dollars and appearance fees. No need to show up for Wimbledon or the Australian Open. No need to lay off that Coke, burger and fries 45 minutes before taking the court. Just keep the hair long, the threads flashy, the bandanna flapping, the earring glinting, the jaw unshaven, the emotions bared. Just be the rock 'n' roll racket-rippin' rebel, the sassy foil for staid Pete Sampras. Just let Madison Avenue use that rebellion against a father that's never actually occurred, by a champion who's never actually won a major championship, by a rock 'n' roller who actually listens to Barry Manilow—to tap into a desire that every consumer has felt to tell his father or boss to go to hell.

So now he's living *someone else's* image of someone else's image of him. He gets the Lamborghini, the Ferrari, the Vector, the Corvette, the three Porsches, the JetStar airplane, the 727. He gets the Lamborghini girlfriend, Brooke. Nothing holds his interest. He sells the cars, sheds the airplanes, shears off all the hair. Blows off tennis, then feels lost without it. Sends himself on missions—brewing the world's best cup of coffee, procuring the planet's finest hair clippers, pouring the ultimate margarita—narrowing the world to one thing, tunneling to its bottom, then moving to the next. A second dream crowds his sleep: the dream of his tongue rubbing relentlessly against his teeth, pushing until one tumbles out. Even teeth don't last.

Canon asks him to say three words. He thinks they pertain to a camera—literally—not to a philosophy or to anything to do with *him.* He still has tunnel eyes, can't see the big picture: that Madison Avenue's calculation will come off as *his* calculation. Three words tied in a nice neat noose, just what everyone suspects of the Slamless Wonder: *Image is everything.*

The cynics don't see the multimillionaire sitting for hours on a weight bench in the ramshackle garage of Gil Reyes—the trainer who has turned his life into a study of body and spirit—wringing truth from the wise old soul as if his life depends on it. They don't see the rebel flying home from tournaments, driving straight from the airport to the home of a songwriting minister named John Parenti and driving circles around the glitter of Vegas all night, questioning, trying to find a gentler God, a comprehensible father, a reliable Andre.

One day Perry, his oldest friend and new manager, suggests that Andre enter the thorniest place: psychotherapy. Because nothing has ever been resolved between Andre and his father. Andre's first phone call after he finally wins that first Slam at Wimbledon? Dad. Dad's first words? *Should've won in four sets.*

But everything he has comes from his father. Who knows where therapy might take Andre or what it might demand that he do? Besides, he explains to Perry, it feels like a shortcut. *I'm bound and determined to eat experience,* he says. *If you give me an option to cut a corner, I take more than I should. But if I make it hard, if I face it at its worst, then I stay focused and driven and it only gets better from there. I need to be in the thick of process. So I can't let myself have shortcuts.*

Rather than dwell on what Dad took from him, he decides to help someone else with what Dad gave him. To turn millions of endorsement dollars into a 25,000-square-foot building, a Boys & Girls Club where thousands of children might find their own gifts.

Rather than stir old pain, he creates new pain. He digs at his cuticles and picks at his lips till they bleed when his strokes aren't perfect. He starts setting the fires that his dad's not there to set, lighting wads of paper on hotel balconies after he loses, and on a restaurant table in Toronto, where an infuriated waiter extinguishes the flames. He puts lit matches in his mouth, making his jaw glow like a jack-o'-lantern. Sure, that burns his palate and fingers sometimes. That's O.K. That's better than *numb*.

No, the forest he's wandering through isn't thick enough. He needs to dig *under* it, to create the tunnel that his father's not there to dig. He cocoons himself in process, obsesses over what tension his rackets are strung at, tweaks them each day according to temperature, humidity, wind. Fixates on his forehand or backhand even when they're fine, three days of drama involving everyone in his camp until, yes, he's figured it out, moved his hand an eighth of an inch. . . . No. Wait. It's the balls. Too much fuzz. They don't feel right. No. It must be the court. Damn, it's so exhausting, no wonder he's always on the verge of dropping the shovel and walking away. Quitting tennis altogether. Because it's always so near, that urge. One slight shift in perspective, one glance out of the tunnel. . . .

Like that October day in 1995, up 6–4 against MaliVai Washington in Essen, Germany, when the sole of his sneaker flaps off and Andre has to borrow a shoe from a friend while someone races to his hotel room for a backup pair—but too late. He's already floating up, glimpsing the big picture, seeing himself down there playing tennis in a stranger's shoe, living a stranger's life, and it's adios, Andre, 6–1, 6–1 in the next two sets, and for most of the next two years.

HE DECIDES to marry the beautiful woman. Because . . . well, because marriage forces a man—doesn't it?—to be what Andre aches to be: the rock. But Brooke's an actress, a model: Image is her job. At night she wants to go to parties and premieres at which movie and TV people gather, to make the new friends she needs to succeed. Andre loathes that life, longs for something real. He becomes, he says, *a dry, empty husk of myself.*

Maybe that's why he risks a transformation that other athletes never do: because he, unlike them, isn't sure he wants to *be* an athlete. Somewhere in the wilderness, as lost as he's ever been, he gets an idea. O.K., maybe it's not *his* idea. Maybe it's his unconscious's: To go backward, as near as possible to where he entered the forest, and shatter *everyone's* image of him. To regress to No. 9 in the world, then No. 29 ... 74 ... 102 ... 141. It feels so awful back there. It feels so hopeless. It feels so ... *perfect*. At last he can choose his life and start over.

At age 27, in his 11th year as a pro, Andre Agassi signs up for tennis.

He begins in the satellite tournaments with the nobodies and neverweres. *Number 122....*

He reenters therapy. He's finally going to see the big picture, finally going to confront—well, no, he's not. He'll go for a year and a half, on and off, and skirt what happened in his childhood, but damn, he's trying. *Number 87....*

He lifts the blinds on his gym window, overlooking the house he built for his parents. He watches his old man, with a heart that's squeaked through quintuple-bypass surgery, hitting balls spit from a machine for an hour and a half on 100° days on his backyard court, and Andre feels something that he could never quite see: that it's *bigger* than him. That it's not personal. That this fire was set long before he was a child and still blazes long after he's become a man. *Number 71....*

He meets with Tony Robbins, the oracle of accountability, and gives himself a crash course in dreams, so he can learn to defang the hallway apparition and escape the endless loop of the tongue and the crumbling teeth. *Number 50....*

Each morning he awakens and writes two or three goals for that day in a notepad, then checks at night to make sure he accomplished them. *Number 31....*

He becomes the best-conditioned athlete in tennis, pares all motion between points except those that hasten the next point, to grind his huffing opponents to dust. *Number 21....*

At last he fully embraces the methodical game that Brad Gilbert, ever since replacing Bollettieri, has been pushing him to play, to stop gambling and start letting his opponents lose points instead of his having to win every one. *Number 13. . . .*

He decides that the Boys & Girls Club and the 3,000 kids he's helped clothe aren't enough. He seizes on Perry's idea of a charter school and commits to building the Andre Agassi College Preparatory Academy. *Number 6. . . .*

One more thing must be resolved: his inauthentic marriage. As he leaves his wife that night in 1999, as he grabs the world's best coffee beans and shuts the refrigerator door, his eyes fall on the picture there that Brooke cut out because she admired the graceful legs of the woman in it. *Her.* The undanced dance. The holy grail.

SHE'S *here.* He can see Steffi's balcony from the condo he rents six weeks later on Fisher Island, Fla., where he's staying while he plays in the Key Biscayne tournament. What if . . . ? Nah. She's already said no. She's had the same boyfriend for seven years. But if the guy hasn't sealed the deal by now. . . . Besides, the guy's not here!

Go down swinging, Andre tells himself. You're not the same guy she turned down eight years ago. He goes to work. Huddles with his old pal John Parenti and starts preparing that first phone call to Steffi as if it's a State of the Union address. Recruits the Fisher Island ferry operator to report her comings and goings. Discovers her practice time, with help from Brad, so they can accidentally schedule Andre's practice right after hers. Contact! They hit together for a half hour! He's aching to tell her what's still a secret—that he and Brooke have split—and the *other* secret bursting in his heart. But he doesn't want to blow it. He floats back to his room. He blows it. He orders a bouquet of roses too big for the lobby of the Ritz-Carlton. He paces, bleeding over every word in the note to go with it, calls Perry to help him revise it again and again and finally sends the bouquet to her room. He watches her balcony window, spying . . . dying. . . .

At last Steffi staggers out under the megabouquet and deposits it, of all places, on her balcony. That can't be a good sign. He waits. Forever. The phone rings. He pounces. "I want no misunderstanding between us," she says. "Don't come near me now. My boyfriend is here."

Here? He blanches. Reconnaissance failure! He parses every word she uttered. *Don't come near me now.* His mind swims. His game drowns. He loses his first match and heads home, his whole life rising and dipping on the kite string of that one word: *now.*

Two months later, on the clay he's never solved, he learns how much he can rely on himself. Down two sets against Andrei Medvedev in the final of the French Open, he wins in five sets, drops his racket and weeps: At 29 he's the first man since Rod Laver in 1969 to win all four Grand Slam singles titles. Seven years after his first attempt, he feels like a man who deserves Steffi Graf.

It's just the start of a 27–1 run in Grand Slam matches, the best since Jimmy Connors's 20–0 in '74; three majors in less than a year. On the flight to Wimbledon a few weeks after Paris, he scissors out a picture of a barn and a field from an airline menu, turns it into a birthday card, rolls it up, ties it with a ribbon and gives it to Steffi's coach to pass on. It's so sweet she has to call him. Boy, is our boy ever ready. *I want no misunderstandings,* he says. *I'm sure you've heard by now about Brooke and me. I think you're beautiful and fascinating and I have a tremendous amount of respect for what appear to be the pillars of your life. Can we have lunch or dinner or coffee, take a walk, I don't care—I just want to get to know you better.* Bull's-eye! She green-lights him to call her after Wimbledon.

One month later, two days before she plays the final match of her career at age 30, they go out to dinner in La Jolla, Calif., and Steffi gets a surprise: Andre's not at all like his *image.* They end up running on the beach and start discovering that somehow they're completely different. . .and uncannily the same. That Steffi, too, has a foundation for children, one that addresses the psychological scars from violence all over the world. *Her* dad's a fanatic for tennis, boxing and soccer? Precisely the same as his! *Her* favorite musicians are George Michael, U2 and Prince? Exactly his! When she asks him his favorite alltime movie a few weeks later, she lets go of the phone and screams. It's hers, *Shadowlands,* the story of C.S. Lewis finding his soul mate late in life and then losing her to cancer. Steffi, too, is a seeker—she planned to travel the globe to photograph animals until Andre began laying siege—but the big difference between them, the saving one, is this: Once she finds an answer, she trusts it. She leaves it alone.

She flies to Vegas to see his world. She approaches Andre's father for the first time. He's on his tennis court, of course. Andre tenses— remembering how Dad disdained his marriage to Brooke, how he walked out on their wedding reception—still yearning to be part of a family that's *whole*.

Steffi walks right up and wraps her arms around his father, an embrace so warm that it melts the old man . . . and more of the ice between him and his son.

HERE'S WHAT happens when a man finds a lens that makes every choice in his life clearer: Will it make my wife proud? Here's what happens when a boy raised to win more Grand Slam tournaments than anyone else on earth ends up with not even half as many as the woman in his own bed, and he's so damn grateful for it that at night he writes on a chalkboard in their kitchen the things he noticed and admired about her that day. Here's what happens when that gratitude begins swelling, rippling outward from that bed and kitchen.

He starts having children, and they turn his churning energy outward, and his meltdowns become rarer and rarer, and he starts playing some of the best tennis of his life, outlasting all the peers who'd been far more dedicated to the game. And in his children's faces he sees the child he didn't get a chance to be, and the faces of all the children who lose that chance, and he begins adding more classrooms to his school for kids from broken homes. He lifts his own kids to hold them so often that it aggravates a condition in his back, caused by a vertebra that's slipped over the one below it, and so then, to get things right with tennis that he got wrong all those years, he has to do it with pain shooting down his sciatic nerve.

And suddenly he's in front of the world in the first round of the 2005 French Open with his back killing him and a far lesser player taking him apart, but rather than quit and call off the embarrassment as he would've before, he fights to the end and then explains why with such conviction and such appreciation of the fans who'd paid to see him that an ESPN editor includes it on *SportsCenter*.

It reaches the eyes of a man on his back in California recovering from a kidney transplant, the hot television comedian George Lopez, who feels so moved that he sends a text message that ricochets from his TV producer to Perry to Andre. "Because," says Lopez, "you could tell Andre's words came from a man who has traveled the world and found compassion. A man who said *Image is everything* is now saying, *Humanity is everything*." And so, of course, Lopez accepts Andre's invitation to take the stage at his annual fund-raising gala last October, where he joins Robin Williams and Céline Dion and Barbra Streisand and a slew of other celebrities who come to Vegas to auction off their time and perform for Andre's cause, which raises $7.5 million in one night, prompting Andre to bound to the microphone and round off that number, from his and Perry's pockets, to *$10 million*, so that all the kids at his academy can walk into a brand-new high school that'll open this fall.

HOW DO you move on when you've finally found the sweet spot? He couldn't say farewell to the game during the first six months of this year, even as back pain and inactivity from a severe ankle sprain kept driving him out of tournaments in the first round or before they even began. It wasn't so much the tennis he'd be losing but the cocoon of all that *process*. Finally on June 24 at Wimbledon, the field of grass he once couldn't bother to play, he swallowed hard at 36, said *enough* . . . and felt liberated.

He insists he's not worried about a void after tennis, once he's done playing several hard-court tournaments and the 2006 U.S. Open, because he's learned by watching how his wife moved on without a hitch. Sure, his new life will probably have a lot to do with the academy, perhaps trying to replicate it around the country. Sure, it'll have even more to do with his own kids, but not likely on a tennis court unless they *really* want it. Already his father's telling him that Jaden's not playing enough and that Andre needs to start dropping the boy off at Grandpa's house at sunrise and picking him up at sunset, to which Andre just nods and says, "Yeah, I might do that, Dad" . . . and never does.

Andre: *I just hope the kids find something to pour all of themselves into because that's where the marrow of life comes from. If it's tennis . . . wow, I'd take a deep breath. I'd have to hand it to Jaden if he did that. He'd have to have a mighty big pair of. . . .*

Steffi: *It would work out, Andre. Just trust your instincts. You'd do it right.*

Andre: *Yeah ... but my instinct is to NOT trust myself.*

Even now. After the magic thing happened.

That fifth set. Last September against James Blake in the U.S. Open quarterfinals. The changeover as Blake prepares to serve for the match. The crowd rising, love thundering from the highest seats like a waterfall, gathering volume as it rolls. Love for the battle Andre has waged, digging out of an 0–2 grave in sets against Blake, and for his 20 U.S. Opens, and for more than that: for his arc, for who he has become. He's as deep in the tunnel as he's ever been, but he looks up and around, and for the first time in his life he sees and hears everything outside the tunnel. He sees his friend James instead of the distant blur that his opponents have always been. He sees what he's never seen in the audience: actual faces, individual joy. He hears not the fuzzy din that he has all of his career but each syllable growing louder and louder: *An-dre! An-dre! An-dre!*

Chills run through him. He battles from behind once more and beats Blake. It's O.K., he says now, that Roger Federer defeats him four days later in the final because Federer's the best he's ever seen, and besides, being No. 1 never was what his journey's about. It's O.K., he says, because he finally knows what it's like to be totally absorbed in yourself and yet feel part of everything.

He shakes his head. All that trekking, only to find out that where you get to means nothing. To find out that all that matters is how you *look* at the forest.

I used to look at it as something overwhelming, he says, something separate from me that I had to find my way through. Now I see myself as part of it. When you start out on the journey you think it's all about taking in experiences to fulfill yourself. But it's not. The greatest experience is changing someone else's experience of life. And once you come to that realization, it becomes your foundation, the ace in your pocket, who you are. It's the opposite of what you think it is. When you see the world through the lens of others, that's when you find yourself.

But I still can't see the big picture. I still can't see things in context. I swear I can't. ...

THE FIRE'S out. The world's best margarita blender's empty. The man yawns and rises. You thank him for taking you on the journey and wish him luck on the second leg, the new path. The one where the man who learned to see learns to trust his eyes.

———————

POSTSCRIPT: *Two years removed from his last professional tennis match, Andre Agassi, together with his wife Steffi Graf, is managing an extensive portfolio of business projects, including a luxury hotel, a chain of sports clubs and a furniture line. "It's been my philosophy that you don't invest in things, you invest in people," Agassi says. He considers the charter school he opened in Las Vegas in 2001 his greatest investment. The Andre Agassi College Preparatory Academy will graduate its first class of students in '09. Agassi says he hopes to spread the model to other cities across the country.*

Damned Yankee

*John Malangone had all the tools—a can't-miss athlete destined to succeed
the great Yogi Berra as catcher for the New York Yankees. But his torment over
a dark family secret kept him from fulfilling his prodigious promise.*

EVERYTHING YOU WILL READ ON THE NEXT 22 PAGES
revolves around one photograph. The rest of the old
man's past, you must understand, is all but gone. The
framed baseball pictures were smashed by his hammer. The scrapbook thick with newspaper clippings was fed to the furnace in the basement of the Sears, Roebuck in Paramus, N.J. The trophies, with their figurines of ballplayers and eagles and angel-like women, were placed on a portable table in the middle of a ball field and annihilated, one a day, by the old man's rifle arm. Have you ever heard the popping sound an angel makes when it's struck by a fastball?

Surely the other artifacts that survived are too few and too baffling to be trusted. The death certificate of a seven-year-old boy ... the tattered letter from the New York Yankees front office ... the 1955 Louisville Slugger with the name *John* misspelled on the barrel. Without the photograph, who could watch the gray-whiskered man with no laces in his shoes rummage through his trailer and not wonder if his tale is too fantastic to be true?

But then John Malangone, with a funny look on his face, a mixture of pride in the thing he's holding and an eagerness to be rid of it, thrusts in front of you the picture, snapped on a sunny spring training day 32 years ago. You stare. No. It wasn't a dream. The old man hasn't gone mad. If it hadn't been for the horror, he really might have filled Yogi Berra's shoes. Look at the picture. Just look at it.

"*Kid! Come over here. Wanna take your picture.*"

"*Who, me? You don't want my picture.*"

"*Come on! Gonna put you right between the two Hall of Fame catchers, Dickey and Cochrane. You're gonna be plastered all over the* Daily News."

"*The* Daily News*? Naw, get somebody else.*" "*Somebody else? You crazy, rookie? You're gonna be a helluva star.*"

How many of us possess a photograph of the very instant when our lives reached the top of the mountain and then, with the click of the camera—*because* of the click of the camera—began their descent? Look closely at John Malangone, in the middle. It's 1955. He's 22. Touching his glove, anointing him, are the fingertips of perhaps the two greatest catchers in the history of baseball: Mickey Cochrane, on the left, a 51-year-old Yankees scout and camp instructor, and Bill Dickey, a 47-year-old Yankees coach. John has just homered in an intrasquad game. He's fresh from leading the winter league in Venezuela in home runs, RBIs and doubles. Casey Stengel has tabbed him "the probable successor to Yogi," even though Berra would be the Yankees' regular starting catcher for four more seasons.

John remembers the words the tall photographer uttered just before he took the picture. John remembers the panic spreading through his stomach as he squatted between Cochrane and Dickey, the fear that someone on his block in East Harlem would see this picture in the next day's paper and call the *Daily News* and tell what occurred on that summer evening 18 years before, insist that what John really deserved was a seat in a chair humming with a couple of thousand volts. John remembers everything, because memory is the whip he has used to flog himself for 60 years. . . .

ORLANDO PANARESE was blond and he was bashful and he was handsome and he was seven, and when he and John trampolined on the bed they usually shared, they jumped so high they nearly banged their heads. It was perfect, having your best buddy be your uncle. Having your mom's little brother living just one floor up in a tenement on 114th Street, so your family was his family and all of you, aunts and uncles and cousins and grandparents, ended up on the roof with Uncle Duffy's pigeons every summer Sunday, playing checkers and eating linguini with red sauce bare-chested, if you were a boy, to save your mother from spending Monday scrubbing shirts. So you could float in and out of each other's apartments at any hour and end up in pj's pounding each other with pillows while Mom and Grandma rolled pasta or talked another cup of coffee to death. *Zi*, John called Orlando, shortening the Italian word for uncle. They would slip downstairs at sunrise, while Grandma

Panarese dressed for church, and earn apples for her by helping the Italian fruit peddlers pry open their crates. *"Grazie*, Orlando. *Grazie*, John," she would say when they delivered the apples to her, bowing formally to the little boys.

They were upstairs talking, Mom and Grandma, that July evening in 1937. They couldn't keep their eyes on five- and seven-year-old boys all day, could they? Eleven years had passed since Grandma had lost her first Orlando, her eight-year-old son who was tagging along with his older brothers to the movies when one of them fibbed, "Go home, Orlando, Mommy's calling you," and the little boy turned back to cross the street and was killed by a truck. A mother can't run scared every minute for 11 years, can she?

John found the broken umbrella rusting in the basement of his six-floor tenement. He and the boys on his block pulled off one of its metal spokes and lashed it, with rope, to a shorn-off broomstick handle. Excellent. A javelin. A new contest for the first-generation Italian-American children teeming on the streets of East Harlem. John took the javelin, paced down 114th Street and eyed his goal: the pile of sand the peddlers would shovel onto the wooden ramp leading into the stables next to John's apartment building, so their horses wouldn't slip in their own urine. The other boys stood in a group in front of the candy store and watched.

John reached back and threw himself, all of himself, into that javelin. Maybe it flew a little off the side of his hand, and maybe it went farther than anyone thought a boy his size could throw it. Every time he has seen it happen ever since—on the sides of water glasses, on cabinet doors, on outfield walls—he has squinted and tried to discern whether it was a misjudgment of his might or a flaw in technique. But he knew, as he watched the javelin arc, that he was in trouble, and he knew when he heard the boys gasp that it had hit someone, and he knew when he approached the tight circle of children and frantic adults and saw two small feet protruding—one sock of solid color and one sock striped—that it was Uncle Orlando. Because when he looked down at the ground, the other striped sock and the other solid one were on his own feet.

A boy turned to John. "You're in trouble," he said.

GARY SMITH

"Spell that name for me."
"Huh?"
*"Your last name, kid. You pronounce it Mal-an-go-nee, right? Gotta make
sure they spell it right when they run this picture. M ...A ... is it two l's or
one in Malangone?"*
"Uh ... yeah ... two ... two l's."

He remembers cringing that day as the photographer scribbled in his
notepad. Another secret they were closing in on. Another secret that each
line drive off his bat, each shotgun throw from his arm to rub out a runner
stealing second was leading them closer and closer to discovering: The
22-year-old Yankees hotshot couldn't read or write. Oh, they would find
out why, sure as the sunshine beating on his shoulders when he crouched
between Cochrane and Dickey.

He had shoved it out of his mind since the day he had signed, but now,
as the shutter clicked, he could smell it: the beginning of the end. The
story of the lovable homegrown Italian boy laying siege to the position of
the lovable, aging Italian Hall of Fame catcher, the story of a kid as strong
as thunder and flakier than snow, able to awaken from a dead sleep in
December and out-malaprop Berra, out-Yogi Yogi—you don't think the
New York tabloid wretches, the chroniclers of the greatest dynasty in
baseball history, are going to crawl all over that? You don't think they're
going to find out how his brain shut down because of the accident and
how neither he nor all the letters and numbers he stared at could ever
stay still after the *next* shock?

You can't figure on anything in life. You can't figure on a javelin flying
through the air and hitting someone's skull, let alone your uncle's. And
then, once it does, you can't figure on him pulling it out with his own
hands, and, oh, thank God, standing up. And walking home with the help
of his mother, barely bleeding because it's a puncture wound, and looking all right for a few days, *thankyouthankyouGod* ... until the small red
swelling appears. Nobody ever told John that the wound became infected
and that Orlando was taken to a hospital and that he underwent surgery
to relieve the swelling but that the infection kept spreading because the
use of penicillin was still four years away; Jesus Christ, it's so easy to
hoodwink a five-year-old boy. Nobody told him anything, not even what

all the commotion was upstairs in Grandma's apartment and why all the adults looked so sunken-eyed. They forgot all about John for a moment, and he wandered up the steps and through the door and into a room where he saw a box surrounded by white drapes and flowers. He stared at it, too short to see its freight. He moved closer, closer. He stepped up onto the kneeler. Orlando. . . ? God, he looked beautiful. Why was he sleeping there? *Zi, what's wrong? ZI, WAKE UP!*

That was how John learned what his right arm had done. That was when he screamed, and his right eardrum popped, and his tongue nearly went down his throat, and the corner of his mouth and his right hand went numb for the first time. That was when he lost half of his hearing and, for nearly a year, every word of English he had learned. That was when Grandma burst into the room and found the catatonic boy and shrieked at God, "No, not this one too!" And rushed him to the room in her apartment that she had turned into a chapel and held him near the candles and the crucifix and the statues of St. Anthony and Mother Mary and Baby Jesus, her fumbling fingers pouring olive oil into a small bowl and dropping into it a piece of wool torn from mattress stuffing, then striking a match to light the wool and warm the oil, and thrusting her thumb into the liquid and using it to rub tiny signs of the cross on the boy's forehead, his nose, his chin, his temples and behind his ears, murmuring ancient words that had been passed down to her, until her eyelids slowly sagged and a great yawning fatigue overcame her, as it always did when she healed the old way.

"Shhhh. Don't say a word," they said to each other when the boy finally fell asleep. "He's quiet now. Don't say a word about any of this—ever—do you hear me? He's only five. He'll forget everything if no one ever says a word."

GO BACK to the photograph. Perhaps you see it now: the uncertainty in John's smile, in his eyes. Perhaps you see what John sees when he looks at that picture today. "Half of that boy is missing," he says. "That's just a body there. That's just a shadow I was casting. That's just a shell."

The police arrived at John's apartment after Orlando's death. The five-year-old boy climbed out the back window and hid on the fire escape until they were gone. He had evaded them, he thought. *For now.* But then a kid on the street called him Killer. A woman who saw her daughter talking to John cried, "Stay away from him!" One of the Mafia members who ruled his block slapped him on the back and said, "Ya got one under ya belt, kid!"

And then no one saw him. The alleyways behind the tall tenements became his home. On his way to and from school he could go for blocks scrambling over the seven-foot mesh fences that separated one building from the next, never seeing the sun except when he darted over a cross street to the next alley. He could go for hours hurling balls in the shadows at a clock he drew in chalk on an alley wall, aiming first at one o'clock until he nailed it on the button, then one by one around to 12, over and over and over, taming the arm that had betrayed him. Then he would line up two dozen bottles, hurling anything when his rubber ball had disintegrated—rotten apples, oranges, stones—exulting silently when the bottles exploded and the noise shattered off the walls. Soon he was turning his back on his target, spinning and blindly throwing, throwing, throwing. . . . When at last he grew weary, he would grab a stick and imagine that he was conducting an orchestra, sending waves of beautiful music swelling up the tenement walls.

When it snowed and the block was empty, the boy would emerge. The people would hear a relentless scraping noise, and when they peered out, the sidewalk up and down 114th Street between First and Second Avenue would be bare.

He risked exposure only in exchange for exhaustion. He would race to the coal yards three blocks away, and for a quarter—but not really for a quarter—he would take some malingerer's shovel and do the man's task all day. He would continue waxing and polishing the Mob's black Chryslers, long after they were already gleaming, in the alley behind their clubhouse. He went to the basement where the old paisanos made wine, and he hand-cranked the press until his arms screamed. He stood on three empty soda cases and pounded the speed bag in the Silver Star boxing club, just down the street from his apartment building. He mucked the peddlers' stables, wrung water from neighboring women's wet laundry with his thickening wrists, wrung so tightly he sometimes ripped the clothing, trying so hard to please everyone around him and to fatigue the creature into tongue-hanging silence.

The creature?

Yeah. You know. The thing. The hunchback, just behind John's shoulder. Can't you see it in the photograph? The one that could show up at any moment when John wasn't throwing or shoveling or mucking or wringing or punching. The beast he would suddenly hear laughing faintly and mumbling so softly that John had to lean to make out the words. *You. . . . You killer, you. . . . You know what you deserve. . . .* He would shut his eyes, clutch his head, cover his ears, and still he'd sense it, still he'd hear it. It looked like . . . yes, almost exactly like Quasimodo, the terrifying humped creature with half a sunken face whom John kept returning to the Cosmo Theater to stare at in *The Hunchback of Notre Dame* . . . only somehow the eyes and nose and mouth of the hunchback stalking John were his own.

His head would begin to throb. His throat would tighten; he couldn't swallow, he couldn't breathe! His right ear would pop and begin to ring, his throwing hand would go numb, the right edge of his mouth would curve up, his arms shiver, his equilibrium vanish, his vision tunnel and blur. And now, upon whatever surface his eyes fled to, he would see and hear the javelin arcing through the air, making that terrible swishing sound, and then the coffin, looming larger and larger as if he were a small boy again, stepping nearer and nearer to it, and then, Orlando's beautiful face inside it. And John's fist or his baseball bat would lash out at the image, and suddenly there was a hole in the wall or the cabinet or the wardrobe in his bedroom, and his mother was scurrying to find someone to patch it before his hot-tempered father came home.

"Why?" he would hear his father scream at his mother. "Why did you leave him alone that day? It's *your* fault!" But never, ever, was the subject mentioned when John was in the room. The boy might go two nights, three nights in a row without sleep, and when at last he dozed he would dream that he was running down 114th Street, racing against the javelin, reaching up to catch it before it landed, and then he would awaken, shouting "Orlando!" in a puddle of urine and sweat.

He knotted two dark socks together and tied them around his head, over his ears, to keep that maddening swishing sound from entering his ears whenever the wind blew, or whenever he tried to outrun the son of a bitch, all the way from East Harlem to Greenwich Village. . . .

Still mumbling. Still there.

Maybe he could drown the bastard. Maybe, if he jumped into the Harlem River off the Willis Avenue Bridge and stayed underwater for one minute . . . two minutes. . . .

Still laughing. Still there.

Maybe if he stuck his grandmother's sewing needle into his throwing arm. . . .

He felt nothing. Still there.

Maybe if he careened down the ramp off the Triborough Bridge on a bicycle with no chain or brakes, he could shatter the hunchback.

He broke his leg.

Maybe he had to pinpoint the demon's location first. Maybe if he turned swiftly when he walked through snow, he could see footprints, the same way the police finally located and killed the Invisible Man in the next movie that obsessed John at the Cosmo. Maybe fabric would reveal the creature's whereabouts, as it did in the film. Maybe if John stood in front of a mirror nonchalantly and suddenly tossed one of his grandmother's black veils over his shoulder, it would land on the demon's head, and then John could whirl and throttle it. Maybe if he heaved a handful of his mother's baby powder over his shoulder. . . . No! Nothing! Damn him!

There were only two things to be done. Hurry to the arms of his mother, Josephine—she hugged him, soothed him without ever saying what she was soothing away and led him to her own mother, who would stop the pounding in his forehead and temples by rubbing them again with warm olive oil. Or he could race to Mount Carmel church and go up into its tower to sit with the bells, just like the hunchback did in the movie to escape his enemies. Inside the church, where the demon couldn't pursue John, he would light a votive candle and pray feverishly, "Make him stop, God! Make him go away! Please, God, I'll do your work, I'll help people, please!"

He would give the shoes off his feet to a beggar. He planned to become a priest, choke the demon with the collar, but he couldn't even cut it as an altar boy. Instructions bewildered him; he just couldn't concentrate. He would turn the wrong way at the altar, forget what part of the Mass was coming next, spill the wine, exasperate the priest. It was the same story in school, where the letters and numbers swam, and he would end up in the back of the classroom, the perennial dope, lovable but hopeless.

No one could stay mad at him—except his father, the barber. Sylvester Malangone would come home and find his wife gone again, always upstairs with her mom; her guilt over her son's killing of her mother's son had turned her into Grandma's slave. Sylvester's jealous rage would begin to boil, and at the slightest excuse he would seize the thick barber's strap he kept on a hook and rip into his eldest son, John, knowing that the thumps and cries would bring his wife racing downstairs in tears, back where she belonged.

After the rat the beatings grew worse. John awoke to an earthquake one night when he was 10; his father was heaving the mattress right off the bed on which John and his brother, Sylvester Jr., were sleeping, and lunging for a rat of terrifying size. Now John's dad had the rodent where he wanted it, shrieking behind the radiator, just enough space between the radiator's ribs to insert one of the boys' bed slats and pin the rat against the wall. The shrieking grew ghastly, almost human, and sweat erupted from the father's pores as his two sons cowered behind him, but he drove the slat home and blood spattered them, and the father swooned and cried out and began to shake. He ended up in a straitjacket at Bellevue, and when he came home a month later, his fury at John had somehow grown larger.

Five decades would pass before John would learn that his father, too, carried a terrible secret. Fifty years of silence and rage until John learned about the day that his dad, then just a seven-year-old boy, had been so happy to see his own mother coming home from another long day at a sweatshop that he and his two brothers had thrown a bear hug around her legs on the street, toppling her backward onto the jagged edges of a steel garbage can, causing a wound that became infected, just like Orlando's, and killed her. And John, when he finally heard the story, understood instinctively that everything he had turned in on himself, his father had turned outward—upon John, the son who had also killed a loved one accidentally.

The beatings stopped all at once when John was 15. His father grabbed the strap one day, enraged at John's younger brother for a change, after the boy had knocked the family's radio off the counter and broken it, and cocked his arm behind his ear to let the boy have it, when ... *huh*? The barber yanked down, and yanked again, but it was as if the strap were nailed to a ceiling beam. He looked over his shoulder and saw John clutching the strap with one hand. "You son of a bitch!" Sylvester Sr. shouted. "So you want it!" And he yanked and yanked, until it dawned on him that his boy was a 5' 10", 195-pound man, arms and thighs like a stevedore's from all the frantic shoveling and mucking and punching, and his strap would remain where it was for all time if John so willed it.

The barber grew small before John's eyes. John let go of the strap. His father opened a window and flung the strap into the alley.

Sylvester Sr.'s eyes widened: Out the door John darted, returning in seconds and placing the strap back on its hook.

He needed the lashes. They made him feel good.

YOU CAN'T see Paul Krichell. He was just a few feet out of the picture that day, wearing a proprietor's grin. "You make me proud, John," Krichell told him just after the *click*. It wouldn't be long now, the 72-year-old scout realized, until the press began pestering him for details of that improbable spring day in 1950 when he strolled onto the field at East Harlem's Jefferson Park in his sunglasses, straw hat and white cotton jacket, looking for someone else.

He had positioned himself on the first base line that day to assess a player from Ben Franklin High. Krichell was the man who had found Lou Gehrig, Charlie Keller, Red Rolfe, Phil Rizzuto, Whitey Ford and a fleet of others, a calm, assured gentleman who knew that everyone knew he was Krichell, the great Yankees scout.

He took no notice of John as the teenager finished laying the strip of lime down the leftfield line. John, academically ineligible, had never played on the team. He was in the hammer-and-nail class at Ben Franklin, the 1940s version of special ed, and served as a gofer for the varsity coach. "Wanna throw, Paulie?" John asked.

"Sure!" said Paulie Tiné.

The two boys had met six years before: Paulie with the disfigured face and John with the mutilated soul, clinging to each other with the static electricity of pain. Paulie was two years older, his cheeks ravaged by a case of acne so severe that John believed him when he claimed he had been burned in a fire. Alleys? Sounded good to Paulie. Baseball all day across the East River at Randall's Island, or on the field at Jefferson Park that was farthest from 114th Street, where no one would likely recognize them?

Suited Paulie just fine. The moment that kids from John's block showed up, Paulie would scent his buddy's fear and say, "I'll race ya, John!" The moment girls started pointing at Paulie and shrieking and hiding behind each other's backs, calling him the Mummy or the Phantom of the Opera, John would say, "I'll race ya, Paulie!" And lickety-split they were off, almost faster than shame, Paulie a heartbeat ahead at first and then John pulling even as they neared the 107th Street Pier and headed straight for the edge, diving blindly into the East River—goners if there had been a log or a boat below.

Has there ever been a friend so loyal as Paulie? When John couldn't read a sign, Paulie lied, "Don't worry, John. I can't read that either." When John threw a BB from deep left, Paulie pogoed across the field, screaming, "Didja see that throw? *John Malangone! What an arm!*" He was the admiring audience John had never had, couldn't have—not after what happened when a cop talked him into joining the Police Athletic League at 13 and he froze on the mound in his first and only game, unable to throw a single pitch for fear he would kill the batter. But even to Paulie, John never told his secret.

They were throwing to each other for distance on an adjacent field when Krichell's hungry eyes roved. *What?* Did he just see what he thought he just saw? One kid had just thrown the ball from home plate and hit the leftfield fence, near the sign that said 368! Krichell's legs began to move.

"How old are you, kid?" Krichell asked.

"Seventeen," replied John.

"Where do you play?"

John hesitated. Loaded question.

"Anyplace!" Paulie piped.

"Come to Yankee Stadium tomorrow. We're having a tryout."

"How do I get there?" asked John.

Krichell's eyebrows took a slow walk. An East Harlem teenage boy who didn't know where the Stadium was? What hole had this kid been hiding in? "What's your address, kid? We'll pick you up."

The tryouts had been going on for weeks, the legion of young prospects already whittled from hundreds to 40, when John entered the Stadium, believing he was about to participate in a distance-throwing contest. The Yankees' coaches blinked at the lefthander's glove, one of Paulie's, that

John had been jamming onto the wrong hand for years, and gave him a righthander's mitt. The first day, John sat the entire practice game with Paulie at his side. The second day, he was sent to the mound in the seventh. For three scoreless innings he threw blurs. As the Yankees brass stood to leave in the bottom of the ninth, he approached the batter's box. The first pitch came in . . . and went out, ricocheting in the upper deck's empty seats, *whack, whack, whack.*

"What do you think about playing pro ball?" Krichell asked moments later.

"Sure!" crowed Paulie.

Half the block was out on 114th Street three days later, surrounding the big black car, as word went from window to window: The Yankees are here. *What for?* To sign Malangone. *Malangone?*

MARK THIS sentence with your thumb. Go back to the photograph. Take a look at the *ain't he hot stuff?* look on Cochrane's face. Priceless. See, Mickey smelled smoke, but he had no idea he was crouching beside a volcano. Just smoke, because he knew the whiff of pain and anxiety well. He had suffered a nervous breakdown in 1936, lost a son in World War II. Sure, this kid he was tutoring, Malangone, was an original—first player Mickey had ever seen run to the outfield during dead time and hit fungoes to himself. But when it was quiet and the kid was unaware, gazing into space, Mickey saw fear . . . and mistook its source. "You're gonna make it," he kept reassuring John. "You're locked in. Stop worrying. If not this year, next year for sure."

Hell's bells, the kid had the goods. "Stronger than a bull," recalls Johnny Blanchard, one of John's catching rivals in the Yankees' farm system. "A rifle arm. Power out the ying-yang. He was a big Yogi Berra."

For the first two years the Yanks hid John on local sandlot teams, converting him from a pitcher to a catcher to take advantage of his stick, watching with a wary eye as he piled up MVP trophies in weeklong tournaments. They were fearful it would be discovered that they had signed him before he had graduated, but unable to send him away to one of their farm teams; he kept freezing on the train platform when it came time to leave his mother's arms, his grandma's healing fingers. Finally, in the spring of 1952, just shy of John's 20th birthday, Paulie poured him onto a bus and he went to Trois Rivieres in the Canadian Provincial League.

"Listen up, men!" Trois Rivieres manager Frank Novosel barked to his team of youngsters as their bus rolled through Montreal, hours after he had made his final cut. "The guys on this bus are the guys who've made the ball club. This is the group that's going all the way. You got it? There's no turning back now, men!"

And suddenly, with those words, John felt the shivers and the sweats again, the ringing and mumbling in his ear, the choking in his throat, the numbness in his throwing hand: The hunchback had crossed the border! He rose, struggling to breathe—no, not here, on a moving bus with nowhere to run. He stumbled to the front. He knew what happened when he felt trapped.

It was the same feeling he had coming out of anesthesia after a double hernia operation just a few years before, when he reached down and felt the surgeon's clips and thick bandages all over his groin and abdomen and suddenly became sure they were the beast's hairy hands and fingernails. He screamed and ripped open the entire incision, trying to tear the creature from his groin, then reached up and tore at his face. There was blood every-where, and a nurse rushed through the door and shrieked. He hurled her across the room. Two orderlies charged in. Two orderlies flew out. It took six men to straitjacket him, and he lost so much blood that he nearly died.

And now his new teammates and the Trois Rivieres bus driver blink-ed at him, unaware of such terms as *panic attack* and *post-traumatic stress disorder*; in 1952 there were only lunatics and maniacs. "I need a church!" John panted.

"What're we here for?" the bussie grunted. "To play or pray?"

"Take him to a church!" growled Novosel. "When *you* can hit like him, we'll go where you want to go."

A few turns, a few blocks, and the most glorious sight in John's life ap-peared: Montreal's huge cathedral, St. Joseph's Oratory. Between games, for the rest of the season, he was at church, praying and holding holy oil over the candles he had lit and rubbing it where Grandma had. He hit .302 with 17 home runs and 90 RBIs that season. The fans loved him. One day he might be missing a sock, the next a belt, then a hat. He played without shoelaces. "My feet are tight," he told the skipper. Truth was, he couldn't concentrate enough to tie a bow.

Just before the team's last game, the manager pulled him aside. "The Yankees have called you up for four days," said Novosel. "You probably won't get to play, but you'll get a taste of the big leagues. Then you're going to Venezuela for winter ball. Congratulations!"

"Skip, can't I stay here with you?"

"Are you crazy, son?"

THE PICTURE'S a damn lie, and Bill Dickey knows it. Go back and look—you couldn't have caught it on the first glance or the second. Sure, Dickey's smiling, but it's only for form's sake. He's smiling at nothing. He isn't looking at the kid.

Dickey didn't care what Stengel or Cochrane thought, or how many four-baggers John hit. He didn't give a flip that John was fresh from two years in the Army, where he'd won a medal for saving a drowning soldier. He didn't give a damn that the glove on John's left hand was given to him four days earlier by Berra himself. Nobody with a head like Malangone's was going to inhabit the soil behind the plate that Dickey, for 17 years with the Yankees, had made holy.

And he was right. He just didn't know how right until that photo hit page 66 of the *Daily News* on February 23, 1955—Malangone misspelled with two *l*'s in the caption beneath it—jangling John's telephone with calls from relatives, friends, Louisville Slugger and Bazooka, and stirring his darkest fear: A locker in The House That Ruth Built was awaiting him, and with it, a chair just up the river at Sing Sing.

Suddenly the disintegration began, and no one in Yankees management could figure out why. So innocently, it started. "Just sign your name here," said the Louisville Slugger representative, handing John a form. "We'll use that signature on your new line of bats." John froze, uncertain how to spell even his first name, terrified that the world would learn he was illiterate. He stalled, begged Paulie to jump on a plane to St. Petersburg to sign for him, but a snowstorm in New York had canceled all the flights, and besides, Paulie had already bailed him out that spring, driving to Tennessee to retrieve John when he misread the road signs on the way from New York to Florida and got lost for three days. Jhon, he finally scrawled on the Slugger form. Someone at the company noticed at the last minute and tried to etch over it, but his teammates snickered and Yankees brass scowled when the bungled bats appeared. John snickered too. That was always the best way to cover his confusion: Giggle, play the buffoon, act crazy, man, so no one suspects you're *going* crazy!

He came to the plate in an intrasquad game brandishing a rake instead of a bat. He noticed a motorboat with keys in the ignition, jumped in and gunned it for a joyride, forgetting to untie the rope. The dock and the boat both splintered. The Yankees' front office got a call.

John bought a motorcycle. He wrecked it one day later. In retaliation for a prank, he cackled and hurled oranges at his teammates in the Yankees' hotel, splattering seeds and juice, shattering an exit sign. "I did it, Skipper," John volunteered at the next morning's team meeting.

"Why, John?" asked Stengel.

"I was warming up, Skipper."

"Yeah?" said Casey, rolling his eyes. "Who was your catcher?" On the golf course just outside the hotel, John noticed a pond full of golf balls. He filched a dozen pillowcases and filled them with balls, placing them in the lobby beside the baskets of oranges and grapefruits for the guests. Stengel got another belligerent call. Finally, a day passed without trouble, and John mock-swooned in relief onto his roommate's bed. A slat splintered in half and tore right through the roommate's expensive suitcase, and the roomie went straight to the brass. What more did John have to do to make the Yankees see what he saw when he looked in the mirror?

Sooner or later, Stengel and the front office had to see what Dickey saw: that the catcher was the nerve center of a ball game, and that you couldn't have a guy there, no matter how powerful his arm or catcherlike his body, who flashed signs that were incomprehensible to his pitchers.

John's teammates—the nonpitchers, at least—loved to gather around him in lounge chairs beneath the stars that spring and reenact his latest fiasco. They crooned the song they always crooned to guys about to walk the plank—*Dear John . . . I sent your saddle home*—and were agog that day after day, by sheer dint of talent, his saddle remained right where it was. They marveled at Malangonese, a language in which an RBI might be an IBM, and treading water was *threading* water. The great Joe DiMaggio, John addressed as Charley. Correcting him was pointless. "O.K., tank you," John would say in his thick Noo Yawk accent. "I got it now. Got it down to a teeth."

One evening during that pivotal spring of '55, the players were buzzing about the change that had come over pitching coach Phil Page. "Didn't you hear what happened?" a player told John. "He killed his friend over the winter in a hunting accident."

John blanched. Then came the cold sweat, the hair rising from his flesh. He lurched away from the group, hesitated and then bolted for Page's room. Finally, for the first time in his life, he was going to tell someone his secret. Finally there was someone who would understand, someone whom John could perhaps even help. He rapped on the coach's door. Page opened it. John's mouth opened. Nothing came out.

"What do you want?" the coach demanded.

"Maybe I . . . " John stammered. "Maybe I can help you."

Page's eyes narrowed. The buffoon, he thought, was mocking him. "You?" he said. "You can't help yourself." He shut the door, and the words that might have saved John never left their vault.

Camp broke. The confounded Yankees chiefs assigned John to the Double A Birmingham Barons. The Barons had a new manager. His name was Phil Page. A few days later, as the Barons played their way from Florida to Alabama in a string of exhibitions, John was sitting in the stands an hour before a game and needed to use the rest room. Confused by the lettering on the doors, he waited and watched. A door opened. A woman emerged. John headed through the other door, not realizing that the ladies' room had two doors. A woman screamed. Page refused to believe it was an honest mistake.

Only a couple of weeks had passed since the click of the camera, and now John and his Mercury were lost on the road again, in search of the Class B Tars in Norfolk, Va. A place where he and the hunchback could hit .326 without running the risk of being called up to Yankee Stadium.

IT GROWS more and more unnerving, the idyllic photograph—doesn't it? A few weeks later John walked into a doctor's office in Norfolk. "My nerves are bad," he told the physician. "I think too much."

"Take off your clothes," the doctor told him. "I'll be right back." While the doctor was gone, John fled. For four years, from Norfolk to Portsmouth to Montgomery to Knoxville to Amarillo to Charlotte to Winston-Salem and back to Knoxville again, he fled. Every city, his ritual was the same. First, he would search for a church, a place to drop a 50 and run the whole rack of candles. Second, he would find lodging, preferably in a migrant worker's shack on a farm a few miles from his teammates, so they wouldn't know what happened when he chanced to see an umbrella or a pair of striped socks, so they wouldn't notice him roaming the roads at night gathering rocks to throw at poles and trees. Then he would look for a day job simonizing cars or hauling blocks of ice or collecting golf balls at a driving range, anything to demolish dead time. Dead time was killer time; why was baseball so riddled with it? He would count mosquitoes during games, do push-ups, run sprints, squeeze his crucifix, rattle off Hail Marys, do anything to stave off another flashback, meanwhile losing all track of minor things such as strikes, balls, outs, base runners, signals, score. *You don't tag up with two outs, Nuts 'n Bolts, you run on anything! Get your head in the goddam game!* He was cut from the team in midgame in Winston-Salem—what's a manager to do with a guy who rips two straight doubles and gets picked off both times?

He couldn't possibly explain it to anyone, not even himself. Each time he slunk out of the office of another furious manager, he felt humiliated . . . and *relieved*. Relieved because when he went a week or two without punishment, his guilt would eat at him like acid; he was cheating, getting away with something. And yet he lived in dread of pushing the Yankees brass too far, of being separated once and for all from the game he loved, from the rickety minor league clubhouses and stadiums where he was so popular.

For years he tiptoed this precarious ledge between stardom and banishment. One night he would leave a gaping hole in Norfolk's centerfield fence, attempting to snag a fly ball in his Mercury at 40 mph. The next night he would batter the plywood-bandaged wall with line drives. He would go AWOL for two weeks. He would hit .356 at Winston-Salem. He would ground out and continue running up the rightfield line, all the way to the fence, and smash it with his fist. No one ever dreamed that he was swinging at a flickering image of a javelin, a coffin, a child's face.

He lived for those weeks when Paulie would join him. In between he befriended the old black groundskeepers and locker room janitors in all those Southern towns, helping them to rake the field, dig mud from cleats, scrub the floor. They too were outcasts, and they never tried to get too close. In '57 he married a knockout from East Harlem named Rosemary

Chique, whom he had met—where else?—in a church. He turned everything over to her: checkbook, money and responsibility for the children they would have. Everything—except the secret. Even when things were great, when it was just the two of them and her skin on his skin felt like heaven's grace, the mumbling might start: *What about Orlando? You're alive right now, too alive, but he's just dust beneath the ground.* John would have to turn and roll away, the life all gone from him.

And then, in the spring of '59, still without a single big league at bat, his career was over. It ended in a flash when he wiped out his third motorcycle, broke his leg . . . and knew that he had finally run out of ways to make absolutely certain that he failed.

THIRTY-TWO YEARS walked by. The photograph remained forever young, hanging on a wall in the house John and Rosemary bought in Little Ferry, N.J., right across the street from St. Margaret's church. But everything else changed.

Paulie was shot on the street by a mugger and died on the operating table calling John's name. John stood on the 107th Street Pier and screamed back Paulie's.

John's father died of lung fibrosis. "You never forgot, did you, John?" the old man said just before he expired, and the two of them cried. But they never spoke of *what* John never forgot.

Rosemary bore John five children through their on-again, off-again marriage, but he was afraid to hold them or play with them, afraid he would hurt them and lose them . . . and so, of course, for long periods of time, he did. He always seemed to be gone, working two full-time jobs, repairing and installing New York City fire hydrants from dawn till midafternoon, running to his mother's house in the Bronx for an hour and then off to his night job as a mechanic in Sears's automotive department. They called him the Santa Claus of Sears, he gave away so many repair jobs, still hoping against hope to convince God to call off the beast. But, of course, John needed the beast, so who could say that any of its visits came without a whistle from somewhere deep inside John?

He turned to drinking and totaled five cars, but he and the demon always walked away. When his despair, at last, was more than the candle racks at St. Margaret's could bear, he took it to a therapist in the early

1980s. He spoke of grief, of anxiety, of the ticket to the bigs that he had torn to bits, of everything but the hunchback and the secret. "You're reminiscing too much," the therapist told him. "You need to get rid of all those trophies, plaques and pictures."

He began the destruction with sledgehammer blows of his bat, but that was too impersonal, too swift. He needed to involve the killer that hung from his right shoulder; he needed to make sure he was still in command of it. The children playing at Moonachie Park in northern New Jersey kept looking at each other and shaking their heads. Day after day, a gray-whiskered man wearing a wool pullover hat in the dead of summer because of the swishing sound the wind made inside his ear, wearing a coat because the warmth took him back to his grandmother's candles, would set up a table in front of home plate and place a trophy on it. Then he would lay cobblestones to steady the trophy and blocks of wood to shield all of it but the metal figurine. He would walk 30 or 40 strides with a bucket of balls. Only the finest, most accurate 55-year-old arm in the country could hit the tiny target from that distance. Only John Malangone could nail his past right on the head.

THERE'S NO need to leave you, dry-mouthed, on that ball field, because that's not how the story ends. On a February day in 1991, a 53-year-old man from Manhattan named Ron Weiss got directions to the Sears in Paramus, N.J., where John worked. Ron's son had just been cut from his school baseball team. Ron's life had just been shaken by his retirement after 30 years as a phys-ed teacher and coach. Ron's heart was still racked by regret that he had never taken a shot at the big leagues. And the one shiny thing that he kept clutching was a compliment from a teammate on a sandlot team he had played for in 1965, an anvil-armed power hitter who had told Ron that his infield play reminded him of a couple of guys he had rubbed elbows with a few years back, a couple of guys named Tony Kubek and Bobby Richardson.

Ron ignored John's reluctance. Ron kept coming back, asking John to turn his son into a ballplayer, asking John to be a friend. "You don't know who I am," John finally said. "You can't trust me with your son."

"Why not?"

Perhaps it was because Ron was virtually a stranger. Perhaps it was because of Ron's childlike trust. How do you figure that after a lifetime of holding it in, a guy whom John had given an offhand *attaboy* 26 years earlier would be the one to whom he would finally spill his guts? The javelin, the coffin, the demon, everything. And mercy, Ron didn't recoil, not an inch.

They went together to John's mother. The 80-year-old woman began to sob when Ron spoke Orlando's name. "You're gonna get him sick!" she told the stranger.

"Mom," said John, "I've been sick for a long time." She cried some more, and they talked through their tears and their shudders for hours. When they finished, John wanted to dance.

He and Ron took another trip, to the Manhattan Bureau of Records. They asked for the death certificate of Orlando Panarese, and John nearly vomited as he waited to see if the word after *Cause of Death* was *Murder*. The clerk handed Ron the medical examiner's report. Ron cleared his throat and read: "I further certify that I have viewed said body and from Partial Autopsy and evidence, that . . . the chief and determining cause of his death was Brain Abscess following perforating fracture of the scalp, skull and brain: that the contributing causes were Accidental." John hugged Ron. John wept.

He needed to tell someone from the Yankees his secret. He tracked down Johnny Blanchard at the Plaza Hotel in Manhattan, where Blanchard had gone to sign autographs. John told him everything. "I was paralyzed," says Blanchard.

A week without the hunchback passed, then another. The damnedest craving came over John. "Ron," he said, "ya know what I wanna do now? I wanna play ball. Play ball with a clear mind, for the first time in my life. C'mon, let's join a team."

John squeezed hand grips to bring back the wrists. He swam laps at the Y. He spent hours taking cuts in batting cages and playing catch with Ron's son. John pitched and Ron played second base in a New Jersey league for men over 40. By 1994 they found themselves in Florida, playing in the Roy Hobbs World Series. John won two games on the mound and singled home Ron for the run that won the national title for the New Jersey Wonderboys.

John lives in a trailer today, retired from his two jobs and separated from his wife, spending his days fixing cars for friends, playing ball with three or four teenagers whom he has taken under his wing to make sure they never give up, and learning, with Ron's help, how to read. "Symphonics," John calls their method.

Rescued? John almost thought so, but in truth, he had only reached a reef where the rescue might *begin*. One Sunday morning last March, on opening day of the 1997 over-40 season, Ron miscalculated the power of guilt. He gave John a few articles he had clipped, one about a Houston Oilers defensive lineman who killed himself with a shotgun in 1993 just moments after losing control of his car and causing a crash that killed his best friend, and one about a girl whose face was impaled by a javelin at a high school track practice.

You know what happened next. John couldn't play ball for three months, so fierce was the volcano, but then he staged another comeback, on a Sunday three months ago. The oldest pitcher in the league took the hill for the Bergen Rockies and twirled a four-hitter against the Bergen Cardinals for a 14–1 win, and he was so damned excited each time he returned to the dugout, so full of hope—honest-to-God 65-year-old half-scared-to-death hope—you just wished to hell someone had been there to take a picture.

POSTSCRIPT: *John Malangone pitched on three championship teams at the Roy Hobbs World Series. "I even hit 79 on the radar gun," he says now from his home in Little Ferry, N.J. In 2002, Malangone had an accidental fall, damaging his spinal column and leaving him temporarily paralyzed. After successful surgery, Malangone made a full recovery, but hasn't thrown a baseball since. In '07, a documentary film about his life,* Long Road Home, *won the best film award at the second annual Baseball Film Festival held at the Baseball Hall of Fame in Cooperstown, N.Y.*

The Sorcerer's Apprentice

Mike Veeck, the wizard of the minor leagues, passed along both
his love of baseball and his penchant for comic spectacle to his blind teenage
daughter, Rebecca. She taught him a few things too.

A MAN WITH A SALT-AND-PEPPER GOATEE WALKS alone through an airport. Pick an airport. Any airport. He has walked alone through them all. He's thinking about his five minor league baseball teams. He's thinking about putting on the world's largest pillow fight on the field after a Hudson Valley Renegades game; hatching a reality show to find the next Natural of either sex for the St. Paul Saints; spraying green paint over the bald spots on the Charleston RiverDogs' field; holding BALCO Night at a Sioux Falls Canaries game and handing a small plastic cup of Mello Yello to every fan at the gate; and, yes, sad to say, staging a Tommy James and

351

the Shondells concert at a Fort Myers Miracle game . . . when suddenly his eyes close. Just to see what it feels like to be his daughter. Again.

They close partway—no, that's cheating—then tighter until it's all gone: the harried commuters and zigzagging children and jostling luggage. He sends his left foot, slowly, into the blackness . . . then . . . his right foot. There it goes, the bottom dropping out of the pit of his gut. Now the left foot again. He takes three steps . . . four . . . five. . . .

His eyelids open. He chickens out. Darkness 1, Veecks 0.

HIS DAUGHTER stands in their yard. None of the neighborhood boys are lurking. At least, none she can see.

She lifts her right leg, folds it back at the knee, and takes a hop across the lawn on her left foot. Just to see what it felt like to be her grandfather. Again.

She takes a second hop and a third, begins to teeter and feels her right foot twitch down to keep her balance—no, that's chickening out, that's cheating. She yanks it back up and pitches forward, hop-hopping wildly, like her grandpa under the moon on the beach on his third six pack of beer, 'til she tumbles to the grass, squealing laughter.

Darkness 1, Veecks 1. Extra innings. . . .

THIS IS a 100-year story, covering four generations of one baseball family, but don't panic. There are only four characters to follow, and they're all named Veeck, and only two of them, the two still breathing, truly concern us. We'll even provide a genealogy, the way Russian novelists do—

William Veeck
↓
Bill Veeck
↓
Mike Veeck
↓
Rebecca Veeck

—and deliver you midgets and Martians and mimes being pelted with hot dogs, which Tolstoy never did.

Mike's in a taxi. Pick a taxi. Any taxi. He's ridden in them all. He's thinking about the five *other* minor league teams he consults and writes ads for, besides the five he partly owns. A nice little wad fattens his pocket. It's a Vegas taxi. He never used to give the slots the time of day, but that was before he discovered their secret: They make everything go away. They make you forget.

The first half of his life was hand-to-hand combat with his father's shadow. Booze, drugs, jail, divorce, a heart attack—he tried all the classic routes to escape or annihilate it . . . and himself. But that was nothing compared with the second half: mortal combat with his daughter's shadow, the literal one descending over her eyes. Everything's a weapon now. Every trick, hustle, gag and audacity—the entire Veeck kit and caboodle—he's pulling out of the attic, dredging out of the gene pool, taking to the plate. He's 54 and swinging from his heels at something he can't even see.

He calls the RiverDogs' office from the cab.

"Charleston RiverDogs, Rebecca speaking, how may I help you?"

It's her. He braces. He never knows what's coming. The effects of the disease may have worsened. Or some jerk at school may have soaked the bathroom floor again and given her a shove, and then Mike will beat himself to a pulp for being 2,000 miles away. He wings it, alters his voice, hopes for the best.

"Yes, ma'am, this is Elvis Presley. I'm out here in Vegas with your father."

"*Daddy!* Heyyyy, Groove Thing! You're my pop! You're in—*da da da da de daaah*—Las Vegas! How are ya, Elvis? . . . Laaaahs Vegas! Did you win? . . . *Thirty-six hundred!* Viva my money! . . . O.K., love you dearly, but I must get back to work because the phone is ringing, and please tell Elvis I said hi. Bye-bye!"

That's Rebecca. She's working the phones. She's got retinitis pigmentosa. She's 13. She's blind.

Oh, yes, she's a ham . . . with honey mustard glaze and melted cheese. She wants to be a singer and drummer in a rock-and-roll band, a Broadway actress, a dancer, a pianist, a writer, an equestrienne—"Hey, wanna see a blind kid ride a horse? I love an audience!"—and then, when she's gotten all those out of the way, she wants to be, just like her great-grandfather, grandfather and father, "a baseball guy."

Mike pockets his cellphone. His eyes cloud with tears. He hates being away from her 15 days out of the month, keeping all these crazy crap games afloat. He loathes the road. He needs the road. Was born for the road. He feels guilty when he's not out there making money and flogging the cause—raising funds and awareness of Rebecca's disease everywhere he travels. Guilty when he's not back home by her side. What's a man, the father of a jewel like her, supposed to do?

HIS OWN father is a one-legged legend, a Hall of Famer, the damnedest owner sports ever saw: Bill Veeck. The one responsible for ivy on the outfield walls at Wrigley Field, for the Chicago White Sox' last American League crown, for the Cleveland Indians' last world championship, for record attendance figures, exploding scoreboards, postgame fireworks, names on the backs of jerseys, a midget pinch hitter named Eddie Gaedel, a 43-year-old rookie named Satchel Paige, belly dancers at home plate, circus acts at second base and an outfielder named Minnie Minoso dressed as a matador as he waved a cape at a fake bull on Mexico Fiesta Night—all while Bill's polishing off five books a week, three packs of cigarettes and a case of beer a day, fathering nine children and hosing down the infield before ball games in his swimming trunks on a wooden right leg.

Mike spends his toddler years living in an apartment *inside* a baseball stadium, Sportsman's Park in St. Louis; the bullpen's his first sandbox. He moves 11 times in his first 11 years, the new kid always trying to fit in, and then moves once more at age 16: out of his own home in Easton, Md., into the family's studio apartment a couple of hundred yards away, just to get away from his old man, the one whom everyone—rich men, poor men, sportswriters, thieves—except Mike and a dozen buttoned-down major league owners find the most engaging man on earth.

Mike starts hitchhiking in high school. The only hitchhiker in Easton who doesn't care which way the driver's going, because *going* is all that matters. Who doesn't care if there isn't even a driver, or whether that's not hitchhiking, son, that's larceny. It costs him only a few nights in jail.

Then one day in 1975, three years after Mike graduates from Loyola College in Baltimore, his old man calls out of the blue, invites him to a 12-hour liquid lunch at a saloon, and at the end of it says, "McGill"—

GARY SMITH

Bill calls him that out of affection for Cornelius McGillicuddy, the ancient owner-manager of the Philadelphia A's better known as Connie Mack—"McGill, I'm going to buy the White Sox again. You might want to come check it out. It's going to be interesting." And Mike, an English major/philosophy minor/rock band drummer and guitarist adrift, realizes he's being offered a job in the Show, a shot at the bigs, a place at the legend's elbow.

Hot damn. Double dip: He finds Dad. He finds himself. Some of Dad's best promotional ideas are actually Mike's ideas, because the kid's got a couple of quarts of zany in the blood too. Then, in his second year on the job as promotions director, Mike uncorks a whiz-banger. He's sitting in a Chicago saloon one summer night at 3 a.m., relishing the 20-stage disco-dancing contest that just juiced the gate at a White Sox game, when he remembers two things: his abhorrence of disco and his old man's marketing mantra—*think opposites*. So he blurts, "What about an *anti-disco night?*" Before he knows it, it's July 12, 1979, and he's got 60,000 fans inside 52,000-capacity Comiskey Park, another 15,000 pounding on the ticket booths and 15,000 more gridlocked on the Dan Ryan Expressway, all for Disco Demolition Night. He's got vinyl Bee Gees 45s whizzing through the air, a dumpster behind second base crammed with the crowd's old disco albums, explosives about to blow them to kingdom come . . . and a mushroom cloud of marijuana smoke wafting overhead with the second game of a twi-night doubleheader against the Detroit Tigers yet to be played.

Down goes the detonator, up goes ABBA and—ohhh my *Waterloo! Finally facing my Waterloo!*—there goes Mike's career. Onward they surge, Pillage People and Travolta Revoltas, climbing over the dugouts and fences, shimmying down the foul poles, storming the field, torching the field, cartwheeling the batting cage across it. When the Night Fever subsides, six people are injured and 39 arrested, and the 14th forfeited game in modern major league history has been declared. A travesty, howl the media and Sox season-ticket holders. When the following season ends, Dad sells the team—forced out of the game by runaway costs as the free-agent era explodes—and Mike is so radioactive that not a single baseball mogul will touch him.

For a half-dozen years he bangs around in Florida, sending unanswered

355

application letters to the bigs, hanging drywall and promoting a jai alai fronton, pretending not to miss baseball, not to wonder if he was just his father's creation, not to notice the disappointment of all the strangers when they find out that he's Mike Veeck, not Bill. It all crests in the mid-'80s. He's drinking a bottle of whiskey a day, inhaling recreational drugs and watching his marriage unravel. His heart starts skipping beats. He starts blacking out. He goes to the hospital to take a Lamaze class to help his soon-to-be-ex-wife give birth and has a heart attack there instead. The doctor gives him two years to live unless he changes. His first child, Night Train, is born. His father dies. He cries so hard that his glasses fly off his face. His father's shadow doesn't die. Mike gets divorced. He goes into debt. He loses the battle for joint custody of his son.

Then comes Veeck Demolition Night, when a cop in Fort Lauderdale pulls him over and pours him into a cab instead of a jail cell. The bleary glimpse he catches of himself, on his hands and knees clawing under sofa cushions and through underwear drawers for nickels and dimes as the cabbie waits in Mike's town house, is so degrading that the next day he weaves on his bike to the local Alcoholics Anonymous chapter, then stands outside paralyzed for hours until an old woman named Mary comes out and reels him in.

One hundred fifty AA meetings in the next 90 days, 100 hours of bike-riding a week—they help, but it's really baseball that makes the shadow go away. Baseball, ringing him up out of the clear blue in 1989 after a New York lawyer named Marvin Goldklang buys a wreck of a minor league franchise named the Miami Miracle and bumps into Baltimore Orioles general manager Roland Hemond, who tells him, "If you're crazy enough to buy the Miami Miracle, you're crazy enough to hire Mike Veeck." So Goldklang does. Mike unleashes a decade of pent-up promotion, the franchise moves to Fort Myers and it becomes, financially, its nickname: a Miracle.

No. It's really Libby Matthews, a plucky pharmacist's assistant who shows up in his life the same year that baseball does, who makes the shadow go away.

No. It's really the firecracker they produce together, blue-eyed Bec.

No. The shadow doesn't go away. It just gets swallowed by a deeper, darker one.

HER FIRST baseball job, before turning two, is team greeter. Rebecca squeaks the same salute, 16 or 17 per customer, to everyone entering the St. Paul Saints' front office:

Hi!

Hi!

Hi!

She collapses from hospitality prostration in Libby's arms in the seventh inning each night in the stands behind third base. By age four she's a ballpark rat, darting from bleachers to concession stands to broadcasting booth to gift shop to jump castle to groundskeeper's tractor to her pal in the stands behind home plate, Saints fan Peter Boehm, who reads books to her between innings. She and the team's mascot, a pig, deliver baseballs to the home plate umpire wearing matching tutus, clown suits or rabbit ears. "Oh, it's embarrassing," she'll concede, "but it's baseball. So it's O.K." She and the pig take between-innings spins across the field on a remote-controlled motorcycle. She's slapped with a three-game suspension by her father for excessive waving to the crowd. She dresses up in a miniature San Diego Chicken costume when the real Chicken shows up, follows him across the field, and right on cue, lifts her leg and pretends to pee on the ump, bringing down the house.

By age six she's answering the front-office phone. "St. Paul Saints, Rebecca speaking, how may I help you?"

"How old are you, Miss?" a caller grouses. "Aren't there laws against child labor?"

"Oh, well," she replies, "I'm doing what I love!"

She fits right into the menagerie that Mike assembles on the Saints, the second minor league team that the Goldklang Group—Marvin, Van Schley, actor Bill Murray and singer Jimmy Buffett—asks him to run. There's Darryl Strawberry, recovering from drug addiction; J.D. Drew, baseball's No. 2 draft pick, recovering from a ruptured negotiation with the Philadelphia Phillies; Ila Borders, the first female pitcher in pro baseball history; Dave Stevens, the second baseman in training camp with no legs; Don Wardlow, the radio color man with no eyes; Sister Roz, the nun who gives fans massages on the dugout roof; Rebecca, the radiant urchin . . . and Mike himself, walking to centerfield when the ballpark's empty, asking his dad for advice.

St. Paul eats it up. Joint's packed every game, 2,000 on the season-ticket waiting list. HBO and *60 Minutes* bring their cameras to gawk. Mike turns his father's philosophy into a way of life: Fun Is Good. He empties another cup of coffee, leans back in his chair. The eyebrows start hopping, feet jiggling, fingers wriggling as if something's coursing through him that he can't contain. Here it comes: another shenanigan. Give away a funeral to a lucky customer. Give away a vasectomy on Father's Day. Give away minibats and invite Tonya Harding. Give away seat cushions with Don Fehr's and Bud Selig's faces on opposite sides so fans can sit on the one they blame. Wrap fans in rubber fat suits and have them sumo wrestle between innings. Hire improv actors as ushers, post signs prohibiting neckties and the Wave, offer free admission to pregnant women on Labor Day, hold Lawyer Appreciation Night and charge attorneys double, have a blue Spanish cockatiel trained to croak *Ball!* and *Strike!* and *What are ya, nuts?* over the P.A. system.

Betty Crocker's lab kitchen gone berserk, he calls it. Childish? What's better than being a child, asks the man who on one of his weekly outings with Night Train pours a jar of maraschino cherries down his pants in a grocery store to make his son giggle, who rides bikes with the boy through a car wash to make him guffaw. Ain't no stopping him in St. Paul; he's on a roll. He stations mimes on the Saints' dugout roof to provide instant replays, a stunt so heinous that the crowd smashes concessions sales records in its frenzy to turn hot dogs into missiles: Even Bad Is Good. The Saints win three Northern League championships between 1993 and '97. During one of the title celebrations Mike races onto the field and scoops up Rebecca to save her from being trampled by the players.

The lights never go out in Veeckville. He works all day and all night, just as his father did, keeps his staffers up till 4 a.m. strumming his guitar, regaling them with the story about the time Dad dressed his midget ex-pinch-hitter, Gaedel, and three dwarves in Martian costumes and lowered them from a helicopter onto the field at Comiskey to deputize the White Sox' diminutive double-play combo, Luis Aparicio and Nellie Fox, as honorary Martians in their battle against the giant Earthlings. The next day, when Mike's dazed employees sag at work, he lights an M-80 firecracker and rolls it down the office corridor, his laughter as loud as the *ka-boom!* Funny, though, that laugh of his, that wheezing, honking eruption. It always ends so abruptly. As if someone yanked a plug.

He still hasn't *made* it. It's still not the bigs. The Goldklangers buy the Sioux Falls, Charleston and Hudson Valley teams, making Mike part-owner and president of all three as well as the Saints and the Miracle. Impossible. Nobody could have that much energy. Nobody except a man trying to carry his father's torch and escape his father's shadow . . . at the same time.

Twenty-five million bucks. That's the net worth of the business Mike and his Mischiefmakers are building, enough doubloons to glitter in the eyes of the major league stuffed shirts who've snubbed him for two decades. And so at last, in 1998, it happens: The Tampa Bay Devil Rays ask Mike to be their senior vice president in charge of marketing and sales. He pops the champagne and dances Libby around the living room. At 48 he's back in the Show. Without Daddy. On his own.

A month passes, just enough time for Mike to start finding his way around paradise. He zips up to St. Paul to emcee a charity event on the day that Libby takes seven-year-old Rebecca to Emory University Hospital in Atlanta to find out why she couldn't read the top line on an eye chart. His cellphone rings. It's Libby. Something's wrong with Rebecca's eyes, something unpronounceable and unthinkable. There's no cure. No way to stop it from killing the photoreceptor cells in her retinas. The lights are going out.

WHAT SCARES her most is awakening in the pitch black, alone, and not knowing if the pitch black means it's happened—she's gone blind. So the little girl with retinitis pigmentosa, her central vision already vanishing, keeps taking her pillow and blanket to the hallway outside her parents' bedroom to sleep on the floor beneath the painting of Grandpa Bill. Her guardian angel, she tells people. He'll look out for her.

Mike looks down at his sleeping daughter. Then up at the painting of his smiling father. Dad *knew*. He was born into a house of shadows, to a mother still wrecked by the death of her seven-year-old son, Maurice, by a bullet accidentally fired by his best friend five years before Bill was born. Bill's father, William Sr., buried himself in his work as a sportswriter for the *Chicago American* so effectively that Cubs owner William Wrigley, upon reading William Sr.'s series of articles about what was wrong with the team, said to him, "All right, if you're so smart, why don't you come and do it?" and named him Cubs vice president in 1918 and president one year later, launching the Veeck family on its blazing trail across baseball's sky.

Somehow, Bill ran faster and harder than his father, even on an ankle smashed to bits by the recoil of a 50-mm antiaircraft gun during a Marine training exercise in the South Pacific during World War II. The ankle became infected and, doctors kept telling him, required amputation. Instead Bill kept pouring cologne down a hole in his cast to kill the stench and kept running, parlaying a stake in a minor league team, the old Milwaukee Brewers, into the purchase of the first of his three major league teams, the Indians. Relenting at last to the knife and inviting a thousand people to a coming-out party for his new wooden leg, dancing every dance until the pressure split open his stump and he had to crawl back to his apartment, trailing blood, on his hands and knees. Oh, well. "Suffering is overrated," he declared. "The only thing we have to fear is fire and termites!" Running his whole life, on three hours' sleep a night, through a failed first marriage, 36 operations on his right leg, emphysema and lung cancer, running with a children's rhyme—he confessed in his memoirs, near the end—forever echoing in his head: *Run, run, as fast as you can. You can't catch me, I'm the gingerbread man.*

So what does Mike do as the world goes dark on his daughter? Buries himself in his new Off the Wall advertising campaign to pump everyone up about the Devil Rays, in his 16 hours a day of work and his dozen speeches a week—his overnight bag always packed and ready in his car so he can bolt *justlikethat.* He's lying in bed one Friday night, recuperating from himself, when Bec runs in wearing new battery-powered glasses that whir and telescope, like a zoom lens, to magnify objects. "Sharp!" he enthuses. "Space-age!" Then he pulls the sheet over his head against the wave of despair and remains in that bed, with his work notepad and phone, the whole weekend.

One evening a half year after the diagnosis, Mike comes home from work and tells Libby how frustrating his day has been, how all the petty politics and stuffed shirts are gumming up his Betty Crockery. Libby explodes. *His* day? What about *her* day, running from doctors to vision technologists to Braille tutors to teachers' conferences? What about the two crowns she's fractured, grinding them in her sleep from the tension of go-ing to war alone? "Our lives are going to change!" she cries. "If you want to continue to be a man driven by your career, you can. But you're going to miss something. You can lose your second child the way you lost your first. There's this whole other world out there, and you're missing it."

Him ... blind? He cringes, staggers around for another week, delivers another Fun Is Good speech to another roomful of enthused local citi-zens and is trudging back to work afterward when a thought hisses in his head: *You're a liar. This isn't fun.* He quits the next day. Walks away after seven months from the thing he craved for 20 years. Now what?

He wants to change. He wants to turn and face this new shadow ... but how? He keeps finding himself in front of that painting of his father, above his sleeping girl. It's all there inside that man, the malady and the anti-dote, coiled one around the other, nearly impossible to disentangle. It's all still there, deep in Mike's memory....

The swimming pool. He *must* have seen that amputated stump before, he must have, but the first time it dawned on him, his first consciousness of it, was at a pool as his father stripped to his trunks. Mike's eyes filled—not quite with tears, his mother, Mary Frances, would recall, but with a *luminousness*—and in that same instant Bill grasped what was occurring and began to hop on his good leg, flapping the stump in a crazy dance and singing, "Daddy's little leg ... Daddy's little leg. ... " And what was rising up the little boy's throat came out as laughter instead of a sob, and ... that was it. From that day on Mike was proud to be the one to whom his father handed the wooden leg at the ocean's edge so the boy could run it back to their towels before they dived into the waves. Tickled when his dad gathered the gawking children around him, hammered a nail into the wooden leg and snorted, "Now go home and see if your fathers can do that!" Delighted when his dad carved out a hollow in the wooden leg and used it as his ashtray.

Yes, it occurs to Mike. That's *it*. The way to confront the thing he's been fleeing, Bec's loss, his loss. *Dad's* way. Hammer it with humor. He starts to sway and sing, to the tune of the 1962 hit *Johnny Angel*, "Ret-in-i-tis. ... " Rebecca takes the cue and sings, "pig-men-to-sa. ... " Back and forth they go until it's their song. He bangs his head into the front door, pretending he didn't see it; she mimics him and they collapse in a heap, laughing. "What's the matter with you, kid?" he yelps. "You blind?"

"Yeah," she croaks. "What do ya expect out of a blind kid?"

"Oh, I see. . . . So you're *still* blind."

They both play hooky: she from school, he from work. The Veecks hit the road for most of '99. "I want you to see all the things that are wonderful," Mike tells her, swallowing those three extra words: while you can. They go to Yosemite and the Badlands, to Bermuda and Ireland and Guadalajara and New England and New York City. They see snow in the Grand Canyon, ride horseback in Death Valley. They jump fences to bury their noses in rose fields, to pick cotton and almonds and pecans and pistachios, to harvest life and save scraps of it in her wooden memory box. He lowers the roof of their rented convertible, pulls Rebecca into his lap so she can grip the steering wheel and know what it feels like to drive the Pacific Coast Highway, big breakers crashing the cliffs on her left, sea breeze whipping through her hair and the oldies station cranked. "Car dance!" he bellows, jiggling the wheel left and right as she whoops.

He spoon-feeds her Grandpa's spirit, every story he can remember, as they roam. Did you know, Rebecca, that once when your grandfather owned the minor league Brewers, back in the '40s, they played at a ballpark in Columbus, Ohio, that was so dark they could barely see? And instead of getting mad he turned it into fun by having his players wear miner's lamps and his first- and third-base coaches hold up lanterns and his second baseman take light-meter readings? Not that Grandpa was averse to darkness, because another time, when his Brewers were losing a critical game, he had his electrician short out the stadium lights—*zap!*—sorry, game's canceled, a shame it'll have to be replayed.

Mike and Rebecca pull into Cooperstown to see Bill's plaque in the Hall of Fame. Mike lifts his daughter to see a picture of his dad beside Larry Doby, the African-American ballplayer whom Bill chose to break the American League's color barrier with the Indians in 1947. The little girl presses her face to the photo of the middle-aged white man and the young black outfielder, runs her fingers over it, turns her head to the side to see if her peripheral vision can do any better. Then she asks the most bittersweet question that Mike ever heard: "Which one is Grandpa?"

Mike can sense it beginning to happen, the slow melting of ego. A glimpse of the world through the eyes of someone who can barely see.

Rebecca looks up at the blue sky one day, holding his hand, and says, "It's O.K., Daddy, if I go blind, because I'll always have you and Mom to tell me what you see."

IF YOU'VE ever stood inside a chalked box with a 1–2 count against a fastball pitcher in a big league ballpark in the late afternoon, then you know. A man, after considerable anxiety, can adjust to a shadow, but almost as soon as he does, the shadow moves. So he can never relax.

Mike returns to his minor league empire. Rebecca goes back to school. The sun moves across their blue sky. The shadow shifts.

The black holes in the center of Rebecca's vision grow larger and begin to devour the periphery as well. The closed-circuit TV monitor that magnifies her school texts to 10 times their size is no longer enough. The schoolwork grows more complicated. Each test she must study for, each homework assignment, takes twice as long for her as for her classmates. All those straight-A report cards and honor-roll ribbons disappear from the Veecks' refrigerator door. She hits puberty. It's a different condition, blindness at 13, from blindness at eight. A whole new kind of darkness for her and her dad to navigate.

Now she yearns, more than anything in the world, just to be like the other kids at her middle school just outside of Charleston. Yearns to smash the Braille typewriter that clacks out the difference between her and them. Yearns to ditch the full-time adult aide who accompanies her to every class to help her take notes. Yearns to read one of the notes that kids pass in class, just once, so she can know what they're giggling about. Yearns to walk the hallways without worrying if a book bag's waiting on the floor to send her sprawling. Dammit, she won't use that white cane that her orientation-and-mobility tutor keeps urging on her. Won't take people's arms unless she has no choice. Won't admit she missed that plot turn on the movie screen. And don't you dare mention a school for the blind. She's mainstreaming, no matter how big and crowded and confusing high school will be next year. "I like big!" she gushes. "I love crowds!"

She says, "I'll be fine. I'm a Veeck." That means no retreat. That means you scoff at your handicap, like Grandpa, never give in. Damn, it's confusing for a kid. A couple of times a month she'll say something that makes her dad look at her in awe and say, "You're *him*." Grandpa. Re-incarnated. Both blue-eyed, blond-haired lefties overloaded with sauce and smarts and spunk. It floods her with joy when he says that. She'll Google Grandpa and hear the robot voice on her Jaws software read the text about Bill's legendary tenacity. She'll hop on her left leg in her yard, just to know what it felt like to be him. But now her teachers and Braille tutors and parents are telling her that *damn the torpedoes* won't work, that she's got to accept her blindness, use the cane, use the Braille, stop the bluffing, let people know that she can't see and needs a hand before she finds herself in deep trouble.

She concedes, finally. Once. The Veecks are changing planes in Atlanta last summer with Mike on crutches, his femur fractured in three places from his attempt to ride his bike, catch a basketball thrown behind him and shoot at the same time—why not? The foot traffic is pitiless, bumping the blind girl and her hobbling father. Rebecca finally halts, thrusts out her jaw, jerks off her backpack, yanks out the telescoped white cane and takes the lead, tapping and shouting as she goes, "Coming through! Cripple coming through!" Meaning her father, of course.

"I accept that I'm blind," she says, "but I never totally accept it. You can't. You don't. Because pride will be lost if you totally accept it. Accepting it means I'm O.K. with it—and I'm not. You give in if you accept it totally. One percent of me—no, one and a *half* percent of me—doesn't accept it. I keep that one and a half percent for me. I want my sight back. I'm only 13, but I'm sick of waiting. I just want my vision back. I'm at the age where I'm realizing I'm not going to be able to drive or maybe even see my own kids when I have them. I think God did this for a reason. I just don't know what it is yet."

Some days it all piles up on her: the cruelty of classmates who yank chairs out from under her, the certainty that she's the only 13-year-old girl on earth who hasn't been asked out by a boy, the geography test for which she has to identify all 50 states, their capitals and all the squiggly rivers and mountain ranges in between from studying a map that she alone has never seen. She storms upstairs. Slams the door. "Why did you do this to me?" she screams at the ceiling. No! That can't be her. She's a Veeck. She collapses onto her bed, picturing all the kids who have it worse than she does, picturing the ones in Iraq with their limbs blown off, scalding out her self-pity and anger. Then she gets up and cranks up the music, dances and sings and weeps.

Days like that, the darkness sifts down and settles over Mike. He's not sure anymore when to crack a joke or sing a song about her blindness, when to bump into the front door or run into a tree and titter on one of their two-hour tandem bike rides. She might laugh. She might explode. She's the Dalai Lama one minute. The next she's the kid who insists there's a Santa Claus and a Tooth Fairy and a cure for retinitis pigmentosa right around the corner. She's a *teenager.*

It kills him to hear her upstairs sobbing. Kills him that it was his recessive gene that coupled with Libby's and wrought this. Kills him to have to tell her she can't try out for the basketball team or the cheerleading squad or ride her bike anymore. Kills him to kill off the child in her, the believer, even though he knows, for her good, he *has* to. Kills him because his whole life's about making and marketing magic, awakening the child asleep in us all. Kills him that he has to get up at six the next morning, board another plane and leave her for five days to fight her fight without him.

"It's the life we choose," he tells her as he lifts his suitcase.

"It's the life we choose," she echoes. "I know you're good and you've got to go show your tricks to the world."

"I'm strong like bull," he says.

"I'm strong like baby bull," she says.

Then her fingers search the air, trying to find his cheek, and she kisses him, and he turns for the door. Because worse than leaving is the helplessness he feels if he stays. He can do nothing here to save her, but if he climbs on that plane, if he launches another madcap marketing campaign, if he gives another speech that makes another 50 men laugh and cry and feel what it feels like to watch the lights go out, if he signs and sells another hundred copies of his new book, *Fun Is Good,* if he goes on three hours' sleep until he grows so surly that he has to crawl into the tub and take another three-hour bath, then maybe he can salt away enough money to make sure his daughter never knows a day of need, and maybe, just maybe, he can hand the Foundation Fighting Blindness or Charleston's Storm Eye Institute another fat check that'll help make a miracle appear beneath a microscope. It's the only shot he's got at relighting Rebecca's world: his father's torch.

And so he goes, harder than ever, but for a higher purpose—for her—cutting corners on each road trip to get back earlier, buying a stake in a private plane so he can fly home at any hour to catch her piano and dance recitals, so he can sit in the audience holding it all in, the pride and the panic, when she pirouettes across the stage: Does she know she's one step away from the edge? God, does she know?

And keeps telling himself that no matter how hard this is, no one could be better equipped for it. Because they've got Libby, the warrior. Because they've got Don Wardlow, the blind man Mike hired long before his daughter's diagnosis, who showed Rebecca during his six years as color man in the Saints' and the RiverDogs' radio booths that nothing's impossible. They've got laughter, they've got music—the piano and drums and guitars at home that Mike and Rebecca love to play—and there they go again, crooning that Temptations verse they love to croon: *I've got sunshine on a cloudy day.*

But facts are facts. The days, in all likelihood, will only grow cloudier, and Santa Claus won't walk through her bedroom door and pull up the blinds. So she pops another one of the Great Classics—she's already got more than 100 recorded books under her belt—into her player and listens away the rest of the day, knowing that her mind is her treasure and that blind men like Ray Charles, the one she loves most, have seen something beyond and dragged the whole world there with them. Reminding herself of the dream she had years ago, before the eclipse even began, in which a little girl, one who looked like her but wasn't quite her, came up to her, touched her eyes and said, "I'm sorry . . . but you have a path to take."

THERE'S ONE place where she can see. One place where Rebecca knows every stairway and doorway so well, it's as if she weren't blind. Where she has freedom to wander, and family at every turn: Dad in the seats beyond third base kibitzing with fans, Mom in the office lending a hand, half brother Night Train on the ball field supervising between-innings mayhem, and dozens of employees doubling as her uncles and aunts.

When school's out and the RiverDogs are at home, she works a few games each week and then just roams the park during a few more. She mans the guest-services booth near the entrance. She sells programs. She keeps the little kids smiling while they wait in line for the jump castle.

She escorts Charlie the RiverDog, who can barely see through his costume's headpiece—the blind leading the blind. She dresses up as characters on Geek Night and '80s Night. She does radio ads for the team and occasional player introductions on the P.A. mike. She plays Twister with eight-year-old fans but gives them fair warning: "I'm gonna beat your booty!" She's all empathy and charisma while handling callers on the office phone, until one fan too many on a rainy night demands to know when the downpour will stop and the ball game begin. "What am I?" she blurts. "A psychic or somethin'?"

She loves the smells. She loves being the last human being who still yells, "Charge!" when she hears the tape-recorded bugle. She loves the aura around the game she can barely see. "My real job," she confides, "is to keep everyone at the ballpark happy. To keep everyone alive. Especially when my dad's not here. He tells me I'm his secret eyes when he's gone. I let him know when something's not right."

Sometimes she sits alone in the stands when the ballpark's empty, tilts her head so the edges of her retinas, where not all the photoreceptor cells are dead, take in that beautiful sweep of fuzzy green. "I can feel it when I stare at a baseball field," she says. "I've got stuff to do, something big to help people, something that has to do with a baseball field. The world is stupid, so stupid—it fights and kills over land. I look at a baseball field, and I see this piece of land that's everybody's land. And every field I see has a piece of my family in it. I know this sounds corny, but I see my grandfather out there walking on the grass on his peg leg. I see this place where you can run and be a child somewhere besides your own home. And who made this place that way? My dad! I *love* him for that.

"I like to think about what I'll do if I run a team some day. I want to come up with crazy ideas, because ideas are great. If you can make 'em, wonderful. If you can't, I'm sorry for you. People are too serious. People need to loosen up. Like I've got this one idea where you put Slip 'n' Slides all along the sidelines of the field, and you soap 'em up and let kids slide and sit in the sun while the ball game's going on right beside them, and I know you'd probably have to put a net up to protect them, and I know the idea needs a little work, but. . . ."

The closest she's come to that, her hands-down favorite ballpark moment each season, is Big Splash Day, when she puts on her bathing suit and climbs onto a platform over a water tank, baiting bystanders to ante up a buck to hurl three balls at the bull's-eye and dunk her.

Mike watches her from a distance. He's sure it could be like this at big league ballparks, no matter what the stuffed shirts say. No matter that he's taken two more cracks at it, with the Florida Marlins and the Detroit Tigers, neither job lasting long because divine lunacy can't last in a bureaucracy, because of the usual turf battles, and because he insisted on commuting from Charleston to be here for moments like this.

"Ahhh, you throw like a girl!" she taunts a fan. Mike grins. Swear to God, he's never seen her so alive.

"What's the mattah wit' ya!" she bellows. "Ya must be blind!"

Bang! She *kerplunks* into the water, spluttering and laughing herself silly.

POSTSCRIPT: *Rebecca Veeck, now 16 and starting to think about college, still works for the RiverDogs, in the box office and in customer service. She and her father continue to raise funds for the nearby Storm Eye Institute in Charleston and participate in events for the Foundation Fighting Blindness. In May 2008, the FFB announced what it calls "the biggest advancement" in the organization's 37-year history: Thanks to an experimental gene therapy procedure, three young adults who previously had virtually no vision can now read an eye chart and see in dim light. Says Rebecca, "It's a huge thing for the next generation."*

Escape from Jonestown

*Could there be a more improbable tale of deliverance from the horrors
of that Guyanan jungle than being saved by a game? How basketball gave life
to a son and grandson of the infamous cult leader Jim Jones.*

ELL ME, DOES IT GET SWEETER THAN THIS? THE big handsome kid gliding to the glass in warmup drills, that's your son. He's the best high school player in the city. One look at the visitors, who've come from 40 miles away, tells you all you need to know: He's the best player in the house tonight.

Better still, your two brothers are in town, right beside you. All three of you grew up together on a basketball court. All three of you were starters on the same team. You can see it on their faces. They're reliving it too.

Everyone filing in, it seems, calls or waves to you, the friendly father

369

of the star. Your kid looks up and gives the slightest nod. He's dedicating this game to your side of the family. Got to love that too.

You all rise for *The Star-Spangled Banner*. Then your son and the other team's big man crouch at midcourt for the tap. Your eyes, like your brothers', like your son's, lock on the basketball. As if you owed your lives to that thing.

Which all four of you do.

O.K., there's something else going on here. The kid's dedicating this game to your sister—his aunt, Suzanne—who just died of colon cancer. No, not a pretty way to die, but far more dignified than facedown in the mud on the edge of a South American jungle, like your mother, your father, your wife, your unborn child, two brothers, a sister, four nephews and a niece.

None of you here tonight should exist. Not you, Jim Jones Jr., the one who carries *that* name. Not your brother Stephan, the one who carries that blood. Not your brother Tim, the one who carries the visual memory of your relatives and friends among the 910 bloated bodies lying shoulder-to-shoulder, the largest mass suicide in modern history.

And no, not your son down there. The Reverend Jim Jones's grandson.

You were spared that day: Saturday, November 18, 1978. You, Stephan and Tim were teenagers, 150 miles away, playing against Guyana's national basketball team. You were saved by this sport.

But then . . . if you hadn't been away that day, maybe you could've stopped it. Maybe you'd have stood up to your father when he ordered everyone in the Peoples Temple to drink the cyanide-laced powdered grape punch in Jonestown, Guyana. Maybe you could've saved your family, saved everyone. You were cursed by this sport.

HIS SON controls the tap. Archbishop Riordan High begins to run a play. Jim Jones Jr. looks around the gym. This is the last place he dreamed he'd be in his mid-40s, in December 2006. This is the last sport his child was supposed to play.

The kid misses a four-footer, gets whistled for climbing a defender's back on a rebound, then flings a pass out-of-bounds—all before the game, against San Ramon Valley in the final of the Crusader Classic, is 45 seconds old. *Focus it*, thinks Jim. *Focus that fire.*

His son knows how much Suzanne meant to Jim upon his return from the massacre. Knows that a game's more than a game. He barrels in for three layups, then slashes across the lane and feathers in a turnaround jumper, igniting Riordan to a 17–8 lead. He's settling down now, becoming who he is: RobJones, San Francisco's reigning high school player of the year. RobJones, the kid who keeps that loaded last name glued to his first one so that nobody will ever lose sight or sound of it.

Who would he be now if he *didn't* know? Yes, this had been the million-dollar question for Jim and his surviving siblings after their children were born: Would they tell the kids of the horror, and of their relation to one of the most diseased men and moments in U.S. history? Would the next generation of Joneses have to carry the stain?

Jim glances at Suzanne's two adult children, cheering for their cousin. Only on her deathbed, a few months ago, had Suzanne disclosed her family history, though she'd dropped out of the Peoples Temple long before its hasty flight from San Francisco to the jungles of Guyana in 1977. Surely Jim could've tried to bury his past too. Could've started life over far from the Bay Area, the cult's home base, and disowned the legacy, sealed it from his three sons. Jones, after all, was the fourth most common name in the U.S., and he, unlike the notorious father who had adopted him and made him his namesake, was black.

But Jim's an extrovert, the life of the party, not the keeper of secrets: a lousy vault. Hell, he'd named Rob, his firstborn, after the father of his teenage wife, Yvette Muldrow, who'd drunk the cyanide and died along with their unborn baby. When Rob was a toddler, Jim marked the anniversary of Yvette's death by taking him to the mausoleum where her ashes are interred and letting him play while Jim sat near the urn, devoured by shame that he was alive and she wasn't . . . because of a game.

He knew that one day he might have to pass on his story to his son. But how could he ever pass on his game?

WAIT A minute. Where's Jim? He's not sitting with his brothers in the upper section anymore. He's down in the lower section, beside his wife, Erin. He winces as his son misses a chippy, outmuscles everyone for a putback that misses as well, and then, dammitall, goes up again . . . *yes!* Jim raises his fist as Rob takes a feed a moment later and slams. The kid's 6'5½", 230, a furniture truck with springs and speed.

But Jim remembers the pipsqueak he could lift overhead. Back when he still thought he had plenty of time to figure out how and what he'd tell his son; hell, the kid was only four . . .

. . . when Waco happened. A 51-day FBI siege of another sect—the Branch Davidians in Waco, Texas—that left 82 dead in 1993 and kept TV commentators harkening back to the last American cult horror: Jonestown. "Jonestown?" echoed little Rob in front of the TV. "There's a town named after us? I want to go there!"

Oh, God. For 15 years Jim had been going there and fleeing there in his head, and finally—he'd thought—found refuge, a nice numb little cove. At first, of course, that had been impossible. A Secret Service agent, a customs agent and a Treasury agent were assigned to him and each other player on their way home to the U.S. He'd been interrogated in an airport hangar the moment he'd set foot in America, then placed under police surveillance for months while he lived in Suzanne's Bay Area apartment. For weeks he'd been mobbed by reporters on his way in and out of federal courthouse hearings on the Jonestown tragedy, his picture splashed across San Francisco newspapers and, when people pointed at him in malls, made to feel like a leper. He was 18 years old.

He'd swallowed his fears and shown up at a half-dozen funerals for temple members whose bodies had been shipped back to the Bay Area. Then the mother of one of the dead, at a postfuneral gathering, put a gun to his head and hissed, "Why should you be alive when my daughter's dead?"

"I don't want to be alive," Jim replied. "Kill me now."

Mourners grabbed the gun and gave him some advice: Stay away from the survivors; they'll blame you. Hell, he blamed himself, mostly for having sent Yvette, the pregnant bride who had wanted to stay at his side, back to Jonestown a few weeks after their wedding in Georgetown while he remained in the Guyanese capital to do public relations and liaison work for Jonestown's economic and outreach projects, including the basketball games against the host country's Olympic team.

"So you're Jim Jones, huh?" said his boss at his first job in his new life, as he prepared to head out on his route as a bank courier. "You going to pick up some Kool-Aid on your drive tonight?"

"That's not funny," said Jim. "That's my *father.*"

"What?"

"That's my father."

"You can't be serious. Jim Jones was white."

"I was adopted by him."

His boss looked at him. "You're fired," the man said.

The stain was deeper than Jim had feared. He tried college but quickly dropped out. Too much mind static. He tried the office-furniture delivery business alongside brothers Tim and Stephan and former Jonestown teammate Johnny Cobb. He tried Buddhism, Islam, Pentecostalism and Catholicism. He tried Telisa and Alice and Danette, hasty engagements to three tall, light-skinned, curly-haired African-Americans born under the sign of Scorpio . . . just like Yvette. He became the last thing that his socialist father could've imagined: a Republican.

Why not a new identity—or his original one? He considered changing back to his birth name. He settled on James Jones, safe but not a lie, and winced through 11 years of Kool-Aid jokes from people who never dreamed that a man so likable, a black man, could be the mega-killer's son.

Then one day in 1989, after he'd gotten a two-year degree in respiratory therapy from California Pacific College and gone from hospital orderly to respiratory therapist to director of cardiopulmonary services at a San Mateo hospital, he stared at the name affixed to his new office door. Apparently all the certification initials listed after his name—CRT, CPFT, RCP—had made James Jones Jr. too long for his name plate, and someone had shortened it. To Jim Jones Jr.

No, he thought. People would find out. He'd have to have that changed.

Something stopped him. Jim Jones Jr. was who he was. Sure, it would be risky. The woman he loved, a neonatal nurse named Erin Fowler, had bolted from his car on their first date, just a few years earlier, when his relationship to the Rev. Jim Jones had spilled out of him. But she'd calmed down. Even married him.

He began introducing himself as Jim Jones and letting a few people know that he was the cult leader's son. The dispassion with which he spoke of it sometimes perplexed them. But they'd marvel at the miracle that a man who'd lived through what he had could come out the other end as successful and affable as Jim. He felt a little better. For a while, at least.

Two places remained off-limits. The first was the basketball court. The sport that had taken him away from where 24 members of his family had died still flushed him with guilt. The second place was inside himself. He refused psychotherapy. "The mind's a dangerous neighborhood," he'd say. "Don't go there unless you have to." He wouldn't, he couldn't disturb the buried pain, because then he couldn't be *Jim*, the charismatic guy with the deep, rich voice that boomed down hospital corridors. Besides, it was just too difficult to convey to a stranger, even a hired empathizer, what it felt like to be him. The closest he could come was this: Imagine there's a painting of you, he'd say, with the background all there, right behind you. And 20 years later, you're still there in the painting, but all the background's gone. There's nothing behind you. The people, the setting, your way of life and belief system—gone.

He'd sink into depressions each November, the anniversary of the tragedy. He'd dream Yvette back to life, then watch her vanish each time he drew near. He'd dream that his father was coming after him. Then wake up, go to work and crack the Kool-Aid jokes himself. But now it was '93—with Waco on everyone's lips and Jonestown suddenly disinterred—and the coworkers to whom he'd confided his past kept asking, "You O.K., Jim? You O.K.?"

"Are *you* O.K.?" he started snapping back. Something was bothering him, something stirred by Waco—so many children, dead again—something that he just couldn't reach. And now his child was asking about Jonestown. He could dodge it, keep the kid in the dark. But that carried an explosive risk too.

He swallowed hard and started in the shallow end. He started with the story of a minister and his wife entering an Indianapolis orphanage in 1961 to adopt a Caucasian baby girl, only to be distracted by a wailing 10-week-old African-American boy whose unwed mother, age 15, couldn't raise him. Jim told Rob what his adoptive mother had told him, how Jim had stopped crying the moment Marceline Jones lifted him into her arms, and how she and her husband decided right then to make him the first black child in Indianapolis ever adopted by a white couple, and to consecrate their belief in racial equality by giving him his father's name.

Jim tried to humanize that man with raven hair and sunglasses and the Chairman Mao cap. He told Rob about the gentle side of the Reverend Jim Jones, his hugs and kisses, his ability to make Jim Jr. feel unique, prized, *chosen*. Then one day Jim peeled an old family portrait from a scrapbook, framed it and placed it on the mantel. "See, Rob?" he said. "They called us the Rainbow Family. Seven of us eight kids were adopted, and we came from all over." He pointed to Agnes, an elder sister who was part Native American. Then to Suzanne and Lew, both adopted from Korea, and to Tim, a close family friend whom the Joneses ended up adopting as well. Then to Stephan, their one biological child. Then Jim told Rob about the two who weren't in the picture: Goldie, the eldest, who married and broke ties with the family before Jim was adopted, and Stephanie, another child adopted from Korea, who died in a car crash.

He told Rob about the adventures of the Rainbow Family, the years abroad in Brazil, Argentina and Hawaii, and the long caravan that formed in 1965 when Father—as everyone in the church called Jim Jones Sr.—led 70 Indiana families to the Peoples Temple's new home, a tiny hamlet in the vineyards of Northern California. About the orphanages his dad ran, the soup kitchens, free clinics and senior citizens' homes he opened, the theaters, restaurants and hospitals he desegregated. About his dream that their church would be the seed for a new world, one without barriers between rich and poor, races and sexes and ages.

Little Rob didn't need to hear the messy details. Not yet. Didn't need to know that it was Grandpa's raging paranoia that drove the Rainbow Family to Belo Horizonte, Brazil, and then to Redwood Valley, Calif.—two sites listed in a 1962 *Esquire* article as among the likeliest to survive a nuclear holocaust. That it was his lust for greater power that sent the family and the temple to San Francisco in '72, and that it was published stories about his alleged abuse of church members that stampeded them to Guyana in '77.

The kid was way too young for that, and besides, Jim had learned something. When he spoke well of his father by day, his father stopped stalking his dreams at night.

ROB CAN feel it now. No one here can stop him. He whirls and powers through two defenders to score, giving Riordan a 30–19 halftime lead. But where's Jim?

That's him, slipping outside the gym and lighting a cigarette, sucking hard so he'll have time to light and suck a second one. Always dropping out of sight when he can't be the wonderful guy everyone knows. But no, it's nothing like it used to be, back when Rob was four, when Jim started heading out for work or an errand. . . .

... and vanishing. He would drive for hours, tearing at himself. Dammit, he'd been on his father's security team, protected *him* from danger. Walkie-talkies, earphones, weapons, code words, the works. He would park his car at the beach and pour from a bottle into a plastic cup, hoping vodka worked as a solvent on the stain. He'd skulk back home, wrung out and ragged, a day or so later.

Waco had started the slide, then his eldest son's questions about Jonestown, then that thing that began to appear in the boy's hands, that round thing wrapped in dimpled leather, that ... basketball. "Dad," he'd ask, "can we play?"

Jim took the ball in his hands. All the old guilt and remorse began to seep from it. *Selfish. So damned selfish to have been off playing basketball on his family's day of reckoning.* . . . See, that was the problem: Jim's father had pounded that basketball guilt into his sons even before Jonestown, and then, in the sickest possible way, proved himself right! He wouldn't forbid them to play. He was a master at knowing just how far he could push people, and he seemed to sense that basketball was the boys' outlet from the demands of temple life. He'd shame the boys instead, snort, "What a folly! What a waste of time when the world's in shambles and we need to be changing it." Didn't Jim, of all the boys in the Rainbow Family, see how exploitative the sport was, how it kept blacks from using their minds to smash the shackles of a repressive capitalist society?

The Jones boys' basketball guilt was laced, of course. Laced with liberation, a feeling that they were thrusting a middle finger at the holy hypocrite every time they shoveled snow or swept leaves off their concrete patio court and went at it. They'd come home from a two-hour practice at Ukiah Junior High, grab a ball and play again. *Normality.* That was the game's gift. A couple of hours to feel like regular kids instead of the cult loonies who'd invaded Redwood Valley.

That's what they were doing, playing pickup ball at a temple picnic back in the early '70s, when they heard that gunshot and froze, and saw Dad lying on the ground, clutching his chest, his shirt soaked in blood, then waving frantic temple members away once they'd carried him into his house ... so he could resurrect himself and have the shirt framed as a temple relic.

If only Jim had exposed the fraud when even he started seeing it a few years later. But he'd bought into his dad's vision of a just world, swallowed the ol' end-justifies-the-means snake oil: the larger Father loomed, the farther the word spread, the more converts—nearly *20,000* ultimately—rushed to the ramparts. Hell, nobody in the temple would've listened to young Jim anyway. Its members had turned over everything to that man: their children, their life savings, their homes. And no one owed him more than Jim did. That man had rescued him from an orphanage, perhaps saved him from the life of drugs and prison that would eventually befall two of Jim's three biological brothers . . . and then saved his life again. Laid his hands on six-year-old Jim's dead body after a drunken driver hit the Joneses' station wagon, causing Jim to fly out the backseat window, across the hood of the spinning car and back in through the opposite window! That's what he'd grown up being told, anyway, that his soul had left his body until Dad prayed over him, reviving him long enough for doctors to mop up the job.

And so when Dad took him to the theater one day when he was 12 to see a documentary about an evangelist, Marjoe Gortner, who'd begun wowing tent-revival throngs at age four, and told Jim that he had the charisma, rich voice and near-death anecdote to pull that off, Jim said, well, O.K., why not? He watched the movie a few times, got the groove. When summer came, he and the Peoples Temple began piling into their 13 Greyhound buses to go soul-harvesting at tent revivals and churches across the U.S. In a suit and tie, little Jim would take the microphone, the stutter that sometimes afflicted him suddenly gone, and warm up the people with a few parables sprinkled with parallels between Jesus and Jim Jones Sr. Then he'd downshift into his personal tale, the black boy twice saved by the white father, and whip 'em—mostly African-American mothers and grandmothers—into an "Amen! Go, little Jimmy!" tizzy, then into tears, then into tongues. An offering plate would appear, followed by the white father himself, emerging to conduct faith healings, often involving removals of tumors that were actually raw chicken giblets.

How had he ever let himself get swept up in . . . *"Dad! Hey, Dad, are you listening?"* his three sons would yammer, tugging at him on the couch when Erin was working night shifts at the hospital two decades later. Yeah, yeah, he'd reply, but no, he was gone, lost again in lonely guilt, flailing like a flipped turtle to find his way back to sunny-side up.

Good ol' optimism: Jim's favorite cleansing agent. Lasted longer than vodka, got him through 18 years in that dysfunctional family and 18 more in its ashes. That's it, keep dwelling on the positive, keep smiling. Keep standing up at meetings with work colleagues or school parents who might've heard of his lineage and telling everyone, "I'm willing to offer any help I can, except providing the punch." Ha-ha—beat 'em to the punch!

One problem. The more *happy* he slapped on, the less he could feel at all. No pain had a price: no joy. His arguments with his kids and his wife grew sharper. Full of misgivings, he agreed to co-coach Rob's CYO basketball team, but jumped on his son so hard that Erin begged him to back off.

It all came to a head early in '98 when Jim vanished as Rob and brother Ryan, younger than Rob by two years, were celebrating their January birthdays together at a bowling-alley party, leaving Erin to chase their youngest son, three-year-old Ross, and referee two dozen seven-, eight- and nine-year-old boys with bowling balls. Then, on the eve of Rob's CYO championship game a few weeks later, just before the team's final practice, he vanished again. "Where's Coach?" Rob's teammates asked.

Off somewhere with old basketball echoes pounding in his head, with his marriage and Rob's world about to fall apart. That's what he might've replied. But Rob was in third grade. He winced and shrugged in silence.

THERE'S JIM. He has moved again. He's up there on the runway, above and behind the basket. It's perfect. There are no seats up there, no people. No conversations that might become personal.

He looks down and sees Rob bolt ahead of the pack, pluck a long pass overhead without breaking stride, then dunk with such violence as he's fouled that he has to hang on to the rim till the world stops shaking. He lands and bounces, fist-pounds his heart and chest-bumps a teammate halfway to the bench.

There it all is in one five-second burst, why all those big football factories—Southern Cal, Notre Dame, Oregon and Cal—keep calling and sending love letters. Keep craving Rob for the job for which his height, bulk, speed, ferocity, hard head and soft hands are all custom-crafted, the position at which he shattered school records: tight end.

The kid will look right past people who say he's nuts—spitting away a multimillion-dollar NFL career for a sport in which his size and game fit the specs for no particular position—and walk into a tattoo parlor to have the image of a basketball and the words MY PASSION burnt into his right biceps. Then have a single word seared onto his left biceps, beneath a cross and a crown: JONES.

Jim remembers the day when the kid began to grasp the connection. The day, when Rob was eight, that Jim, his wife and three sons stepped out of a small airplane, boarded a truck, bounced across a dirt road, came over a rise . . . and stared at Jonestown.

Or what was left of it in 1998, after scavengers and termites had picked its bones, and vines and weeds had choked it. Jim blinked in the tropical glare. He'd never dreamed he'd be there again.

ABC had asked him to go back to film a segment for a *20/20* special on the 20th anniversary of the tragedy, and after his initial shock, he'd agreed. Maybe there, somehow, he would find an answer to the *why?* that had wrought such havoc in his life, and threatened now to rip apart his family. But hell, he was still playing games with himself. Three days before his departure he had yet to apply for his passport; the panicking network had had to pull strings to ramrod it through.

It thrilled little Rob to be handed a machete to hack through the bush. Jim grabbed one too. He'd remained in Georgetown after the slaughter, never returned to Jonestown or laid eyes on the bodies. That had both preserved him and kept the carnage unreal, kept him from ever confronting it head-on. He began walking through the ruins and searching for something he could touch.

He approached the remnants of the pavilion where his father had gathered his tribe beneath the thunderclouds on that frantic final day. He probed the underbrush and earth with his machete. The blade struck something. He began to dig. Even with all the rust, he recognized it: the oil drum that temple members had sawed in half and soldered handles to, the container that the cyanide, powdered punch and water had been mixed in and spooned from into paper cups. . .

He scooped dirt away from it and stared. Now he had something tangible, an artifact not only from the tragedy but also from all the meals the community had shared there, back when Jim was still a teenager, still full of hopes and plans to head off to medical school in Havana with his soon-to-be bride, Yvette. Back when he, his brothers and lifelong temple pals would gather on their makeshift basketball court—still there, rotting in the weeds on the other side of the settlement—and lose themselves in the old sweet rhythm of the game.

Stephan had revived it for them, one bleary day after another of the "white nights." Sickened by those vigils—when their father's amphetamine- and barbiturate-blurred mind would concoct the threat of imminent attack to spread fear through his disciples, harangue them with all-night rants on the P.A. system and test loyalties to see who'd fight to the death or drink poison in suicide drills that always turned out to be hoaxes—Stephan had resorted to his old closet rebellion, erecting a backboard and rim alongside the abandoned flooring of a storehouse whose walls and ceiling had never been built. It was only the size of two Greyhound buses parked side by side, and it was raised four feet off the ground to protect it from the torrential rains, making each drive to the basket a dangerous adventure and each errant pass a pain in the ass. But the boys' game, each day for hours until the sun sank, was back on.

Their father, anxious to improve strained relations with his host country, gave grudging approval to the boys' proposal for a series of games against Guyana's national team. Blue-and-white uniforms were ordered, and Jonestowners cheered as the squad ran laps and three-man weaves in the fields to prepare for battle. But the team, as it departed on its overnight boat journey to Georgetown, sensed an uneasiness among the thousand settlers as they bade the boys farewell. There was talk that California congressman Leo Ryan might soon pay a visit, accompanied by reporters and former temple members hoping to reclaim loved ones from the cult, and Jones's lifelong fear of betrayal and abandonment had begun to throb. Who would stand up to Father, should the congressman's visit turn ugly, now that the athletes were gone?

The first game against Guyana was a calamity. Out of sync and out of shape to play a full-court game, Jonestown's 12-man team was devoured by 30 points. Jim, a long-armed 6' 4" center whose specialty was rebounding and shot blocking, seemed as lost as his teammates against taller foes who'd been training and competing for years.

Two days later Ryan arrived in Georgetown. Their father's voice crackled over the CB radio in the temple's headquarters in the capital, where the team was bunking, and demanded they return. Nobody dreamed what was brewing. Jim and his brothers agreed: hell, no.

The congressman and his entourage departed in a small chartered plane for Jonestown. Jones Boys & Co. took on Guyana once more in Georgetown. Suddenly, from all their years together, they remembered the music. Point guard Johnny Cobb began running the pick-and-roll and hitting the open man. Rail-thin Stephan's sweet outside shot bloomed again, Tim found his old ferocity and his running one-hander, and Jim did the dirty work on the boards and in the lane. The Guyanese coach, his players trailing in the first half, called a timeout to rant at them.

Late in the game Guyana's conditioning and depth wore down the Americans, and it won by 10. But the Jones boys walked off the court knowing it was only a matter of time, lung- and legwork: They were going to take that team down.

Most of the squad went to the movies the next day, Nov. 18. Jim was the only Jones at their lodging when his father radioed again. "Where are the others?" he demanded.

"At the theater," said Jim.

"Go get them!" he ordered. Congressman Ryan's entourage had just left Jonestown with several defectors, and Father said he had sent "avenging angels" in a tractor to pursue them to the airstrip in nearby Port Kaituma.

"Why?" cried Jim. "Why are we doing this?"

By the time his brothers returned from the theater, the killing had begun. The avenging angels had jumped off the tractor with rifles, blown away Ryan, two NBC newsmen, a *San Francisco Examiner* photographer and a female defector, and left a host of others wounded in the dirt.

Jim, his brothers and their teammates stood around the radio, frozen. Their father's voice came from the speaker once more. "We're going to see Mrs. Frazier," he declared. Their eyes jumped to the nearby crib sheet that translated the code. My God. Mass suicide was about to begin.

"No, Dad, why?" they cried. "It's not that drastic! Is this real?"

He ordered them to use knives, medicine or piano strings on themselves if they had no poison. Jim felt as if he were watching it all unfold from somewhere else. "There's got to be another way!" he heard himself saying. "Why? *Why?*"

The boys ran to the U.S. embassy. Maybe, somehow, they could get help and arrange a chartered flight to Port Kaituma. The Guyanese guards at the gate, who'd just received reports of the shootings at the airstrip, refused to let them in. The boys were helpless, with no way to reach Jonestown, where Father was summoning his flock to the pavilion over the P.A. and informing them that there was no escape, that the senior citizens and children would be tortured by U.S. soldiers, that their only choice was to drink from the vat and die in dignity, commit "revolutionary suicide" that would show the world the depth of their beliefs before para-troopers began raining from the sky. They were all so weary from months of his manic alerts. Armed men, members of Father's inner circle, fanned out around them, and their will to live began to wane.

One by one, except for the 85 who melted into the jungle, they drank and lay down. So many kids, so many earnest and passionate friends and loved ones with whom Jim had prayed, danced and sung, so many people who had invested everything in an idea and couldn't see a way out now that the dark sky had smothered it so suddenly. . . .

Jim and his teammates returned to their lodging and found more hor-ror. Four other temple members who'd been living there—a mother and her three children—were dead, their throats slit. Guyanese soldiers poured into the complex with M-16s and took up posts, two to a room. The Jones boys, crying one moment, staring into nothingness the next, weren't teen-age basketball players anymore. They were orphans and suspects in an epic massacre, under house arrest.

They spent five days that way, being awakened at night and interro-gated by soldiers, wondering if they were about to be thrown into a roach-and rapist-infested Guyanese prison. Stephan *was*, for three months, the police thinking at first that he had some hand in the four Georgetown deaths. Tim and Johnny Cobb were flown to Jonestown to help authori-ties identify the 910 bodies there, which included Jim's father—dead of a gunshot wound in his head—and 23 of Jim's other relatives. . . .

But maybe they hadn't really died. Even now, on a sunny day 20 years later, Jim kept looking toward the trees, half-expecting them to walk out of the jungle now that the coast was clear.

SHARD BY shard, young Rob began piecing together his father's and grandfather's stories. Jim showed his sons the National Sports Hall in Georgetown, the site of his final game. He showed them the house where the floor had fallen out of his life. It began to hit Rob: the enormity of what his dad had lived through and lost. The stay of execution granted to his father, and the breath of life granted Rob, by basketball. He remembers feeling awe.

When they got home from Guyana, Jim set down his baggage but didn't empty it for a few days, putting off the trip's end just as he'd put off its beginning. At last he pulled out the shoes that he'd walked in at Jonestown and stared at their soles. Yes, he'd found the vat there, but no clarity, no answer, no why. The only thing he'd brought back, it struck him, was the dust in those soles . . . the red dust of Jonestown.

That was the *click* that opened the lock. He buckled and wept. He finally knew it now, in his gut and gasping chest: There were plenty of whys for what had happened, but no *why*. No answer. No closure. *Ever*. What had happened couldn't be made rational. It could only be felt. Now that his heart understood that, it freed him to stop asking—and dodging—the question.

The tears and anger he'd clenched back for years kept flowing for weeks. The dreams returned and gnashed his sleep. His wife, who'd withstood so many storms as a neonatal nurse, didn't flinch. For six months Jim saw a counselor and attended Alcoholics Anonymous meetings. He stopped disappearing. He began to feel again. And he finally saw the lonely little boy—the son of a World War I vet who'd been mustard-gassed in Europe and returned an aloof alcoholic—inside the monster his dad became. He forgave his father. "I had to forgive him," Jim says, "to forgive myself."

Forgive himself for what? Jim's eyes mist. "For still living."

The red dust of Jonestown would remain with him forever, Jim knew, working in crevices so narrow no brush could ever reach it. But now another realization arose from that dust. The only answer to what had happened lay in the future, not in the past. It lay in his sons.

Jim began playing more ball with Rob, banging with him one-on-one, testing his grit. The kid flared—why, it wasn't fair that his old man was heaving his 250 pounds against a fourth-grader. "You'll survive!" his father would reply. "We're Joneses! Our name demonstrates to the world, *We survived*. What doesn't kill us only makes us stronger!" Rob had heard that from his father before. But now he understood exactly what it meant.

Jim knew his limits as a coach, and what his son's would be if the boy kept playing suburban-white-boy ball. He knew he'd have to take Rob to where Jim didn't want to go, the place he'd avoided for two decades: the Fillmore District in San Francisco, the African-American neighborhood where Jim had played high school ball and lived on the third floor atop the Peoples Temple.

Jim and his fourth-grader got in their car one day in 1999. Jim began to drive toward Fillmore, where an AAU team, High Hopes, played ball. Rob was dying to play for it. Jim's dread grew. He turned onto Geary, his old street. So many memories still living there—of people who were dead. So many friends and relatives of those dead people still living there too. What if they saw him and challenged him? The sneaker was on the other foot. Now Rob and his love for basketball were testing Jim's new grit, tugging him further and further . . . back toward himself.

Rob made the team. Nobody raised the ghost of Jonestown, but sometimes Jim saw it in people's eyes and felt it on his skin. He blocked it out and began, in that ever-cheery, High Hopes way of his, to help the team raise money, to work the ticket table and concession stands. That didn't hurt, but nothing helped like knowing that the team *needed* your kid.

One by one—gym by gym—Rob and his new team pulled Jim to the old haunts, the last playgrounds of his innocence before it had been crushed. They had plenty of car time now to talk. Now and then Rob would pop a question, each a level deeper. *How did it feel to lose both your parents when you were only 18? Why did your dad kill all those people? Why didn't you name me Jim Jones?*

Jim would take a deep breath and answer as best he could, each airing of the issue diminishing its charge. So that Rob, by the time he was a high school junior, would suffer only a moment's indecision when the subject of cults and Jim Jones Sr. suddenly reared itself in a Life Issues class, then raise his hand and declare, "That's my grandfather." And only wince in a bookstore checkout line when his eyes fell on *100 Most Infamous Criminals* and he opened it to find Grandpa nestled among Hitler, Charles Manson and Jack the Ripper.

WHERE'S JIM? He's moved again. He's on the floor now, alone beneath the opposite basket.

It's late in the fourth quarter. Riordan's rolling. Rob's got 30 points and 17 rebounds. Jim looks up. The students are chanting, "Rob who? RobJones! Rob who? RobJones!" Jim's nephews and nieces are waving and making faces to try to get Rob to smile. Forget it. The kid's still breathing fire. Damnedest thing. . . . Jim spending his life trying to turn a white-hot ember into ashes. Rob spending his turning an ember into flames.

The kid knows he's going to need all that fire. He knows that college is not going to be like tonight, knows the knock that has kept the big-time college coaches away. He's a 6' 5½" forward with a power game, a bull entering a land of gazelles and giraffes, and only a few such men have excelled at the modern game's highest level—Adrian Dantley, Mark Aguirre, Charles Barkley—men whose furnaces had to be as large as their haunches to pull it off. Why, RobJones wonders, don't the big-time coaches understand that his *is*?

Controlling the flames—that's his challenge. Jim has seen it happening, watched his son's investment in basketball grow so deep that he'd run to the court near his house with ankle weights, a jump rope and cones for a half hour of conditioning before his two hours of shooting practice began, that he'd sprint even when coaches called for three-quarters speed, that he couldn't understand it, couldn't bear it, when teammates bungled the fundamentals and derailed his team. He'd slam walls, slam lockers, slam mates—"You guys are terrible! You lost that game!"—until finally, in his sophomore year, coach Rich Forslund had had enough and benched him for an entire game. That's when his game took the big jump.

Riordan wins 59–46. There's Jim, standing off to one side as Rob and his teammates sing their alma mater to the crowd. There's Rob's brothers, Ryan and Ross, well on their way to being just as comfortable as Rob with their family's past. There's Tim and Stephan watching from above, relishing the paradox of their nephew's personality. "So soft-spoken and humble and gracious off the court, such a ready smile," says Stephan. "But on it? He's a warrior. It's his court. He gives no ground and leaves nothing on the court. He has a hero's heart."

Rob doesn't tell his uncles. He doesn't tell his dad. It's an AAU coach, who also happens to be named Rob Jones, whom he'll confide in during a long heart-to-heart in a hotel room after an AAU tournament game. "People," he tells his coach, "are going to forget about Jonestown."

"How?" asks Rob Jones.

"I'm going to make them forget it," says RobJones.

HE'S A freshman starter at the University of San Diego now. His coach, Bill Grier, calls him the cornerstone of the program he's building. His point guard, Brandon Johnson, calls him the Beast, and his scratched and bruised teammates shake their heads at the intensity and aggression he brings to practice every day. "He's like a young wild animal," says Johnson. "He goes to the basket with collision on his mind."

"This sport gave me life," says Rob. "That's made basketball more personal. My dad went through so much pain and suffering, and he didn't let it stop him. He went through so much bad, something good has to come out of it. His life taught me that you've got to be able to get over something. You've got to let it go and build something new.

"By my success I can show people that things can be changed, that nothing has to stay as it was or as it is. It's giving me more fuel for the fire—that I can help people feel motivated and make my dad feel better about his life too.

"My father became open about everything, and it's been a positive in his life, so why shouldn't I? If you try to hide something, people can use it against you. If you're open, it shows you're not scared. You can make it part of life. It doesn't feel like a burden. It's one of the better feelings I've had in my life. I'd have been fine if they'd named me Jim Jones. That would've intensified it even more."

He's ready, he says. Ready, should any fan or opponent be so small, so enormously small, as to hurl Jonestown at him during a game. "Taunts rally me," he says.

"This kid," says Brad Duggan, the former University of San Francisco coach who spent months honing Rob's skills in private sessions after his junior season, "will end up being a president of a bank, or mayor of San Diego, or senator from California. That's the kind of kid this is."

Jim Jones Jr. gropes for words. How can the son of such a father explain what it means to be the father of such a son? How can he explain what happens inside a man after he's been spared and stained forever in the same instant—the obligation to justify that sparing, the despair that one man could ever cleanse that stain. And then one day he realizes that someone, almost without knowing it, is doing just that. And it's his son.

"I spent half my life," Jim says, "trying to tell people that there was a different side to Jim Jones and Peoples Temple. No one wanted to hear it. But Rob embodies that difference. He plays like a lion, but even more, he's such a substantial person off the court. I don't have to explain it anymore. I just have to say, *Look. There he is.*

"I'm so proud of all three of my sons. When they're born, you wonder: Will they have to carry the legacy of Jim Jones? But there's no stigma on Rob. There's no stain."

Nowadays Jim sells biofeedback technology, which helps doctors quickly identify heart attacks. But he catches himself, at age 47, daydreaming about retirement. A daydream, unimaginable just a decade ago, in which he sees this old guy with a grizzled beard pulling up in front of an old city gym each morning, balancing a coffee and a newspaper as he pulls out a ring of keys, and letting in a bunch of neighborhood kids. Then sitting courtside, reading his paper and sipping his coffee while they play, just some old guy living out his last breaths to the bounce of a basketball. Nobody paying him, nobody remembering his name, unless, of course, his eldest son stops by to pay a visit, and then maybe they'll remember. Yeah, that old guy . . . Rob Jones's dad.

———

POSTSCRIPT: *Rob Jones averaged nine points as a freshman forward for the University of San Diego, which upset Gonzaga to win the West Coast Conference championship and earn a trip to the NCAA tournament. His father, Jim, was in the stands. After the game Rob pushed through the crowd to his father, lifted his jersey to reveal his Jones tattoo, slapped it and pointed to his dad. Says Jim, "That was the moment I knew that, yeah, he's O.K."*

Ali and His Entourage

The champ and his followers were the greatest show on earth; from the woman who cooked his meals to the man who was his muse, they all played their parts with passion. Then the show ended—but life went on.

ROUND MUHAMMAD ALI, ALL WAS DECAY. MIL-dewed tongues of insulation poked through gaps in the ceiling; flaking cankers pocked the painted walls. On the floor lay rotting scraps of carpet.

He was cloaked in black. Black street shoes, black socks, black pants, black short-sleeved shirt. He threw a punch, and in the small town's abandoned boxing gym, the rusting chain between the heavy bag and the ceiling rocked and creaked.

Slowly, at first, his feet began to dance around the bag. His left hand flicked a pair of jabs, and then a right cross and a left hook too, recalled the ritual of butterfly and bee. The dance quickened. Black sunglasses flew from his pocket as he gathered speed, black shirttail flapped free, black heavy bag rocked and creaked. Black street shoes scuffed faster and faster across black moldering tiles: *Yeah, Lawd, champ can still float, champ can still sting!* He whirled, jabbed, feinted, let his feet fly into a shuffle. "How's that for a sick man?" he shouted.

He did it for a second three-minute round, then a third. "Time!" I shouted at the end of each one as the second hand swept past the 12 on the wristwatch he had handed to me. And then, gradually, his shoulders began to slump, his hands to drop. The tap and thud of leather soles and leather gloves began to miss a quarter-beat. . .half-beat. . .whole. Ali stopped and sucked air. The dance was over.

He undid the gloves, tucked in the black shirt, reached reflexively for the black comb. On stiff legs he walked toward the door. Outside, under the sun, the afternoon stopped. Every movement he made now was infinitely patient and slow. Feeling . . . in . . . his . . . pocket . . . for . . . his . . . key. . . . Slipping . . . it . . . into . . . the . . . car . . . lock . . . . Bending . . . and . . . sliding . . . behind . . . the . . . wheel . . . . Turning . . . on . . . the . . . ignition . . . and . . . shifting . . . into . . . gear. . . . Three months had passed, he said, since he had last taken the medicine the doctor told him to take four times a day.

One hand lightly touched the bottom of the wheel as he drove; his clouded eyes narrowed to a squint. His head tilted back, and the warm sunlight trickled down his puffy cheeks. Ahead, trees smudged against sky and farmland; the glinting asphalt dipped and curved, a black ribbon of molasses.

He entered the long driveway of his farm, parked and left the car. He led me into a barn. On the floor, leaning against the walls, were paintings and photographs of him in his prime, eyes keen, arms thrust up in triumph, surrounded by the cluster of people he took around the world with him.

He looked closer and noticed it. Across his face in every picture, streaks of bird dung. He glanced up toward the pigeons in the rafters. No malice, no emotion at all flickered in his eyes. Silently, one by one, he turned the pictures to the wall.

Outside, he stood motionless and moved his eyes across his farm. He spoke from his throat, without moving his lips. I had to ask him to repeat it. "I had the world," he said, "and it wasn't nothin'. " He paused and pointed. "Look now. . . .'

Black blobs of cows slumbering in the pasture, trees swishing slowly, as if under water rather than sky. Merry-go-rounds, sliding boards and swings near the house, but no giggles, no squeals, no children.

"What happened to the circus?" I asked.

He was staring at the slowly swishing trees, listening to the breeze sift leaves and make a lulling sound like water running over the rocks of a distant stream. He didn't seem to hear.

And I said again, "What happened to the circus?"

THE DOCTOR

A MAN of infinite variety. Medical doctor, jazz connoisseur, sports figure, confidant of the great.

—EXCERPT FROM FERDIE'S PACHECO'S PUBLICITY BROCHURE

"This is a painting of myself when I was 30 and living alone and messing around with a German woman who loved it when there was sweat and paint all over me . . . and this is a screenplay that I've just cut down from 185 pages to 135 . . . and this one here is a 750-page epic novel, a very serious look at the immigrant experience in Tampa . . . and this is a painting I did of Sherman's March—that stream of blue is the Union soldiers . . . and that one is a screenplay I just finished about two Cubans who steal a Russian torpedo boat, and a crazy Jewish lawyer—Jerry Lewis is going to play the part and direct it—picks them up in a boat. . . . "

In one way, Ferdie Pacheco was just like his former patient Muhammad Ali: He needed laughter and applause. He led people to each of his paintings, lithographs, cartoons and manuscripts the way Ali once led them to continents to watch him talk and fight. Both worked on canvas: Ali, when his was not near to dance on, used parlor magic tricks to make eyes go bright and wide; Pacheco, when his was not near to dab on, told long tales and jokes, dominating a dinner party from escargots to espresso with his worldliness and wit.

In another way, they were not alike at all. Ali lived for the moment and acted as he felt, with disregard for the cord between action and consequence. This allured the doctor, whose mind teemed with consequence before he chose his action. "In an overcomplicated society," he says, "Ali was a simple, happy man."

Twenty-five years ago Pacheco was a ghetto doctor in Miami. Today he can be found in his home, white shorts and paint-smeared white smock covering his torso, blue Civil War infantryman's cap atop his head, stereo blaring Big Band jazz, telephone ringing with calls from agents, reporters and TV executives as he barefoots back and forth, brushing blue on three different canvases and discoursing, for anyone who will listen, upon the plot twist he has just hatched for chapter 16 of his latest novel. He receives a six-figure salary from NBC for commenting on fights, has quit medicine, has become a painter whose works sell for as much as $40,000, and has completed 600 pen-and-ink drawings converted into lithographs, six books (two of which have been published, including *Fight Doctor*), eight screenplays (four of which have sold) and a play that may soon be performed in London. He has also formed a Florida-based film production company and appeared across the country as a speaker. "But on my tombstone," he says, "it will say 'Muhammad Ali's doctor.' It's like being gynecologist to the queen."

In our time, will we see another comet that burns so long and streaks so fast, and whose tail has room for so many riders? "The entourage" some called the unusual collection of passengers who took the ride; the traveling circus, the hangers-on, others called it. "These people are like a little town for Ali," his manager, Herbert Muhammad, once said. "He is the sheriff, the judge, the mayor and the treasurer." Most were street people, thrown together on a lonely mountaintop in Pennsylvania where Ali built his training camp, until they burst upon the big cities for his fights. They bickered with each other over who would do what task for Ali, fist-fought with each other at his instigation—two of them once even drew guns. And they hugged and danced with each other, sat for hours talking around the long wooden dinner table, played cards and made midnight raids on the refrigerator together. "That's right," said Herbert Muhammad. "A family."

Because they were there for Ali, he never had to worry about dirty underwear or water bills or grocery shopping; he could remain an innocent. Because Ali was there for them, they could be mothers and fathers to the earth's most extraordinary child.

For a decade and a half he held them together, took them to the Philippines, Malaysia, Zaire, Europe and the Orient, their lives accelerating as his did, slowing when his did, too. But among them one was different, the one who obeyed the law of consequence. Ferdie Pacheco ejected while the comet still had momentum, and made a missile of himself.

"I had an overwhelming urge to create," he says. And an ego that kept telling him there was nothing he couldn't do. "On napkins, tablecloths, anywhere, he'd draw," says his wife, Luisita. "I shouted 'Help me!' when I was delivering our child. He said, 'Not now'—he was busy drawing me in stirrups."

Few knew him in the early Ali days: What reason was there to consult the doctor when Ali was young, physically unflawed and all-but-unhittable? Pacheco was the son of Spanish immigrants, a first-generation American who had established a general practice in Miami's black Overtown district and become a regular at Miami Beach boxing matches, where he met cornerman Angelo Dundee and began to treat Dundee's boxers for free. One day, a patient named Cassius Clay came to him. And Pacheco became part of the entourage.

"It satisfied my Iberian sense of tragedy and drama," he says, "my need to be in the middle of a situation where life and death are in the balance, and part of it is in your hands. Most people go out of their way to explain that they don't need the spotlight. I see nothing wrong with it.

"Medicine—you do it so long, it's not a high-wire act without a net anymore. At big Ali fights, you got the feeling you had on a first date with a beauty queen. I'd scream like a banshee. It was like taking a vacation from life."

The first signal of decline was in Ali's hands. Pacheco began injecting them with novocaine before fights, and the ride went on. Then the reflexes slowed, the beatings began, the media started to question the doctor. And the world began to learn how much the doctor loved to talk. Style, poise and communication skills had become the weaponry in the land that Ali conquered: A member of the king's court who could verbalize— not in street verse, as several members could, but in the tongue the mass markets cried for—and foresee consequence as well, could share Ali's opportunities without sharing his fate. The slower Ali spoke, the more frequently spoke the doctor.

Ali reached his mid-30s stealing decisions but taking more and more punishment; Pacheco and his patient reached a juncture. The doctor looked ahead and listened, heard the crowd's roar fading, the espresso conversation sobering. His recommendation that Ali quit met deaf ears. The same trait that drew him to Ali began to push him away.

He mulled his dilemma. Leave and risk being called a traitor? Or stay and chance partial responsibility for lifelong damage to a patient who ignored his advice?

Pacheco followed his logic. He wrote Ali a letter explaining that cells in Ali's kidneys were disintegrating, then parted ways with him and created laughter and applause on his own. Ali followed his feelings and went down a different path.

Today the ex-fighter turns dung-streaked canvases to the wall and the ex-doctor covers his wall with new canvases. In his studio, Pacheco shakes his head. "I feel sorry for Ali," he says, "but I'm fatalistic. If he hadn't had a chance to get out, I'd feel incredibly sad. But he had his chance. He chose to go on. When I see him at fights now, there's no grudge. He says, 'Doc, I made you famous.' And I say, 'Muhammad, you're absolutely right.'"

THE FACILITATOR

WHAT IF a demon crept after you one day or night in your loneliest solitude and said to you: "This life, as you live it now and have lived it, you will have to live again and again, times without number; and there will be nothing new in it, but every pain and every joy and every thought and sigh and all the unspeakably small and great in your life must return to you. . . . The eternal hourglass of existence will be turned again and again—and you with it, you dust of dust!" Would you not throw yourself down and gnash your teeth and curse the demon who thus spoke?

—FRIEDRICH NIETZSCHE

Warm Vegas night air washed through the '76 Cadillac convertible. "We had fun, mister," said the driver. "We *lived*, mister. Every day was history. Millionaires would've paid to do what I did. To be near *him*."

He fell silent for a few blocks. The lunacy of lightbulbs glinted off his glasses and his diamond-studded heavyweight championship ring. "When I was a little boy, I used to watch airplanes in the sky until they became a dot, and then until you couldn't even see the dot. I wanted to go everywhere, do everything. Well, I *did*. Europe, Africa, the Far East, I saw it all. He was pilot, I was navigating. Hell, yes. The most exciting days of my life. Every day, I think about them. We were kids together, having fun. He was my best friend. I think I might have been his."

The car stopped at an intersection. A woman, thick in the thighs and heavy with makeup, walked across the beam of his headlights. His eyes didn't flicker. Frantically, hopelessly, the blinking lightbulbs chased each other around and around the borders of the casino marquees.

"You could feel it all around you, the energy flow," he said. His foot pressed the accelerator, his shoulders rested back against the seat. "When you're with someone dynamic, goddam, it reflects on you. You felt: Let's go *do* it. I met presidents and emperors and kings and queens and killers, traveling with him. Super Bowls, World Series, hockey, basketball championships I saw. I was big in the discos, Xenon, Studio 54. There was myself, Wilt Chamberlain and Joe Namath: the major league of bachelors."

Quiet again. The traffic light pooled red upon the long white hood. Dead of summer, down season in Vegas. The click of the turn signal filled the car. Then the click-click-click of a cocktail waitress, high-heeled and late for work. He peered into the neon-shattered night. "What could I find out there tonight?" he asked. "A girl more beautiful than I've been with? A girl more caring than I've been with? What would she tell me I haven't heard before? What's left that could impress me? What's left I haven't done or seen? It burnt me out, I tell you. It burnt me out for life. . . . "

Gene Kilroy had no title. Everyone just knew: He was the Facilitator. When Ali wanted a new Rolls-Royce, Kilroy facilitated it. When he wanted to buy land to build a training camp, Kilroy facilitated it. When a pipe burst in the training camp or a hose burst in the Rolls, when Marlon Brando or Liza Minnelli wanted to meet Ali, or Ali wanted to donate $100,000 to save an old-folks' home, Kilroy facilitated it.

At hotels he usually stayed in a bedroom that was part of Ali's suite. As soon as they entered a city, he collected a list of the best doctors, in case of an emergency. He reached for the ever-ringing phone, decided who was worthy of a visit to the throne room. He worried himself into a 10-Maalox-a-day habit, facilitating. "Ulcer," he said. "You love someone, you worry. Watching him get hit during the Holmes fight, I bled like a pig—I was throwing it up in the dressing room. And all the problems before a fight. It was like having a show horse you had to protect, and all the people wanted to hitch him to a buggy for a ride through Central Park."

The trouble with facilitating was that it left no mark, no KILROY WAS HERE. He has covered the walls of his rec room with 50 Ali photos. He reminisces every day. He watches videos of old Ali interviews he helped facilitate, and sometimes tears fill his eyes. "I wish I had a kid I could tell," he said. And then, his voice going from soft to gruff: "I'll get married when I find a woman who greets me at the door the way my dogs do."

The Vegas casinos knew what Kilroy might be worth. All those contacts around the world, all those celebrities who had slipped into the dressing room on a nod from the Facilitator: perfect qualifications for a casino host. First the Dunes hired him, then the Tropicana and now the Golden Nugget.

Each day he weaves between blackjack tables and roulette wheels, past slot machines and craps tables, nodding to dealers, smiling at bouncers, slapping regulars on the back, dispensing complimentary dinners and rooms to high rollers and "How are ya, hon?" to cocktail waitresses. He no longer gambles: All the lust for action is gone. All that remains is the love of arranging a favor, of helping other members of Ali's old "family" when they hit hard times, of facilitating someone else's wants now that his are gone.

"As you know, I was all over the world with Ali," he said to a multi-millionaire as he led him into one of the Golden Nugget's suites. "I got the royal gold-carpet treatment everywhere. But this"—he swept his arm across the room—"solidifies the epitome of luxury. *Look.* Your Jacuzzi. Your sauna." Again and again his beeper would sound, and he would be connected with another wealthy client. "Sure, I'll have our limo pick you up at the airport. . . . Your line of credit is all set, $100,000."

Whenever Ali comes to Vegas to see a fight, he will mix with high rollers at Kilroy's request or sign a couple of dozen boxing gloves, a stack of a hundred photographs, mementos Kilroy passes out to favored clients. In his world, Ali souvenirs are currency. "One man was so proud of the things I'd given him," he said, "that when he died, he was buried with his Ali picture and boxing gloves. I can give people their dreams."

When Ali is near, Kilroy looks at him and remembers what the two of them once were. Sometimes he feels helpless. How can he facilitate away Ali's great fatigue with life—when he, too, feels sated and weary? "I remember one day not long ago when he was signing autographs, and I was standing next to him. We heard someone say, 'Look at Ali, he's a junkie.' Muhammad's eyes get kind of glassy sometimes now, you know. I wanted to choke the guy. But Ali nudged me and kind of smiled. God, I hope he wins this last fight. . . .'"

On an impulse he picked up the phone and dialed Ali's number. "Hello, it's Gene. . . . You've been out walking, huh? I wish I could walk with you. . . . I can just barely hear you. . . . I said, I wish I could walk with you. . . . It's good you're walking; you'll feel a lot better. . . . Hey, wouldn't it be nice to have a reunion at Deer Lake? Get everybody together— Sarria, you, me, Bundini, Pat, Lana. Get Lana to cook a roast, potatoes, gravy, everything. Wouldn't it be?. . . No, not bring back *old* memories. Bring back *great* memories. . . . Yeah. . . . O.K., well, get some rest. See you, champ. . . . "

He hung up the phone and stared at the wall. He glanced at his watch. Another day was nearly finished, a day of facilitating rooms and meals and money for men who still had the appetite, and he knew what he would do with the night. "I could call and have three girls if I wanted," he said. Instead he would drive past the riot of blinking lights, past the ads for bare-legged showgirls and sequined singers, through the warm night air of Vegas to his home in the suburbs. His three dogs, all boxers, would jump up and lick him, and he would let them, and he would call hello to his 80-year-old mother, eat dinner and settle back for an evening of TV amid the Ali photos. "The foxhole," he said. "I'm going back to the foxhole."

THE COOK

"NEXT! HOW many? Two? O.K., let's move it, please! Next! You gettin' big, honey! How come you don't stop by more to see me? Soup! Chicken noodle soup, anybody? Next! Hey, Eskimo, what you doin'? Ain't you beautiful? You want two? Gonna kill yo'self, storin' up all them fat cells. Next!"

She stood in a food-splotched apron in the basement cafeteria of a private school on East 70th Street in Manhattan, stuffing pita pockets with barbecue and rolling her hips to the music from the radio. Her hips, her soul and her name—Lana Shabazz—are those of a jazz singer, but the gaze she gave the children was that of a mother.

Hardly none of 'em down here know. That's nothin' off my teeth, no need for 'em to. I got my own life, I don't need 'em fussin' over me. Get up at five every

396

mornin', draw me a bath, get dressed in my whites for work. Still live out of suitcases—that's from being with him. Then I go drink coffee in a deli or a restaurant. Nice to sip and socialize with folks. By seven, I'm down here workin' myself tired to the bone runnin' this kitchen, the kind of tired you got to soak out in another big hot bath at night. Ain't easy, but I'm happy, 'course I am.

"Lana," the headmaster called, "do you have some tea?"

"Lana," a teacher said, "you got any of that broiled fish?"

"Lana," said the memo on the wall, "'a reminder that we will need coffee and Danish for parent tours next week."

"Mama," said the little boy. "I'm hungry. What's to eat?"

Mama, that's what the young ones call me. Three hundred and fifty kids needin' me here every day . . . but all of 'em needin' together can't never need me like he did. He'd come in at midnight, I'd have his dinner ready. He'd wake up at five a.m. and say, "Lana, get me a cuppa tea," I'd get up and do it. He'd travel, I'd pack up and cook in his hotel suite. Made sure he got all the live enzymes. Cooked without butter to save the calories—had to allow for his sweet tooth. Made him cookies and cakes, then hid 'em so he wouldn't eat 'em all at once. He'd swallow what I made so fast I'd wonder if he had teeth in his stomach. Then he'd go back to his cabin, and I'd worry about the cold from the air conditionin' hittin' his chest, he kept it so high. What a beautiful man. I'd feed his kids at camp, break up their fights—they treated me like a mother. Nobody else couldn't a did what I did for that man.

She looked up and saw the first- and second-graders fill the cafeteria like a burst of happy swallows. They swarmed at her legs and tugged at her white bell-bottom trousers. "Mama, do you have cookies? Mama, can we have a cookie?" She told them she couldn't do that, stroked their heads, then grinned and sneaked them each a big one.

One time, man read my cards and looked at me funny. He said, "There's more of Ali's cards showin' than yours." That scared me—I'd almost lost myself to him. All I thought of was Ali. But he gave so much of himself to the world, I told myself, he needs someone to take care of him. And that was me. Veronica, his third wife, she sat there combin' her hair while Earnie Shavers was punchin' on him, but I couldn't bear it. I had to get up and go back to my hotel room, where I prayed and screamed so long, God had to let him win. Psychic told me that in another life, I was his mother. Gets me to wanna cry, thinkin' about him. But I won't though. No, I won't.

She did a little samba around the butcher block, disappeared into the pantry and reappeared bopping out a bongo beat on a shiny ice bucket. When she leaned to dip a spoon and test the soup, her gold earrings shook. She straightened and pushed her big eyeglasses back up her steam-slick nose.

A teenage boy entered with a gift—a pair of stuffed grape leaves. She laughed from her belly and thanked him. A teenage girl said goodbye and kissed her on the cheek. "You be a nice girl," she said softly to the girl.

Even when I was 15, back in Bessemer, Alabama, I still kept my dolls on my bed. My first husband pushed them off and said I wouldn't need 'em now I had a real one in my belly. Guess I got that motherin' instinct—can't get rid of it. Been takin' care of people all my life. Took care of my mother 'fore she died. Raised up my two little girls. Cooked for Malcolm X, for Elijah Muhammad and then for Ali. Funny thing, people trust you when you feed 'em, and folks always seem to trust me. Sitting on buses, I end up telling strangers next to me what foods they need to eat. I read nutrition books all the time when I'm layin' alone in bed.

At four o'clock she took off her white work shoes with a sigh, slipped on her sneakers and overcoat and walked out into the chill. She wedged inside the 101 uptown bus, left the million-dollar condos of the Upper East Side behind and went home to Harlem. She stopped at the post office, then sat over coffee at the Twin Donut Shop, the way she does every evening, and read her mail. Soon she would return to her apartment—her daughters live in Chicago and Miami and she is divorced—and draw a bath. "Hey, how you doin', Lana?" someone called to her. "Doin' great," she said. "Doin' great."

'Course, maybe if you looked closer, you'd see the hurt in my eyes. Know what it feels like to think of somebody all the time, and suddenly they ain't there? Like losin' a child. Maybe he's sick because he ain't eatin' right. Maybe he ain't gettin' the right enzymes. I see other people 'round him now. Why we ain't there? We the ones made sure he was champ. Don't wanna say my life's empty. . .no, but. . .I have dreams about him. One where he's sick and doesn't want nothin' to do with me. Then he's all better and he's so happy to see me. Sometimes I think about that poem I wrote when he was young. Wrote that somebody like that could never live to be old.

I love him, but sometimes I get mad at him, too. People say that after wor-

kin' with him all those years, I shouldn't need for nothin'. . .and I'm flat broke. If they'd only have set up a retirement fund for us, we'd have no problems now. He used to say he was gonna buy me a house when he retired. If I'd asked him, he'd a done it. But I never asked for nothin'. And maybe that's best. Maybe if I had money I'd lose my love for people.

Some days, though, I just have to hear his voice. I call him, ask him what he's eatin'. People ask me all the time how he's doin'. Know how that feels, when people ask you how's your child, and you don't know what to say?

THE MASSEUR

THE GATE ot the fence that surrounded the little yellow house in northern Miami was locked. "Sarria!" I called from the sidewalk. "Sarria!" From inside the house a dog barked, then a second dog barked, a third, a fourth. And then the whole house exploded and shook with barking, a dozen, no, two dozen different timbres and pitches, the baritone bark of big dogs, the staccato yelp of small ones, the frenzied howl of the thin and high-strung. My knuckles whitened on the chain-link fence; how many could there be? "Sarria!" I cried again—he *had* to be in there, people said he was a shut-in—but my shout was lost in the din.

I swallowed hard. Such a sweet old man, everyone had told me. I began to scale the fence.

This the dogs seemed to sense and take as an insult; the whole house seemed to snap and snarl and salivate. My eyes darted, my stomach clenched. I shifted onto the balls of my feet, approached the door, reached toward it from a few feet away and knocked—my god, I couldn't even hear my own rapping. *Bang!* The door shuddered, but not from my knocking. *Bang-bang!* The metal meshing put up inside to protect the windows shook as the beasts hurled themselves at me.

I counted the strides it would take to flee back to the fence—how could the gentle old man live *here* ?—then held my breath, reached over a bush and rapped on a bedroom window. *"Sarriiiiiaaaaa!"* In reply came the asylum howl, the door thumping as if about to splinter, the flash of teeth and eyeballs and fur in the window. I ran back to the fence and had just jabbed a toe in the meshing when, weakly, beneath the fury, came a muffled human grunt.

Five long minutes passed. Then I saw the rush of snarling black. I froze, then whirled, clawing to climb. *"Negrita!"* I heard someone call. *"Ven! Ven!"* The dog hesitated, charged again, hesitated. I looked back. The old man—thank god!—was reaching out to wave me forward.

His hands, splayed from long, long arms, were broad and black and powerful from years of hacking Cuban sugarcane. I remembered them, working endlessly up and down the smooth ripples of Ali's body, rubbing until Muhammad drifted off to sleep on the table and then rubbing some more out of love. His hands I remembered, but I could not remember *him.*

His shoulders hunched, his head poking turtlelike from those shoulders, Luis Sarria moved in hobbling increments toward the steps in front of the house. He sat, and the bottom of his puppy-chewed pantleg hitched up to show the swathes of tape that wrapped his left leg. It had been chronically ulcerated since he stepped on a sea snail while fishing as a boy, but now the wound had grown threatening. At the gym near his home, where he worked until a year ago when the leg became too painful, they wondered if the germs carried by the great pack of dogs inside his house were what kept reinfecting it; and they wondered how much longer the 76-year-old man would last.

His wife, Esther, a Jamaican with small, happy-sad eyes, came out and sat next to him. Sarria picked up the black dog and hugged it to his chest. "She is his favorite," his wife said, "because she never wants to come back in the house, and so he gets to lift her like a baby."

They are childless, she explained, and need money badly, barely making it each month on Social Security. The gentle old man can neither visit friends because of his leg, nor have them in because of his dogs. "They would rip people up," his wife said. "There are 25 of them."

"But why keep so many?" I asked.

She shrugged. "They say Liberace left 25 dogs."

"How could there be room for them all in your house?"

"They live in the living room and one of the bedrooms," she said. "We live in our bedroom now. We had to move all the furniture out of the living room because they were destroying it. They broke the record player chasing rats. They dug up Sarria's garden. Dogs eat pumpkins. Did you know that?"

"How can you afford to feed them all?"

"We can't. I spend five dollars a day to buy chicken backs, turkey parts, rice. I mix it with their dog food. We spoil them. But dogs are better than people. Sarria loves to caress them."

Sarria rose gradually and hobbled to the house holding the black dog. "He is sad," she said, watching him go. "Because he cannot work, he is losing force." She glanced at the fence. "If Ali would come to that gate and say, 'Let's go to Manila,' Sarria would be young again."

I remembered how reporters used to gather in Ali's dressing room after a workout, recording every word from the champion's lips, moving then to the corner man, Angelo Dundee, or perhaps to the street poet, Bundini Brown, or to Dr. Pacheco. Never did anyone exchange a word with Ali's *real* trainer, as some insiders called Sarria. It was almost as if no one even saw him. "Even in Spanish," said Dundee, "Sarria was quiet."

He had flown to America in 1960 to train Cuban welterweight Luis Rodriguez and never returned to his homeland, yet he never learned English. He felt safer that way, his lips opening only wide enough to accommodate his pipe, and Ali seemed to like it, too. Surrounded so many days by con men, jive men, press men and yes men, Ali cherished the morning hour and the afternoon hour on the table with the man who felt no need to speak. For 16 years, the man physically closest to the most quoted talker of the '70s barely understood a word.

Sometimes Ali would babble at Sarria senselessly, pretending he spoke perfect Spanish, and then in mid-mumbo jumbo blurt out "*maricon!*" and Sarria's eyes would bug with mock horror. Everyone loved the silent old one. They swore his fingers knew the secret—how to break up fat on the champion's body and make it disappear. "And the exercises he put Ali through each morning! Sarria was the reason Muhammad got like this," Dundee said, forming a V with his hands. "He added years to Ali's boxing life."

The extra years brought extra beatings. And, likely, the Parkinson's syndrome. "I used to ask God to help me introduce power into him through my hands," Sarria said in Spanish, sitting once more on the front step. He rubbed his face. "Never did I think this could happen to him. I feel like crying when I see him, but that would not be good for him to see. To tell a boxer to stop fighting is an insult. I did not have the strength to tell him, but I wish to God I had."

"Oh, Sarria," said his wife. "You have never talked."

"If I had spoken more, I might have said things I should not have. Perhaps they would have said, 'This Cuban talks too much,' and I would have been sent away...." Or perhaps today he would be standing in Sarria's Health Spa on Fifth Avenue, massaging corporate lumbars for $75 an hour.

He ran his fingers across a paw print on his pants and spoke softly again of Ali. "Ambitious people ... people who talk a lot ... perhaps *this* is what happens to them."

Behind us, the dogs began to snarl and thump again. "Shhhhh," Sarria pleaded. "Shhhhh."

"Sarria," I said, "how did you get so many dogs?"

From his pocket he pulled three photographs. Two of them were yellowed ones of him and Ali, clipped from newspapers. The other was a color glossy of a little girl. Tears misted his eyes, then his wife's. And the two of them took turns explaining the story of the 25 dogs.

Fourteen years ago they had taken in the three-day-old daughter of a relative who was unable to raise her. For 11 years she gave them someone to hug and care for, to take to ballet lessons and help with homework, to fill the hole left when Ali departed their lives. And then, just like *that*, the relative reappeared and took her away. "Oh, how Sarria cried," said his wife. She turned away and clamped her lips.

"Just before she left us," she went on, "the girl brought home a stray dog. We named it Alfi, and then she brought home a second one—we named it Kelly. When she left, we couldn't give away her dogs, you see. And then they started to make babies...."

THE BODYGUARD

CLANKING AND jangling with walkie-talkie, nightstick, pistol and keys, Officer Howard (Pat) Patterson swung his 220-pound body out of patrol car No. 511 on the far south side of Chicago, and the shouting match began.

"Officer, this mother's in my face."

"You reported a battery? What's your name, ma'am?" Patterson asked calmly.

"'Miss Jones. I went to jail for this mother---- , and now...."

"I didn't touch her!" hollered the man. "I called her a name!"

"I might kill him!"

"Wait a minute, both of you."

"She got my chain, officer!"

"You mother---- ! I was locked up last summer for your honkie ass."

"Did he hit you, Miss Jones?"

"No, but he was in my face!"

"She pulled the chain off my neck. I want my chain!"

"Look," said Patterson. "You assault him, miss, and I'll lock *you* up. You're both high. Sir, you go take a walk. Let her cool off. And you stop screaming like that, Miss Jones."

Officer Patterson stepped back into the car and shook his head. "Lot of police would put them both in jail," he said. "I know before I was Ali's bodyguard, I'd put folks in jail 10 times faster than I do now. Now I just try to help them solve their problems and send them home. My attitude's different since seeing the world and rubbing shoulders with Ali."

When the comet ride with Ali began, Patterson was a 31-year-old cop on the streets of Chicago. When it ended, he was a 45-year-old cop on the streets of Chicago. He had two children, a loving wife, a close-knit family, 50 scrapbooks and a couple of walls of photographs that a ghetto kid never dreamed he would have, and for all of that he was grateful.

He got the bodyguard job through a chance meeting. The day in the mid-1960s he was assigned to protect the leader of the Black Muslim movement in America, Elijah Muhammad, he stuck a gun into a face coming out of the darkness: Herbert Muhammad, Elijah's son and Ali's manager. Herbert wanted just such a businesslike fellow to protect his boxer, and Patterson became the Bodyguard. He worked primarily during the weeks of fights until '74, when he was put on permanent loan to Ali by Chicago mayor Richard Daley.

Whenever they met, Ali made a game of guessing where Patterson's gun was hidden. One time it might be the Colt Diamondback strapped to his ankle, the next time, the 9-mm automatic tucked under his suit coat; then again, if it was cold enough for an overcoat, the Colt *and* a .38 would be buried in his pockets. Upon reaching Ali's hotel suite, the Bodyguard would hide the pistols in a flower vase or beneath a sofa cushion, so he would always have one near, along with the shotgun he kept in a closet or under the bed. In a briefcase he carried as much as $50,000 in cash— spending money for the champ.

His protective instinct was fierce. At Yankee Stadium on the night of the fight against Ken Norton in 1976, he had a $400 leather suit ripped to shreds while fighting off a mob from the fender of Ali's limo. He turned down four-figure bribes from people desperate to get past his checkpoint in hotel hallways and see Ali. When Ali entered a public bathroom, Patterson went, too. "If anything at all happened to Muhammad," he said, "I figured it would be my fault."

During fights, he always kept his hand clamped over the water bottle so no one could sabotage Ali. But the Bodyguard had to sit on the corner stool and watch helplessly when his man needed protection most, in the ring when the end was near. "Watching him get hit was like watching someone stick my mama with a knife," Patterson said. "Ali fights stopped being a party. I tried to tell him to quit. . . . "

He drove the patrol car through the streets as he reminisced, head continually swiveling, eyes sweeping, ears listening for his number on the radio. The recruit he was training listened to the stories silently. Now and then a wino or a pimp called from the sidewalk, "Hey, Patty, how's Muhammad?"

"Traveling with Ali opened up the whole world for me," said the Bodyguard. "I'll admit it, I was afraid of flying before I got on that first airplane to meet him in Toronto. I never thought of going to other countries. Now I feel like there's nothing I can't do; my wife and I travel all the time.

"With him I saw that people all over are the same—trying to educate their kids and get enough to eat—just like us. Only most of them don't have as much as we do. That changed me, too. I used to worry about being a success, getting a promotion. Now that's not important. Seeing how somebody as powerful as Ali never used force to get things done, I learned from that. I'm not a police officer anymore, I'm a *peace* officer. I'd rather drive a drunk home or give somebody five dollars to solve an argument than stick them in jail. People need help, not jail."

Not long ago, he was in London with a tour group when a disheveled, unbathed man approached and asked for money. The others averted their eyes and edged away. "There's a sucker," some said when Patterson gave the beggar a bill and talked with him, but they didn't understand. He wasn't safeguarding a man anymore, he was safeguarding an idea.

"Whenever he saw someone old or sick or in trouble," said the Bodyguard, "Ali always wanted to help them. He'd say, 'Who knows? Some day I might be that way.'"

GARY SMITH

THE MANAGER

THE LAST man to enter the Chicago mosque was short and round and rumpled. His sport coat was two sizes too baggy, his shirttail spilled out across the seat of his pants. His shoes were unbuckled, and his face was stubbled with whiskers. He looked not at all like the man who had reached into his pocket for a million dollars to buy the land and build the mosque he stood in.

The others at prayer stood near the front. He slipped off his shoes, padded to the back and dropped to his knees behind a pillar. Few were aware of it, but he remembered well a passage in Muslim scripture advising worshippers to pray behind an object, an obstruction for the devil.

All his life Herbert Muhammad has hidden behind pillars. As a young man he was the quiet, respectful houseman and chauffeur for his powerful father, Elijah Muhammad. Then he became the manager of Muhammad Ali, taking 33% of Ali's multimillion-dollar purses but remaining so obscure that bouncers at Ali workouts sometimes barred his entry to the gym. "I never wanted to be a leader," he said. "I never wanted to be a target. My role is to support those in the lead."

Now he was 58, and he had trouble. His pillar was crumbling, his point man fading away. His dream of building 49 more mosques like this first one, using the money Ali and he could generate, was drifting further and further from his reach. Ali slurred words and shook and didn't want to be seen on television. Ali didn't care about making money anymore.

Herbert remained Ali's manager, and he wasn't going to give up his dream without a fight. Beneath the untucked shirt, unshaven face and tufts of black hair was a man burning with determination not to be forgotten when the Muslim history in America is written. Perhaps not equal to his father nor to his younger brother Wallace, whom Elijah anointed as successor, but close. "Fifty mosques," said Herbert. "Allah said if you build him a mosque in this life, he'll build you a paradise in the next life. My father established 200 mosques, my brother 250. But they didn't *pay* for them. I want to *pay* for 50. That would make my father proud. Every day my wife tells me to relax. How can I? I want to go till I drop. If I can't do something meaningful, take me now."

He sighed. The Muslim movement had changed since Elijah died in 1975; it had dropped the black separatist thrust and become rounder,

405

softer—more *Herbert*. Big-name athletes weren't changing their names to Abdul and Rashad as they did in the '60s and '70s. The glamour years were gone, and now it would take the quiet, behind-the-scenes work—the kind Herbert was cut out for—to keep the movement growing.

"Seemed like we were always doing something back when Muhammad was fighting," he said. "Building buildings, schools, starting mosques, buying buses, helping people. Now everything has quieted down with Ali, but I still got the taste of it in my mouth."

The irony was pungent. For years the Manager tried to restrain Ali. Now Ali was restraining the Manager. "I'd beg him not to be so proud, not to mess around with women, not to say, 'I am the greatest,' " Herbert said. " 'I am the greatest' was an insult to God—in our prayers, we say *'Allahu akbar,'* God is the greatest. That was when I was trying to make him more meek and religious. Back then I had to run to keep up with him when he walked. But this sickness stopped him dead in his tracks. Now everything's in slow motion. Now he's a hundred times more religious and meek than I ever thought he'd be. His whole life is his prayers. But he doesn't seem to care about anything. . . . "

The Manager had ushered in the era of million-dollar sports contracts, brilliantly playing promoters Don King and Bob Arum off against each other. Now he has an agreement for 25% of the cut if he negotiates a product deal with Ali. "If he wanted it and he wasn't sick, he could be making $20 million to $30 million a year in endorsements," said Herbert. "He's probably making a couple a hundred thousand. Last year I made $500 dollars from him."

Still, the Manager keeps busy. Between his five trips to the mosque each day to pray, he occasionally brokers deals for Third World sellers and runs a catering business in Chicago. But Ali was, and is, the key, and Herbert knows it.

Now and then the fighter leaves his 88-acre farm, which Al Capone once owned, in Berrien Springs, Mich., and makes the two-hour drive to meet Herbert at a Chicago hotel coffee shop. Ali genuinely liked Herbert and his easy laugh: He was the only nonfamily member Ali said he would ask along if he could take only five people to the moon. On one visit to the city, Ali sat in the coffee shop as the Manager made plans, listening with blank eyes. The Manager, sharp and angular beneath the round body and the baggy sport coat with the elbow patches, tried everything to wake him. If Ali were dead, could Herbert feel completely alive?

"I tell him, 'Joe Frazier ain't sitting around,'" he said. "'If you lost some weight and took your medicine, you could make a whole lot of money. You could even fight.' I know he can't fight, but I say it just to motivate him. He won't take his medicine, he hates to depend on anything. I think his problem is getting worse. He's shaking more. Sometimes it's hard to be in his presence, like someone sick in your family. I love that man. He is quicker to help a stranger, he has more inner compassion than any human being I've ever met. But I'm afraid he's losing the values of this earth. Allah said to do everything in your power to seek an afterlife, but not to neglect your share on this earth. Ali gave away that big house of his in Los Angeles, he gave away cars. He's giving up things *too* easy. I don't want to push him, but I have got to make him realistic. His mother, his father, his eight children, what will he do about their expenses, the kids' college educations? And he shouldn't dress the way I dress. He should have a suit and a tie, and he should have his hair groomed, because he represents something to people.

"He says, 'I don't need no car, I'll just ride a bike.' I say, 'That's as crazy as a guy making $400 a week driving a Cadillac.' One night when he stayed over in Chicago, he slept on the floor of the mosque instead of getting a hotel. I told him, 'People are going to think you've lost all your marbles or your money—and neither one is good.' The whole world rallied around Islam as a universal religion because of Muhammad Ali. But if he doesn't watch it, he's going to become a monk."

One day last summer the Manager received a call from Mexico City. It was Ali, seeking counsel: Should he chance a new form of brain surgery that might cure his illness? Two of the 18 patients who had undergone the operation—in which adrenal cells are placed inside the brain to help make dopamine, a brain chemical essential to controlling voluntary body movement—had died shortly thereafter, but others had shown marked improvement. Ali might be Ali again!

Ali's fourth wife, Yolanda, cried on the telephone and begged him not to risk it. Herbert Muhammad closed his eyes and thought. He so hated to see Ali hurt, he used to keep his head down and pray during fights.

"I felt if he put his trust totally in God, the operation would be a success," said Herbert. He looked down at his hands. "But I didn't tell him that. If he turned out like a vegetable, it would be seen as my decision. People would think I said yes just because I wanted more paychecks from Ali. So I told him to listen to everybody but to make up his own mind."

Ali decided to wait until American doctors had become more familiar with the surgery. Part of him was afraid to be what he was again, filled with an energy that needed lights and action and other people's eyes. The illness, he sensed, was a protection against himself. And because of this, the Manager closed in on 60 feeling the way Ali did toward the end of his career, still able to visualize himself doing what he wanted to do, but unable to do it.

"Not just 50 mosques," said Herbert Muhammad. "But 50 mosques with day-care centers and schools and old-folks' homes attached to them. I keep telling Ali, Let's get back in the race. How could I have ever dreamed I'd have to beg Muhammad Ali to *go*?"

THE MOTIVATOR

THE SCENE: A small motel room in downtown Los Angeles that costs, at monthly rates, $5.83 a night. A little bit of afternoon light makes it through the curtains, falling on a tablecloth etched with the words GOD—MOTHER—SON. *On top of the television stands a small statue of Buddha, its head hidden by a man's cap. Four packs of playing cards and a Bible lie on the head of the bed; tin dinner plates are set on a small table. Affixed to a mirror are a photograph of a young Muhammad Ali and a leaflet for a play entitled* Muhammad Ali Forever.

On the bed, propped against a pillow, is a 57-year-old black man, slightly chubby, with black woolly hair on the sides of his head and, on the top, a big bald spot with a tiny tuft of hair growing at the very front. As he talks, his eyes go wide and wild . . . then far away . . . then wet with tears.

His name is Drew (Bundini) Brown, the ghetto poet who motivated Ali and maddened him, who invented the phrase, "Float like a butterfly, sting like a bee" and who played bit parts in The Color Purple *and* Shaft; *who licked Ali's mouthpiece before sliding it in but never said a yes to him he didn't mean; who could engage the champion in long discussions of nature and God and man, then lie in the hotel pool before a fight and have his white woman, Easy, drop cherries into his mouth; who, when he felt good, charged*

two $300 bottles of wine at dinner to Ali's expense account and then made Ali
laugh it off; and who, when he felt bad, drank rum and shot bullets into the
night sky at the mountain training camp in Pennsylvania—a man stretched
taut and twanging between the fact that he was an animal and the fact that
he was a spirit.

Oh, yes. A visitor sits in a chair near the window of the motel room, but
often Bundini Brown talks as if he is ranting to a crowd on a street corner—or
as if he is completely alone:

The old master painter from the faraway hills,
Who painted the violets and the daffodils,
Said the next champ gonna come from Louisville.

I made that up 'fore we was even champion. Things just exploded in
my head back then. Guess that's why Ali loved me. I could help him create new things. See, he never did talk that much. People didn't know that
about him, 'less'n they slept overnight and caught him wakin' up. All that
talkin' was just for the cameras and writers, to build a crowd. He was
quiet as can be, same as now. But now people think he's not talkin' 'cause
of the Parkinson's, which is a lie.

I remember when he fought Jerry Quarry, after that long layoff. Going from the locker room to the ring, my feet wasn't even touchin' the
ground. I looked down and tried to touch, but I couldn't get 'em to. Like
I was walkin' into my past. Me and the champ was so close, I'd think,
"Get off the ropes"—and he'd get off the ropes! Man, it made chill bumps
run up my legs. We were in Manila, fightin' Frazier. The champ came
back to the corner crossin' his legs. Tenth or 11th round, I forget. Angelo
said, "Our boy is through." I said, "You're goddam wrong, my baby ain't
through!" I was deeply in love with him. Ali tried to fire me every day,
but how he gonna fire me when God gave me my job? So I stood on
the apron of the ring, and I said out loud, "God! If Joe Frazier wins, his
mother wins, his father wins, his kids win. Nobody else! But if Muhammad lose—God!—we *all* lose. Little boys, men, women, black and white.
Muhammad lose, the world lose!"

And you know what? The nigger got up fresh as a daisy. Everybody
seen it! Got up fresh, man, *fresh!* And beat up on Frazier so bad Frazier

couldn't come out after the 14th round! God put us together for a reason, and we shook up the world!

(He picks at a thread on the bedspread.) People'd see us back then and say, "It's so nice seein' y'all together." We made a lot of people happy. I was a soldier. *(His hands are shaking. He reaches down to the floor, pours a glass of rum as his eyes begin to fill with tears.)* I was happy then. It'd be good for Muhammad if I could be with him again. Be good for me, too. Then I wouldn't drink as much. By me being alone I drink a lot. Always did say I could motivate him out of this sickness, if me and the champ was together. He needs the medical thing, too, but he needs someone who truly loves him. If we were together again, more of the God would come out of me. *(His voice is almost inaudible.)* Things used to explode in my head. . . . I'm kind of runnin' out now. . . .

He asked me to go stay on the farm with him. *(His eyes flare, he starts to shout.)* What you goin' to do, put me to pasture? I ain't no horse! I don't want no handouts! I got plans! Big things gonna happen for me! I gotta get me a job, make some money, take care of my own family 'fore I go with him. If I don't love my own babies, how in hell I gonna love somebody else's?

First thing I'd do if I had some money, I'd go to the Bahamas and see my baby. King Solomon Brown's his name. Made him at Ali's last fight, with a woman I met down there. He was born on the seventh day of the seventh month. There's seven archangels and seven colors in the rainbow, you know.

I brought him to America and lived with him until he was one. Then he went back to the Bahamas with his mother. Didn't see him for a year and a half, then I went back. Wanted to see if he'd remember me. I said, "A-B-C-D-E-F-G—dock-dock" *(he makes a sound with his tongue and the roof of his mouth)*—that's what I always used to teach him—and he *remembered*! He ran and leaped into my arms—I mean, jumped!—and we hugged, and it wasn't like I was huggin' somebody else, we was one body, we was one! *(He wraps his arms around himself and closes his eyes.)* I'll never forget that hug. Couldn't bring him back to America, I had no house for him to come back to. Stayed eight weeks and went broke. Came back and after that I'd see kids on the street and think of my kid and I'd start to cry. . . . Why don't you get up and leave now? Put two eggs in your shoes and beat it. You stirrin' up things, you know. *(The visitor starts to stand.)*

I'll make some money. I'll get a home he can come to, and put him in school. Got two grandchildren, too, and I wanna be near 'em. They're by my son, Drew, he's a jet pilot in the Persian Gulf. And I have another son, Ronnie, here in Los Angeles. One son black, one son white, born a day apart. And then Solomon. I'm a boymaker. Don't see my kids like I want to. Can't go back to my babies till I got somethin' to give 'em. Right now, I'm broke. I said, *broke,* not poor, there's a difference. *(He glances across the room and speaks softly.)* I know one thing. You get used to good food and a clean bed, hard to get used to somethin' else. Why don't you leave now? Please?

(He rises and goes to the door, shredding a piece of bread and tossing it outside to the pigeons.) People don't know it, but feedin' the birds is like paintin' a picture. . . . Some people think Muhammad's broke, too. He ain't broke. He's brokenhearted. He hasn't found himself in what he really want to do. Maybe he just be in the freezer for a few years. Maybe he's going through this so he has time to think. Last time I was with him, his 15-year-old son said to him, "Daddy, Bundini is your only friend, the only one that doesn't give up on you." Muhammad looked at me, and we started cryin'. But this is not the end for Ali. Somethin' good gonna happen for him. Maybe not while he's still alive on this earth, but Ali gonna *live* for a long time, if you know what I mean. Like my kids, even when I'm gone, I'm gonna be livin' in 'em . . . if I can be around 'em enough to put my spirit into 'em. Go fishin' with 'em. There you go again, you got me talkin' about it. Didn't I ask you to leave? *(The visitor reaches for his shoulder bag.)*

It ain't nothin' for me to get up and walk down the street and have 15 people yell, "Hey, Bundini, where's the champ?" That one reason I stay in my room. *(He pauses and looks at the visitor.)* You think I'm alone, don't you? Soon as you leave, God's gonna sit in that chair. I call him Shorty. Ha-ha, you like that, don't you? By callin' him that, means I ain't got no prejudice about religions. I was born on a doorstep with a note 'cross my chest. It read, "Do the best you can for him, world." I had to suck the first nipple come along. I didn't run away from home—I been runnin' *to* home. I'm runnin' to God. And the nearest I can find to God is people. And all around me people are fightin' for money. And I'm tryin' to find out what makes apples and peaches and lemons, what makes the sun shine. What is the act of life? We all just trancin' through? Why can't we care for one another? There's a lady that come out of church the other day and got shot in the head. I want to know what the hell is goin' on. God, take me home if you ain't gonna give me no answer. Take me home now. If you're ready to die, you're ready to live. Best thing you can do is live every day like it's the last day. Kiss your family each day like you're not comin' back. I want to keep my dimples deep as long as I'm here. I want to see people smile like you just did.

(His lips smile, but his eyes are wet and shining.) The smarter you get, the lonelier you get. Why is it? When you learn how to live, it's time to die. That's kind of peculiar. When you learn how to drive, they take away the car. I've finally realized you need to be near your kids, that you need to help 'em live better 'n you did, that you can live on by feedin' your spirit into your babies. But now I ain't got no money and I can't be near 'em. Back when I was with the champ, I could fly to 'em anytime. See, I was in the Navy when I was 13 and the Merchant Marine when I was 15, and they was the happiest days of my life, 'cause I was alone and didn't have no one to worry about. But now I'm alone and it brings me misery. . . . C'mon now, get on up and leave. Talkin' to you is like talkin' to myself. . . .

See this bald spot on my head? Looks like a footprint, don't it? That come from me walkin' on my head. Don't you think I know I'm my own worst enemy? I suffer a lot. If my kids only knew how I hurt. But I can't let 'em know, it might come out in anger. And 'fore I see 'em, I gotta have somethin' to give to 'em. I owe $9,000 'fore I can get my stuff out of storage. *(He bites his lip and looks away.)* One storage place already done auctioned off all the pictures of Ali an' me, all my trophies and memories from back then. Strangers have 'em all. . . . *(A long silence passes.)* Now the other storage place, the one that has all Ali's robes from every fight we ever fought, every pair of trunks we fought in, lot of jockstraps, too, enough stuff to fill a museum—I owe that place $9,000, and I'm talkin' to 'em nice so they won't auction that off, too, but I don't think they'll wait much longer. Sure I know how much that stuff's worth, but I can't sell it. That's not right. I want that stuff to be in my babies' dens some day. That's what I'm gonna give my babies. I can't just sell it. . . . *(His head drops, he looks up from under his brow.)* You know somebody'll pay now?

(He rubs his face and stares at the TV set.) You stirrin' it up again. Go

on, now. You know if you just keep sittin' there, I'll keep talkin'. Pretty please? *(He gets to his feet.)* You can come back and visit me. We friends now. I can't go out, I gotta stay by the phone. I'm waitin' on somethin' real big, and I ain't gonna get caught off-guard. Somethin' big gonna happen, you wait and see. . . .

A few days later, Bundini Brown fell in his motel room and was found paralyzed from the neck down by a cleaning woman. And then he died.

SEVEN YEARS ago, when the group broke camp at Deer Lake for the final time, everyone contributed money for a plaque that would include all their names. They left the task to Bundini Brown and departed.

Today the camp is a home for unwed mothers. In front of the log-cabin gym, where babies squeal and crawl, stands a tall slab of gray granite, chiseled with 16 names and surrounded by flowers. Bundini Brown had bought a tombstone.

POSTSCRIPT: *Lana Shabazz, Luis Sarria and Pat Patterson have died. Herbert Muhammad underwent successful open-heart surgery in 2004. Gene Kilroy, still a fixture in Las Vegas after 30 years, works at the Luxor. He delivered eulogies at the funerals for Shabazz and Patterson. Dr. Ferdie Pacheco has had success as an author and painter in Miami; he's written 16 books, several of them on boxing. As for Ali? "I saw him about a year and a half ago," says Kilroy, "and it was sad because of the Parkinson's. But he told me he's not in any pain, and he always thinks about those good times we had."*

Acknowledgments

YOU DON'T get many chances to publicly high-five the people who made your life and your work possible. So I'll leap to it, starting with Jean and Harry Smith, the parents who created and controlled the nine-child asylum I grew up in, and who still own up to it at 84.

In an industry in which the long narrative is gasping, I'd have long ago staggered elsewhere for oxygen if not for Terry McDonell, the editor of SPORTS ILLUSTRATED who provided me the freedom and space to keep breathing.

But I wouldn't be a magazine writer at all if not for two men. John Walsh, the Buddha of both print and TV sports journalism, flung open the gates to the kingdom at *Inside Sports*. His lieutenant, Jay Lovinger, flung open the doors in my head as to what a magazine story could be. Should you ever find a mentor who's both kind and brilliant enough to walk around all night taking apart your story as if it were a car engine, grab him with both hands and don't let go.

Mike Sisak! Stan Hochman! Thanks for yanking me into the big leagues at the *Philadelphia Daily News* and letting me do stuff that 20-year-olds have no business doing, and to Hal Bodley and Matt Zabitka for making a scrawny 16-year-old think he belonged at the *Wilmington News-Journal*.

It would be splendid to say all the stories in this book were my ideas— a splendid lie. If not for SI colleagues such as Greg Kelly, Melissa Segura and Richard Deitsch, half of these stories would never have germinated. Chris Hunt has been my deft frontline editor and Rob Fleder my brainstorming partner for two decades; and Rob, Peter Carry and Mike Bevans have been the editing closers. I wish I could acknowledge all the fact-checkers by name, but there have been too many.

My wife Sally, a former scribe, and my writing amigo, Cal Fussman, pushed me to slog the extra mile on every one of these stories. And my artist friend, Duke Hagerty, played a bigger part in them than he knows.

Lastly, I thank David Bauer and Stefanie Kaufman for all the work and care they've poured into editing this book, and Rick Reilly—who has much better things to do—for writing a beauty of an introduction.

Wait. I must also acknowledge the principal characters featured in these stories. Without their trust and vast patience, this book would be called *Staying Shallow*.